Strategic Human Resource Management

Strategic Human Resource Management

Catherine Truss
University of Kent

David Mankin
Academic Consultant

Clare Kelliher
Cranfield School of Management, Cranfield University

OXFORD
UNIVERSITY PRESS

OXFORD
UNIVERSITY PRESS

Great Clarendon Street, Oxford OX2 6DP

Oxford University Press is a department of the University of Oxford.
It furthers the University's objective of excellence in research, scholarship,
and education by publishing worldwide in

Oxford New York

Auckland   Cape Town   Dar es Salaam   Hong Kong   Karachi
Kuala Lumpur   Madrid   Melbourne   Mexico City   Nairobi
New Delhi   Shanghai   Taipei   Toronto

With offices in

Argentina   Austria   Brazil   Chile   Czech Republic   France   Greece
Guatemala   Hungary   Italy   Japan   Poland   Portugal   Singapore
South Korea   Switzerland   Thailand   Turkey   Ukraine   Vietnam

Oxford is a registered trade mark of Oxford University Press in the
UK and in certain other countries

Published in the United States
by Oxford University Press Inc., New York

British Library Cataloguing in Publication Data

Data available

Library of Congress Cataloging in Publication Data

Data available

Typeset by TNQ Books and Journals Pvt. Ltd.
Printed in Italy
on acid-free paper by
L.E.G.O. S.p.A.—Lavis TN

ISBN 978-0-19-958306-5

10 9 8 7 6 5 4 3 2 1

Outline contents

Detailed contents

Preface

In today's globalized world, human resource (HR) professionals are under pressure from three different sources in relation to the way they go about managing their employees. First, irrespective of whether employers are in the public, private, or voluntary sectors, they are under pressure to maximize the value created through people. Research evidence is mounting that human resource management (HRM) can contribute to organizational success and so many employers are seeking ways to enhance and professionalize their people management practices. Second, employers are under pressure from governments, unions, and lobbying groups to address the issue of employee wellbeing and health at work, recognizing not only employers' responsibilities towards their staff, but also the economic costs of absence and labour turnover. Third, employers are under pressure from professional bodies and international institutions to organize and manage themselves in a way that is sustainable and ethical from the human and the environmental perspectives. The recent global economic crisis has focused the attention of HR professionals on the role they have to play in determining the employment relationship and ensuring ethical management practices and long-term sustainability. These three pressures combine to create an imperative for HR professionals today to focus on issues of strategic human resource management (SHRM) that go beyond traditional administrative and bureaucratic approaches to managing people.

Not surprisingly, much of the debate about the theory and practice of HRM and SHRM has been dominated by Western perspectives. It is likely that, as the 21st century progresses, indigenous perspectives will emerge, for example in the BRIC economies (i.e. Brazil, Russia, India, and China).

The aim of this book is to present a comprehensive and thematic overview of the thinking and research evidence in the area of SHRM. This will enable students of strategic SHRM to develop their own understanding of the field, and to inform their practice as HR professionals. The book consciously seeks to build on students' prior knowledge of the HRM field at an operational level, and takes a strategic perspective that focuses on key overarching themes at the strategic level.

Throughout the book you will encounter a wide range of terms and abbreviations, including the jargon that is a perennial characteristic of any profession. Consequently, a glossary of terms is available at the back of this book. As you will discover, a number of organizational stakeholders, including senior executives, line managers, HR professionals, and employees, all have a role to play in helping to develop a strategic approach to HRM.

Pedagogical features

Our original aim was to write a textbook that would demystify the concept of SHRM and explain different aspects of the concept in an accessible and student-friendly manner. We hope that we have achieved this aim. Various pedagogical features have been used to make the content more interesting and to encourage readers to find out more about specific topics:

- Key concept boxes provide succinct explanations of concepts important to developing an understanding of HR development.

- Case study boxes contain examples of practice relevant to a chapter's content. Some of these are taken from primary sources, such as HR professionals who we have interviewed for the book. Others are based on material drawn from secondary sources such as academic journal articles and other textbooks. Each has associated activities for you to undertake. You should use a mix of academic and media sources to answer these questions. Where possible, share this with fellow students.

- Review questions at the end of each chapter provide an opportunity to check understanding.

- We have recommended further reading sources, involving a wide range of books and articles for you to select from to improve your understanding of a chapter's content.

- There is a case study at the end of every chapter and these have been kept relatively short so that they can be used for group work in the classroom.

- The Oxford University Press web pages provide further material and links so that learning from the book can be enhanced. Some topics date very quickly, such as those covered in Chapter 1. Consequently, the web pages will contain updates, new cases, and additional insights into practice and media-watch items. Tutors will be able to access PowerPoint slides which can be used in lectures and seminars.

- The glossary of terms provides easy accessibility to definitions of all the principal concepts contained in the book.

Structure of the book

The book comprises four parts which cover different aspects of SHRM.

Part 1 (Chapters 1–3) discusses the context of SHRM from an external and internal perspective. Specific implications for the theory and practice of SHRM are highlighted in the first two chapters. The third chapter provides some conceptual foundations of strategic management so that you can better understand the complexities of different perspectives on SHRM, which are covered in *Part 2* (Chapters 4–8). *Part 2* explains the theories, concepts, and models that underpin SHRM. There is coverage of a wide range of issues that HR practitioners need to better understand about the strategy-making process. *Part 3* (Chapters 9–15) is intended to illustrate the changing nature and scope of SHRM by focusing on the role of the HR function in relation to HR development, talent management, employment relations, employee engagement, knowledge management, corporate social responsibility, and the management of change. These topics reflect current thinking on the scope of SHRM in terms of theory and practice. *Part 4* (Chapter 16) looks to the future and explores potential new forms of strategic HRM.

Chapter 1 focuses on the external context of organizations and the implications of globalization for the practice of SHRM. Key themes are the effects of economic globalization, changing demographics, trends in communications and information technologies, and changes to organizational structures.

Chapter 2 is concerned with the changing context for SHRM. It examines contextual factors which bear upon both the nature of the workforce and the nature of work. It includes consideration of changing labour market patterns, demographics, and orientations to work. It also explores the implications of the growth in service work, including increased focus on emotional and aesthetic labour, workplace flexibility, and changing management practices.

Chapter 3 is devoted to the concept of strategic management. The chapter covers some of the fundamentals of strategic management and acts as a foundation for the discussion of SHRM in the Part 2 chapters.

Chapter 4 provides a detailed discussion on the role of the HR function and the HR professional in the modern organization. Reference is made to some well-known models and theories of HR functional roles and we consider the choices open to HR professionals in how to structure and organize the department.

Chapter 5 introduces the concept of SHRM and examines in what ways SHRM differs from HRM or personnel management. Some of the more widely known theories such as the best-fit and best-practice perspectives on SHRM are introduced.

Chapter 6 develops the theoretical underpinnings of SHRM further by examining the contribution that the resource-based view of the firm has made to our understanding of SHRM. We also introduce the institutionalist approach to SHRM which has emerged recently and that seeks to embed notions of SHRM in a broader societal context.

Chapter 7 focuses on HR strategy. In particular, we examine the choices open to HR professionals when seeking to develop and operationalize an HR strategy, from both the content perspective (what the strategy contains) and the process perspective (how it is developed).

Chapter 8 brings together the themes explored in this section of the book by examining the debate on the link between HRM and performance outcomes. We evaluate the research evidence on whether HRM can impact directly on performance, and explore some of the theories that have been developed to explain how the relationship might work.

Chapter 9 focuses on the concept of HR development which encompasses a range of individual, group, and organizational learning processes such as training, learning and development, career development and lifelong learning, and organizational development.

Chapter 10 explores the concept of talent management which has developed as an important and separate strand to HR development. This reflects the increasing importance of attracting and retaining those employees who underpin the organizational capabilities that provide organizations with their competitive advantage.

Chapter 11 provides an introduction to employment relations and discusses how this relates to strategic SHRM. The chapter explores the choices open to managers in the way in which they manage employment relations and the factors likely to influence these choices. Whilst not concerned with the detail of legal regulation, the ways in which managers may respond to regulation is also discussed. The chapter also examines various forms of employee voice and considers some of the challenges associated with implementation.

Chapter 12 examines employee engagement. Engagement has been the focus of considerable interest in recent years, as there is growing research evidence that highly engaged employees perform better, are less likely to quit, are more innovative, and enjoy higher levels of wellbeing. We explore what engagement is and evaluate the research evidence.

Chapter 13 explores the implications of knowledge management for HR functions. The chapter argues that HR practitioners can play an important role in facilitating knowledge formation processes within and between organizations (e.g. knowledge creation, knowledge sharing and knowledge transfer).

Chapter 14 discusses the implications of corporate social responsibility for the practice of strategic human resource in a range of organizational settings. This is a relatively neglected area in the literature on strategic HRM despite the importance and topicality of ethical and socially responsible management.

Chapter 15 looks at the importance of change management for HR professionals. We examine some of the well-established models of organizational change and consider their relevance for the HR professional. We also look at some of the research evidence on HR's role in managing change.

Chapter 16, the final chapter in the book, considers possible future directions for SHRM. It examines a number of scenarios which have been put forward for the future of business and discusses the implications of these for approaches to SHRM and for the competencies required by HR professionals.

Acknowledgements

A great many people have helped all of us directly and indirectly in the writing of this text-book. We would all like to thank the team at OUP and in particular our editor Fran Griffin for her unerring support and guidance and for providing us with invaluable feedback. We would also like to thank all the reviewers who also provided very detailed and useful feedback on each of the chapters.

Those who have helped us indirectly are too numerous to mention and have already received our thanks in person.

We are grateful to *People Management* and the following authors for permission to repro-duce copyright material from the magazine: [to be completed from permissions list]. [Other permissions to be added]. We would also like to thank those who gave up their valuable time to participate in interviews with us to provide new case study material for the book.

There are several other people each author would like to thank.

Catherine would like to thank Alex Michael, Eric Collins, Joyce Henderson, Mark Moorton, Tim Miller, and Raffaela Goodby for assistance with the case studies. Thanks are also due to Kerstin Alfes for her very helpful feedback on earlier drafts. She would also like to thank the many friends and colleagues who have contributed to the development of the ideas dis-cussed in this book over many years, and to extend heartfelt thanks and appreciation to Edward, Jemma, and Sebastian for their patience, love, and support whilst this book was being written.

Clare would like to thank Mike Clancy (Deputy General Secretary) and David Luxton (Na-tional Negotiator) at Prospect, Andy Brierley (Group HR Director) at QinetiQ, and Melanie Flogdell (Head of HR Policy) at Centrica for assistance with the case studies. She would also like to thank Mike Emmott (Advisor, Employee Relations) and Vanessa Robinson (Head of HR Practice Development) at the CIPD, and Edward Irwin (Head of Marketing, Human Resource Services) at PWC. Thanks are also due to Jayne Ashley at Cranfield School of Management for assistance in producing the manuscript.

David would like to thank his co-authors for their patience and consideration through the writing of this book. He would also like to thank his wife Kay for her unending support and patience.

We are grateful to the following for permission to reproduce copyright materials:

Chapter 2 end-of-chapter case study, reproduced with kind permission of Mel Flogdell and Centrica plc. Figure 2.4 reproduced from Riley, M.W. and Riley J. (1994) 'Age integration and the lives of older people'. *The Gerontologist*, with the kind permission of the publisher, Oxford University Press. Chapter 2 case study *How labour migration patterns in China affect the avail-ability of the 'must have' Christmas toy in Europe* adapted from BBC News at bbc.co.uk/news. Chapter 2 case study *Pizza Express* © Louisa Peacock / The Daily Telegraph. Figure 3.2 from Whittington (2001: 3) *What is Strategy – and Does it Matter?* Cengage. Figure 4.1 reproduced from John Storey, Developments in the Management of Human Resources (1992), with kind permission from the publisher, John Wiley & Sons Ltd. Figure 4.2 and table 4.2 adapted and reprinted with permission from *Human Resource Champions: The Next Agenda for Adding Value and Delivering Results* by Dave Ulrich. Harvard Business Press, 1996. Chapter 4 case study *Michael Chivers* used with the permission of the publisher, The Chartered Institute of Personnel Development, London and Michael Chivers, Vice President Human Resources, Sony Ericsson. Figure 4.3 and table 4.3 reproduced with kind permission of the *Harvard Business Review*. Figure 4.4 and table 4.4 reproduced with kind permission from the publisher, John Wiley & Sons Ltd. Chapter 4 case study *Cambridgeshire County Council* adapted from McLuhan *Personnel Today*, 27th November 2007, used with permission. Chapter 4 end-of-chapter case study *Reed Boardall* reproduced from *HR Magazine* 1 April 2009 © A&D media, part of the Mark Allen Group. Figure 5.1 reproduced from Wright and Boswell, 2002 *Journal of Change Management*, reproduced by permission of SAGE Publications. Chapter 5 case study *Tarmac* adapted from www.thetimes100.co.uk, used with permission. Chapter 5 case study *Hennes and Mauritz* adapted from: Deepu Prakash, Hennes and Mauritz (H&M) Case Study, In: ideasthoughts.com. With kind permission from Deepu Prakash. Chapter 5 end-of-chapter case study reproduced with kind permission from Mark Moorton and Specsavers Ltd. Chapter 6 case study Delta Airlines adapted from Wright and Snell, *Human Resource Management Journal* 2005: 177-181, reproduced with kind permission from the publisher, John Wiley & Sons Ltd. Chapter 6 case study *Nuclear Decommissioning Authority* www.thetimes100.co.uk © MBA publishing. Figure 7.3 used with the permission of the publisher, The Chartered Institute of Personnel Development, London. Chapter 7 McDonald's case study used with permission from McDonald's Corporation. Chapter 8 case study *Pace* from Churchard, C. (2010) 'In the Top Set', *People Management*, 8 April, pp. 18-21. With permission of the publisher, the Chartered Institute of Personnel and Development, London. Chapter 8 case study *Nick's Pizza and Pub* adapted from *Improving Employee Performance in 3 Simple Steps: A Restaurant Case Study*, with permission from Greg McGuire, Halogen Software Talent Management and Employee Performance blog, 16th March 2011. Figure 8.1 used with the permission of the publisher, The Chartered Institute of Personnel Development, London. Chapter 8 end-of-chapter case study *DWP* used with kind permission of Joyce Henderson, People Insight Consultant. Table 11.1 from Salamon, *Industrial Relations: Theory and Practice* © Pearson Education Limited. Figure 11.1 from Kitay, J. and Marchington, M. (1996) 'A review and critique of industrial relations typologies'. *Human Relations*, 49, pp. 1263-1290, Reproduced by permission of SAGE Publications. Table 11.2 from Hyman, J. and Mason, B. (1995) Managing Employee Involvement and Participation. London: Sage Publications. Reproduced by permission of SAGE Publications. Chapter 11 end-of-chapter case study reproduced with kind permission of Andy Brierley, Group HR Director, QinetiQ and David Luxton, National Negotiator, Prospect. Figure 15.1 reproduced from Balogun, J. and Hope-Hailey, V. (2004) Exploring Strategic Change, 2nd Ed (London: Prentice Hall), with permission from Pearson Education Ltd. Figure 15.2 from Alfes, K., Truss, C., and Gill, J. (2010) 'The HR Manager as Change Agent: Evidence from the Public Sector'. *Journal of Change Management*, 10, 1, 123. Reproduced by permission of SAGE Publications. Chapter 15 *Six Steps in Managing Change* Hayes, The Theory and Practice of Change Management 2e. 2006: 54-59. Reproduced with permission of Palgrave Macmillan. Chapter 15 case study *HR's Role in Managing a Merger* from Martindale, N. (2007) 'Delivering Major Change'. *Personnel Today*, 27 November, pp. 30-31. Used with permission. Figure 15.3 Based on Adams et al (1976) *Transition: Understanding and*

Managing Personal Change. London: Martin Robertson & Co. Reproduced in Balogun and Hope-Hailey (2004: 142). Used with permission from Pearson Education Ltd and John Wiley & Sons Ltd. Figure 15.4 from Goodman, J. and Truss, C. (2004) 'The Medium and the Message: Communicating Effectively during a Major Change Initiative'. *Journal of Change Management*, Vol. 4, no. 3, p. 225, with permission from the publisher. Chapter 15 Crail, M. (2007) HR's role in managing organisational change, *IRS Employment Review*, November 19, 2007, used with kind permission from Mark Crail, Head of Salary Surveys and Benchmarking Services, XpertHR.

Guide to the Book:

Our original aim was to write a textbook that would demystify the concept of strategic human resource management and explain different aspects of the concept in an accessible and student-friendly manner. We hope that we have achieved this aim. Various pedagogical features have been used to make the content more interesting and to encourage readers to find out more about specific topics:

 Key Concept

Strategy is a plan that integrates an organization's vision, mission, goals, and objectives, and determines how

Key concept

Boxes provide succinct explanations of concepts important to developing an understanding of human resource development.

 Case study 3.2 Tata Motors

Over the last 20 years US car producers have been focusing on trucks and sport-utility

Case study

Boxes contain examples of practice relevant to a chapter's content. Some of these are taken from primary sources, such as HR professionals that we have interviewed for the book. Others are based on material drawn from secondary sources such as academic journal articles and other textbooks. Each has associated activities for you to undertake. You should use a mix of academic and media sources to answer to these questions. Where possible share this with fellow students.

 Review questions

1. What is the relationship between an organization's vision and mission

Review questions

At the end of each chapter provide another opportunity to check understanding.

 Further reading

Mintzberg, H. (1987) Crafting strategy. *Harvard Business Review*, July–Aug.

Recommended further reading

Lists a wide range of books and articles for you to select from to improve your understanding of a chapter's content.

End-of-chapter case study Tesco, Kraft Foods, and Haier: comparing strategies

Case studies

At the end of every chapter include questions to answer and can be used for group work in the classroom.

Glossary

Added value Added value is about identifying what really matters to key stakeholders and delivering the

Glossary of terms

Provides easy accessibility to definitions of all the principal concepts contained in the book.

Guide to the Online Resource Centre:

The Online Resource Centre includes resources for both lecturers and students.

http://www.oxfordtextbooks.co.uk/orc/truss/

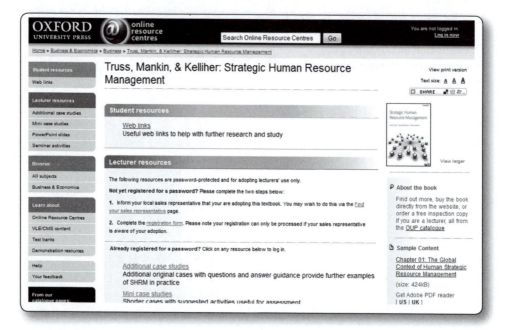

For students:

Annotated web links provide a useful guide to helpful material.

For registered lecturers:

Truss, Mankin, and Kelliher: *Strategic Human Resource Management*

Case study: Google in China

Google came into existence in March 1998 when two Stanford University students, Larry Page and Sergey Brin, set up the shop in a friend's garage to work on their big idea for a search engine. Today, Google is one of the most admired companies in the United States; and in 2009, appeared for the first time on *Fortune*'s list of most admired companies in fourth

Additional original cases with questions provide further examples of SHRM in practice.

Learning objectives

By the end of this session you will be able to:

- Define and explain the concept of globalization.
- Discriminate between different perspectives on globalization

A suite of adaptable PowerPoint slides accompanies each chapter along with supporting notes and seminar questions. These can be easily customized to match your teaching style.

Truss, Mankin, and Kelliher: *Strategic Human Resource Management*

Seminar activities

Activity 2

Lynda Gratton argues in her book *The Future of Work is Already Here* (published by Harper Collins) that we need to change how we work in the future by doing the following:

- use technology and globalization to develop new networks of collaborators
- co-operate and pursue balance in our lives

Seminar activities and discussion questions can be used in class to generate debate and promote critical thinking.

Part 1

The context of SHRM

1

The global context of strategic human resource management

Learning Objectives

By the end of this chapter you should be able to:

- Define and explain the concept of globalization.
- Discriminate between different perspectives on globalization.
- Understand the relationship between globalization and free-market capitalism.
- Understand the principal causes and consequences of the global recession.
- Explain how globalization is impacting on work and organizations.
- Appreciate the implications of globalization for the practice of strategic human resource management.

Key Concepts

Globalization and global trends
Supply chains
Free-market capitalism
Unitary ideology
Strategic human resource management (SHRM)

1.1 Introduction

This chapter is intended to provide an overview of the global context and how particular global trends are impacting on organizations. Trends include the rapid development of different information and communications technologies, increased competition in global markets, changing organizational structures, and the emergence of new business models. Examples of specific implications for the nature and style of strategic human resource management (SHRM) across a range of sectors are highlighted in the final section. In order to appreciate global trends it is necessary first to have an informed understanding of globalization and the principal concepts associated with it, such as free-market capitalism. Globalization is a term widely used to explain the apparent global convergence of political, economic, social, and technological trends over the last few decades. It is an emotive and highly contentious concept that is characterized by a polarization of viewpoints, essentially around the economic and social: the integration of global markets can be viewed as an opportunity to create wealth in both developed and developing nations or as a process that exploits low-paid workers in developing nations. Economic globalization is driven by consumerism and the demand for ever cheaper products and services, ranging from clothes to electronic goods. As a consequence, more people in India, China, and South-East Asia aspire to the lifestyle choices available to citizens in the developed, predominantly Western, nations, so more people are lifted out of poverty and into the middle classes (Nair, 2011). Unfortunately, the availability of cheap labour in Asia now threatens the prosperity of Western workers (Brown et al, 2011).

The current phase of globalization can be traced back to the 1980s, a decade that witnessed the deregulation of markets and the privatization of public sector services. Since then global trade has become increasingly integrated as old business models and organizational forms have been replaced with new ones. Increasingly supply chains are being extended as production and service facilities are outsourced to other companies [such as specialist small to medium sized enterprises (SMEs)] and other countries (especially China and India). Much of this has been enabled through the utilization of increasingly sophisticated information and communications technologies, symbolized by the internet. The extent to which global markets are now integrated is aptly illustrated by the recent global recession that was triggered by a financial crisis in the US and which quickly engulfed nations around the world (including the UK and Europe, the Middle East, Asia and Australasia, and South America).

 Key Concept

The **supply chain** is the network of organizations that are involved in the processes that create value for customers in the form of products and/or services (Mankin, 2009).

The period since 2007 has been characterized by reduced demand in developed nations for a wide range of services and products. Workforces have been culled, wages frozen or reduced, and homes repossessed in the US and Europe (e.g. Ireland, Iceland, Spain, Portugal, Greece, France, and the UK). Arguably this is indicative of fundamentally flawed economic policies (Moyo, 2011). Asian countries have fared better. This contrast in economic fortunes reflects the extent to which traditional industrial powers are in relative decline (Lynn, 2011). Whereas job losses have been particularly acute in the US (Sullivan and Marvel, 2011) and the US struggles to recover its pre-recession dominance of the global economy, China is in the process of creating a new economic model (Naisbitt and Naisbitt, 2010). However, it is far too early to predict that China will definitely replace the US as the world's dominant economy (Magnus, 2011). The recession has also impacted on the levels of investment in eco-friendly initiatives needed to create low-carbon economies (e.g. wind farms, recycling). Competition between nations for natural resources is becoming more intense as the world's energy needs are predicted to rise by 50% by 2030 (Kaplan, 2010). This problem is compounded by the failure of governments to agree a workable policy strategy for curbing the causes of climate change (Victor, 2011).

These trends have profound implications for the theory and practice of SHRM. The chapters in Part 2 of this book explore a wide range of perspectives on SHRM. However, for the purposes of this introductory chapter, SHRM will be defined as the vertical and horizontal alignment of HR strategy, policies, plans, and practices with an organization's corporate or business strategy. Vertical alignment is the process by which HR strategy, policies, and plans are aligned with an organization's strategic goals and objectives. Horizontal alignment is the process by which HR strategy, policies, plans, and practices are aligned with each other as well as with other functional strategies, policies, plans, and practices such as marketing and health and safety which, in turn, are also vertically aligned. In effect HR has a shared responsibility with other functions, such as Finance, IT, and Marketing, to 'ensure corporate systems and corporate thinking are uniform, with set reporting mechanisms to facilitate collation and consolidation of data to allow more robust, rapid decision making at the centre [of the organization]' (Matthewman, 2011: 96). The chapter will argue that SHRM has been impacted in a number of ways, including the need to use HR policies, practices, and processes to help the organization: develop global leaders who can think and act from a global perspective; develop adaptable and flexible organizational structures; manage increasingly complex supply chains and the implications of increased levels of outsourcing and offshoring; manage increasingly diverse workforces; update and apply core competencies and skills; support innovation and knowledge sharing processes; as well as develop other aspects of knowledge management systems.

1.2 Globalization

Whilst the concept of globalization is not new, the breadth and depth of the current phase of globalization and its social, economic, and political impact are greater than ever before. This is the result of several factors including population growth (demographics), information and communications technologies (e.g. digital technologies, the internet), and the deregulation of markets (e.g. free flow of financial capital, speculative investments, increasingly complex financial instruments, and the spreading of financial risk across the globe). The global convergence of social, economic, and political factors has led some observers to argue that we are in the process of creating a form of cultural homogeneity, as once disparate communities are connected together in a new, global society (Kingsnorth, 2008), a trend Gray (2000) refers to as *de-localization*. A specific example of this is Wong's (2010) observation that 'IKEA's Scandinavian aesthetic is changing Beijing's style, promoting Western ideals of domestic space and décor' (p. 148). However, this perspective needs to be treated with caution. For instance, foreign direct investment (FDI) companies are still confronted by wide-ranging differences in legislation, business practices, and cultural values and norms.

From an economic perspective globalization is about the primacy of an integrated global market which transcends national markets and frontiers (Wolf, 2005). The underpinning principle is that global markets create competition which ensures better products and services at

Key Concept

Globalization is about the creation of a borderless global economy that allows unhindered movement of finance, products, services, information, and people (Mankin, 2009).

better prices (Marquardt, 2005). For this to work there needs to be deregulation of markets: organizations need to be able to compete freely against each other and without the hindrance of any trade restrictions. Restrictions have included national trade barriers and tariffs such as import quotas, product standards, subsidies, voluntary export restraints, and licensing (Spulber, 2007). While the advocates of economic globalization promote the benefits of wealth creation, the detractors of the concept, usually referred to as anti-globalists, tend to focus on social and environmental consequences, pointing out that as each year passes the world's population grows by 78 million, thus placing further strains on global resources and infrastructures.

 Case study 1.1   Globalization and the crime 'industry'

As far back as the 1930s gangsters have been adopting, often unknowingly, management principles. For instance, one of London's most infamous post-war crime bosses, Jack Spot, reflecting on his experiences in prison in the 1930s explained that: 'One fact became increasingly obvious to me. No one man is capable of possessing all the various skills that the perfect criminal needs. But to achieve perfect robberies, beautifully executed and with no fear of failure, the separate skills of all these men should be welded together into one concentrated effort. . . . Then perfection in crime could be achieved'. It could be argued that Jack Spot failed to appreciate the fallibility of management models. Jack Spot's criminal empire generated income primarily through illegal gambling and protection rackets. Today the three principal income streams for organized crime are the smuggling of drugs, arms, and weaponry, and the illegal trade in animals (the latter is worth billions). Other major sources of income come from human trafficking and illegal gambling. More recently, organized crime has grown in tandem with the globalization of the world's economy. In today's globalized world, 'One group of people . . . saw real opportunity . . . [and] understood instinctively that rising living standards in the West, increased trade and migration flows, and the greatly reduced ability of many governments to police their countries combined to form a goldmine. They were criminals, organised and disorganised, but they were also good capitalists and entrepreneurs, intent on obeying the laws of supply and demand. As such, they valued economies of scale, just as multinationals did, and so they sought out overseas partners and markets to develop industries that were every bit as cosmopolitan as Shell, Nike or McDonald's. They first became visible in Russia and Eastern Europe, but they were also exerting an influence on countries as far away from one another as India, Colombia and Japan'. The adoption of innovative information and communications technologies has been an important facilitator in the expansion of organized crime beyond traditional geographical boundaries (which limited the scope of earlier gangsters such as Jack Spot cited above). However, not everyone agrees with this globalized interpretation of organized crime. For instance, Varese (2011) argues that it is actually difficult for crime bosses to establish and monitor overseas 'branches' effectively: 'A reputation for violence depends on long-term relations, cemented within independent networks of kinship, friendship and ethnicity. It is next to impossible to reproduce them in a new land'.

Sources

Clarkson, W. (2002) *Hit 'em Hard: Jack Spot, King of the Underworld*. London: HarperCollins Entertainment, pp. 40–41.

Lunde, P. (2004) *Organised Crime: An Inside Guide to the World's Most Successful Industry*. London: Dorling Kindersley.

Glenny, M. (2009) *McMafia: Seriously Organised Crime*. London: Vintage Books, pp. 5–6.

Varese, F. (2011) *Mafias on the Move: How Organised Crime Conquers New Territories*. Princeton, NJ: Princeton University Press, p. 4.

Activity

There is a growing body of academic literature on organized crime. What does this tell us about the ways in which criminal organizations and their 'employees' are managed by crime bosses?

Not surprisingly the detractors of economic globalization portray business corporations as villains, driven solely by the need to generate profits (Bakan, 2004; Stiglitz, 2007). In many companies the uptake of corporate social responsibility (CSR) policies may simply be a rational (or in some cases cynical) decision aimed at satisfying stakeholder expectations rather than as a legitimate concern for social and environmental issues. Klein (2008) argues that even natural disasters are now being viewed as market opportunities, a trend she describes as 'disaster capitalism', while Diamond (2005) cites genocide and violent crime as some of the consequences of globalization (primarily in Third World countries). Addressing these issues is a complex and challenging task, especially as the global political context is growing increasingly unstable (Rachman, 2010). Presently, social and political instability is affecting countries across North Africa and the Middle East (e.g. Afghanistan, Iraq, Pakistan, Tunisia, Libya), while Iran and North Korea are viewed by the West as unstable regimes.

The different perspectives on globalization have been summarized as 'pro-globalization' and 'anti-globalization' in Table 1.1.

Finally, it is evident that indigenous business models are evolving in emerging economies such as China (Naisbitt and Naisbitt, 2010), although it is still difficult to assess the effectiveness of HR practices in many of these countries (Mankin, 2009). Asian countries such as South Korea are characterized by a strong work ethic and a collective spirit (Kim and Jaffe, 2010) which suggests that new forms of employee engagement and other HR practices are likely to evolve as competition from other Asian countries intensifies. As Matthewman (2011) observes: 'emerging markets are full of over-engineered Western management philosophies which in many local firms have failed because they were not tailored or amended to fit local work culture' (p. 124). Yet despite all of these trends it is still the US that the rest of the world turns to for global solutions to global problems (Brooks and Wohlforth, 2009).

Table 1.1 Different perspectives on globalization

Pro-globalization	Anti-globalization
Globalization provides an integrated global market through the removal of barriers to free trade.	It is a flawed economic concept that has failed to deliver on its early promise (proven by the collapse of free-market capitalism as a result of the global recession). It is characterized by a process of homogenization that poses a threat to individual nation states (e.g. the erosion of national cultures and the distinctiveness of the local communities that make up nation states).
It removes the need for trade barriers.	There are still many examples of trade barriers that restrict nations, such as those in Africa, from increasing GDP through exports. There are fears of increased protectionism as a result of the global recession.
It promotes the mobility of financial capital across the globe.	The movement of financial capital from the rich developed nations to the poorer developing nations has been relatively modest. There is an increasingly polarized global distribution of income and wealth between the nations of the North and South. Wealth remains in the North.
FDI by multinational corporations stimulates the transfer of technology and management practices to less developed countries.	FDI by multinational corporations is actually restricted to a few countries.
Economic convergence over time results in an equalization of wages across the globe.	There is a lack of any economic convergence: income inequality between the developed and less developed nations is actually increasing. Wages may have increased in developing economies but are not keeping pace with wages in developed countries. Also there are downsides: lack of job security, long hours, and poor working conditions. The migration of low-skilled work to Asia and the Far East also means that supporting low-skilled indigenous workers in Western countries is becoming unsustainable. The increased use of technology (e.g. mobile technologies) has contributed to the intensification of work, resulting in higher incidences of stress and other related physical and psychological health problems. The global recession has resulted in increases in global poverty.
Global markets create competition which ensures better products and services at better prices.	Global markets are producing cheaper products, but manufacturing processes are posing a threat to the world environment: they are characterized by a competitive exploitation of natural resources and a lack of adequate conservation strategies. They are unlikely to deliver the sustainable technologies needed to tackle environmental problems.
Globalization is best driven by a Westernized form of free-market capitalism.	Globalization should not mean the Americanization of other economies and cultures. The global recession highlights the need for a return to the Keynesian mixed-economic model.

Table1.1 *(continued)*

Pro-globalization	Anti-globalization
Globalization can be a force for good: economic integration is a prerequisite for tackling global issues such as poverty.	An economic focus is too narrow: globalization should be seen primarily as a social process. The short-term financial interests of developed countries do not always coincide with the needs and wellbeing of citizens in developing nations. Free-market capitalism has failed to deliver on sustainability.

Source: adapted from Mankin (2009) using additional sources: Burke and Cooper, 2008; Collier, 2009; Shiller, 2009; Wolf, 2009; Brenner et al, 2010; Harvey, 2010; Naisbitt and Naisbitt, 2010; Brown et al, 2011.

1.3 The relationship between globalization and free-market capitalism

In the modern era globalization has been inextricably linked with the concept of free-market capitalism which is characterized by the free markets, privatization, and deregulation. In theory free-market capitalism is characterized by self-correcting mechanisms that avoid any necessity for state intervention. These mechanisms are embedded in a globally integrated financial market which has been made possible through advances in technology. It is the belief that a free-market economy has an inherent ability to correct itself that underpinned government decisions in the West's leading economies to initiate a process of financial deregulation following an era of strict regulation (Soros, 2008). In turn, free-market capitalism is associated with what is termed neo-liberalism. Put simply this is an ideology that puts its faith in technological advances in order to drive economic development which, in turn, creates and sustains a liberal, democratic society (Gray, 2009). Critics of the neo-liberal approach argue that there is still an important role for government intervention in free markets, as highlighted by government bail-outs of banks around the world in 2008 and 2009. At the turn of the century Gray (2000) suggested that the neo-liberal belief in free-market capitalism was 'a Utopia that can never be realised' (p. 2), claiming that 'its pursuit has already produced social dislocation and economic and political instability on a large scale' (ibid). In the light of the post-2007 global recession these words appear highly prescient. Contrary to many of the statements made by politicians that no one could have predicted the recession, there were many individuals whose warnings were ignored. As far back as the mid-1980s Minsky warned that free-market capitalism was seriously flawed (Minsky, 2008 [1986]). Although it is argued that the belief in the infallibility of the market has been exposed as a myth (Fox, 2010) the concept of neo-liberalism is by no means dead (Harvey, 2010).

Whilst it is outside the scope of this chapter to provide an in-depth discussion of the recession, the principal causes and effects are summarized in Table 1.2.

 Critical Reflection

Identify at least two articles written by Milton Freidman, a prominent American economist, and critically analyse the strengths and weaknesses of his position on free-market capitalism.

Table1.2 Causes, contributory factors, and consequences of the global recession

Causes	Contributory factors	Consequences
Free-market capitalism, which underpins globalization, is an inherently flawed concept. The view that the concept is infallible ignores the reality of historical boom–bust cycles.	Complacency of key stakeholders who believed that the cycle of boom and bust was at an end; credit being readily available to businesses and consumers; greed and arrogance of bankers and traders.	Banks and financial institutions brought to the brink of bankruptcy; huge bail-outs provided by governments around the world; loss of consumer faith in the banks and other financial institutions.
Deregulation and decline in corporate governance. The process of deregulation can be traced back to the 1980s, with the principal political proponents being Margaret Thatcher in the UK and Ronald Reagan in the US.	Governments, central banks, and financial regulators failed to regulate the activities of financial institutions and credit-rating agencies [e.g. Labour government, Bank of England, and Financial Services Authority (FSA) in the UK; recent US Democratic and Republican presidents, and Alan Greenspan at the Central Bank of America in the US]; an over-reliance on debt; increasingly complex financial processes and mechanisms (e.g. securitization) which many executives in the banking sector did not actually understand; over-reliance on technology to support the increasingly complex financial processes and mechanisms (e.g. computer systems for calculating credit risk).	Controls on lending removed; increased levels of consumerism; low-income families encouraged to take out mortgages they could not afford to pay back (the subprime mortgage).
Human behaviour: greed and arrogance of bankers and traders. Massive bonuses based on risky short-term decisions and the accumulation of debt—referred to subsequently as 'toxic assets'.	Lack of regulation; changing social values (increasingly materialistic from the 1980s onwards); the appointment of senior managers of banks and financial institutions who lack banking and financial qualifications; lack of a long-term perspective.	Reckless lending; destabilization of the banking industry; increased bankruptcies (firm and personal); collapse of financial markets and share prices; sharp decline in exports; sharp increase in the number of homeowners in negative equity; the emergence of protectionism. These all contributed to a breakdown of trust and a sense of panic and insecurity as confidence in financial markets and senior executives' competence dwindled.

Table1.2 *(continued)*

Causes	Contributory factors	Consequences
Human behaviour: consumer greed and complacency. A belief that the era of 'boom and bust' was truly over; changing social norms—increasingly materialistic.	Ready availability of credit; low inflation and relatively low interest rates; banks and financial institutions encouraging homeowners to treat equity as an untapped resource to borrow against (e.g. between 2000 and 2007 American homeowners borrowed $2.8 trillion against their homes).	Increased levels of debt disproportionate to income levels; consumers no longer able to meet monthly payments for mortgages and bank loans; collapse in consumer spending impacting on retail outlets and other types of business; increased poverty in developing countries.

Sources: Cooper, 2008; Klein, 2008; Morris, 2008; Peston, 2008; Soros, 2008; Akerlof and Shiller, 2009; Barbera, 2009; Cohan, 2009; Elliott and Atkinson, 2009; Reich, 2009, Shiller, 2009; Tett, 2009; Wolf, 2009; Birkinshaw, 2010; Fox, 2010; Harvey, 2010; Boyd, 2011; Brown et al, 2011; Buckley, 2011; Eichengreen, 2011; Lybeck, 2011; Martenson, 2011.

The alternative view to free-market capitalism can be traced back to the work of John Maynard Keynes whose economic model was adopted in the middle decades of the last century before becoming discredited or unfashionable (depending on your point of view) in the 1970s (Morris, 2008). Keynesian economics requires the government to play an active role in the management of the economy (Gray, 2000) and is associated with the doctrine of liberalism (Morris, 2008). In effect, it involves a triad: a combination of welfare, state management of the economy, and private enterprise (Elliott and Atkinson, 2009). Friedman (2006) argues that state intervention in the form of protectionist policies would be self-defeating for the US government; rather, state intervention should be a combination of a domestic policy that is focused on 'upgrading the education of every American' and a foreign policy that can open 'restricted markets all over the world' (p. 263).

1.4 The impact of globalization on organizations

The efficacy of the traditional organization structure, based on the division of labour, hierarchy, mass production, and large size, has lost ground to alternative structural principles (Alvesson, 2004) which can offer organizations greater levels of flexibility and adaptability. Divesting production operations to create a more agile organization underpinned Acer's business strategy in 2000–01 (*New York Times*, 2009a), while in 2009 Shell was planning to reduce layers of bureaucracy by merging divisions and creating two new units, one covering the Western hemisphere and the other the rest of the world (*New York Times*, 2010). Flexibility is critical for sustaining innovation in global markets (Sparrow et al, 2004). The ability to innovate and compete in global markets, regardless of the size of the organization, is closely linked to advances in information and communications technology. New ways of working and competing have been opened up through e-commerce. Therefore with the emergence of the internet and the ready availability of software that can support collaborative projects it is not surprising to find that since the turn of the century there have been signs of a transfer of power from the multinational corporation to the individual (Friedman, 2006). It is now possible for individuals to collaborate and compete globally. Size is no longer a determinant of whether an organization can be described as global. Indeed technology has made possible collaboration among large numbers of workers, thus enabling some companies, such as General Electric, to be described as **talent-intensive** mega-institutions (Bryan and Joyce, 2007). Sparrow et al (2004) argue that the impact of e-commerce in this century will be as significant as the impact of mass production methods in the last century. However, it should be noted that:

> Hierarchies may have gotten flatter, but they haven't disappeared. Frontline employees may be smarter and better trained, but they're still expected to line up obediently behind executive decisions. Lower-level managers are still appointed by more senior managers. Strategy still gets set at the top. And the big calls are still made by people with big titles and even bigger salaries (Hamel, 2007: 4).

The rate of change and the type of changes taking place around the world can become easily exaggerated and subjected to hype and speculation. Not surprisingly, a wide range of changes are being predicted: from customers being replaced by 'prosumers' who co-create rather than simply consume goods and services (Tapscott and Williams, 2008) to the use of 'service-oriented architecture' to design and deploy software that supports business activities (Merrifield et al, 2008). This theme is developed further in the final chapter.

As can be seen from Table 1.3 the principal drivers of globalization are: advancements in technology and communications, global competition, and changing organizational structures:

- **Current trends in technology:** these include the speed at which technological changes are occurring, the gains in efficiency as processing speeds increase, the increasing degree and complexity of connectivity, and the greater ease with which organizations can produce customized products and services (Ulrich and Brockbank, 2005). Friedman (2006, 2008) and Fung et al (2008) argue that technology and communications have helped to make the world become 'flatter' as people make connections across organizational and national boundaries and collaborate and compete in real time on a 24/7 basis. The emergence of e-commerce has been fundamental in helping SMEs to carve out niche markets on a world stage. For instance, Finland has been particularly adept at exploiting the internet for e-commerce, having one of the highest internet connection rates globally (Ohmae, 2005). Technology is also helping emerging economies to develop much faster than their Western counterparts were able to in the past (Turner, 2001).

- **Global competition**: markets around the world are now characterized by global competition (Schuler et al, 2008) as more and more businesses flood the markets with their products and services. In particular, China and India are not only experiencing rapid economic growth but also developing their own indigenous forms of capitalism rather than replicating the prevailing Westernized model (Ferguson, 2004). Both countries have been focusing on different sectors: manufacturing, construction, and transport in China, and services and software design in India. China has adopted a classic Asian strategy of exporting low-priced manufactured goods to the West (Das, 2006). Her competitive advantage comes from a combination of cheap labour and modern production facilities

Table 1.3 The impact of economic globalization on organizations

Drivers of globalization	Organizational requirements
Technology and communications	• Workforce demographics (diversity: gender, ethnicity, age)
• Digital technology (speed, efficiency)	• Health (longer life spans in developed countries)
• Portability (laptops, palmtops, mobile phones)	• Global leadership (understanding global markets; matching management practices to the needs of a global business)
• Workflow/collaboration software (24/7 working, higher productivity)	
• Connectivity (internet, intranets)	• Adaptable and flexible organizational structures (e.g. flexible firm; integrating offshore and outsourced elements of the firm; matching structure to innovation requirements)
• Customization (products, services)	
Global competition	
• Integrated global market	
• Free-market capitalism (US model)	• Managing supplier chains (implications of outsourcing and offshoring; preparing managers for international assignments)
• Asian indigenous business models	
• Global brands	
• Deregulation	• Managing a diverse workforce (external and internal labour markets)
• Offshoring (labour intensive and low automation)	
• Outsourcing (low value-added activities)	• Updating core competencies and skills
• Disintegration of supply chains and fragmentation of production processes (having different parts of the process carried out in different countries in order to minimize costs)	• Innovation (better products and services but at a lower cost; shorter product life cycles)
	• Knowledge management systems for knowledge creation, sharing, and transfer
Organizational structures	• Retention of intellectual capital
• Mergers, acquisitions, and alliances	• Cost reduction (e.g. labour)
• Restructuring	• Increased productivity (quality of service)
• Migration of work (manufacturing, services, and specialist/knowledge functions)	• Market expansion

Sources: Mankin (2009) plus additional sources: Naisbitt and Naisbitt, 2010; Chesbrough, 2011; Matthewman, 2011.

(Kynge, 2006). The country has been transformed from a rural-based economy to an urban state-controlled version of capitalism (Huang, 2008) that reflects China's rejection of Western democratic values (Deng, 2008). Meanwhile India has been concentrating on services and software design and has relied on domestic rather than export markets (Das, 2006). As a result the software development sector in India has grown significantly and is diversifying from offering basic services to developing high-level software development. Leading companies, such as Motorola, Hewlett-Packard, and Cisco Systems, now rely increasingly on Indian software development teams for next-generation products, with Bangalore becoming India's own 'Silicon Valley' (Mankin, 2009). However, just as the US and old USSR were locked in a power struggle that centred on Europe between 1945 and 1989, today the Indian Ocean has become the site of a trading rivalry between India and China (Kaplan, 2009). Elsewhere, Russia has been using its vast supply of natural resources for political leverage in Eastern Europe (Goldman, 2008), while Brazil appears to be well placed to weather the global recession.

- **Changing organizational structures**: organizations have had to make structural changes in order to keep pace with global trends. The increase in mergers, acquisitions, and alliances reflects the extent to which multinational corporations are using size and brand name to exploit global markets. At the same time many organizations have had to relocate or outsource elements of the supply chain in order to take advantage of lower labour costs in other countries.

 ## Case study 1.2   Do we need a new business model?

The economic rise of the BRIC countries (i.e. Brazil, Russia, India, and China) is being accompanied by the emergence of new, indigenous business models that are starting to challenge prevailing Western models of how businesses should be managed both operationally and strategically. This trend was strengthened by the global financial crisis which demonstrated flaws in the West's adherence to free-market capitalism. Many of these new models will reflect greater interaction between businesses and government and a more pragmatic attitude will see Western firms trying to find new ways to make this changing situation profitable. James Fleck, Dean of the Open University Business School, agrees that the financial crisis has affected business profoundly; in particular, it has demonstrated the limitations of existing ideas about how business should be managed. He believes that the concept of management has not yet reached maturity and what is needed from people in organizations is the ability to take a much more holistic view of what the organization is and how it should be managed. Arguably, his emphasis on a holistic view reflects an Asian perspective. However, Western business failed to appreciate the holistic nature of the total quality management (TQM) philosophy imported from Japan in the 1980s and 1990s. Businesses tended to select certain ideas only, such as quality circles, and failed to appreciate the need for these to be integrated with a wider system that was predicated on a distinctive Asian culture. For instance, the Toyota Production System is underpinned by **challenge** (requiring empowered employees), *kaizen* (continuous improvement), *genchi genbutsi* (go and see), **respect** (which is built on trust), and **teamwork** (including quality circles). These are underpinned by a distinctive set of beliefs and values which Kaoru Ishikawa, one of Japan's most well-known 'quality' gurus, argued were alien to Western thinking. As Fleck points out, people may believe that the current dominance of the Anglo-American model of business is the culmination of management thinking, but actually the failure of this model has been its inability to engage with the broader issues of governance of a business operation. Poor governance has been a characteristic of Western business models, as illustrated in Chapter 14 on corporate social responsibility. Fleck also argues that these changes will have major consequences for HR in its role of developing, motivating, and acclimatizing people to different organizational cultures. How prescient these views are is still unknown. If Raghav Bahl is correct when he argues that the West has seriously underestimated the level of China's drive and ambition, it may not be that long before we find out.

Sources

Ishikawa, K. (1985) *What Is Total Quality Control? The Japanese Way.* Harlow: Prentice Hall.

Liker, J.K. and Hoseus, M. (2008) *Toyota Culture: The Heart and Soul of the Toyota Way.* New York, NY: McGraw-Hill.

People Management, 30 October 2008, p. 18. © James Fleck, Dean of the Open University Business School and Professor of Innovation Dynamics.

Bahl, R. (2010) *Super Power? The Amazing Race Between China's Hare and India's Tortoise.* New York, NY: Portfolio/Penguin.

Kaletsky, A. (2010) *Capitalism 4.0: The Birth of a New Economy.* London: Bloomsbury.

Magnus, G. (2011) *Uprising: Will Emerging Markets Shape or Shake the World Economy?.* Chichester: John Wiley and Sons.

Activity

1. How is government intervention in business different in China than in the UK or US?

2. Can you identify a firm in each country that illustrates a particular difference revealed by your answer to the first question?

1.5 The implications of globalization for HR

The greatest challenge facing HR professionals working in an international capacity is how to operate effectively at both a global and a local level (Hall, 2005); to have the ability to **think globally** but **act locally** (Hatcher, 2006). This is important because it has been increasingly recognized that country and local context influence the HR practices of multinationals (Cooke, 2004a). Although many smaller organizations now operating in the global market-place tend not to employ specialist HR professionals there is still a need for managers to think in this way.

 Key Concept

The **unitary ideology** promotes a common purpose and shared values and ways of behaving. Teamwork and employee commitment are emphasized. Anyone who challenges this ideology is treated as dysfunctional and subjected to training or disciplinary action.

The concept of free-market capitalism is associated with profit maximization and individual rewards (Klein, 2008). Individual rewards are a characteristic of the closely entwined relationship between HR and a unitary ideology (particularly in larger organizations), while profit maximization has driven the need for HR functions to demonstrate they add value to an organization (and that their activities contribute to sustaining competitive advantage). Whilst profit maximization may not be important to public sector and non-profit organizations, the maximization of performance (against budgets) and the drive for added value certainly are (Mankin, 2009). Globalization presents HR professionals with the opportunity to deliver a wide range of HR interventions that add value to an organization. In order to achieve this they need to work in partnership with key stakeholders at both a strategic and operational level. Managing these stakeholder relationships is a challenging and complex task and is influenced by how the HR function is structured (see Chapter 4). To be successful HR professionals must understand global trends and the issues that matter most to stakeholders (Ulrich and Brockbank, 2005). This knowledge needs to be integrated with an understanding of the global economy regardless of the size of an organization and the sector it is operating in. In larger organizations the ability of managers to integrate and coordinate organizational structures and processes that are globally dispersed is becoming ever more critical (Lasserre, 2007). This has major implications for HR practices that involve organization development, management development, and work design.

Much of the existing literature on the role of HR is dominated by Anglo-American perspectives. However, there are important differences in practice between the US and the UK in areas such as employee relations, human resource development (HRD), and employment legislation (Larsen and Mayrhofer, 2006). Indigenous responses to HR are now emerging across the Middle East, Asia, India, and China. For instance, there are examples of sophisticated indigenous approaches to HRD in the developing economies of India and China, although training costs are minimized in the Chinese manufacturing sector (Mankin, 2009). FDI companies invest in HR more than indigenous companies and this is helping in the transfer of HR practices between developed and developing economies. This trend is not restricted to Western multinationals. For instance, the South Korean car manufacturer Hyundai has applied some of its own HRM policies in India, particularly training programmes which have been designed to reinforce employee loyalty to the company (Lansbury et al, 2006).

The impact of the global recession has highlighted HR's role in decision-making processes that affect the short- and long-term viability of an organization (e.g. redundancies and retention respectively). The retention of key employees (often referred to as 'core' or 'knowledge' workers) is critical in most organizations and sectors. The retention argument was used by some banks as a justification for continuing the practice of paying huge bonuses. In contrast, companies such as Motorola, Fedex, and Caterpillar 'slashed' salaries and bonuses for executives (Guerra and Chung, 2009). The global recession has prompted a more critical examination of the HR function and the extent to which it adds value or is simply expendable.

Unfortunately there has been limited and inconsistent evidence that HR interventions do add value by impacting positively on employee and organizational performance. A major research study for the Chartered Institute of Personnel and Development (CIPD) by Purcell et al (2003) revealed that it is possible only to discern some positive associations between specific HR practices and performance (e.g. training, career development and communications). Maybe this is why HR functions still have a relatively poor track record in evaluating the effectiveness of HR strategies, policies, and practices. Those functions that have been able to demonstrate added value have been better placed to 'ride out' the economic storm (as illustrated by organizations that sustained pre-recession levels of investment in learning and development in order to maintain competitive advantage. You may find it useful at this point to refer to Chapter 8 on the outcomes of SHRM.

Table 1.4 sets out the key organizational requirements that HR functions need to address. All the themes covered in the table will be discussed in subsequent chapters. Although these requirements are biased to multinationals, many affect other types of organization to a lesser or greater extent. For instance, non-profit organizations operating in several countries or

Table 1.4 Implications of globalization for the HR function

Organizational requirements	HR implications
The development of global leaders with a global perspective Developing leaders who can think and act from a global perspective is a critical success factor for organizations operating in global markets. There is a view that organizations need to create a unique leadership brand.	• Management and leadership development initiatives that focus on the development of leadership skills. This includes in-house and external programmes. • Regulating an organization's CSR policy. • Educating managers to behave in ethically and socially responsible ways. This can be achieved through workshops, courses, conferences and seminars, mentoring programmes, and executive coaching. • Identifying and developing less senior managers who demonstrate potential senior managerial talent. This can be linked to organizational systems for career development and succession planning. • Building employee commitment to the organization's objectives, values, and norms. • Sustaining employee engagement. • Designing, implementing, and sustaining effective approaches for recruitment and selection, promotion, reward, and retention. • Promoting ethical management and leadership as part of daily activities (HR professionals as role models). • Informal mentoring and coaching (can include upward coaching).
Adaptable and flexible organizational structures There are an increasing number of mergers, acquisitions, alliances, and joint ventures, often involving cross-national and cultural boundaries. Management need to help ease any transition and counter engrained attitudes that may hinder the process of change. Organizations of all sizes seek some degree of flexibility.	• Creating and sustaining new forms of organizational structures with cultures based on cooperation and collaboration. • Implementing an appropriate reward strategy. • Regulating work design. • Management training in change management processes. • Keeping departments and employees affected by an impending merger or acquisition informed about the change using multiple communication channels (reflecting an organization's communications policy in conjunction with its employee involvement or employee participation strategy). • Educating management about potential reorganization options and the implications for the organization and its workforce of those options. • Designing and sustaining performance management systems. • Keeping departments and employees affected by an impending merger or acquisition informed about the change using informal communication channels.

(continued)

Table 1.4 *(continued)*

Organizational requirements	HR implications
Managing supply chains The offshoring and outsourcing of parts of the supplier chain (e.g. production) has resulted in the dispersion of core assets and the creation of competence clusters around the globe. The number of global organizations has continued to rise and the number of employees, primarily managers, relocating abroad continues to increase. However, there is a lack of consistency in preparing managers for international assignments. For instance, many US companies are sending employees abroad without any preparation.	• Creating and sustaining new forms of organizational structures. • Building global teams that can handle problems of diversity and distance. • Training local customer service/call centre staff in British or American language and voice skills (as well as product and customer skills training). This is important as it helps create empathy with the customer. • Training local, indigenous managers in modern management techniques and behaviours. • Cross-cultural training for managers: educating them in 'cultural fluency' (i.e. the ability to work effectively within and between multicultural environments). • Increasing the cultural competence of employees generally. • Preparing employees and managers for expatriation. • Promoting fairness and equity of treatment. • Facilitating the activities of global teams. • Preparing employees and managers for expatriation.
Managing a diverse workforce Internal and external labour markets are becoming increasingly diverse. For instance, the skills needs of immigrant workers; the rising number of female workers; and employees working beyond the traditional retirement age. It is likely that those organizations with cultures that support diversity will be better positioned to retain the best talent needed to remain competitive. There is also a need to improve basic literacy and numeracy skills among low-skilled and low-paid employees.	• Diversity education and training programmes. These communicate the importance of diversity and help to remove barriers, such as employees not understanding the value of diversity. • Designing appropriate recruitment and selection processes. • Designing and implementing diversity and equal opportunities policies. • Developing cross-cultural teamworking and communication skills. Cross-cultural training, traditionally restricted to preparing employees for expatriate assignments, can be used to help domestic employees interact with colleagues from diverse cultural backgrounds. • Training immigrants in technical and customer service skill. • Re-skilling and retraining of older employees beyond the traditional retirement age. • Providing employees with opportunities to improve their basic literacy and numeracy skills to give them the potential to break out of the low-wage cycle. • Adjusting the design and management of performance management systems in multinationals to reflect how performance is impacted by different cultural contexts. • HR professionals acting as role models in the promotion of cultural sensitivity. • Helping employees to understand how they can learn from team experiences.

Table1.4 (*continued*)

Organizational requirements	HR implications
Updating core competencies and skills The core competencies and skills needed by employees are changing rapidly as new forms of technology are introduced, new products and services are developed, new markets are opened up, and suppliers are sourced from around the globe.	• Systems for the identification and monitoring of core competencies and skills (particularly an effective performance management system). • Training and development programmes to enable employees to upgrade or learn new competencies and skills. • Linking skills updating to retention strategies (e.g. promotion/succession planning; rewards). • The promotion of lifelong learning. • Developing alliances with regional and national institutions (e.g. Learning Skills Councils in Britain; labour-market partnerships in the US). • Ensuring management development initiatives are developing new capabilities and not simply reinforcing old ones, which may have human and ecological consequences. • The promotion of lifelong learning and facilitation of informal workplace learning.
Innovation and knowledge sharing The need for innovative products and services. The life cycles of many products and services are becoming shorter and shorter, which places increasing demands on the ability of organizations to be innovative. For instance, Google has achieved its market position by offering superior products, and needs to keep innovating in order to sustain its competitive advantage.	• Developing a global culture of continuous learning, engagement, and commitment which instils employees with a spirit of innovation. • Helping employees to unlearn old behaviours and skills and to learn new ones. • Creating new ways to work. • Supporting technological entrepreneurship (i.e. activities that support innovation through the creation of new resource combinations). • Promoting the role of informal groups and social networks as sources of innovation and problem solving. • Facilitating the activities of informal groups and social networks.
Knowledge management systems Knowledge management (KM) systems are needed to ensure the effective creation and sharing of knowledge within an organization and transfer around the globe. The latter, in particular, requires sophisticated technology.	• Developing employee competencies in knowledge creation, sharing, and transfer and linking this to retention strategies (e.g. rewards; personal development). • Creating a learning infrastructure that maximizes opportunities for organizational learning and knowledge sharing between organizations. • Improving employee familiarity with technology-based KM systems through the utilization of new technologies to deliver e-learning programmes around the globe. • Facilitating KM processes involving both electronic and face-to-face interactions. • Identifying and improving opportunities for knowledge creation, sharing, and transfer.

Source: adapted from Mankin (2009) with additional sources: Rigg, 2007; Burgelman et al, 2008; Marin, 2008; Varma et al, 2008; *New York Times*, 2009b; Ulrich et al, 2009.

regions and competing for funding need senior managers to have effective global leadership skills; and all organizations operating in global markets, from small business to multinationals, need to understand about change management (Mankin, 2009).

 ## Conclusion

This chapter has provided an overview of the global context and explained how several specific global trends are impacting on organizations. These trends include the rapid development of different information and communications technologies, increased competition in global markets, changing organizational structures, and the emergence of new business models. In order to appreciate global trends it was necessary to discuss globalization and the principal concepts associated with it, such as free-market capitalism. Globalization is a term widely used to explain the apparent global convergence of political, economic, social, and technological trends over the last decades. However, as was highlighted, it is an emotive and highly contentious concept that is characterized by a polarization of viewpoints, essentially around the economic and social perspectives on globalization. Following this discussion, the final section highlighted, in tabular format, examples of specific implications for the nature and style of strategic human resource management (SHRM) across a range of sectors. Many of the issues covered by the table will feature more prominently in subsequent chapters.

 ## Summary

This chapter has discussed the global context in respect of several issues:

- The two principal perspectives on globalization (economic and social) and the dominance of the economic perspective .
- The drivers for globalization (e.g. advancements in technology and communications, global competition and changing organizational structures) along with the implications of these drivers for organizations.
- The causes and consequences of the global recession.
- The emerging economies of China and India and the potential for a shift in economic power from the developed nations of the West to these developing nations in Asia and the Far East.
- The potential for HR professionals to deliver a wide range of HR interventions that add value to an organization in a global context.

 ## Review questions

1. What are the principal perspectives on globalization and to what extent are they convergent or divergent?

2. What are the principal causes and consequences of the recent global recession?

3. Summarize how globalization is impacting on organizations generally.

4. What are the principal implications of globalization for the human resource (HR) function in larger organizations?

5. To what extent are Western business models and HR practices relevant to emerging economies such as China and India?

End-of-chapter case study   AirAsia: a Malaysian success story

AirAsia, the international budget airline, is often touted as one of Malaysia's success stories. Malaysia is a relatively small but high-growth economy and is one of the most resource-rich countries in the world. Malaysia underwent a major privatization programme between 1983 and 2000 which achieved mixed results. Malaysia Airlines, the principal competitor of AirAsia in Malaysia, is an example of a company that was privatized and then renationalized when it nearly went bankrupt. Despite such setbacks, Malaysia, in common with many other developing countries, is now on the brink of graduating to the level of more advanced economies such as Korea, Taiwan, and Singapore. However, this progression is potentially at risk from competition from lower-wage economies such as China, India, and Vietnam. There are also potential internal threats to the country's political stability.

AirAsia had two Boeing 737-300 aircraft and RM40 million (approximately £8 million) debts when it was bought by Tony Fernandes for RM1 (approximately 20 pence) in 2001. The firm was relaunched with three aircraft in 2002 and within 7 months it was making a profit. Since then the company has gone from strength to strength by adopting and then adapting the low-cost business model that was working successfully in the US and Europe (e.g. South-western Airlines, Ryanair). By 2009 the airline had 7,500 employees and was making a net profit of RM506 million (approximately just over £100 million). In the same year the firm's long-haul carrier, AirAsia X, was chosen as the World's Best Low-Cost Airline for 2009 by more than 16.2 million travellers in a survey conducted by London-based consultancy Skytrax. The airline continues to expand rapidly and in March 2011 announced the launch of a new joint venture company with the travel firm Expedia which will offer a range of value flights, hotels, and holiday packages in the Asia Pacific market.

Tony Fernandes believes that 'the biggest, most important thing to my passengers is the low fare'. However, to make sure the low-cost model works 'you have to make sure you have the right people, focus and discipline'. He argues that it is pointless doing something just because other airlines are doing it: 'being on time, safe and efficient are important. The rest are really added frills'. Consequently, AirAsia has dropped any services that cost extra money such as free in-flight entertainment, free meals, and refreshments. Customers are encouraged to purchase tickets online. The firm always looks for the cheapest airports to land in and lands as far away from the airport lounge as possible because this reduces landing fees; passengers have to walk to the lounge as buses are not provided. The firm schedules most of its flights so that the same personnel can work on both legs of a journey and return home on the same day, thus eliminating the need to pay for overnight hotels and meals. Longer flights are only considered if they make business sense. The firm does not own any technology such as computers and mobile phones as it is cheaper to rent the equipment. Tony Fernandes describes this strategy as the 'ultra low cost business model'. In terms of the firm's commitment to its employees it has published a range of commitments, such as to develop a safety culture and provide employees with appropriate training, and clearly defines for all employees their responsibilities and accountabilities. The firm has also set up the AirAsia Academy, which trained over 15,000 employees in 2009.

Sources

Vincent, J.R. and Rozali, M.A. (2005) *Managing Natural Wealth: Environment and Development in Malaysia*. Washington: RFF Press.

Telegraph (2007) http://www.telegraph.co.uk/finance/markets/2807593/First-Asian-low-cost-carrier-heading-this-way.html (accessed 4 May 2011).

Tan, J. (2008) *Privatisation in Malaysia: Regulation, Rent Seeking and Policy Failure*. Abingdon: Routledge.

Ze, S. and Ng, J. (2008) *The AirAsia Story: How a Young Airline Made it Possible for Everyone to Fly and Became a Runaway Success Practically Overnight*. Kuala Lumpur: Kanyin Publications.

AirAsia (2009) Annual Report. http://www.airasia.com/iwov-resources/my/common/pdf/AirAsia/IR/AirAsia_AR09.pdf (accessed 4 May 2011).

Ang, J.B. (2009) *Financial Development and Economic Growth in Malaysia*. Abingdon: Routledge.

Pepinsky, T.B. (2009) *Economic Crises and the Breakdown of Authoritarian Regimes: Indonesia and Malaysia Comparative Perspective*. New York, NY: Cambridge University Press.

Hill, H., Yean, T.S. and Zin, R.H.M. (2011) *Malaysia's Development Challenges: Graduating from the Middle (Routledge Malaysian Studies Series)*. London: Routledge.

New York Times (2011) http://markets.on.nytimes.com/research/stocks/news/press_release. asp?docTag=201103291840PR_NEWS_USPRX___SF73786=Search (accessed 4 May 2011).

Case study questions

1. What are the potential business implications for AirAsia of the trends identified in this chapter?

2. What are the potential HR implications of AirAsia's low-cost business model?

 Further reading

Bahl, R. (2010) *Super Power? The Amazing Race Between China's Hare and India's Tortoise*. London: Portfolio/Penguin.
This is probably the best comparative text to date on this topic.

Cappelli, P., Singh, H., Singh, J. and Useem, M. (2010) *The India Way: How India's Top Business Leaders Are Revolutionising Management*. Boston, MA: Harvard Business Press.
An excellent account on the indigenous management practices that are emerging in India.

Kaletsky, A. (2010) *Capitalism 4.0: The Birth of a New Economy*. London: Bloomsbury.
An informed analysis of the evolution of modern capitalism.

Magnus, G. (2011) *Uprising: Will Emerging Markets Shape or Shake the World Economy?* Chichester: John Wiley and Sons.
This focuses on the thesis that without significant political and economic reform in the emerging economies, including China and India, the US will continue to be the world's dominant economy.

Stiglitz, J. (2007) *Making Globalisation Work*. London: Penguin Books.
There are many texts on the subject of globalization, but this one offers a particularly searing critique.

 For additional material on the content of this chapter please visit the supporting Online Resource Centre www.oxfordtextbooks.co.uk/orc/truss.

2 The changing context for SHRM

 Learning Objectives

By the end of this chapter you should be able to:

- Explain recent global labour market trends.
- Understand changes in the nature of the workforce and critically evaluate the implications for SHRM.
- Understand the changing nature of work and work relationships and critically evaluate the implications for SHRM.
- Discuss how HR managers might develop strategies to take account of these changes.

 Key Concepts

Emotional labour
Aesthetic labour
Workplace flexibility

2.1 Introduction

In this chapter we will examine a range of contextual factors which have implications for the strategies adopted in managing HR. First, we focus on what has been happening to the workforce. We will examine population and demographic trends and also changes in attitiudes to work and how people see work in the context of their broader lives. Second, we focus on what has been happening to work. We will look at where people work and what that work involves. Third, and related to the above, we will examine the growing phenomenon of flexibility, both from the point of view of organizations which seek flexibility to improve their competitive position and from the view of employees who seek flexibility to help them balance their work and non-work activities more effectively. Finally, we will briefly explore the trend towards greater individualism and the concern for productivity in the way in which HR are managed. The chapter explores each of these developments and discusses the wider implications for developing HR strategies.

2.2 **The global labour market**

A major concern of employing organizations is to be able to recruit and retain the right number of staff with the appropriate skills and experience. As will be discussed in Part 2, both the quality and costs of labour can play an important role in the delivery of an organization's strategy. Hence it is important for organizations to be aware of the factors that impinge on their ability to obtain the appropriate numbers and quality of HR at the right price. In this section we will examine factors concerning the availability of labour, by examining both population trends and social trends that influence working patterns and attitudes towards paid employment.

An examination of trends in world population gives an indication of whereabouts in the world potential labour is, or will be located in the future. Recent years have seen a number of changes taking place in the distribution of the world's population, which have important implications for those concerned with developing HR strategies. In 2010, world population was estimated to be in the region of 6.9 billion. Table 2.1 shows the top ten countries by population in the world. China and India have by far the largest populations and together have more than one-third of the world's population.

If we examine the distribution of world population between the different continents, we see that there have been some shifts in recent decades; these trends are forecast to continue. Figure 2.1 compares the population between continents for 1960, 2005, and forecast figures for 2050. Looking at this 90-year period we see the continued dominance of Asia, growth in the share based in Africa, stability in the Americas, and the relative decline of Europe as a centre of world population. Changes in population distribution are influenced by both birth rates and life expectancy in different parts of the world. For example, in much of Western Europe birth rates are decreasing, whilst in other parts of the world they remain static or are increasing. Equally, although there are large differences, in many parts of the world life expectancy has increased. In Japan, life expectancy in 2009 was just under 83 years, whereas in Zimbabwe it was less than 45 years (United Nations, 2009). Overall, since 1950, life expectancy has increased globally by 21 years from 46.6 in 1950–55 to 67.6 years in 2005–10 (United Nations, 2009).

If we look more specifically at the population distribution within Europe, we also see significant differences between countries (see Fig. 2.2). France, Germany, Italy, the UK, and Turkey are the largest nations, all with a population of more than 50 million. Taken together, France, Germany, Italy, and the UK account for more than half of the EU-27 population.

Population figures are of course not a direct representation of the labour force or of those available for employment, since a proportion will be in the pre- and post-normal employment age groups. However, knowledge of population trends can inform decisions for global organizations about where to locate their production and/or service delivery facilities. For example, an organization that requires a plentiful supply of low-cost labour may choose to locate in a country with a high population and where labour costs are relatively low. It is clearly no accident that many manufacturing companies have chosen to locate plants in China and that many call centre services are outsourced to India.

Table 2.1 World population—top 10 nations 2010

	Country	Population
	China	1,330,141,295
	India	1,173,108,018
	United States	310,232,863
	Indonesia	242,968,342
	Brazil	201,103,330
	Pakistan	184,404,791
	Bangladesh	156,118,464
	Nigeria	152,217,341
	Russia	139,390,205
	Japan	126,804,433

Source: US Census Bureau, International Data Base.

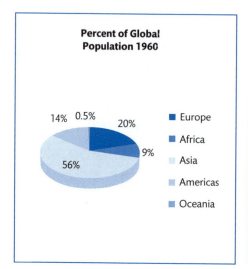

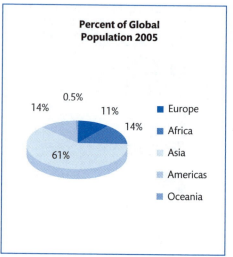

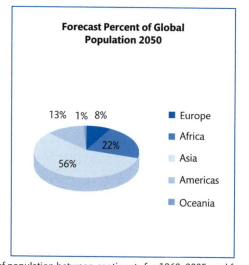

Figure 2.1 Comparison of population between continents for 1960, 2005, and forecast for 2050.

Source: Eurostat (2010) *Europe in Figures, Eurostat Yearbook 2010.* Luxembourg: Publications Office of the European Union.

Knowledge of these trends is also important for employers in those countries where the labour force is set to decline, or where there are existing labour shortages. Even if they are unable to relocate where their work is carried out, it will help them identify those countries where there may be surplus labour which can be attracted to migrate for work. Data on the age distribution of the population also give an insight into the future availability of HR, since it can be gauged well in advance of the time at which people are likely to join and leave the labour force.

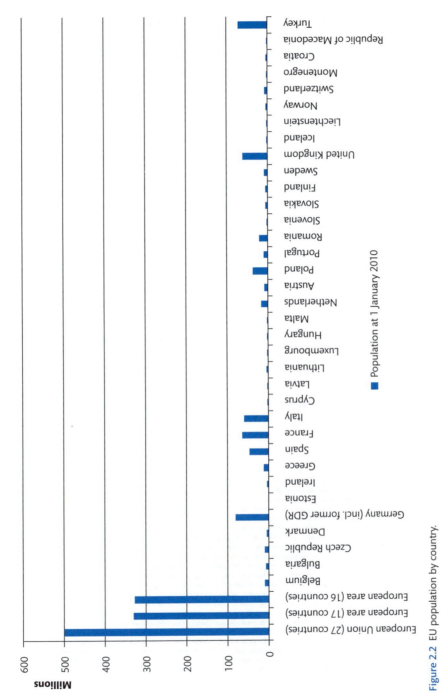

Figure 2.2   EU population by country.

Source: Eurostat. © European Union, 1995–2010. http://epp.eurostat.ec.europa.eu/portal/page/portal/eurostat/home/.

2.3 The changing character of the workforce

Over and above the changes in population trends, there have also been a number of social changes in recent years, which influence the way in which people participate in paid work. A major area of change in many Western economies is the point at which people join and leave the labour force. Patterns in joining and exit times give an indication of how long people will be available for employment. In many countries the amount of time spent in full-time education has increased and consequently the average age at which new entrants join the labour force has also increased. This applies to both compulsory education and participation in voluntary further and higher education. In the UK the recent expansion of participation in higher education means that the entrance to the workforce has been delayed. Furthermore, the Education and Skills Act 2008 has increased the minimum age at which young people in England can leave education or training to 17 from 2013 and 18 from 2015. This development has important implications for employers who have traditionally recruited school leavers, since 16-year-olds will no longer be eligible to undertake full-time employment. The counter side to longer periods of time spent in education is of course that the workforce is more highly educated and this may influence the amount or nature of training that employers need to offer to new entrants to the workforce. This may also impact on wage levels.

At the other end of the age spectrum we have witnessed a trend over a number of years of early retirement from paid employment. Figure 2.3 shows the average age at which people exit from the labour force across EU countries. Although there is some variation in normal retirement age between the countries, these figures show that for the EU the average age for exiting the labour force in 2006 was 61.2. Consequently, many people in the EU are no longer in paid employment during their sixties. Early exit from the labour force may be through choice, to pursue an alternative lifestyle, but it may also be as a result of discrimination, where

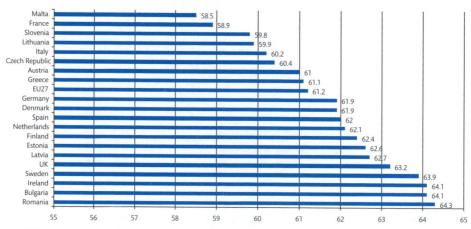

Figure 2.3 Average exit age from the labour force, 2006 (in years).

Note: No data for Belgium, Cyprus, Hungary, Luxembourg, Poland, and Slovakia.

Source: European Foundation for the Improvement of Living and Working Conditions (2008) *Annual Review of Working Conditions in the EU 2007–2008.* Luxembourg: Office for Official Publications of the European Communities.

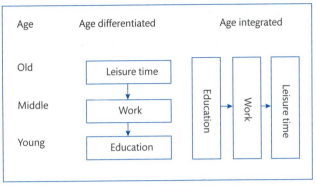

Figure 2.4 Life-course structure.

Source: Riley, M.W. and Riley, J. (1994) Age integration and the lives of older people. *The Gerontologist*, Vol. 34, pp. 110–115.

an older worker is unable to gain or retain employment. This, however, is an area where we are likely to see further change in the future. It is likely that we will see some increase in the average age for exiting the labour force. A number of countries, including France and the UK[1], have increased their normal retirement ages. This move has been in response to increased life expectancies (discussed above) and the resulting financial costs associated with long periods of retirement. In this vein the EU's Lisbon Strategy developed in 2000 set a goal of achieving a 50% rate of employment amongst older workers across the EU. Employers who wish to attract and retain older workers need to think about strategies for the group. The end-of-chapter case study presents the approach adopted by Centrica to managing older workers.

Changes to time spent in education and retirement age reflect more general changes to lifestyles which have implications for employment. In the past the so-called 'age-differentiated' model of employment was prevalent, where a linear approach to life course is taken—education followed by work, followed by leisure. More recently, however, we have seen a trend towards combining these activities in an age-integrated model (Riley and Riley, 1994). For example, students in full-time education may work part-time, or older workers may reduce their commitments to ease themselves into retirement (Loretto et al, 2005). The age-differentiated and age-integrated models of life course are depicted in Fig. 2.4.

Taken together these trends suggest that in some countries the numbers available and willing to work may decline and this may result in labour shortages. Faced with the inability to recruit the right numbers and quality of staff, employers may opt to export jobs or to import labour. Under these circumstances, factors such as average wage costs and employment rates in different countries need to be taken into account. Average wage costs and levels of employment may inform decisions about whether to export jobs to a particular country. Employment levels will also help employers establish the likelihood that they will be able to persuade people to migrate from their home country for work elsewhere. For example, in recent years high levels of unemployment in Poland have influenced the willingness of Polish workers to move to other countries in the EU for work.

---

[1] By 2020 the age at which the state pension is payable will increase to 66 years old in the UK.

Whether or not an organization has the flexibility to export jobs will depend in part on the nature of its activity. For example, a manufacturing company may have considerable geographical flexibility, especially if its product is easy to transport. Equally, back-office and call centre activities may be amenable to being offshored. However, businesses that are more location specific (e.g. retail, hospitality), may have less choice over the location of their workplaces, and instead may respond to labour shortages by importing labour. There is of course a dynamic element here. As labour migrates from a country there will be an impact on employment rates, and as a result in the longer term this may reduce the numbers of people who are willing to move country in search of employment. Similarly, as labour becomes scarcer in a country, average wage rates are likely to increase and as a result the country may become a less attractive source of labour.

In the EU there has been significant migration as countries have opened their boundaries to economic migrants. For a number of European countries a significant proportion of the workforce population is made up of migrant labour. Eurostat (2010) reports that 6.4% of the EU population in 2009 were not living in their country of citizenship. Overall, more than a third of these are citizens of other EU countries. Figure 2.5 provides details of the composition of the population for EU countries. The distribution, however, is not even, with 75% of migrants in the EU residing in France, Germany, Italy, Spain, and the UK. See the case study below for an example of how labour migration patterns in one part of the world can influence business in another.

 Critical Reflection

- Consider what types of business activities best lend themselves to offshoring.
- What might be possible impediments?
- Consider what types of business activity might be best able to make use of migrant labour.
- What factors might employers need to take into account when employing migrant labour?

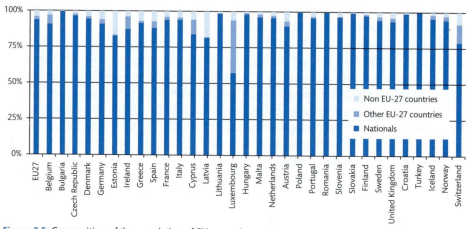

Figure 2.5 Composition of the population of EU countries.

Source: Eurostat (2010) *Europe in Figures, Eurostat Yearbook 2010.* Luxembourg: Publications Office of the European Union.

Case study 2.1 How labour migration patterns in China affect the availability of the 'must have' Christmas toy in Europe

'This year we think Buzz Lightyear is going to be very big. . .', predicts Gareth Davies Marriot, manager of Hamley's toyshop in London.

Each year toy retailers face the challenge of spotting the 'must have' Christmas present toy and ensuring that they have sufficient stocks to satisfy demand.

However, this year it is anticipated that retailers will face an additional challenge to getting sufficient supplies and the source of this is rooted in labour migration patterns in China. A significant proportion of the toys sold in Europe and North America are made in China, particularly in the southern coastal provinces of Guangzhou, Shenzhen, and Zhuhai. In the past these factories have relied on a steady stream of cheap, migrant labour from other parts of China where work has been less available.

However, as a result of government policy to support development in other inland regions in China, the supply of migrant labour to these areas has started to dwindle. Apparently, three million Chinese workers didn't return to the toy factories in southern China following the Chinese New Year holiday in 2010. As a result the factories have had to reduce production. This means that, not only are they producing fewer toys, but also they will be less able to respond quickly to the changing forecasts of toy retailers, who want to ensure that they have sufficient supplies of that 'must have' toy.

'Last year we would have been able to react to customer demand in September and still have goods on our shelves in time for Christmas . . . this year we would probably have needed to have ordered in July in order to get stock in on time', acknowledges Alan Simpson, Managing Director of retailer Toytown.

Source

Adapted from http://www.bbc.co.uk/news/business-11757618.

Activity

Consider other circumstances where patterns of labour migration may have implications for organizations.

In addition to the changes identified above, it has also been observed that people who have entered the workforce in recent years, the so-called Generation Y, approach work with a different attitude and a different set of expectations (Cates and Rahimi, 2003). The term Generation Y has been used to describe those people born between 1978 and 1994 who are now entering the workforce. Generation Y, it is argued, are distinct from Generation X (1962–77) and the 'baby boomers' generation (1945–61) with whom they share the workplace. Commentators suggest that Generation Y's attitudes and values have been shaped by the environment in which they grew up—one of technological advancement and economic prosperity—and as children experienced 'being on the move' and constant stimulation. Observers suggest that they are concerned with issues such as CSR and work–life balance and with what they will gain from employment, such as marketable skills and rewards which are based on meritocratic principles. They are not seen to be loyal to employers and do not expect to stay with one employer (Barr, 2004). These factors suggest that employers may need to take a different approach to the management of Generation Y.

Critical Reflection

- What issues might Generation Y raise for the recruitment and retention of younger workers?
- What issues might arise for other members of the workforce (Generation X and baby boomers) if employers shape their employment policies and practices to fit with the needs of Generation Y employees?
- What might be the consequences of not doing this?
- Is Generation Y a Western concept, or might it also be applicable in other parts of the world?

2.4 The changing nature of work

The nature of work has been subject to some changes in recent years and this has had implications for the ways in which HR are managed. First, as a result of broader economic changes, we find in many countries that the majority of the workforce is employed in service organizations and alongside this we have also seen a significant growth in knowledge work. Second, and in response to increasing competitive pressures, we have seen employers utilizing labour in different ways. For example, in some countries there has been an increase in the use of temporary and part-time contracts, in order to enable employers to match the supply of labour more closely with the demands of their business. We have also seen the growth of forms such as 'virtual teams' in businesses that operate on a global basis; such teams may be made up of employees who work in different locations and in different time zones, working together via the use of some form of communications technology. Linked to the growth in service work, we have seen increased importance placed on what has been termed 'emotional' and 'aesthetic' labour, where employees are paid to manage their emotions and to appear in a prescribed way (for example, customer-facing staff may be expected to smile and be polite and staff may be expected to maintain a standard of dress in line with the company image). If employers are looking for different things from the workforce, this would suggest that there may be a need to change the way they are managed.

2.4.1 The growth of service work

The contribution of services to the European economy has continued to grow as restructuring in many European economies has resulted in a shift away from industrial to service activity (Eurostat, 2010). Across the EU services account for 70% of total employment (European Foundation for the Improvement of Living and Working Conditions, 2007) and in the US this figure is even greater, with services accounting for 78% of total employment (US Bureau of Labor Statistics, 2010). Korczynski (2002) identifies five attributes of services that distinguish them from primary, secondary, manufacturing, and agricultural sectors. These are:

- Intangibility—services have an intangible element which cannot be touched, e.g. quality of service in a restaurant.
- Perishability—service work can be stored or stockpiled, e.g. sales staff in a shop can only sell when customers are present.

- Variability—customers may vary in their expectations of and actions within services.

- Simultaneous production and consumption—the employee produces at the same time as the customer consumes, unlike manufacturing where production and consumption are normally separate.

- Inseparability—customers cannot be separated from the service process, e.g. a healthcare procedure cannot take place without the patient being involved.

However, Korczynski notes that service work is wide-ranging and that not all service work will possess all of these attributes, especially where work is associated with information rather than customers, when it will possess fewer of these. For example, back-office work is less likely to be perishable, because information can be saved to be used on another day. Frenkel (2000) has identified a number of characteristics of service work that have implications for the management of HR. These include the following: first, service work tends to be labour intensive and therefore containing labour costs is likely to be a management priority. Second, symbolic behaviours (attitudes, dress) and the social skills of employees form part of the product and therefore need to be considered in job design and the way in which HR are managed. Third, service work may involve others, typically the customer in work tasks (e.g. internet shopping) and this may present communication and motivation challenges. Fourth, service work is often required 'on demand' and many require complex coordination of different specialists to deliver the service. Where the demand for labour occurs on demand, it may also be difficult to maximize the productivity of labour. Fifth, the nature of services may mean that some degree of customization is needed and therefore there may be limits to the extent to which work can be standardized and therefore may require a different form of work and employment relations. Finally, performance management may be problematic since the experience of the service recipient is central. With services, Boxall (2003) argues that the match between competitive strategy and HR strategy is of greater importance than in manufacturing (see Chapter 5 for further discussion of the relationship between business strategy and HR strategy). He has developed a typology that relates market characteristics in services to competitive dynamics and HR strategy. This suggests that where competition is cost-based in mass services, competition tends to drive out any advantage derived from adopting a more sophisticated approach to managing people. However, beyond this environment there is scope for sustained competitive advantage to be derived from the quality of the human capital and organizational processes used.

In service environments employees may be required to perform emotional and/or aesthetic labour as part of their jobs. Emotional labour, identified by Hochschild (1983) in her book *The Managed Heart*, describes circumstances where employees are expected to manage their emotions as part of their paid employment. Emotional labour takes place in the context of social interaction in the conduct of work. Employees are expected to manage their emotions in order to engender a state of mind in another person (normally the customer). As such, employees are expected to, for example, smile, laugh, be polite, or display caring behaviour towards the customer. In a study of airline stewardesses Hochschild (1983) describes how it is part of their job to smile and be polite and equally to disguise fatigue and irritation in order not to impair the customer experience. Other studies have examined how emotional labour is part of the work of call centre staff (Korczynski, 2003; Lindgren and Sederblad, 2003), holiday company tour representatives (Guerrier and Adib, 2003), nurses (Lewis, 2005), and barristers (Harris, 2002). More recently, studies have examined how emotions are managed in dealing with not only customers but also colleagues and subordinates as part of a managerial role (Clarke et al, 2007; Humphrey et al, 2008).

See the case study below for details of a training programme implemented by Pizza Express to train staff to flirt with customers.

 Key Concepts

Emotional labour is where employees are required to manage the emotions they display (both express and conceal) as part of their paid employment, normally designed to engender a particular response in others.

Aesthetic labour is where employees are required to look (dress, self-presentation) or sound (voice, language used) in a particular way as part of their paid employment, normally in order to match the desired image of the organization.

 Case study 2.2   Pizza Express teaching staff to flirt with customers

Pizza Express has recruited classically trained actor Karl James to teach flirting and the art of chit-chat to staff to help them to 'butter-up' the restaurant's customers.

Mr James is running a series of bespoke workshops with Pizza Express employees to help them improve the way they interact with people.

A source close to the company said: 'With social media and texting reducing our face-to-face interaction, Pizza Express has enlisted the help of a conversation expert who is incorporating flirting and unique conversation techniques into its new staff training scheme to help completely redefine the restaurant experience for customers.'

Mr James has played a key role in designing Pizza Express's new training and recruitment process, including teaching staff 'how to flirt (subtly) with customers so they feel more comfortable and relaxed', he said.

He added that the hectic pace of modern life often prevented people from having a quality conversation. But somewhere among the pizza ovens, pushchair ramps, and oversized pepper grinders the art of banter was a 'teachable skill' which would help staff 'get the most from every interaction, with colleagues and customers,' the source said.

Source

Adapted from an article by Louisa Peacock, Jobs Editor, *The Telegraph*.

Activity

1. How well do you think staff can be trained to undertake this type of behaviour?
2. How might managers control and appraise emotional labour?

In a related vein, the term aesthetic labour has been coined by Warhurst et al (2000) to refer to circumstances where physical appearance and 'embodied capacities and at-tributes' form the basis of employment. In other words, part of paid employment is con-cerned with how people look, sound, and present themselves. Warhurst et al argue that these embodied capacities and attributes which individuals possess are then mobilized, developed, and commoditized by employers. As such they recruit, select, and train staff to suit a predefined corporate style. They report on how employers use phrases in job adver-tisements, such as 'smart appearance', 'well spoken', and 'very well presented', to signal the kind of people they wish to employ.

Managing these kinds of work may raise new challenges for managers. In the case of emo-tional labour, managers need to define and prescribe what is an appropriate interaction and develop mechanisms to monitor these. In call centres this may be done by recording calls so that the interaction can be reviewed, but in other cases (such as airline cabin crew and retail staff) interactions may be less amenable to supervision and monitoring. Performing emo-tional labour where employees may have to deal with rudeness, discrimination, and/or in-nuendo is likely to be stressful for staff (Bolton and Boyd, 2003) and as such there may be a need to provide mechanisms to help staff cope with these situations. Aesthetic labour may raise issues in relation to discrimination if staff are recruited on the basis of physical attributes and presentation.

2.5 Workplace flexibility

In recent years the issue of flexibility has become a significant one for many organizations. Flexibility in organizations can be viewed in two main ways—flexibility for organizations and flexibility for individuals. Alis et al (2006) have made the distinction between flexibility *of* and flexibility *for* employees. The first of these is where organizations look for flexibility in the way in which they utilize labour so that they can match the supply with their need for labour more closely. This need to manage labour in flexible ways stems from an increasingly competitive business environment, where employers need to manage labour and related costs as efficiently as possible. Individuals, by contrast, look for flexibility in the way in which they work in order to help them achieve an acceptable relationship between work and non-work activities. Interest in achieving a work–life balance is as a result of social change, both in relation to the way in which work is considered and as a result of increased participation rates of parents, particularly mothers in paid employment.

The flexible use of labour by organizations may take a number of forms (Atkinson, 1985). Numerical flexibility allows employers to adjust the number of workers or the number of hours worked in line with variations in demand. This is likely to be of particular relevance in service industries where employee productivity is determined by demand. Examples of nu-merical flexibility include part-time jobs and temporary jobs. Temporal flexibility allows the employer to vary the time at which work is done and might take the form of compressed working hours or annual hours contracts.

Functional flexibility occurs where the employer is able to redeploy employees across a range of different tasks in line with demand. In order to maximize the performance of

Key Concepts

Workplace flexibility involves changes to the amount, timing, and location of work and may also involve different organizations. It may be designed to meet the needs of the employer or the employee. Examples of changes to the timing of work are as follows:

- **Flexitime** refers to a situation where employees are able to exercise some choice over their working hours, usually based around required core hours; for example, they may be able to choose to start working any time between 7 a.m. and 10 a.m.

- **Compressed working hours** refers to a situation where employees complete the normal hours for the job in fewer but longer periods of time, for example by working normal weekly hours in 4 days, or a 9-day fortnight.

- **Annual hours contracts** refers to a situation where the employer and employee agree a total sum of hours to be worked on an annual basis. The employer then has some flexibility, normally within an agreed set of rules, to vary the number of hours worked according to the demands of the business. For example, employees may be asked to work longer days at some times without being paid overtime and shorter hours at others when demand for labour is low and to avoid 'idle time'.

employees when they are redeployed, functional flexibility normally requires an investment in training to allow the employee to become multiskilled. The strategies of using labour in more flexible ways have been shown to deliver productivity and efficiency gains (Casey et al, 1999). However, it has also been noted that numerical and some forms of temporal and functional flexibility may have negative consequences for employees (Purcell et al, 1999; Nolan et al, 2000; Green, 2004; Kelliher and Gore, 2006), which may in the long run impact negatively on employee outcomes such as job satisfaction and organizational commitment.

Flexibility *for* employees allows individuals to exercise some degree of choice over where, when, and how much they work. The essential difference between these two forms is that here it is the employee, not the employer, who exercises choice. Employees may choose to reduce the hours they work, to work remotely (from home or other location) for some or all of their working week, and/or to work at different times from those that are 'normal' in the workplace. In the UK there has been significant growth in the number of employers offering flexible working options to employees in recent years (Kersley et al, 2006). This increase may be in part explained by legislative support provided for flexible working in some countries. For example, in the UK 'the right to request flexible working' provisions were first introduced in 2003 for parents of young or disabled children by the Employment Act 2002. However, employers may also choose to offer flexible working options in order to improve their competitive position in the labour market (Rau and Hyland, 2002). There is widespread evidence that being able to exercise some degree of control is highly valued by employees (Bloom and Van Reenen, 2006) and therefore may be an attractive offering to help recruit and retain staff, and it is noteworthy that many employers have developed policies offering flexible working to all employees, not just parents as required by the legislation. This desire for choice over where, when, and how much work is done is in line with the social changes discussed above, where employees want to be able to achieve a satisfactory integration of work and non-work activities, in contrast to the so-called ideal worker (Rodgers and Rodgers, 1989) who is able to devote his or her time to work without conflicting demands. Generation Y also view the work–life relationship as important and take this into consideration when evaluating potential employers (Gerdes, 2009). Research shows benefits accruing from the use of flexible working, such as positive impacts on organizational commitment, job satisfaction, and employee performance (Cranfield School of Management, 2008). However, the decision to implement flexible working in practice may be more complicated than it may seem at first glance. Whilst for many types of work, particularly those where some form of communication technology is used, the location of the employees may not be significant, other roles may not be amenable to remote working. Where work requires face-to-face interaction between customers and staff, employees are required to be physically present at least for that element of their work. It is also important that where flexible working is implemented that HR policies and practices are reviewed to ensure that they are appropriate for employees who are physically distant from the workplace or present at different times from their managers and co-workers. For example, a performance management tool needs to ensure that it has an outcome focus, since if employees are not present managers may find it hard to judge their performance.

 Critical Reflection

- Consider what issues might arise for organizations with the implementation of **employer**-driven flexible working practices.
- Consider what issues might arise for organizations with the implementation of **employee**-driven flexible working practices.
- Consider whether it might be possible for employers to match their own needs for flexibility with those of employees.

2.6 Changes to management practices

Over recent decades we have also seen an increasing trend towards the individualization of the employment relationship in some parts of the world (Brown et al, 1998; Pollert, 2005). This has been in part as a result of the decline in trade union membership in a number of countries (European Commission, 2011), but also as a result of deliberate action on the part of employers wishing to take a more individualized approach to the employment relationship. This individualized approach is in line with a unitary perspective (see Chapter 11) and the thinking behind HRM (see Chapter 5).

In harmony with this approach, we have also seen growth in the use of and interest in so-called high-performance, high-involvement, and high-commitment work systems or practices (see Chapter 8). Although there are some differences in emphasis in each of these approaches, there is much similarity and the terms have been used interchangeably (Lepak et al, 2006). In essence they are concerned with approaches to HRM that deliver superior organizational performance (Whitener, 2001; Lepak et al, 2006) and are appropriate for organizations in a globally competitive environment. It has been argued that this focus on how HR practices and the organization of work may influence organizational performance was stimulated by a debate in the US about future economic performance competitiveness, where it was argued that, in addition to technological advances, changes to work systems were required to maintain competitiveness (Boxall and Macky, 2009).

Whilst there has been some discussion about the specific practices involved in high-performance work systems (HPWS), it is generally seen to involve an emphasis on teamwork, training (including the development of skills in teamwork and interpersonal interaction), and employee motivation (including job security, internal career progression prospects, variable pay schemes, and skill-based pay). Butler and Glover (2010), building on the work of Bélanger et al (2002), argue that more generally high-performance management comprises three main dimensions. The first, production management, is concerned with productive flexibility and process standardization, a hard approach to quality management. The second dimension is concerned with the organization of work, centred on teamworking and breaking down traditional skill demarcations. The third is concerned with a commitment-based employment relationship, in order to support the first two dimensions. Thus terms and conditions need to be designed to secure commitment and foster alignment with wider organizational goals.

Boxall and Macky (2009) point to the arguments concerning the systemic affects, which suggest that performance gains are greater where organizations adopt a set of complementary practices (Appelbaum et al, 2000). They argue that whilst there is a need for HR practices to be complementary, there is also a need for account to be taken of the broader management system at the workplace and challenge the notion that a universal set of practices delivers enhanced performance, irrespective of context (Boxall and Macky, 2009).

 ## Conclusion

This chapter has presented a summary of recent changes which have been taking place in the world of work and which have implications for the development of HR strategies. This has included changes to both the nature of the workforce and the nature of work. In relation to the workforce we have examined the global labour market and the geographical distribution of the workforce. We have also examined changing orientations to work, including those of the so-called Generation Y. In relation to changes in the nature of work we have explored factors such as the growth of employment in services, the emergence of emotional and aesthetic labour, and the desire for greater flexibility on the part of both the employer and the employee, and changing employer approaches. In each case we have explored the implications of these changes for the way in which people are managed and the development of HR strategies.

Summary

- Changes in the distribution and nature of the workforce have important implications for the development of HR strategies.
- Increased time spent in full-time education and early exit from the labour force have reduced the availbality of labour in some EU countries.
- Changing social attitudes have impacted how people participate in work and what they expect from their employers.
- Changes in the nature of work have important implications for the development of HR strategies.
- The increasing prevalence of employment in service work presents different priorties and challenges for the managment of HR.
- Both employers and employees seek flexibility in the organization and conduct of work.
- The employment relationship has increasingly been individualized and practices have been shaped by a concern for performance.

 ## Review questions

1. Explain how knowledge of world population trends might influence the development of HR strategies.
2. How have social trends influenced the way in which people participate in work and what are the implications of this for SHRM?
3. What factors might influence whether an organization opts to export jobs and/or import labour?
4. Examine the implications of greater use of emotional and aesthetic labour for the way in which HR are managed.
5. Why might organizations offer flexible working options to employees and what factors need to be considered in implementation?

 ## End-of-chapter case study   Centrica: managing an older workforce

(Based on an interview with Mel Flogdell, Head of HR Policy, Centrica)

Centrica is a top 30 FTSE 100 integrated energy company with almost 37,000 employees, including over 6,000 in the US, operating in seven countries across the globe. British Gas is the UK 'downstream' arm of the company. It supplies gas and electricity and installs and maintains central heating and gas appliances and low-carbon and energy-efficient products and services to UK residential and business customers. British Gas employs over 28,000 of Centrica's people. Under the company's Business Principles they make a commitment to respect human rights and to value their employees; as part of this commitment Centrica has developed an active diversity strategy.

In recent years, faced with the changing demographics of the labour force, Centrica has been concerned to ensure that it has a strategy in place that allows the company to meet its current and future HR needs. The company recognized that although the economic downturn has meant that employers have a larger pool of potential employees to choose from, 'candidates of choice' have become more discerning when looking for their preferred employer. Having an age-diverse workforce was seen as an important element in sustaining business success and as a response a number of initiatives were put in place to attract and retain an older workforce. Employing greater numbers of older workers was also seen as a way of more closely reflecting the community and customers the company serves. Centrica decided to build its reputation as an employer of older workers and to position itself as an employer of choice in later life. When age discrimination legislation was introduced in the UK, Centrica's approach was to embrace the principles behind it and to create a positive environment for an age-diverse workforce.

The company started by reviewing its HR policies and procedures in order to be confident that it was 'age-friendly' and that older workers were not disadvantaged. Subsequently three main initiatives were put in place—an extensive programme of flexible working; the removal of the upper age limit for entry to Centrica's apprenticeship and trainee schemes; and the introduction of a healthy ageing programme.

Centrica monitors training, promotion, and turnover rates by age and has also developed a number of training programmes for all staff in the areas of diversity and age awareness. Currently in the region of a quarter of Centrica's workforce is aged 45–65.

Eighty-eight per cent of employees who have requested to carry on working beyond the default retirement age have had their requests granted.

Flexible working

Flexible working was introduced as part of the Work:wise programme, a set of policies designed to accommodate employees' changing needs throughout their working life. The opportunity to work in a more flexible way was offered to all employees, and a communications programme, including roadshows and workshops, was launched to explain the options to employees and managers. It was considered important not only to explain what was available to employees, but also to support managers and to deal with concerns they might have about employees working in different ways. The company estimates that in the region of 75% of employees now have some form of flexible working arrangement, with 42% having a formal arrangement. With figures in this region, it is seen to be part of Centrica's culture and part of the way it does business.

The company also recognized that employees of all ages have various and changing non-work demands on their time. Lifestyle contracts have allowed employees to alter their roles or the hours that they work.

Age limits

The British Gas Academy recruits and trains staff for British Gas Services. In order to increase age diversity in the engineering workforce, a decision was made to remove the upper age limit for their apprenticeship and trainee positions. They reworded their print and online recruitment material, removing words such as 'young' and 'experience' in order to avoid any age bias. In addition to increasing the pool of recruits, the company was keen to attract older people into the engineering workforce to take advantage of their already developed life skills. The removal of the upper age limit for entry into the British Gas Apprenticeship scheme has resulted in approximately one-third of apprentice engineers now being over 25 on entry to the scheme, with the average age of apprentices having risen from 21 to 24 years old. Trainers have reported that older trainees have a positive impact on group dynamics of trainees and that some of the older recruits have acted as life mentors to the younger recruits.

There were, however, some costs to the company of recruiting older apprentices, since government funding was reduced (a smaller grant is offered for training people over 24), but this is seen to be outweighed by the benefits gained. Centrica is aware that having older people join the company in jobs historically undertaken by young people has brought about a culture change in the organization.

Healthy ageing

The healthy ageing programme is based around the strands of *be* well, *stay* well, and *get* well and information on health is available to employees via a dedicated portal. The programme aims to help employees of all ages maintain good health and to give them practical support to recover from ailments. For example, engineers are given information on how to avoid injury (backs and knees being particularly vulnerable), diet, and exercise including the provision of personal coaches at local gyms. These programmes have resulted in a reduction in absence amongst engineers, from 25% to 2%. Where employees require medical interventions, the company provides assistance to ensure that employees receive early attention, both to reduce their pain and minimize time away from work. Spending resources in this way is seen by Centrica to provide a good return on investment.

Case study questions

1. What might be some of the challenges of managing an older workforce?

2. Consider how organizations might attempt to change the culture to avoid age discrimination.

3. What other strategies might a company like Centrica pursue to meet the challenges posed by changing demographics of the workforce?

 Further reading

Barr, D. (2004) *Get it Together—Surviving your Quarterlife Crisis.* London: Hodder and Stoughton.
This is an easy-to-read book and includes sections on how Generation Y relate to the world of work.

Bolton, S.C. (2004) *Emotion Management in the Workplace.* Basingstoke: Palgrave Macmillan.
This book examines emotion in the workplace and explores emotion work and emotion management.

Eurostat (2010) Europe in Figures, Eurostat Year Book 2010. Luxembourg: Publications Office of the European Union.
This yearbook provides a range of statistics covering countries in the EU.

Fineman, S. (2003) *Understanding Emotion at Work.* London: Sage Publications.
Fineman's book takes an interdisciplinary look at emotions at work and explores both the positive and darker sides of emotion in the workplace.

Kelliher, C. and Richardson, J. (2011) *New Ways of Organizing Work: Developments, Perspectives and Experiences.* London: Routledge.
This edited text includes chapters dealing with changes to the organization of work brought about by globalization, increased competitive pressures, changing social attitudes, and developments in ICT.

US Bureau of Labor Statistics. http://www.bls.gov/ilc.
This site provides a range of statistics on work and employment in the US.

 For additional material on the content of this chapter please visit the supporting Online Resource Centre www.oxfordtextbooks.co.uk/orc/truss.

3 Strategic management

Learning Objectives

By the end of this chapter you should be able to:

- Define and explain the concepts of strategy, strategic management, business strategy, and competitive strategy
- Critically evaluate the role of vision and mission statements.
- Understand the relationship between business strategy and competitive strategy.
- Appreciate the importance of competitive advantage and the different ways in which this can be achieved.
- Define and explain the concept of strategic alignment.
- Critically analyse key trends in strategic management.

Key Concepts

Strategic management
Business strategy
Competitive strategy
Organizational structure
Organizational culture
Strategic alignment
Resource-based view (RBV)

3.1 Introduction

In recent years vision and mission statements have become a popular way of summarizing and communicating an organization's strategic direction. The vision is an aspirational statement about what the organization will look like in the future. It is used by some chief executive officers (CEOs) to inspire employees to higher levels of engagement and performance. Vision statements range from the succinct (e.g. UK retailer Morrison: 'To be the food specialist for everyone') to the more verbose (e.g. US computer company Dell: 'Our future will take us from the desk top, to the data centre, to the cloud and into the hands of billions of potential new customers who are carrying the internet—essentially the world—with them everywhere they go'). In turn, the mission statement is an articulation of the strategic goals and organizational values that underpin the vision. For instance, a strategic goal of Google is 'to provide the best user experience possible'. This contrasts with the strategic goal of the Vietnamese shipbuilder VinaShin which is 'to make Vietnam the world's fourth largest shipbuilder by the year 2018' (Hayton, 2010). This identification with national success reflects the extent to which state-owned enterprises in the developing Asian economies operate a different business model to their Western business counterparts. The implications of this are discussed in section 3.6 on international trends. In terms of values, Finland's Nokia is a typical example: the firm seeks to 'focus on our customer; communicate openly; inspire; innovate; and, win together' (Steinbock, 2010).

Vision and mission statements are most effective when they are expressed clearly and simply (Levis, 2009). For instance, Sunil Mittal's vision for the Indian company Airtel is 'being the provider of very low-cost telecommunication services to a very large population of customers' (Cappelli et al, 2010). This captures the two principal features of India's rapid economic growth in recent years: the success of low-cost business models coupled with the huge potential of India's domestic market as more and more people are lifted out of poverty and join the country's expanding middle class. Levis (2009) adds that vision and mission statements are also more effective when they focus on something that is wrong with or missing from existing markets. However, as Hamel and Prahalad (1996) warn, 'not only must the future be imagined, it must be built' (p. 117). Consequently, the principal purpose of strategic management is to *build* an organization's strategy using the vision and mission statements as the underlying foundation.

The strategy that emerges from this process can be described as a plan that allocates resources to specific projects intended to achieve the organization's strategic goals. Such projects might involve, for instance, mergers and acquisitions, joint ventures, or the innovation of new products and services. The strategic decisions that are made have important implications for an organization's HR strategy and, in turn, HR policies, plans, and practices. For instance, a business that is expanding through mergers and acquisitions is likely to focus on culture change and team-building as part of its HR strategy. Whilst Ulrich and Brockbank (2005) argue that in 'the last decade, HR professionals have worked to become strategic partners and to align their work with business strategies' (p. 1) the reality for many HR practitioners is a lack of strategic credibility in the eyes of managers and other stakeholders (Mankin, 2009). This may be frustrating for many in the HR profession, but it is not particularly surprising when you consider that the HR function is often referred to as a *support* function (Haberberg and Rieple, 2008). Indeed, as Tappin and Cave (2008) observe, 'many CEOs are scathing about the HR profession' (p. 127).

Figure 3.1 presents these elements as a rational, top-down process. Although this is a simplification of what actually happens, it does provide a useful starting point for discussing strategic management and explaining the relationship between HR and organizational strategy (which is developed further in Chapter 4 on the role of the HR function). However, the reality is often very different for two principal reasons. First, the internal contexts of organizations tend to be messy, ambiguous, and conflict laden (Mankin, 2009). Second, external environments range from the relatively stable to the highly unstable; and the latter is a particular feature of global markets. For instance, the oil industry is struggling to adapt to a new and increasingly volatile economy as well as develop technologies for ever deeper drilling (and the inherent dangers of this were graphically illustrated by the BP oil spill in 2010). The challenges facing multinationals are summarized by Dana Wagner of Google: 'we are in an industry that is subject to disruption and we can't take anything for granted' (*New York Times*,

Figure 3.1 Linear strategic process.

Source: adapted from Mankin (2009).

2009b). It is important to remember that public- and non-profit-sector organizations also have to cope with the budget or income-generating implications of these market conditions.

It is impossible to cover all aspects of strategic management in a single chapter. The aim is to provide an overview of the subject so that better sense can be made of the chapters in Part 2.

3.2 What is strategy?

There are many definitions of strategy, ranging from the simple (strategy as a *plan*) to the more complex:

A strategy is the set of actions through which an organisation, by accident or design, develops resources and uses them to deliver services or products in a way which its users find valuable,

Table 3.1 What is strategy?

Processes	Outcomes
Guiding the evolution of an organization.	Delivering services or products.
Making choices about the nature and direction of an organization.	Creating sustained value for shareholders and other stakeholders.
Making decisions about the allocation and development of resources.	Sustaining competitive advantage.
Responding to the changing conditions posed by the external environment and internal capabilities.	

Sources: Freedman, 2003; Kaplan and Norton, 2004; Haberberg and Rieple, 2008; Koch, 2011.

> while meeting the financial and other objectives and constraints imposed by key stakehold-
> ers (Haberberg and Rieple, 2008: 6).

This may lack the simplicity of more succinct definitions, but it does make explicit some of the salient features of the concept (which are discussed below). Table 3.1 provides an initial analysis of this and two other definitions.

An interesting counterpoint to academic definitions is provided by General Electric's famous former CEO, Jack Welch:

> Look, what is strategy but resource allocation? When you strip away all the noise, that's what it comes down to. Strategy means making clear-cut choices about how to compete. You cannot be everything to everybody, no matter what the size of your business or how deep its pockets (Welch, 2005: 169).

Insights from strategic leaders are important because they help us to better understand the *practice* of strategy. In large, complex organizations CEOs have a significant influence on strategy (Porter and Nohria, 2010). Indeed, the CEO role has been described as the *guardian* of strategy (Tappin and Cave, 2010).

 Key Concept

Strategy is a plan that integrates an organization's vision, mission, goals, and objectives, and determines how resources will be used.

It is important to understand that strategy is not a monolithic concept. Whittington (2001) suggests that there are four generic perspectives on strategy—Classical, Evolutionary, Processual, and Systemic—and that these differ along two dimensions: outcomes and processes (see Fig. 3.2). Each perspective offers a different interpretation of strategy:

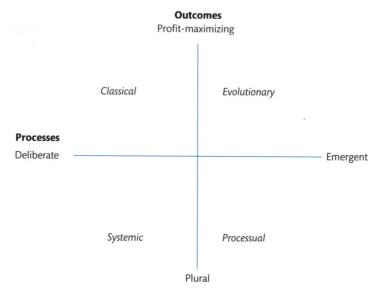

Figure 3.2 Generic perspectives on strategy.
Source: Whittington (2001: 3).

- **Classical** argues that managers can shape strategy through the utilization of rational planning and decision-making methods (usually with a long-term focus). Mintzberg (1994, 1996) refers to this as a **deliberate** strategy. From this perspective the aim of strategy is to maximize profits. However, the notion that strategic decisions rely solely on rational processes at the exclusion of intuition is highly questionable.

- **Evolutionary** is based on a Darwinian interpretation of the market (i.e. natural selection or 'survival of the fittest'). Markets are too volatile for long-term planning and only the best performers will survive. Successful strategies are dependent on the ability of managers to **react** effectively to changes in the market. The aim of strategy is to maximize profits. The work of Michael Porter is associated with this perspective. He argues that there are five principal external forces that shape strategy: the threat of new entrants, the threat of substitute products or services, the bargaining power of buyers, the bargaining power of suppliers, and the level of rivalry between existing competitors (Porter, 2008).

- **Processual** reflects the imperfect nature of organizations and views strategy as an accommodation of internal *and* external factors. Mintzberg (1994, 1996) argues that strategy as a plan, which he describes as an organization's **intended** strategy, invariably fails to materialize, with new strategies emerging (the term **emergent** is often used to describe this perspective). The aim of strategy is to achieve more than one outcome. This perspective reflects how difficult it is to make predictions about the future (Bryan and Joyce, 2007).

- **Systemic** views strategy as being inextricably linked to local social systems and cultures. The aim of strategy is to achieve more than one outcome. Whilst a multinational might have an overarching strategy, the specifics need to be adapted to fit the different local circumstances of its international operations. An example of this was Google's acquiescence to the Chinese government request that some online content could not be made available to Chinese users of the site.

The reality is that organizations often exhibit a blend of two or more of these perspectives. As Kaplan and Norton (2004) argue, strategy 'is developed and evolves over time to meet the changing conditions posed by the **external** environment and **internal** capabilities' (p. 34, emphasis added). Arguably, the challenge is in knowing what the best blend should be at any given time.

 Case study 3.1   A Taiwanese story about strategy and structure

Before 2000 the Taiwan-based company Acer had competing strategies. For 15 years one part of the firm had been building computers for other PC sellers who would put their own labels on the machines, while another part sold very similar computers under the company's own brand. The latter strategy was predicated on direct sales to consumers, which had brought the firm into direct competition with companies such as Dell. However, in 2000 the firm decided to adopt a new business strategy in order to increase its global market share. Acer's manufacturing division was made an independent company (Wistron) and this enabled a smaller and more nimble sales firm to emerge. The strategy based on direct sales was discarded and replaced with a strategy focused on selling as many low-cost laptops and netbooks as possible to consumers but via a network of partners and retailers. A new logo was adopted to reflect this new strategic direction, which had proved very successful despite the industry downturn. By 2008 Acer had replaced Hewlett-Packard as the market leader in Europe, the Middle East, and Africa, partly as a result of Acer's success in the booming netbook market. This strategy enabled the firm to become the world's second largest PC vendor. However, in 2011 tensions at board level over the firm's strategic direction culminated in the resignation of Acer's CEO Gianfranco Lanci. The difference in opinion appears to be about whether the firm's future lay in PCs or mobile devices. Acting CEO J.T. Wang announced that the PC would continue to be the firm's core business. In 2009 the firm had entered the smartphone market with the launch of four different smartphones and the promise of more in the pipeline. Unlike Apple, which has focused on developing one phone only, Acer's strategy is based on targeting each of its phones at a different market segment. In March 2011 Acer announced that revenue projections for the first quarter in 2011 will fall short of expectations by about 10% due to weaker demand in the PC markets in the US and Europe.

Sources

1. *New York Times*, 2009
   http://www.nytimes.com/2009/06/28/technology/companies/28acer.html?ref=business-computing
   (accessed 29 June 2009).

2. *Bloomberg Business Week*
   http://www.businessweek.com/globalbiz/content/oct2008/gb20081016_577701.htm
   (accessed 19 June 2010).

3. *The Financial Times*
   http://www.ft.com
   (accessed 20 June 2010).

4. *PC Pro*
   http://www.pcpro.co.uk/news/366448/acer-ceo-quits-over-strategy-dispute
   (accessed 12 June 2011).

5. *Financial Times*
   http://blogs.ft.com/fttechhub/2009/06/acers-smartphone-strategy/
   (accessed 12 June 2011).

6. http://www.channelweb.co.uk/crn-uk/news/2039010/acer-boss-resigns-strategy-clash
   (accessed 12 June 2011).

7. http://br.acer.com/ac/pt/BR/press/2011/12911
   (accessed 12 June 2011).

Activity

1. Which elements of Whittington's four perspectives can be identified in the case study?

2. What does this case study tell us about the role of the CEO?

3.3 Strategic management

Strategic management is the process that enables organizations to turn strategic intent into action. It comprises four phases: analysis, selection, implementation, and review. These are inextricably linked, as illustrated in Fig. 3.3. Each phase represents a different aspect of an organization's business and competitive strategies; so it is important that you appreciate the difference between these two types of strategy. Business strategy sets out an organization's strategic scope or direction—essentially, the markets it wants to compete in (Grant, 2010). It is important to note that business strategy is often referred to as corporate strategy. Competitive strategy is about *how* an organization will compete in those markets:

> A company's competitive strategy provides a kind of template for day-to-day business decisions but is not itself subject to short-term alteration . . . the template provides a framework for engaging in the market and guiding operational decisions. It sets forward a view on how best to compete over the next three, five, or even ten years (Cappelli et al, 2010: 118).

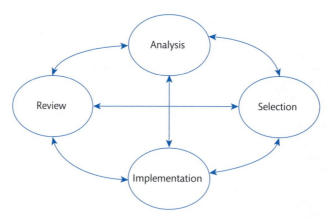

Figure 3.3 Four phases of strategic management

The four strategic management phases provide a route-map for determining an organization's business and competitive strategies:

1. **Analysis:** data from external and internal environments can be analysed to provide information which then informs strategic decisions about business and competitive strategy. External sources include: economic forecasts, market trends, technological changes, labour market and demographic trends, and government initiatives. Internal sources include: business processes, performance metrics, staffing (and skills) levels, financial data, and attitude surveys. This analysis is not the preserve of a single function, although marketing usually plays an important role (Brassington and Pettitt, 2003). A particular problem with analysing information for strategic decision making is 'bounded rationality' (Simon, 1985). It is not possible to know everything about the external environment although it is assumed that people will always choose the best course of action and will make rational decisions based on that information. Any search for information is inevitably incomplete, thus resulting in satisfactory rather than optimal decisions (Simon, 1985).

2. **Selection:** this involves making choices about what the strategy should be (i.e. business strategy) and how it should be achieved (i.e. competitive strategy). Freedman (2003) defines strategy as the 'framework of choices that determine the nature and direction of an organisation' (p. 2, emphasis added). From a business perspective it is about 'winning' (Grant, 2010: 4). The latter reflects the competitive nature of global markets. It is critical that the organization's sources of competitive advantage are correctly identified. Ulrich and Brockbank (2005) provide several examples of these, including: innovating new products and services (e.g. Intel); quality (e.g. Toyota); branding (e.g. Coca-Cola); on-time delivery (e.g. FedEx); and customer service (e.g. Virgin Atlantic Airways). These sources of competitive advantage (or in the case of public and non-profit sectors performance advantage through the delivery of best value) reflect the core capabilities of an organization. This point is developed further in the next section on competitive advantage.

3. **Implementation:** this involves a combination of resource investments in what can essentially be described as strategic projects. These projects lie at the heart of an organization's competitive strategy. However, as Morgan et al (2007) point out, most strategies fail at the implementation phase, suggesting that it is not possible to plan for every possible contingency. It is during this phase that intended strategies are overtaken by events and replaced with new, emergent strategies. The ability of an organization to adapt to any changes is dependent on a combination of internal factors (see section 3.5).

4. **Review:** it is critical that the projects underpinning the implementation phase are reviewed on an ongoing basis (Morgan et al, 2007). The outputs of the review phase become inputs for the analysis phase. Unfortunately, this can be a neglected aspect of strategic practice. Many organizations use the Balanced Scorecard (Kaplan and Norton, 1996) to measure the effectiveness of their strategies. The Balanced Scorecard is intended to encourage organizations to move away from a short-term reliance on financial measures by focusing on four areas: financial, internal business processes, learning and growth, and the customer (Kaplan and Norton, 2004). India's Tata Steel relies heavily on this approach (Seshadri and Tripathy, 2006), while another Indian firm, Wipro, uses a modified version which is used to link individual performance to six rather than four areas (Hamm, 2007).

3.4 Competitive advantage

The aim of competitive strategy is to acquire or sustain competitive advantage. However, there is considerable variation in how organizations can do this. A common strategy is to be less expensive than competitors. A good example of this is the airline sector and low-cost airlines, such as Ryanair in Europe and Southwest Airlines in the US. Other strategies include differentiation, innovating new products and/or services, and occasional cost promotions to undercut competitors for short periods, although the latter is proving increasingly ineffective as companies learn how to respond to such deals much more quickly than in the past (Hall, 2008). Much of India's business success has been achieved through competitive advantage based on a combination of low-cost business models and innovation (Kumar et al, 2009), while multinationals are using different strategies to establish and grow businesses in China (see Case study 3.2 below).

The resource-based view (RBV) of strategy (Wernerfelt, 1984) focuses on the role of organizational capabilities as a source of competitive advantage. These capabilities are intangible assets and represent something an organization does well relative to its competitors (Ulrich

 Key Concept

Competitive advantage involves building a relatively consistent pattern of returns for shareholders (Porter, 1985).

 Case study 3.2   Tata Motors

Over the last 20 years US car producers have been focusing on trucks and sport-utility vehicles (SUVs). This strategic focus derived from the analysis of marketing information on consumers and competitors. Market analysis indicated that there was less immediate competition in the truck and SUV market segments than in conventional cars and this was seen as an opportunity for the greatest short-term profits. In contrast India's Tata Motors was moving forward with a strategy focused on small inexpensive cars even though this was a highly competitive market segment, dominated by Japanese auto-makers. The company's aim was to design a small car that would be significantly cheaper to make and buy than any other model and thus satisfy India's mass market demand for low-cost transportation. The result was the Nano with a sales price of 100,000 rupees ($2,500), which was half the price of its closest competitor in India. Tata Motors achieved this by designing everything from scratch; deleting features that were taken for granted by other auto-makers (e.g. air conditioning, power brakes, radios); using lightweight steel and an aluminium engine; and building in fuel efficiency of 50 miles to the gallon. The car's other important feature was its modular design enabling the Nano to be distributed in kit form and assembled across the country by local businesses. The global reaction to the Nano catapulted the Tata Group into sixth place on the *Business Week*'s list of the world's most innovative firms (behind Apple, Google, Toyota, General Electric, and Microsoft in first to fifth places respectively).

Source

Cappelli, P., Singh, H., Singh, U. and Useem, M. (2010) *The India Way*. Boston, MA: Harvard Business Press, pp. 12–15.

Moving into China

The world's three biggest retailers have adopted different entry and growth strategies. Carrefour has expanded aggressively and set up joint ventures in China's provinces. Walmart has been more cautious in expanding into the provinces. In 2007 the company paid $1 billion for a local chain, Trust Mart, to strengthen its expansion. In 2009 Walmart overtook Carrefour. Tesco bided its time before acquiring a 50% stake in the Hymall chain (which was a subsidiary of a Taiwanese company). This strategic decision was taken because the company viewed it as a way of better understanding China's retail environment, particularly in relation to supply and distribution networks.

Source

Torrens, C. (2010) *Doing Business in China*. London: Profile Books, p. 10.

Activity

1. Compare Tata Motors' approach to competitive advantage with that of a leading car manufacturer in the US, such as Ford or General Motors. What appears to be the principal difference between the approaches adopted by the two firms?

2. What role does the state play in China's corporate sector and how does this impact on the ability of Western firms to penetrate China's domestic markets?

and Brockbank, 2005). Organizational capabilities can also be described as an organization's core competence. This was a popular term in the management strategy literature of the 1990s (Le Deist and Winterton, 2005) and was defined as 'a bundle of skills and technologies that enable a company to provide a particular benefit to customers' (Hamel and Prahalad, 1996: 219). Whilst competitive advantage may be built on a combination of tangible and intangible assets (such as state-of-the-art production facilities and talented employees), 'only valuable, rare, costly to imitate, and non-substitutable resources can be a source of sustained competitive advantage' (Barney and Clark, 2007: 235). Petrobrás, the Brazilian oil producer, has used its technological competence, in the form of groundbreaking technologies in deepwater drilling, to underpin international expansion (Brainard and Martinez-Diaz, 2009). In contrast, Nokia, Finland's leading multinational, was renowned in the 1990s for innovation (Steinbock, 2010) but is now struggling to keep pace with the levels of innovation being demonstrated by its competitors (*Wall Street Journal*, 2010).

 ### Key Concept

The **resource-based view** of the firm is based on the premise that firms can achieve sustained competitive advantage if they secure and effectively deploy resources that are not available to, or imitable by, their competitors.

Core competence is associated with the concept of human capital. For instance:

> Human capital that possesses organisation-specific knowledge is an invaluable asset that has the potential to produce a competitive advantage and sustain it. Hence, firms should be very selective with the employees they decide to train and develop (Carmeli and Weisberg, 2006: 202).

Leading CEOs in India assert that their competitiveness is derived from their firms' human capital (Nilekani, 2008; Cappelli et al, 2010). However, human capital can be leveraged in very different ways. For instance, the two low-cost airlines referred to above, Ryanair and South-west Airlines, have markedly different HR strategies. It is also important to note that this is not simply a large firm response: studies show that intangible factors, such as organizational change, innovation, and HRM contribute to the competitiveness of SMEs (Aragón-Sánchez and Sánchez-Márin, 2005). The current situation is complicated by the fact that many state-owned enterprises (SOEs) in developing countries, such as China and Vietnam, are receiving support, directly or indirectly, from their governments. For instance, state funding enables the Vietnamese shipbuilder VinaShin to win orders by bidding below cost (Hayton, 2010) (see section 3.6 on international trends). Chapter 6 covers the resource-based view and the role of human capital in more detail.

Global competition today is such that it can be very difficult to hold on to competitive advantage. For instance, Sony had long been regarded as the world's leading electronics manufacturer, but in 2002 the firm was overtaken by Samsung. Sony's competitive advantage lay in quality and miniaturization, which were of limited value in the age of DVDs and digital technologies (Chang, 2008). It can be argued that Sony lacked the capability for change.

 Critical Reflection

Two models have been developed to explain options for an organization's business and competitive strategies. The first is Ansoff (1987) who argues that there are four business strategic options: market penetration, product development, market development, and diversification. The second is Porter (1985) who argues that there are four generic options for competitive strategy: cost leadership, cost focus, broad differentiation, and differentiation focus. To undertake this activity you need to source a copy of these two models. You can do so by going back to the original sources (see below) or seeking out more recent journal articles that discuss the two models (both have been cited extensively). You also need to access any sources that can help you answer the following question:

- To what extent do these two models reflect the totality of options available to organizations?

An answer summary can be found on the OUP website at www.oxfordtextbooks.co.uk/orc/truss.

Sources

Ansoff, H.I. (1987) *Business Strategy*. London: Penguin.
Porter, M.E. (1985) *Competitive Advantage*. New York, NY: Free Press.

3.5 Strategic alignment

Strategic alignment is critical to competitive advantage. It combines strategic and operational practices in such a way that both levels are in effect intertwined. This can be seen in firms such as Toyota where managers treat employees as knowledge workers or assets, rather than resources, in order to sustain the firm's strategic approach, which is based on the lean production model (Osono et al, 2008). Many Western firms have tried and failed to replicate the 'Toyota Way' (Liker and Hoseus, 2008) because Western business leaders have struggled to understand the management mindset within Toyota, instead viewing the 'Toyota Way' as little more than a set of techniques (Rother, 2009). However, Toyota also illustrates the fragility of competitive advantage: its capabilities for quality, improvement, and innovation have been compromised by following a strategy based on rapid expansion (Spear, 2010).

Figure 3.4 on the following page illustrates the principal internal factors that need to be aligned. **Strategy and structure** are linked together because an organization's structure is critical to the achievement of business strategy (Bryan and Joyce, 2007). The importance of the relationship between strategy and structure can be traced back to Chandler (1962). An organization should be designed in such a way that its structure supports the competitive strategy (not the other way round). For instance, strategies that focus on close collaboration with customers and suppliers require a strong matrix structure that 'promotes agility and responsiveness' (Morgan et al, 2007: 116). Many of India's leading CEOs believe that strategy drives structure (Cappelli et al, 2010). As K.V. Kamath, Chairman of India's ICICI Bank observes, 'We've always seen structure as living and play about with it as much as we can' (Tappin and Cave, 2010: 40).

As Chapter 1 explained, organizations have become more varied in design as a result of globalization and improvements in information and communications technology. Many organizations are now characterized by flexibility, outsourcing of the supply chain, and virtual working. Brazil's leading construction company, Odebrecht, uses 'a flexible internal organizational structure that devolves as much autonomy—and entrepreneurial decision making—as possible to each manager. Traditional hierarchical structures are eschewed' (Brainard and Martinez-Diaz, 2009: 212).

Arguably, changes in supply chains have had the most impact on the relationship between strategy and structure:

 Key Concept

Strategic alignment comprises two elements. The first is vertical strategic alignment which is the process by which HR strategy, policies, and plans are aligned with an organization's strategic goals and objectives. The second is horizontal strategic alignment which is the process by which functional strategies, policies, plans, and practices are aligned with each other.

As supply chains increase in their complexity, the owners of the work that makes up any given product or service is also accordingly more distributed among an ever-broadening number of organisations . . . [consequently] companies must rely on strategy and communication

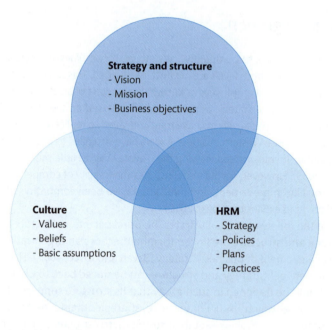

Figure 3.4 The principal internal factors influencing strategic alignment.

Source: Mankin (2009).

across multiple organisations and processes in order to find alignment (Koulopoulos and Roloff, 2006: 23).

Over 300 multinationals, including Pfizer, Microsoft, Sony, and Samsung, have now opened research and development centres in China, while others, such as Hornby, have relocated production there to maximize cost efficiencies (Torrens, 2010). A great many other Western companies have outsourced facilities to take advantage of cost savings. This has enabled countries such as India to build a strong reputation for call centres. Other types of structural change can be more substantial. For instance, in 2009 Shell, the Dutch oil company, announced it was planning to merge its power and gas division with its exploration business to create two new units in order to make the company more nimble by having fewer layers of bureaucracy (*New York Times*, 2009a).

The dilemma facing organizations is that any structure 'hardens eventually' according to K.V. Kamath (Tappin and Cave, 2010: 40). This can result in a loss of competitive advantage. Consequently, organizations need to ensure that the four phases of strategic management are ongoing processes rather than a once-a-year activity.

Definitions of **organizational culture** vary. It can be summarized as the 'collective mindset of the company . . . that is, shared ways of thinking' (Ulrich and Brockbank, 2005: 150) or as 'a commonly held set of beliefs, values and behaviours' (Smith and Sadler-Smith, 2006: 79). Schein's (1992) definition of organizational culture highlights the role of basic assumptions and how these underpin values and beliefs:

A pattern of shared basic assumptions that the group learned as it solved its problems of external adaptation and internal integration, that has worked well enough to be considered valid and, therefore, to be taught to new members as the correct way to perceive, think, and feel in relation to those problems (Schein, 1992: 12).

This definition suggests that it is the basic assumptions underlying culture that drive behaviour in the workplace. These basic assumptions usually exist at a subconscious level, manifesting in a 'taken for granted' fashion. This is why changing organizational culture is one of the biggest challenges confronting strategic leaders. Hewlett-Packard (HP) illustrates the importance of culture. The founders of the firm, Bill Hewlett and Dave Packard, 'consciously developed a caring and consensus-oriented environment that cultivated long-term employees and allowed for bottom-up influence on strategic direction' (Morgan et al, 2007: 95). Many of India's leading CEOs believe that an organization's culture is a key component of structure (Cappelli et al, 2010). Well-known brands such as Apple, Dell, and Google have strong cultures which are a source of innovation, but strong cultures can also be a force for rigidity (Levis, 2009). Again, this can be countered through an ongoing strategic management process.

In turn, if HR practices are going to have any impact they must be aligned with the organization's strategy (Ulrich et al, 2009). Holbeche (2009) highlights the implications of strategic alignment for **human resource management**:

The business context drives the HR agenda, especially as work becomes progressively more knowledge- and talent-intensive. It also drives the transformation of the HR role, organisation, structure and skills sets. Delivering a value-adding agenda requires purpose, focus, a well-formulated strategy and effective methods, as well as effective measurement to ensure the right kinds of impact on organisational performance are being achieved (p. xi).

This requires a form of HR leadership which combines strategic acumen with pragmatism (Holbeche, 2010). CEOs of leading Indian firms emphasize the importance of HRM practices; in particular, employee engagement and culture (Cappelli et al, 2010) are encouraged.

3.6 International trends

To date, the literature on strategic management has been dominated by Western perspectives. This dominance is now being challenged as new indigenous business models emerge from developing nations such as China and India. This trend mirrors changes in the global political context, with America's position as the sole superpower now being challenged by China (Clegg, 2009). It also reflects the extent to which new multinationals have been emerging over the last decade from developing countries: China's Huawei in telecommunications equipment, India's Tata Consultancy Services in information technology services, Brazil's Embraer in regional jets, Russia's Gazprom in energy, and Mexico's Cemex in cement (Ramamurti, 2009). Although business plans and strategies were not really considered in the start-up phase of many Chinese private enterprises, most of them adopted what was in effect a low-cost model (Nie et al, 2009).

The problem for Western multinationals is that they are discovering that what has worked in the West does not necessarily work in countries such as China which is very different in terms of its business practices and competitiveness, as well as language and culture (Nie et al, 2009; So and Westland, 2010):

> Many companies have relied on their strategies for developed markets to operate in the country. For most this has failed, and they have been forced to revise plans to take into account the idiosyncrasies of the Chinese market (Torrens, 2010: 1).

Initially many of China's leading enterprises adopted a Western-influenced strategy but have since grown as a result of emergent indigenous strategies. For instance, the intended strategy for Sina was focused on adapting Yahoo's business model (a diversified approach involving 10–20 services), but over time a new strategy emerged that was based on fewer services [the primary focus being the online aggregation of news (except politics) plus four supplementary services covering lifestyles, finance, entertainment, and sports]: Chinese consumers preferred this less diversified approach (So and Westland, 2010). The competitive advantage of Chinese firms is largely predicated on understanding of their own culture, which outside firms struggle with. For example, when the US travel firm Expedia acquired a majority shareholding in China's eLong, its model floundered because the firm relied on the internet as its primary booking system and its payment system relied on consumers having credit cards; Chinese consumers want a call centre option and few of them have a credit card (ibid).

 ## Conclusion

Strategy is often explained as a rational, top-down process and although this is a simplification of what actually happens, it does provide a useful starting point for discussing strategic management. However, the reality is that the internal contexts of organizations tend to be messy, ambiguous, and conflict laden, while external environments range from the relatively stable to the highly unstable. This means that practice or strategic management is highly problematic. It is one thing to state an organization's strategic direction but a totally different matter to turn this intent into action. The latter is achieved through the adoption of a four-phase approach with all four phases being inextricably linked: analysis, selection, implementation, and review. The outcomes of these four phases is a business strategy (often referred to as corporate strategy), which explains what the strategy is and where it is focused (e.g. on specific markets), and a competitive strategy, which explains how the business strategy will be achieved (i.e. how competitive advantage will be acquired and sustained). Strategic alignment is critical to the success of a competitive strategy as it combines strategic and operational practices in such a way that both levels are in effect intertwined. The principal factors that need to be intertwined are strategy and structure, organizational culture, and HRM processes. This means that the HR function can play an important role in developing business and competitive strategies.

 ## Summary

The chapter has highlighted the importance of strategic management to organizations around the world by discussing the following.

● It is through the adoption of the four phases of strategic management that organizations are able to achieve and sustain competitive advantage.

● Strategic management comprises four phases: analysis, selection, implementation, and review. These are inextricably linked.

- Whittington (2001) shows that there are different perspectives on strategy and each of these has different implications for the strategy that emerges from the strategic management process.

- The strategic management process embraces business and competitive strategies and enables an organization to identify and better understand those factors that contribute to an organization's competitive advantage.

- The changing nature of global markets and developing economies in countries such as India, China, and Brazil means that multinationals can no longer take for granted the efficacy of traditional Western approaches to strategic management.

 ## Review questions

1. What is the relationship between an organization's vision and mission statements?

2. How can the concept of strategy be defined?

3. What is the difference between business and competitive strategies?

4. What does RBV stand for and how is it relevant to the concept of competitive advantage?

5. In what ways are developing economies impacting on global approaches to strategy?

End-of-chapter case study Tesco, Kraft Foods, and Haier: comparing strategies

Tesco

When Tesco announced the early retirement of its CEO, Sir Terry Leahy, the company's share price fell by 3% in a day. He is widely regarded as turning Tesco into a great company through a decade-long strategy of 'organic' growth based on domestic and, in particular, international expansion. Recent overseas acquisitions include the purchase of 38 stores in South Korea for £958 million. Current plans included adding 8.5 million square feet to its operations in 2010, up from 5.1 million in the previous year. It also plans to open nine new shopping malls in China. His explanation for his departure was brief: 'My work here is done', referring to his two ambitions of making Tesco Britain's biggest supermarket chain and taking the business overseas. Today Tesco is the third largest retailer in the world. It operates in 14 countries and has 472,000 employees. The most recent annual performance figures are a profit of £2.34 billion on a sales turnover of £56.9 billion. The decision to grow the business through domestic and overseas expansion had actually been taken in 1995, two years before Sir Terry Leahy was promoted to CEO. But it is under his leadership that an aspiration or vision has been turned into reality, with 4,811 Tesco stores now operating worldwide. Presently, the firm's success in Asia is helping to offset the problem of stalled growth in the UK. What makes the Tesco story so interesting is that the expansion strategy has been characterized by diversification into a wide range of non-food products and services, including electronics, books, music, and financial services. At the same time Tesco has striven to stay true to its underpinning values of simplicity, economy, and excellent service. There is speculation that Sir Terry Leahy's successor, Philip Clarke, may have to preside over the break-up of the company because of increasing concerns that it has grown too big.

Sources

1. Tappin, S. and Cave, A. (2010) *The New Secrets of CEOs: 200 Global Chief Executives on Leading.* London: Nicholas Brealey Publishing.

2. *Wall Street Journal*
   http://blogs.wsj.com/source/2010/06/08/leahys-work-not-yet-done/?KEYWORDS=Tesco
   (accessed 18 June 2010).

3. *The Guardian*
   http://www.guardian.co.uk/business/2010/jun/08/tesco-sir-terry-leahy-steps-down
   (accessed 18 June 2010).

4. *The Telegraph*
   http://www.telegraph.co.uk/finance/newsbysector/epic/tsco/7828868/Tesco-UK-sales-slow-as-petrol-costs-hit-shoppers.html
   (accessed 20 June 2010).

5. *Bloomberg Business Week*
   http://www.businessweek.com/globalbiz/content/jun2010/gb20100614_663341.htm
   (accessed 20 June 2010).

Kraft Foods

In 2009 the US firm Kraft set in motion its strategy for acquiring Cadbury, the long-established British chocolate manufacturer. In February 2010 it was announced that Kraft had acquired Cadbury for £11.4 billion. The takeover was controversial and described as a 'hostile' takeover bid. The takeover was consistent with Kraft's strategy of expanding the business through mergers and acquisitions under the leadership of CEO Irene Rosenfeld. Cadbury was an attractive brand because Kraft needed to expand into emerging economies and 40% of Cadbury's sales were already in these markets. The aim of Kraft's strategy is to improve profits by 9–11% per annum. As part of this strategy, innovation is preferred to cost cutting (indeed Irene Rosenfeld reversed some of the cost-cutting measures already in place when she took over as CEO). She has also focused on decentralizing business decision making, so that the most relevant strategic choices are taken, and implementing incentives that encourage collaboration across the company.

Sources

1. Tappin, S. and Cave, A. (2010) *The New Secrets of CEOs: 200 Global Chief Executives on Leading.* London: Nicholas Brealey Publishing.

2. *The New York Times*
   http://www.nytimes.com/2010/05/28/business/global/28kraft.html?scp=2&sq=Kraft&st=cse
   (accessed 19 June 2010).

3. *Bloomberg Business Week*
   http://www.businessweek.com/globalbiz/content/feb2010/gb2010023_379746.htm
   (accessed 19 June 2010).

4. *Bloomberg Business Week*
   http://www.businessweek.com/globalbiz/content/sep2009/gb2009097_250429.htm
   (accessed 20 June 2010).

Haier

Haier is one of China's leading firms with an annual turnover of over $15 billion. The company manufactures home appliances such as refrigerators and washing machines. When its CEO, Zhang Ruimin, took up his post in 1984 the company was on the brink of bankruptcy. In 2004 it was listed as one of the 'World's Top 100 Brands', reflecting the extent to which its branded products can be bought around the world. Today, under his leadership, it is the world's biggest refrigerator and washing machine maker by volume and is one of the few Chinese companies to expand overseas, starting with a production base in the US in 1999. Haier's strategy, under the leadership of its CEO, Zhang Ruiman, is predicated on a commitment to quality, innovation, and a strong desire to be recognized as a global brand. The firm is now trying to build novel technologies and features into its products rather than emphasize the low-cost advantage it derives from being a Chinese company. Such values are consistent with those espoused by firms in other Asian 'Tiger' economies such as Japan and South Korea. Recent expansion includes a 20% share in New Zealand's Fisher and Paykel Appliances Holdings Ltd for just under $34 million. The company is also benefiting from the Chinese government's $586 billion stimulus package to boost domestic consumption as it includes cash subsidies for purchase of washing machines, refrigerators, and computers.

Sources

1. Schuman, M. (2009) *The Miracle: The Epic Story of Asia's Quest for Wealth*. New York, NY: Harper Business.

2. Nie, W., Xin, K. and Zhang, L. (2009) *Made in China: Secrets of China's Dynamic Entrepreneurs*. Singapore: John Wiley and Sons (Asia).

3. McGregor, R. (2010) The Party: *The Secret World of China's Communist Rulers*. London: Allen Lane.

4. Tappin, S. and Cave, A. (2010) *The New Secrets of CEOs: 200 Global Chief Executives on Leading*. London: Nicholas Brealey Publishing.

5. *Bloomberg Business Week*
   http://www.businessweek.com/news/2010-01-14/haier-may-sustain-10-sales-growth-on-japan-demand-update2-.html
   (accessed 20 June 2010).

6. Chinatoday.com
   http://news.cnet.com/Chinas-Haier-eyes-U.S.-living-rooms/2100-1041_3-6226826.html
   (accessed 20 June 2010).

Case study questions

1. How might you explain the business and competitive strategies for each firm?

2. What appear to be the principal sources of competitive advantage for each firm?

 ## Further reading

Mintzberg, H. (1987) Crafting strategy. *Harvard Business Review*, July–Aug.
This is a seminal article that is still relevant today.

Mintzberg, H. (1996) Five Ps for strategy. In H. Mintzberg and J.B. Quinn (eds) *The Strategy Process*. London: Prentice Hall.
This is a good book chapter for expanding your understanding of Mintzberg's critique of deliberate and emergent strategies.

Mintzberg, H. and Lampel, J. (1999) Reflecting on the strategy process. Sloan Management Review, Spring.
This builds on this chapter's content by introducing you to ten schools of strategy formation.

Porter, M.E. (2008) The five competitive forces that shape strategy. *Harvard Business Review*, Jan., pp. 78–93.
This article discusses in depth one of Porter's principal models for analysing the external environment.

Whittington, R. (2001) *What is Strategy—and Does it Matter?* London: Thomson Learning.
At only 130 pages this is a relatively short book to read for improving your understanding of the author's four perspectives on strategy discussed above.

 For additional material on the content of this chapter please access the OUP website **www.oxfordtextbooks.co.uk/orc/truss.**

Part 2

Strategic HRM

4 The strategic role of the HR function

Learning Objectives

By the end of this chapter you should be able to:

- Explain how the evolution of HR functional roles has influenced the HR department today.
- Outline the elements of the CIPD HR Profession Map.
- Critically evaluate the main frameworks and models that have been developed to analyse the role of the HR function.
- Develop an insight into the role conflict experienced by HR professionals.
- Understand the different structural arrangements available to HR departments and recommend alternatives.
- Appreciate the factors that influence structural decisions.
- Evaluate the factors that impact on the changing role of the HR department.

Key Concepts

Strategic partner
Outsourcing
Shared service centres

4.1 Introduction

When leading HR guru David Ulrich launched a 'new mandate' for HR departments in 1997 with his seminal book *Human Resource Champions* (Ulrich, 1997c), he posed the deliberately provocative question:

> Should we do away with HR? . . . It is often ineffective, incompetent and costly; in a phrase, it is value sapping. Indeed, if HR were to remain configured as it is today in many companies, I would have to answer the question above with a resounding, 'yes, abolish the thing!' (p. 24).

HR professionals are often called upon to justify their activities and explain how they add value. Equally, they are also required to take account of employment law and other legal frameworks, as well as professional norms and standards, in the conduct of their work (Guest and King, 2004). The tasks undertaken by HR professionals can vary from basic administrative procedures right through to involvement in board-level strategic decision making, requiring HR profession-als to have a broad skill set and to operate within complex and often competing frames of reference.

In this chapter, we focus on the role played by the HR department, as well as its structure and contribution. We first chart the scope and evolution of the modern HR function, which sheds light on the dilemmas, contradictions, and choices faced by HR professionals as they negotiate their role among the competing priorities of ethical, managerial, and professional imperatives (Jamrog and Overholt, 2004). We then examine the various models of HR func-tional roles that have been developed by theorists, and finally consider the structural choices open to HR departments in terms of organizing their activities.

4.2 The scope of the HR function

Peter Drucker, the renowned management thinker, observed in the early 1960s:

> Personnel administration . . . is largely a collection of incidental techniques without much internal cohesion. As personnel administration conceives the job of managing worker and work, it is partly a file clerk's job, partly a housekeeping job, partly a social worker's job and partly fire-fighting to head off union trouble or to settle it . . . [they] are necessary chores. I doubt though that they should be put together in one department for they are a hodge-podge (Drucker, 1961: 269–70).

It is interesting to compare the scope of HR activities that Drucker referred to in the 1960s with the most recent and influential framework of HR activities, the UK Chartered Institute of Personnel and Development's (CIPD) HR Profession Map, published in 2009 (http://www.cipd.co.uk). The HR Profession Map details the ten areas in which the CIPD believes practising HR managers should demonstrate expertise:

- **Organization design:** including job design, organization structure, and change.
- **Organization development:** including culture management and development.
- **Resourcing and talent planning:** including resourcing, succession planning, and induction.
- **Learning and talent development:** including training, development, and coaching.
- **Performance and reward:** including performance management and reward management.
- **Employee engagement:** ensuring a positive employee working experience aligned with organizational objectives.
- **Employee relations:** including union relations, disciplinary and grievance procedures, welfare, and legal compliance.
- **Service delivery and information:** including the provision of management information and data, and HR service delivery to the line.
- **Strategy insights and solutions:** including the application of knowledge of strategic issues to the design and delivery of HR strategy.

- **Leading and managing the HR function:** leading and managing a 'fit for purpose' HR function.

  (http://www.cipd.co.uk).

The CIPD developed its HR Map in consultation with leading HR professionals and has used it as the basis for the content of its CIPD professional accreditation courses. Although Drucker regarded the role of HR as too varied back in the 1960s, it is evident that it has grown further still today. We can see that HR's role comprises a range of activities that impact directly on employees' experience of working in the organization, as well as activities at an organizational level. In the CIPD's model, each of the ten professional areas can be undertaken at four different levels of seniority, ranging from basic administration support, through policy development, to strategic leadership.

The CIPD's HR Profession Map provides us with a useful summary of the range of activities that fall within the remit of the HR department today. However, a brief historical overview sets these within a context that can help to explain how and why this mixture of roles, or 'hodge-podge' in Drucker's terms, has come about.

Whilst some writers have traced the roots of the HR role back as far as medieval times, when craftspeople organized themselves into guilds in an effort to improve their working conditions (Jamrog and Overholt, 2004), it is generally accepted that the HR function as we know it today has its roots in the development of industrialized organizations that has taken place since the 1800s (Ogilvie and Stork, 2003). The earliest equivalent roles were those performed by the social reformers and welfare officers who worked, often on a voluntary basis, in the emergent industrialized organizations of the 19th century (Marchington and Wilkinson, 2008). Their primary concern was the welfare of workers in what were often harsh and unhealthy working conditions (Tyson, 1995). Today, this concern with workers' wellbeing is manifest in occupational health, wellbeing at work initiatives, and employee assistance programmes (Torrington et al, 2005), falling within the CIPD's 'employee relations' domain.

Another development that influenced the growth of the modern HR function was the Scientific Management movement of the late 19th century. Scientific Management was concerned with the analysis of jobs to determine optimal efficiency and effectiveness, and was often associated with the breakdown of jobs into discrete elements whose performance could be closely specified and supervised (Buchanan and Huczynski, 2004). HR tasks such as job design, selection, and training were particularly important under this movement (Jamrog and Overholt, 2004) and continue to be elements of the modern HR role under the CIPD's headings of 'resourcing and talent planning', 'learning and talent development', and 'organization design', although overlaid with a more sophisticated understanding of human motivation and performance. Scientific Management principles can still, however, be seen in modern automobile production lines and fast-food restaurants with their clear sequencing and separating of tasks. In Chapters 9 and 10 we explore the core themes of talent management and HR development in more detail.

Along with the growing size of firms was an increasing need for record-keeping in relation to the employment of people, including dealing with job applications and the maintenance of employee records such as sickness absence and annual leave. According to Marchington and Wilkinson (2008), this aspect of the HR role came to the fore particularly during the

1940s as employment legislation started to become increasingly formalized with a focus on justice, fairness, and equity of treatment. The ongoing need for HR departments to maintain accurate records and undertake administrative work can be seen in recent HR functional roles typologies emphasizing the importance of excellence in administrative procedures (Storey, 1992; Ulrich, 1997a) and in the CIPD's heading of 'service delivery and information'.

Whilst other aspects of the HR role that we have looked at so far have been largely unitary in focus and concerned with the management of individual workers rather than collectivities, there has been another important thread dating back to the Industrial Revolution, which has been the responsibility for dealing with unions (Tyson, 1995). This aspect of the HR role became especially prominent from the 1940s onwards and during the 1960s and 1970s when trade union membership and power were at their peak (Torrington et al, 2005; Marchington and Wilkinson, 2008), but continues today to be considered by many HR departments and line managers to be a crucial element of the HR role within workplaces with high levels of unionization or where works councils are in place. Linked with this has been HR's role in the legal side of the employment relationship and ensuring compliance. This aspect of the role came to the fore through the 20th century as employment became increasingly regulated, covering areas such as diversity, equality, and human rights. HR's task is to ensure legal compliance, the fair and just treatment of workers, and the avoidance of costly tribunals and appeals (Flood et al, 1995; Ogilvie and Stork, 2003; Jamrog and Overholt, 2004). The development of employment law as an area of distinctive expertise has helped to create an environment where the occupation of HR manager could be seen as a profession. These tasks broadly fall within the CIPD's remit of 'employee relations', which we explore further in Chapter 11.

One of the most significant developments that has affected the role of the HR department in recent years has been the idea that the policies and practices used by organizations in the management of people should be linked in some way to their overall strategic objectives (Truss and Gratton, 1994; Ulrich, 1997a). This notion that HR management can make a direct contribution to a firm's performance emerged for the first time in the 1980s, during an era when capitalism was undergoing a fundamental shift towards the right-wing ideals espoused by the governments of Margaret Thatcher in the UK and Ronald Reagan in the US. Whilst the idea that people should be managed strategically was not new, the notion that an organization's HR policies and practices could themselves contribute to the creation of advantage was. This has created particular challenges for HR practitioners, as operating at a strategic level is about *shaping* rather than supporting business strategy. To do this successfully, HR practitioners need to develop a range of interrelated skills and an ability to think strategically. This, in turn, needs to be underpinned by business or commercial acumen which includes business understanding and cross-functional experience. The CIPD reflects this in several areas of its Professional Map including the areas of 'resourcing and talent planning' and 'performance and reward'. The CIPD's 'employee engagement' heading also refers to the importance of aligning employees with organizational aims and objectives, and we focus on engagement in Chapter 12.

Alongside the move to make the HR function 'strategic' came the idea that HR departments should also be contributing much more to the management of organizational change programmes (Ulrich, 1997a; Caldwell, 2001; Alfes et al, 2010b). The management of change, whilst clearly linked to ideals of SHRM, went beyond this by suggesting that HR departments should become more involved in the full range of organizational change and transformation activities, not just those directly linked to the HR department. The CIPD's headings of 'organization design' and 'organization development' contain specific reference to the importance of change management, and we explore these topics further in Chapters 9 and 15.

 Critical Reflection

Visit the CIPD website and find the pages relating to the HR Profession Map. Then, for an HR department familiar to you (or, using the internet to look at company websites, explore the HR strategies of two or three organizations), evaluate the relative emphasis placed on each of the ten areas identified in the CIPD Profession Map. Is there evidence that all ten roles are being enacted and, if not, why not? How successful would you say this HR department is and why?

4.3 Typologies of HR functional roles

Whilst the CIPD's HR Profession Map provides a framework developed by leading HR policy-makers and practitioners, academics have also been concerned for some years with mapping out the roles that HR can play. In particular, a focus has been on developing typologies that help to explain and contextualize how the various tasks described above combine into different role orientations.

There are five widely known models:

- Legge's (1978) model of HR power and intervention.
- Tyson and Fell's (1986) building site analogy.
- Storey's (1992) strategic/tactical model.
- Ulrich's original 'HR Champion' model (1997) and his updated typology of HR roles (Ulrich and Brockbank, 2005a).
- Caldwell's (2001) change matrix.

Generally, these models differentiate between strategic roles, and tactical or operational roles (see Table 4.1).

4.3.1 Legge's (1978) HR innovator model

Although writing about the HR department some 30 years ago now, Karen Legge's differentiation between 'conformist innovators' and 'deviant innovators' continues to be widely referenced (Guest and King, 2004). Legge's concern was to explain how HR professionals could effect change within their organization, and she suggested that they could choose between three options:

Table 4.1 Summary of HR roles

Author(s)	Operational (tactical) roles	Strategic roles
Legge (1978)	1. Conformist innovator 2. Problem solver	3. Deviant innovator
Tyson and Fell (1986)	1. Clerk of works 2. Contracts manager	3. Architect
Storey (1992)	1. Regulators 2. Handmaidens	3. Advisors 4. Change makers
Ulrich (1997a)	1. Admin expert 2. Employee champion	3. Change agent 4. Strategic partner
Ulrich and Brockbank (2005a)	1. Employee advocate 2. Functional expert	3. Human capital developer 4. Srategic partner 5. HR leader
Caldwell (2001)	1. Adapter 1. Consultant	3. Synergist 4. Champion

- **Conformist innovator:** using HR expertise to improve organizational performance by 'buying into' the prevailing managerial value-system and suggesting improvements that work within the accepted paradigm, rather than challenging it.

- **Deviant innovator:** encouraging radical change by questioning prior assumptions. This role involves the HR professional seeking to persuade line managers to change their way of working at a fundamental level.

- **Problem solver:** where HR professionals contribute by helping to resolve certain organizational problems through their specialist expertise.

Whilst Legge suggested that few opted for the second, more challenging, route, later research has found that evidence that HR plays a leading role in change of any kind is equivocal (Caldwell, 2001). Legge pointed out the problems arising from HR's relative powerlessness and marginalization from core decision-making processes as compared with other organizational functions such as finance, fostering a reactive and short-term focus which further served to reinforce their subordinate organizational position. Revisiting Legge's work recently, Guest and King (2004) showed that there are still tensions between HR and the line over responsibility for HR, and that senior managers continue to be reluctant to invest in HR interventions. They also noted that the HR function has increasingly become aligned with organizational aims and aspirations, with a reduced focus on employee interests, further curtailing the possibility for 'deviant' innovation; they conclude (p. 420): 'there was little or no evidence of the kind of sophisticated social science-based problem-solving advocated by Legge'. Legge's model is useful for understanding the political arena within which HR professionals operate, and the difficulties they face in achieving fundamental change.

Figure 4.1 Storey's HR functional roles.
Source: Storey (1992).

4.3.2 Tyson and Fell's (1986) building site model

Tyson and Fell (1986) argued that HR functions could essentially be regarded as playing three possible roles:

- **Clerk of works:** this role provided the least opportunity for choice and discretion and was essentially concerned with paperwork and administration.

- **Contracts manager:** the role was found where there was a significant union presence in the workplace and where the role was focused around systems and procedures.

- **Architect:** in some cases, HR departments could play a strategic role integrating the management of people into the core of the business.

Each role could potentially be found at each level in the organizational hierarchy, although Monks (1993) later argued that the roles should be regarded as cumulative rather than discrete. This means that, where there is evidence of HR playing the role of architect, then the other two roles would be present as well. In the late 1990s, Hope-Hailey et al (1997) found that the contracts manager role was most in evidence at business unit level (i.e. within departments rather than at corporate level), with the clerk of works having disappeared. This model was developed on the basis of empirical data as a means of classifying organizations into types, depending on their HR orientation. However, it has now been superseded by later and more holistic models that take account of a broader range of HR functions.

4.3.3 Storey's (1992) strategic/tactical model

Storey (1992), also writing in the UK, undertook a detailed examination of the role of the HR function in 15 large organizations in the late 1980s. He argued that the roles played by the HR function could be plotted against two axes: interventionary/non-interventionary and strategic/tactical, giving rise to four possible roles (see Fig. 4.1).

The advisor role comprised internal consultancy and advice to line managers without being interventionary, the handmaiden role was reactive to line manager requests, the regulatory role included involvement in the development and application of employment rules and policy, and

Figure 4.2 Ulrich's (1997a) typology of HR functional roles.
Source: Ulrich (1997a).

changemakers were both strategic and inteventionary and concerned with SHRM and the management of change. In his study, Storey found that only two of the HR departments were performing a changemaker role, reflecting observations noted above in relation to Karen Legge's model.

Caldwell (2003), in retesting Storey's model with a sample of 98 large firms, found that the advisor role was the most common, cited by 80% of respondents as their main, or one of their main, roles. The next most significant role was change agent, with 67 out of the 98 respondents seeing this as their main or a significant role. However, 38 of the 98 respondents identified no main role for themselves. Overall, Caldwell concluded that HR has changed substantially since Storey's model was first developed, with the growth of the change agent and advisor roles and remodelling of the handmaiden role, which he termed service provider, and this growing complexity often led to tensions and conflicts in the performance of the role, which are discussed further below.

4.3.4 Ulrich's (1997a) 'HR Champion' model

Based on his view of the role that the HR department *should* be playing rather than his observations of what the role *actually* looked like, Ulrich proposed a 2-by-2 matrix similar to that of Storey (see Fig. 4.2). The vertical axis indicated a focus on either the day-to-day role or the future, and the horizontal axis a focus on either people or processes. This gave rise to four potential roles: change agent, employee champion, administrative expert, and strategic partner. These terms have entered the popular lexicon of the HR professional and are frequently used to refer to the different ways in which the HR function can be deployed (Brown et al, 2004).

Ulrich argued that for HR to make a real contribution to the organization, all four roles needed to be fulfilled. It is important to note that he did not claim that the HR department *itself* should necessarily fulfil all four roles, but that the department needed to ensure that, in some way, they were carried out. The four roles are summarized in Table 4.2.

Table 4.2 Ulrich's (1997a) typology of HR functional roles

Role	Description
Strategic partner	Focus on HR activities in supporting the strategic direction of the organization. It is this element of Ulrich's model that gave rise to the concept of the 'HR partner' that has become so prevalent in organizations today. This role is associated with a range of functions: strategic planning; organization development and design; improving organizational productivity; facilitating mergers, acquisitions, and partnerships; scanning the environment; recruitment and selection strategy; employee development; compensations and benefits; management of HR information systems; overseeing trade union negotiations; responsibility for legal and regulatory requirements.
Administrative expert	Focus on ensuring that HR activities and tasks are executed efficiently and quickly, responding to the needs of the line, and demonstrating the value added to the organization by HR. Available evidence suggests that line managers particularly value the role of administrative expert, even though this is perceived as the 'poor relation'.
Employee champion	Focus on the need for HR to manage the wellbeing of individual employees through listening and responding to them, and conversely ensuring that employees are aware of the strategic issues facing the firm. This role is shrinking due to the growing focus on the business partner role, although, conversely, the demand for welfare-related work has been growing due to the degree of organizational change.
Change agent	Focus on the management of organizational change.

Source: Ulrich (1997a).

Caldwell (2003) noted that there is considerable overlap between Ulrich's model and that of Storey's. He criticized Ulrich's model for not taking sufficient account of the potential for conflict between the four roles and concluded that the widespread uptake of Ulrich's model 'should be viewed with considerable caution' (p. 1002), presenting as it does a unitary view of how managers, employees, and HR professionals can collaborate within organizations that does not take sufficient account of the realities of organizational life. Despite its influence, in a recent survey, the CIPD found that in practice fewer than 30% of organizations had introduced Ulrich's model in full with a further 30% saying that had partially introduced it (CIPD, 2008a).

 Case study 4.1 Michael Chivers, Vice-President Human Resources, Global Sales and Marketing, Sony Ericsson

Because Sony Ericsson is a global business, HR business partners are often pulled in different directions. However, a fundamental aspect of their role is to focus on developing the structures and job roles to grow the business. Michael explained:

'As a business, we are not yet recognised as a company associated with mobile phones at the 'low end' of the market. Yet there is a market out there, especially in developing economies . . . the business needs to address this to get a share of the market. Our [HR] role is to understand what the business strategy is and drive the people strategy to meet this. This could be addressing ethnic diversity, different types of structures, and managing talent.'

The priority for strategic business partners is organizational design and global talent management, working out what the issues and priorities are in different countries and being responsive to these.

Michael commented that while salaries, salary reviews, and performance management need to be done, and done well, the HR function does not necessarily need to be doing all of these things themselves, as this type of work is not value-adding. HR can provide the tools for others to use themselves, or they can buy/borrow tools from organizations like the CIPD.

Michael wears several partnering hats. With his corporate HR partnering hat he works with HR business partners in other countries/regions to understand the different business priorities. He then contracts with the business partners on what people solutions will be delivered locally and what will be delivered centrally.

As business partner to sales and marketing managers in different countries, Michael focuses on organizational design and talent management solutions. He provided an example here of a conference he recently organized where he brought together global sales and marketing managers to look at the global talent map. As part of the preparation for the conference, each manager was tasked to look critically at the talent in his or her team and identify potential successors for critical roles.

These data were then presented on a global map at the conference—an approach that had a great impact. Each manager then talked about the talent in his or her own area, so where the talent is and where the shortages are. The event was so uplifting and empowering that as the process evolved managers started to offer up talented people to other areas for new roles. This behaviour is unheard of, as traditionally managers have wanted to hold onto their best talent.

Source

CIPD (2008c: 9).

....

Activity

How would you describe Michael Chivers' role, using the models described above?

4.3.5 Ulrich and Brockbank's (2005a) updated model

Ulrich expanded on his original model by suggesting that there are five core HR roles, rather than four (Ulrich and Brockbank, 2005a) (see Fig. 4.3).

These new roles overlap to a considerable extent with Ulrich's previous model, but the strategic partner and change agent roles are combined into one, 'Strategic Partner', whilst adding two new roles, 'Human Capital Developer' and 'HR Leader', in recognition of the importance of HR providing a role model in the way that it leads its own department. Equally, Ulrich has continued to argue for the importance of the employee champion role (now termed 'Employee Advocate'), although the CIPD (2003d) found that only 6% of HR professionals wanted to play this role primarily. Table 4.3 describes the roles in more detail.

4.3.6 Caldwell's (2001) change matrix

Caldwell's (2001) model focuses on HR's role in managing change (see Fig. 4.4). He argued that the 'Changemaker' or 'Change Agent' role in Storey's and Ulrich's work hid some important complexities in the way in which HR specialists went about managing change. Taking this one quadrant of both their models, he undertook some in-depth research into how the role of

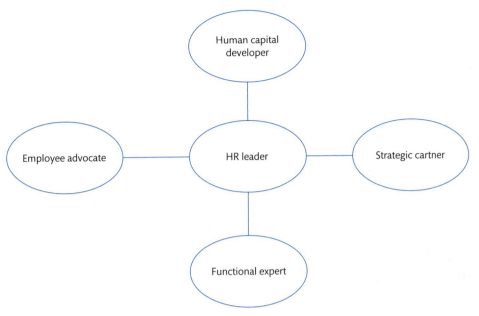

Figure 4.3 Ulrich and Brockbank's updated model.
Source: Ulrich and Brockbank (2005a).

Table 4.3 Ulrich and Brockbank's (2005a) typology of HR functional roles

Strategic partner	Partnering with line managers to add value and help them reach their goals, advise leaders, and help manage change. (Previously: Strategic partner and change agent)
Functional expert	Knowing and applying the body of HR professional knowledge. (Previously: Administrative expert)
Employee advocate	HR professionals spend around 19% of their time on employee relations issues, which involves listening to and responding to employees, as well as communicating with them on behalf of line managers. It also involves caring for employees and advocating on their behalf. (Previously: Employee champion)
Human capital developer	Managing and developing the workforce for the future with a focus on individual employees and matching their wishes with suitable opportunities.
HR leader	Leading and valuing the HR function, and implementing best practice HR initiatives within the HR function itself. This also includes playing a key role in corporate governance and acting as the organization's conscience.

Source: Ulrich and Brockbank (2005a).

change agent was enacted in practice, and developed his own two-by-two model that differentiates the nature of interventions according to whether they are based on HR vision or expertise vs transformative (i.e. large-scale) or incremental (i.e. small-scale) change, giving rise to four potential roles (see Table 4.4).

Figure 4.4 Caldwell's model.
Source: Caldwell (2001: 45).

Table 4.4 Caldwell's (2001) HR roles

Champion	Change champions are high-level executives who lead strategic transformational change programmes.
Synergist	Synergists are senior internal or external HR professionals who strategically coordinate and integrate complex and large-scale change projects across the organization.
Adapter	Change adapters are mid-level HR generalists and specialists who build support for change within business units and functions.
Consultant	Consultants are specialists, either internal or external to the organization, who implement discrete change projects.

Source: Caldwell (2001).

 Key Concept

The term **strategic partner**, also referred to as 'business partner', derives mainly from Ulrich's use of the term in his 1997 model to describe the partnering of HR professionals and executives with senior and line managers in the strategic management of the organization. This can involve both the development of HR policies and strategies aligned with business objectives, and HR's involvement in the overall strategic direction of the organization. Whilst most applicable in private sector firms, the term is also used within the public sector.

Caldwell found that the roles of synergist and consultant were highly problematic, as pressures grow for increasing business unit autonomy and HR expertise becomes more and more fragmented, running the risk of being taken over by non-specialists or outsourced. However, he also argues that this creates an opportunity for HR professionals to reposition themselves through a focus on change at a strategic level.

4.3.7 Summary and implications

We have examined five different models of HR functional roles that differentiate between strategically orienated functions and adminstrative or operational functions. Whilst some were developed through examining evidence obtained from organizations, others, notably Ulrich's two models, are normative. The models provide useful frameworks according to which HR role and organizational contribution can be evaluated. Equally, the CIPD's HR Profession Map provides a holistic overview of the domains of expertise required by HR professionals, overlaid with the consideration that each professional area involves interventions that range from administrative to strategic. Whilst the majority of these models represent 'maps' of HR activity, Legge's model stands out as providing a more critical insight into the political tensions and ambiguities that HR professionals can experience.

Despite the exhortation to move to a more strategic role, the evidence from most recent research is that HR has not become more strategic, and that administrative work continues to dominate (Caldwell, 2003; Guest and King, 2004; Tamkin et al, 2006; Marchington and Wilkinson, 2008). Lawler and Mohrman's (2003) study of 150 large US companies found that, in fact, little changed between 1995 and 2001 in terms of the role that the HR department was playing, and that there was little evidence of an increased strategic role. Overall, they found that 23% of HR time was spent on being a strategic business partner, compared with 31% of time spent on the implementation and administration of HR practices, although the number saying that they were a full partner in the business strategy process had risen from 29% to 41%. It has also been suggested that the HR department may be losing strategic ground rather than gaining it, as more HR work is done by line managers or outsourced, with business partners being marginalized (Marchington and Wilkinson, 2008). Guest and King (2004: 421) somewhat pessimistically conclude: 'it appears that the opportunity that Ulrich identified to seize the initiative and become HR Champions has been passed by'.

However, other studies present a more optimistic view. For instance, Beckett (2005) argues that demand for the business partner role has grown by 30% in 2004, whilst research conducted by the CIPD in 2003 of 1,200 respondents (Tamkin et al, 2006) found that the business partner role was considered the most attractive role for HR practitioners. Of 1,200 HR heads who were surveyed, one-third saw themselves primarily as strategic business partners (with 56% aspiring to be one), one-quarter as change agents, and just 4% as administrative experts (Brown et al, 2004).

The CIPD study (2003d) identified three key strategic challenges facing HR professionals:

- Thirty-five per cent believed that HR is too focused on operational issues.
- Almost half felt that their strategic role was adversely affected by the time they spent on administrative issues.
- Three-fifths believed that line managers had not fully assumed their role in people management (Brown et al, 2004: 4; Tamkin et al, 2006).

 Critical Reflection

Thinking about the five models of HR roles, which do you find most useful and why?

4.4 HR roles: tensions and ambiguities

We saw in section 4.2 the way that historical trends and influences have impacted on HR's role today. Critical to this is an awareness that the various tasks and activities that are now considered to form part of HR's domain of responsibility are rooted in different, and often conflicting, ideologies.

The HR professional is essentially caught between a number of competing demands and priorities (see Fig. 4.5). On the one hand, the pressure to adhere to organizational norms and take the 'side' of the employer in extracting maximum value from employees, as well as performing HR's own role in the most cost-effective way, is very real (Legge, 2005). Right from HR's historical roots in scientific management, through to today's focus on the performance management of the individual worker, HR professionals are expected to have the interests of the organization at heart. Accompanying this is a lack of clarity over the boundaries between HR's role and that of line managers (Guest and King, 2004). We examine this important issue further in Chapter 7. However, HR's welfare roots also create a special relationship with employees, in particular for their wellbeing, as well as broader ethical and moral concerns, which is evident even within Ulrich's most prescriptive work, where HR is urged to act as organizational conscience (Wright and Snell, 2005).

Also relevant is the growth in employment legislation, with HR's legal responsibility to develop and enforce legally compliant HR policies and practices. Sometimes this responsibility runs counter to the wishes of line managers, who may regard HR processes as overly bureaucratic and cumbersome (Guest and King, 2004). Equally, the rise of HRM as a 'profession' has led to a strengthening of norms around how HRM 'should' be done and the body of knowledge that underpins it (Marchington and Wilkinson, 2008).

Caldwell (2003) sums up these potential areas of conflict experienced by HR professionals as follows:

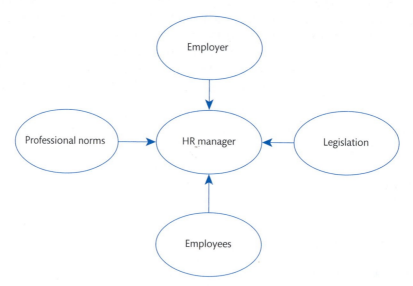

Figure 4.5 Competing pressures on the HR professional.

- **Inter-role conflict**, where carrying out some roles may lead to conflict with other roles; for instance, applying employment legislation which may run counter to the organization's strategic imperatives.
- **Intra-role conflict**, where the expectations of what the HR professional can achieve are in opposition.
- **Value-role conflict**, where the individual's own values or professional values are in conflict with the demands of the job.
- **Old–new role conflict**, where a change of role brings new pressures that may conflict with existing demands.

However, as Tamkin et al (2006: 2) note, the academic field of HRM has 'an unhelpful tradition of navel-gazing and worrying about its place in the firmament'. So perhaps we should expect that some degree of ambiguity and uncertainty is inevitable in any organizational role!

 Critical Reflection

An HR manager in one of my classes recently shared with the group a dilemma he had faced. His US-based company had introduced a new and very favourable maternity leave policy, but he had been told by headquarters that he was not allowed to publicize this policy to staff, although if people asked about it he could tell them, as they were afraid that too many people would ask for the extra leave. He felt torn between an obligation to his line manager, what he perceived to be his professional responsibility as an HR manager, and his wish to be open and honest with staff. What kind of role conflict was he experiencing and, if you were in his position, what would you do?

Source: The authors.

4.5 Structuring the HR department

4.5.1 Structural choices

The question of how to structure the HR department is clearly one that is of great concern to HR professionals. For instance, Peacock (2008) found that 81% of HR departments have restructured in the past 5 years. Ulrich's influence has had a profound impact on the notion of how best to structure an HR department (Tamkin et al, 2006). His advocacy of shared service centres responsible for largely administrative tasks, business partners working alongside line managers, and centres of expertise in areas such as training and reward has led to a widespread advocacy of the so-called three-legged functional design, topped with a small corporate team responsible for strategic issues and policy (Ulrich, 1997c):

- **Shared services:** a single unit handling all routine HR services in areas such as resourcing, payroll, and absence management.
- **Centres of excellence:** teams of HR experts with specialist knowledge, leading innovations in areas such as reward, engagement, and talent management.

- **Strategic business partners:** senior HR professionals working closely with line managers at a strategic level in areas such as long-term talent management planning and the management of change.

(CIPD, 2008a)

However, Tamkin et al (2006) found that there is, in fact, little evidence that this model has been widely adopted, and that organizations are often faced with the practical dilemma of choosing a structural design that best fits with their needs, although it is not always clear what would work optimally. This challenge is evident in the way that organizations alternate between centralized and decentralized structures, and between locating HR staff either together or within business units.

The principal domains where structural choices for the HR department have to be made are:

- **Location:** where should the HR function be situated? Should some or all staff be located out in the business units alongside line managers to facilitate teamworking, or in a central unit which might bring economies of scale and where experience and ideas about best practice can be shared?

- **Reporting lines:** to whom should HR staff report? Functionally, in a direct line through to the HR Director, or to the line managers within the business units, or to both?

- **Areas of responsibility:** which tasks should be the responsiblity of HR staff and which the responsibility of line managers? If line managers are to be asked to take on certain tasks, what support should be provided to them in terms of advice, training and development, on-line support, and so on.

- **Grouping of tasks and responsibilities:** how should tasks be grouped into individual jobs, and how should jobs be linked to one another? For instance, if the role of HR Partner is developed, does the HR Partner take responsibility for some or all HR support for a particular business unit, or act as a first point of contact, directing line managers to a shared service centre or centre of expertise? Should shared service centres or centres of expertise be used at all?

It is generally suggested that the best structure for any HR department is one that fits with the needs of the organization, although it may unfortunately not always be clear how to achieve this (Ulrich and Brockbank, 2005a).

The main structural alternatives for the HR department are shown in Table 4.5.

4.5.2 Outsourcing and shared service centres

 Key Concepts

Outsourcing has been defined as: 'placing responsibility for various elements of the HR function with a third-party provider' (Cooke et al, 2005: 415).

Shared service centres normally consist of a centralized call centre providing advice and support to line managers and sometimes individual employees (Marchington and Wilkinson, 2008). They can be based in one organization or shared across several organizations.

Table 4.5 HR department structural choices

Functional	The whole HR function, or parts of it, can be organized centrally along functional lines, with teams responsible for discrete areas of activity, such as recruitment, training and development, compensation, and benefits.
Geographical	Part or all of the HR department can be organized along geographical lines, with responsibility for particular locations, countries, or regions.
Shared services	Shared service centres can be established, often around a call centre or intranet that is accessible to everyone in the organization and that is set up to answer queries. Shared service centres benefit from economies of scale and accessibility; they can be in-house, part outsourced, or fully outsourced.
Embedded	Each business unit has its own dedicated HR team that reports into it.
Hybrid	A variation or combination of any of the above. Most HR functions in large organizations fall into the 'hybrid' category.

Sources: Mooney (2001); Ulrich and Brockbank (2005a); Marchington and Wilkinson (2008).

Outsourcing all or part of the HR function has become an increasingly popular option over recent years (Cooke et al, 2005; Sako and Tierney, 2007). Some have argued that the most significant trend for HR departments today is outsourcing their non-core, administrative activities whilst retaining a strategic core in-house (Adler, 2003). A PricewaterhouseCoopers survey in 2002 found that over 70% of organizations had outsourced at least one aspect of HR work, compared with fewer than 50% two years before (Marchington and Wilkinson, 2008). In the US, one study found that 94% of large employers were outsourcing at least one HR activity (Tamkin et al, 2006). According to Sako and Tierney (2007), the HR outsourcing market is growing rapidly, from a value of $23 billion in 2005 to $31.7 billion in 2009 and accounts for 65% of the entire back-office outsourcing market. Large organizations such as Centrica, Unilever, BT, IBM, Shell, Standard Chartered Bank, and BP have outsourced significant aspects of their HR activity or set up shared service centres (Tamkin et al, 2006; CIPD, 2008b).

However, it has been argued that most outsourcing is for discrete tasks or functions and is relatively limited in scope and scale (Forth et al, 2006; Pass, 2006). Outsourcing is particularly common amongst SMEs which lack the capability internally to provide the full range of HR services (Klaas et al, 2002). The pressure to develop new forms of HR service delivery comes from several main sources, including technological change, increased globalization, and organizational restructuring, but, of these reasons, cost savings have been cited as the primary driver for outsourcing by over half of respondents to the Workplace Employment Relations Survey 2004 (WERS), followed by improvement in service quality and focus on core business (Tamkin et al, 2006). HR activities that are often outsourced include:

- Payroll/design of compensation system
- Administration
- Training and development
- Communication
- HR information systems

- Succession planning
- Recruitment

Some of the issues that need to be considered prior to outsourcing are as follows:

1. How much HR activity can be outsourced without damaging the business?
2. What impact will outsourcing have on customer service?
3. Which outsource providers will give the best service?
4. What is the potential saving?

(Sako and Tierney, 2007)

Evidence as to whether or not outsourcing leads to cost savings is equivocal (Table 4.6). Sako and Tierney (2007) argue that the average HR cost per employee per annum is cheaper if an outsource provider is used, and Towers Perrin (2005) found that organizations could reduce costs through outsourcing, but this has not been replicated in other studies (Gainey and Klaas, 2002; Cooke et al, 2005). Where outsourcing is used, this inevitably has an impact on the HR function; Sako and Tierney (2007) note that often outsourcing is associated with a reduction of the HR department, or the transfer of staff to the service provider.

As Tamkin et al (2006: 10) note: 'progressive outsourcing of non-core activities can leave the HR function as an empty shell with its heart outsourced'. One study found that nearly

Table 4.6 Potential advantages and disadvantages of outsourcing HR

Advantages	Disadvantages
• Frees up in-house HR expertise in certain areas	• Loss of in-house knowledge and capacity
• Specialist suppliers have economies of scale	• Potential reduction in quality of HR support
• Numerical flexiblity	• Potential higher total cost
• Shifts the burden of administrative work outside the firm	• Loss of employee morale
• Potential cost saving	• Loss of long-term competitiveness
• Facilitates access to new ideas	• Lack of focus on customer needs
• Enables firms to focus on their core activities	• Poor capacity in the outsource provider or complacency towards service provision
• Provides greater flexibility through using subcontractors	• Loss of control
• Shifts the burden of risk and uncertainty	• Lock-in to arrangements that cannot readily adapt to changing organizational needs
• Can create the opportunity for organizational learning	• Erosion of HR's internal capabilities
	• Unanticipated resources needed to manage and monitor the relationship
	• Lack of flexibility on the part of the vendor firm in adapting to organizational needs
	• Potential work intensification for remaining HR professionals
	• Loss of career paths in HR

Sources: Lepak and Snell (1998); Klaas et al (2002); Adler (2003); Cooke et al (2005); Tamkin et al (2006).

two-thirds of outsourcing deals have been renegotiated and almost one in four have been brought back in-house (Birchall, 2006).

 Case study 4.2   Cambridgeshire County Council

Cambridgeshire County Council provides social services, education, and environmental services to a population of 590,000, with an annual budget of £570 million and employs 18,000 staff. The council implemented an e-business tool from Oracle to handle most of its IT, HR, and payroll transactions. However, the continuing need for upgrades was becoming costly, so it decided to create a shared service centre to save money and generate revenue. Partnering with Northamptonshire County Council, it invested £2.7 million over an 18-month period to June 2008. The two councils have created common processes and support teams running the systems on behalf of both organizations. As it is run virtually, it has not involved moving employees, although getting buy-in and securing agreement on common processes, as well as creating suitable legal and commercial agreements, was a challenge. By the end of 2009, Cambridgeshire expected to save £1 million through reducing the cost of corporate services functions and renegotiating the contract with Fujitsu. It also expects income of more than £16 million from the use of its model by other public bodies.

Source

Adapted from McLuhan (2008).

Activity

What do you see as the challenges facing the council in making the shared service centre work?

 ## Conclusion

In this chapter, we have examined the CIPD HR Profession Map and shown how the role of the HR function has developed over time. However, the successful performance of these tasks may lead to role conflict for HR practitioners as they try to juggle the competing demands of the employer, the employee, professional norms, and ethical practice. Various models of HR functional roles have been developed; Ulrich's work has been particularly influential on organizations, but research has shown that implementing his ideas may be problematic for many. Decisions around the structuring of the HR function are complex and involve consideration of such factors as outsourcing and devolution of responsibility for some HR activities to line managers, which is considered further in Chapter 7.

 ## Summary

- The CIPD HR Profession Map outlines ten core HR functions.
- HR's role in today's organization has emerged piecemeal over time.
- These strands of work often lead to experienced role conflict for today's HR practitioners in balancing the competing needs of employers, employees, professional norms, and ethical requirements.
- Several models of HR functional roles have been proposed, many of which differentiate beween a strategic and a tactical role for HR practitioners.

- Although HR practitioners have been exhorted to perform a more strategic role, evidence of uptake is equivocal.
- Various structural options exist for the HR department, and the choice depends on a variety of contextual factors.

 ## Review questions

1. Outline the potential types of role conflict that may arise for HR professionals in their day-to-day work and provide an example of each.

2. Look on the internet for some companies that provide HR outsourcing solutions or shared service centres. What are the main reasons they give for encouraging organizations to use their services, and what are your views on these?

3. David Ulrich's work on HR functional roles has been extremely influential for many HR practitioners. Explain why you think this is the case, and what are the advantages and disadvantages for organizations seeking to draw on his ideas in developing their own HR departments.

4. To what extent do you think HR departments can be held responsible for some of the recent financial failures of firms, and why? What do you think HR practitioners should do differently in future to address any issues you raise?

 ## End-of-chapter case study   Reed Boardall: managing without an HR department

Yorkshire-based chilled and frozen distribution company Reed Boardall is, in many respects, a typical company. It has all the functions a business of 700+ staff expects to have: finance, marketing, PR; all the functions except an HR department, that is.

'The issue here is really that we think line managers should be doing most of the personnel function', explains Chief Executive Keith Boardall. 'Managers and supervisors should have the right relationship with their teams and they can only do this if it's an all-embracing one. Every time there's a problem, you don't want to go through the rigmarole of going through a personnel manager who's slightly to the left of cloud nine and has no idea what he's dealing with.'

Of course, he says, line managers don't do everything. 'Records are centralized, we do have someone who keeps them. But anyone can do filing. However, when it comes to sorting out a fellow's problems, he has to go to his line manager. His manager will know who he is. If I had a workplace problem, I'd want to talk to the person who managed me every day, and who is most likely to understand what's going on.' Boardall adds that individual managers also tend to keep in touch with staff when they leave and handle recruitment.

As well as having managers know their staff well, Boardall believes in having so-called shop-floor HR, keeps the company 'small and accountable', and lets you know whether managers are actually any good. 'What's the line manager for but managing people? When you do appraisals the line manager needs to know everything—for instance, if someone's turning up late, why is that? Are they having marital problems? And when something goes wrong, the line manager has to deal with it rather than just passing it off into HR.'

Boardall also believes that HR can add unnecessary layers of bureaucracy and form filling to an organization. 'I spent 20 years working in companies with big personnel departments and it could get a bit like social services,' he says. 'They were more interested in following procedures than they were with getting things done for people. We live in a bureaucratic age and maybe my view is a bit Victorian. But I believe it's the way to go.'

Source

HR Magazine 1 April 2009. http://www.hrmagazine.co.uk/news/rss/895613/Case-study-Reed-Boardall-no-need-HR-department/.

Case study questions

1. What do you think are the advantages and disadvantages of Reed Boardall's decision not to have an HR department?

2. What arguments would you put forward to persuade Chief Executive Keith Boardall that having an HR department would be better for the company?

Further reading

Brown, D., Caldwell, R., White, K., Atkinson, H., Tansley, T., Goodge, P. and Emmott, M. (2004) *Business Partnering: A New Direction for HR.* London: CIPD.
Useful overview of business partnering for practitioners.

Cooke, F.L., Shen, J. and McBride, A. (2005) Outsourcing HR as a competitive strategy? A literature review and an assessment of implications. *Human Resource Management,* 44(4), pp. 413–432.
Useful source on the theoretical background underpinning the outsourcing debate.

Pass, S. (2006) *The HR Function: Today's Challenges, Tomorrow's Direction.* London: CIPD.
Interesting report giving practitioner views on HR departmental roles.

Ulrich, D. and Brockbank, W. (2005) *The HR Value Proposition.* Harvard: Harvard Business School Press.
Essential reading for understanding David Ulrich's perspective on the HR department.

For additional material on the content of this chapter please visit the supporting Online Resource Centre www.oxfordtextbooks.co.uk/orc/truss.

5 The foundations of SHRM

 Learning Objectives

By the end of this chapter you should be able to:

- Appreciate how the field of SHRM has developed over the past 30 years.
- Outline the differences between personnel management, HRM, and SHRM.
- Explain the core features of universalist (best-practice) approaches to SHRM.
- Understand the diverse ways in which contingency theory (best-fit) has been applied to SHRM.
- Critically evaluate the universalist (best-practice) and contingency (best-fit) perspectives on SHRM.

Key Concepts

Universalist (best-practice) approaches to SHRM
Contingency (best-fit) approaches to SHRM
Horizontal fit or alignment
Vertical fit or alignment

5.1 Introduction

In this chapter we address the issue that lies at the heart of this book: what is SHRM? This may seem like a relatively straight-forward question, particularly to those who are busy practising HRM day-to-day in their jobs, but the enormous number of books, papers, and articles devoted to this issue bears testament to its complexity. We first review the historical development of the SHRM field, before turning our attention to definitions. Then, we examine two major approaches to the topic, universalist theories, which are predicated on the assumption that there is 'one best way' to manage people, and contingency theories, which assume that approaches to SHRM will vary in different contexts. In Chapter 6 we develop the ideas presented here by examining the resource-based view of the firm as it has been applied to SHRM, alongside the new institutionalist paradigm. In Chapter 7, we focus on the concept of HR strategy, and in Chapter 8 we look at the outcomes of SHRM.

5.2 The development of SHRM

The field of SHRM is so extensive that justice cannot be done to its complexity in just this one chapter. Our review of the field will therefore span this and the following three chapters. However, it is useful to take the opportunity now to briefly chart the development of the subject area, so that the more detailed investigations into each of the topics that follow can be set into broader context.

'Human resource management' as a concept originated in the US and first appeared in the 1960s (Kaufman, 2007), when it was used interchangeably with the term 'personnel manage-ment'. However, it was not until the 1980s that research in the field expanded considerably following two highly influential studies in the US (Wright et al, 2005). The first was the devel-opment of the so-called Harvard framework (Beer et al, 1985). Beer and colleagues argued that HRM was an integrative, proactive, and longer-term approach to managing people. They argued that HRM could be seen as a system, comprising 'situational factors', such as organi-zational structure, stakeholder interests, for instance those of trade unions, policy choices in the HRM arena, and short-term outcomes such as performance, alongside longer-term posi-tive societal consequences of firms adopting HRM. According to this model, HRM was regarded as being embedded within an organizational and broader societal context, and as being an arena where distinctive choices were available to organizations in terms of the way they managed people. The model was not normative, in the sense that it did not advocate 'one best way' of managing people, but instead was a map of the HRM terrain.

The second influential study was the 'Michigan model' (Fombrun et al, 1984). This ap-proach, in contrast to the Harvard framework, focused on the links between HRM practices and business strategy. Fombrun and colleagues argued that HR strategies and policies in the core areas of selection, development, appraisal, and reward should be aligned with corporate strategic direction and be explicitly aimed at improving performance. The Michigan model was the precursor for the 'best-fit' or 'contingency' approach to SHRM (see section 5.5).

The question of why interest in HRM came to the forefront when it did is an interesting one. Millmore et al (2007: 62) argue that the crisis in US business performance in the early 1980s in the face of increasing competition from the Far East acted as one trigger. Seeking alterna-tive ways of enhancing performance, the focus shifted to examining in more detail the way in which different styles of people management could foster organizational success. Equally important were societal level changes, such as the trend in Western countries towards indi-vidualism from the 1980s onwards, reflected in decreasing levels of social housing, and the privatization of state-owned industries such as railways and utilities. These were commensu-rate with declining trade union membership and the focus within HRM on the management of individual performance, accompanied by the shift away from more traditional industrial relations-type approaches (Millmore et al, 2007). These changes, alongside the will of HR practitioners to legitimize their role in helping achieve organizational success, paved the way for the development of HRM as an area of policy, practice, and study.

UK-based academics developed an interest in researching HRM in the late 1980s. Here, a particular concern was the distinction between different approaches towards managing peo-ple, distinguishing between 'hard' and 'soft' HRM (Truss et al, 1997; Storey, 2001). 'Hard' HRM was linked with the Michigan model, with the focus on people as resources to be deployed in order to maximize performance. 'Soft' HRM, on the other hand, was associated with the 'human' side of HRM, with a focus on garnering loyalty and commitment in order to raise performance levels (Legge, 1995). Generally, UK commentators have been more sceptical about the notion of HRM than their American colleagues, and some have highlighted the strong managerialist and unitarist underpinnings of HRM which downplay the needs and rights of workers (Legge, 1995) and take insufficient account of issues of power and inequality in the workplace (Watson, 2004).

Although there was a groundswell of support amongst both academics and practitioners for the notion that HRM, if approached appropriately (although no one agreed on what this entailed) could lead to enhanced performance, it was in the mid-1990s that research in HRM received a significant boost due to two major, interconnected developments. The first was the publication of a seminal article by Huselid in 1995, in which the author used a large-scale survey of 1,000 US companies to show that adopting certain HR practices was statistically associated with improvements in performance, share price, and productivity. This article inspired a significant number of studies around the world that sought to shed further light on which HRM approaches were the most important, and how the process of linking HRM and performance worked. This is explored in more detail in Chapter 8.

The second development was the application in this and other publications of the concept drawn originally from economics of the 'resource-based view' (RBV) of the firm to the field of HRM (Wernerfelt, 1984; Barney, 1991). The RBV provided a theoretical justification for the link between HRM and firm performance by suggesting that it is the management of internal firm resources that enhances performance, and that the HRM–performance link could be conceptualized under this umbrella as a means of capitalizing on the advantages that accrue to organizations through effective resource deployment. In light of critiques that have subsequently arisen of the RBV, the pendulum has now swung the other way, and a more balanced view is now being advocated by some researchers that combines a focus on internal firm resources with adaptation to the external environment, particularly in light of the fact that much of the research emanates from the US and may not be generalizable to a European context (Brewster, 1999; Paauwe and Boselie, 2005; Wright et al, 2005). This is explored in more detail in Chapter 6.

Overall, the development of the field of SHRM has been characterized by growing methodological and theoretical sophistication and the accumulation of significant amounts of empirical data (Wright and Boswell, 2002). However, it is also a complex area to understand, not least because of the sometimes confusing array of terminology that is used, the variety of approaches that have been adopted, and the differing levels of analysis.

5.3 What is SHRM?

The first issue that we need to consider is what is meant by the term 'strategic human resource management'? Is it the same as 'human resource management', or even 'personnel management'?

Early commentators were interested in the difference between personnel management and HRM (Martin-Alcazar et al, 2005). Whilst some argued that, essentially, there was no

difference because both were concerned with the way in which organizations go about managing people, others suggested that HRM was distinctive in a number of ways. Legge (1989)
considered HRM to be focused on the management of line managers, to encompass the
management of organizational culture, and to be concerned with organizing resources towards achieving profit. Personnel management, on the other hand, was felt to be more administrative in focus, geared towards developing policies for the entire employee group, and
to be concerned with policy development rather than any notion of how to link the management of people with performance. Others further noted that HRM was essentially unitary in
perspective, in other words, built on the notion that the interests of employees and employers could be readily reconciled, in contrast with the collectivist approach of more traditional
industrial relations, which acknowledged that the interests of all parties may well not coincide
(Guest, 1989; Storey, 1989).

A key distinguishing feature was felt to be the linking of HR practices to the strategic aims
of the organization (Miles and Snow, 1984; Storey, 1992). However, the advent of the term
'strategic HRM' served to muddy the waters (Wright and McMahan, 1992). If HRM is concerned with how HR practices linked with strategy, then what is SHRM (Wright and Boswell,
2002)? Truss and Gratton (1994: 666) suggest the following distinction: 'we should, perhaps,
regard SHRM as the over-arching concept that links the management and deployment of
individuals within the organization to the business as a whole and its environment, while
HRM could be viewed as an organizing activity that takes place under this umbrella'. However, Wright and Boswell (2002: 248) prefer the term 'macro HRM'.

In Table 5.1 we analyse five different definitions of SHRM. These definitions suggest that
SHRM is an overarching approach to people management within the organization in a
broad, strategic sense. The focus is on the longer-term strategic needs of the organization in
terms of its people, rather than day-to-day HR policies and practices. SHRM can be regarded as encompassing a number of individual HR strategies, for instance a strategy for
rewards, for organizational development, and for performance management (CIPD, 2009d).
The notion of SHRM implies that the management of people is critical for organizational
success.

Wright and Boswell (2002) provide a helpful distinction between four different perspectives in HRM research, which further sets SHRM within a broader context of research on
approaches to managing people at work. Their typology distinguishes between:

- The number of HRM practices concerned, whether the focus is on one practice, such as
  recruitment, training, or rewards, or on multiple practices at a systemic level.
- The level of analysis, whether the focus is on the organizational level and firm
  performance, or on the individual level.

The four approaches identified are as follows (see Fig. 5.1):

- **Multiple practices at the organizational level—SHRM:** the focus here is on establishing
  which classifications or configurations of HR practices are best linked with firm
  performance. This is the dominant paradigm within the field, and we review research on
  SHRM in this and other chapters in Part 2 of this book.
- **Single practices at the organizational level—isolated functions:** the focus here is on
  how a particular practice, such as recruitment, rewards, and training, is linked with firm

Table 5.1 Definitions of SHRM

Definition	Interpretation
'A set of processes and activities jointly shared by human resources and line managers to solve people-related business issues' (Schuler and Walker, 1990: 7)	Suggests that SHRM comprises both activities and processes. Also suggests SHRM's focus is on people-related business issues, rather than business issues per se.
'The pattern of planned human resource deployments and activities intended to enable an organization to achieve its goals' (Wright and McMahan, 1992: 298)	Suggests that SHRM is focused on helping achieve organizational outcomes, but SHRM itself is regarded as a 'pattern' observed in organizational practice, rather than an actual strategy.
'Organizational systems designed to achieve sustainable competitive advantage through people' (Snell et al, 1996: 62).	Regards SHRM as an overarching 'system' geared towards competitive advantage, which is not a goal relevant for public or third sector organizations.
'A set of activities aimed at building individual and organisational performance' (Boxall and Purcell, 2008: 5).	SHRM is seen as a set of activities, rather than as an overarching system. Outcome is seen as performance, which is relevant in all sectors.
'A general approach to the strategic management of human resources in accordance with the intentions of the organisation on the future direction it wants to take. It is concerned with longer-term people issues and macro-concerns about structure, quality, culture, values, commitment and matching resources to future need' (CIPD, 2009d: 1).	A more holistic definition that specifies multiple outcomes and suggests the importance of 'fit' between SHRM and organizational goals.

performance. Historically, this approach predominated prior to the development of interest in holistic HRM systems. Much of the research seeking to link individual practices with firm performance has been inconclusive.

- **Single practices at the individual level—functional HRM:** the focus in this strand of research is on examining the impact of individual practices. This might perhaps be most closely associated with traditional personnel management.

- **Multiple practices at the individual level—psychological contract:** here the focus is on the link between systems of HR practices and individuals, such as research into the psychological contract or employee engagement, which we examine in Chapter 12. Wright and Boswell (2002) make the point that SHRM research could usefully draw heavily on theories from the psychology field more than it has hitherto, as this could help to shed further light on how and why HRM practices, policies, and systems impact on people.

Research at the level of SHRM that we are concerned with in this book mainly falls into the top left-hand quadrant of the model shown in Fig. 5.1, with growing numbers of studies encompassing the bottom left-hand quadrant. Research that falls within the remit of the two right-hand quadrants with a focus on individual HR functions can be regarded as having a somewhat less overtly strategic focus.

Number of HRM practices

Multiple   Single

Strategic HRM Research on how HRM systems impact on performance	**Isolated functions** Research on how particular functional areas (e.g. training, appraisal) link to performance
Psychological contract Research on the psychological processes of HRM systems	**Functional HRM** Research on individual HRM functions

Level of analysis — Organization / Individual

Figure 5.1 Typology of HRM research.

Source: Wright and Bosewell (2002: 250).

Critical Reflection

Considering Wright and Boswell's (2002) typology of HRM research, what do you think are some of the main challenges in research in this area?

Next, we explore two important perspectives on SHRM that have been proposed by researchers:

- The universalist approach, which is based on the idea that there is 'one best way' of managing people applicable to all organizations.
- The contingency perspective, which argues that the best way of managing people is likely to vary according to organizational circumstances.

Case study 5.1   Tarmac

Tarmac was established in 1903 and is the UK's leading supplier of building materials and aggregates to the building industry. The company has two main divisions: Tarmac UK, comprising Tarmac Ltd which extracts key building aggregates and materials and Tarmac Building Products Ltd which turns raw materials into products usable in the building sector, and Tarmac International, which develops building products for supply around the world. The company has almost 11,000 employees working in a variety of settings, including quarries and wharves. Tarmac's vision is to 'achieve exceptional value' through five core goals: develop markets, reduce costs, engage employees, act responsibly, and manage assets (DREAM). A particular focus is on setting clear objectives, employee development, and recognition and reward.

Whilst in the past most employees would have been manual labourers, this is no longer the case, since many employees are in high-skill, externally facing roles such as sales and customer service. Workforce planning is therefore regarded as key to the company's HR strategy, particularly in light of the changing skill profile that is needed for the future. Each employee has a personal development plan to help him or her grow personally and professionally within the business. Tarmac takes corporate social responsibility very seriously, as well as issues of health and safety of both employees and the communities within which the company operates.

Source

Adapted from http://www.thetimes100.co.uk.

Activity

Considering the business in which Tarmac operates, what do you think might be some of the key SHRM challenges the company faces? Do you think that the same HR approaches should be used for different types of workers, for instance manual workers as opposed to office workers?

5.4 Universalist approaches to SHRM

Universalist approaches to SHRM are based on the assumption that there is 'one best way' of managing people in order to enhance organizational performance, and that it is the task of the researcher to identify what this is, and the task of the HR professional to implement it (Delery and Doty, 1996). These approaches are held to impact positively on performance for all types of organization. A large number of studies, many emanating from the US, have focused on identifying what the precise components of these approaches are.

 Key Concept

The **universalist approach** assumes that there is one 'best way' to manage people that is applicable across all contexts.

5.4.1 Best-practice approaches

One of the best-known proponents of the universalist approach is Jeffrey Pfeffer, who has published an influential series of books and articles where he describes a set of HR practices that he argues is positively associated with competitive success. In an article published in 2005 in the Academy of Management Executive, Pfeffer outlines 13 interrelated 'best practices' that are derived from his reading and discussions with HR executives:

1. **Employment security:** offering secure employment reflects a long-standing commitment to the workforce and increases the likelihood that they will reciprocate with higher levels of performance.

2. **Selective recruitment:** it is important to select the best people for jobs through a rigorous selection process.

3. **High wages:** in order to attract and retain high-calibre staff, relatively high levels of pay are desirable.

4. **Incentive pay:** provide people with the opportunity to share in the financial rewards of organizational success in order to motivate them.

5. **Employee ownership:** allowing employees to have shares in their company helps to align the interests of employees with those of shareholders and encourages a longer-term view.

6. **Information sharing:** in order to ensure people perform to their best, they require access to all the information they need.

7. **Participation and empowerment:** encouraging the decentralization of decision making and fostering a climate of involvement enhances satisfaction and productivity.

8. **Self-managed teams:** where organizations have used self-managed teams, this can raise levels of performance.

9. **Training and skill development:** organizations need to have a commitment to training and skills development alongside a recognition of the need to change organizational structures to enable the successful deployment of these skills.

10. **Cross-utilization and cross-training:** enabling people to perform multiple jobs can make work more interesting and be motivational. It fosters the cross-fertilization of ideas.

11. **Symbolic egalitarianism:** symbols can act as a barrier to decentralized decision making and self-managed teams. Signalling equality amongst the workforce through eliminating status symbols such as executive dining rooms and parking spaces enhances communication and empowerment.

12. **Wage compression:** ensuring that pay variations within the organization are limited helps foster a climate of collaboration and enhance performance overall.

13. **Promotion from within:** creating a strong internal labour market helps to foster training and skill development, encourages participation, and helps promote trust.

(Pfeffer, 2005)

 Critical Reflection

Look at Pfeffer's list of 13 best HR practices. Imagine first that you are the manager of a fast-food store employing mainly part-time and sessional staff, including several students, to cook and serve food. Now imagine that you are the CEO of a medium-sized law practice, employing mainly highly qualified lawyers. For each of the 13 practices, consider how you might apply them in these two contexts. What do you think would work well, and what would be problematic and why?

Pfeffer (2005) argues that the precise number of best practices is less important than considering the overall approach to managing people [elsewhere he has advocated 16 and 7 practices (Pfeffer, 1994; 1998)]. Although the best-practices approach is very persuasive, several commentators have pointed out the difficulties potentially associated with trying to implement a set of practices such as these within an organization, and the lack of underpinning theory. We look in more detail in section 5.4.3 at the critiques levelled against the universalist approach.

5.4.2 **Configurational approaches**

Moving beyond the relatively simple, list-like enumerations characteristic of the universalist approach, some researchers have explored in more detail the interrelationship between various HR policies and practices, and have suggested that particular configurations of practices impact more on organizational performance than do others (Delery and Doty, 1996). This body of research has focused on high-performance, high-commitment, or high-involvement work practices and systems, and has relied on the use of quantitative techniques applied to large-scale datasets to identify their precise components. The suggestion is that there are patterns of choices available to organizations in their approach to SHRM (Martin-Alcazar et al, 2005), and that where coherent bundles of practices are adopted, then they are more likely to impact positively on performance.

Huselid's (1995) seminal paper explored the link between high-performance HR practices and performance in 1,000 US organizations. He found that two groups of HR practices, termed employee skills and organizational structures (including, for instance, job design, enhanced selectivity, training, participation, and profit sharing) and employee motivation (including, for instance, appraisal linked to pay and focus on merit in promotion decisions), were associated with higher levels of firm financial performance and productivity and lower levels of labour turnover.

Other studies have since explored the potential association between practices such as these and a range of performance outcomes, with very mixed results. This is discussed in more detail in Chapter 8 where we look at the relationship between SHRM and performance. The configurational approach has clear commonalities with the universalist approach, since the implication is that if organizations deploy the best bundle of practices, then performance will be enhanced.

Several commentators have, however, noted that although the notion that organizations should be coherent in their approach to HRM makes sense, empirical research has lent little support to the contention that organizations are in fact adopting consistent bundles of practice (Truss et al, 1997; Wood and de Menezes, 1998). Marchington and Grugulis (2000: 1113) argue that the achievement of some practices may actually undermine others. For example, how can employment security be reconciled with performance-related pay through difficult times?

5.4.3 **Critiques of the universalist approach**

The best-practice view of SHRM is very persuasive, and also very appealing to practitioners keen to ensure they are focusing their energies and resources on the activities most likely to yield positive results. However, the approach has attracted a considerable amount of criticism on several counts.

5.4.3.1 Implementation

- It has been pointed out that there is generally little agreement between commentators as to which practices are the most important (Becker and Gerhart, 1996). First, although some practices tend to be advocated by a number of writers, including training and development, contingent pay and reward, performance management, careful recruitment and selection, job security, and employee voice (Boselie et al, 2005), there is considerable variety in the approaches that have been suggested (Boselie et al, 2001; Martin-Alcazar et al, 2005). For example, whilst Pfeffer's work attaches importance to job security, this is not included in other lists (Marchington and Grugulis, 2000). Furthermore, those practices that are generally advocated tend to be at a very generic level and therefore lacking in any specificity. For example, recommending that 'training' is a 'best HR practice' does not explain much about the type of training or development actually required. Some have therefore argued that the focus should be more on the overarching orientation of the practices, rather than on the detail of the practices themselves (Wood, 2003).

- No account is taken of the potential costs to the firm of adopting high-performance work practices (Marchington and Grugulis, 2000).

- Best-practice approaches may remain aspirational, rather than represent the realities of people management. Several studies have shown that HR management in many organizations tends to be piecemeal and fragmented, rather than to follow the prescriptions of best practice (Guest, 1997; Wood and de Menezes, 1998). For example, in a study of 4,500 employees in seven large organizations based in the UK over 10 years, Gratton and Truss (2003) found that only 20% felt their HR department had a clear strategy guiding its activities.

- Marchington and Grugulis (2000: 1118) argue that there are two sets of circumstances where best-practice HRM is most likely to make a difference: when employee skills are essential to organizational goals, e.g. in high-tech industries, and where the time taken to learn to do jobs effectively is relatively long. In other circumstances, where training time is short, there is a ready supply of labour, or performance can be readily assessed, then the rationale for a costly best-practice approach is less clear.

5.4.3.2 Theory and methods

- The universalist approach has been criticized for being atheoretical; no underlying theory has been proposed to explain why some practices, more than others, might influence performance, or how the process works (Guest, 1997; Martin-Alcazar et al, 2005).

- No account is taken of context. For example, Datta et al (2005) argue that industrial setting or sector may be an important factor in determining what approach to HRM may be most effective. Equally, no consideration is made of corporate strategy, which may be an important determinant of the best HR approach to adopt (Purcell, 1999).

- Methodologically, studies that have examined the relationship between HR practices and performance have important shortcomings in terms of the use of single questionnaires

(Marchington and Grugulis, 2000; Boxall and Purcell, 2008). These are explored further in Chapter 8.

- Studies reliant on factor analysis of responses to large-scale questionnaire surveys sometimes create spurious groupings that are hard to justify in practice. For example, participation and profit sharing emerge in Huselid's (1995) 'employee skills and organizational structures' factor rather than in 'employee motivation', which is difficult to justify in theoretical terms (Marchington and Grugulis, 2000).

5.4.3.3 Broader societal considerations

- Boxall and Purcell (2008) note that the best-practices perspective does not consider for whom the practices may be considered 'best'. For example, downsizing may be in the best interests of shareholders, but would clearly not be in the interests of employees who risk losing their jobs. Simply advocating a best-practices perspective does not allow a consideration or exploration of these tensions (Legge, 1978). Kochan (2007: 604), for instance, provides the example of executive remuneration, which in the US has risen from an average of 40:1 in relation to the average worker salary in the 1960s and 1970s to over 400:1 today. Contingent pay may be welcomed by executives on high salaries who have benefited personally, but the widening gap between the richest and the poorest in Western nations is a matter for social concern. Marchington and Grugulis (2000) comment on the potential for work intensification and insidious forms of control to be masked by the rhetoric of best practices, whilst Hope-Hailey et al (2005) note the damaging long-term effects on performance of neglecting people. Boxall and Purcell (2008) argue that best practices that serve the interests of both shareholders and employees are more likely to lead to sustainable performance over time, to enjoy higher levels of social legitimacy, and to benefit both employers and wider society.

- The notion of a best-practice approach to HRM is culturally specific. For instance, whilst highly individualized approaches such as structured interviewing, performance management, and performance-related pay may be welcomed in a Western setting, such approaches may not fit well within other more collectivist cultures (Trompenaars and Hampden-Turner, 1997; Boxall and Purcell, 2008). Firms are further constrained in their approach to labour management by the prevailing employment law framework, which will vary between countries (Gooderham et al, 1999).

 Case study 5.2 Hennes and Mauritz (H&M)

H&M is a multinational clothing retailer headquartered in Stockholm, Sweden, with presence in over 33 countries and in excess of 53,000 employees. The company's values include having a commercial mindset, simplicity, constant improvement, cost-consciousness, and entrepreneurship. Its long-term goal is to make fashion available to everyone through both increasing the number of stores and sales within each store and maintaining a focus on quality and profitability. The company's HR strategy states that it seeks to be a good employer, including in those countries where employment law falls below the company's expectations. There are therefore global guidelines on diversity, equality, and discrimination. The company has an open-door policy giving all employees the right to discuss any work-related issue directly with management and it also supports employees' rights to organize and decide who should represent them in the workplace. It has agreements with a wide range of trade unions around the world. The company's underpinning values and strategy are global and upheld around the world.

H&M aims to have high levels of employee commitment and responsibility and places emphasis on the 'H&M spirit', where employees are committed to their work and are prepared to take on new challenges, work hard, and collaborate in teams. The structure at H&M is flat, but employees are encouraged to take on new roles and to take personal responsibility for their careers and development within the company. The selection process is aimed at finding individuals who are able to cope with the fast pace of work and who appreciate responsibility and decision making. Training takes place largely in-house; for example, when a new store was opened in Japan, locally recruited staff were sent to stores in Norway and Germany for training. The reward strategy focuses on benefits such as staff discounts and private health care rather than on titles and status. However, store managers have considerable delegated power.

Source

Adapted from: http://ideasthoughts-erruppackal.com/2009/09/hennes-mauritz-hm-an-hrm-case-study/.

Activity

In light of the discussion above concerning universalist approaches to HRM, what elements of HRM 'best practice' can you detect at H&M? Which elements of its HRM approach are contingent to the company?

5.5 Contingency approaches to SHRM

In contrast to universalist approaches, contingency, or best-fit, approaches are premised on the notion that the way in which people are managed in organizations will vary according to circumstances. Whereas the universalist perspective suggests that there is one best way of managing people, the contingency approach takes account of factors such as organizational size, location, sector, strategy, and the nature of work. This is founded in a long history of contingency theory within the social sciences that stresses the importance of setting in influencing management practice.

 Key Concept

Contingency approaches to SHRM suggest that the best approach to managing people will vary according to organizational circumstances, most particularly, corporate strategy.

Over the years, various contingency approaches have been explored. Some have stressed that the most appropriate approach to managing people depends on the stage the organization has reached in the organizational life cycle. For example, Baird and Meshoulam's (1988) model suggests that appropriate HRM approaches will vary according to the different life-cycle stages from start-up to maturity. As organizations grow and mature over time, becoming increasingly complex, so there is a need for increasingly sophisticated HR systems and policies. Kochan and Barocci (1985) propose a three-phase model of start-up, maturity, and decline, and associated HR policies in the areas of recruitment, rewards, development, and employee relations.

More often, though, it has been argued that HRM is contingent upon the strategic direction of the organization (Devanna et al, 1984; Miles and Snow, 1984), and the underlying assumption is that the stronger the degree of alignment between strategy and HR strategy, the higher the level of organizational performance will be (Delery and Doty, 1996). This idea lies, in many ways, at the heart of SHRM, and a key concern has been to explore how the relationship between strategy and SHRM works. Some have approached this by examining the link between popular strategy typologies, such as that of Porter (1985; see Chapter 3), and HRM. This body of literature derives particularly from the work of Beer et al (1984), which first stressed the importance of stakeholder interests and situational factors in HRM decision making. They identified three overarching models which could be combined in complex environments:

- **Bureaucratic model:** with a focus on control and efficiency, using traditional hierarchical models most relevant in stable markets with stable employment conditions.
- **Market model:** where employees are viewed as subcontractors, with a focus on short-term relationships and performance management, most relevant in rapidly changing environments.
- **Clan model:** associated with more diffuse ties based on shared values, teamworking, commitment, and innovation.

Miles and Snow (1984) similarly link HR approaches with the three strategic options of **Defender**, operating in a stable market and concerned with defending their position, **Prospector**, with a strategy of innovation and operating in a dynamic market, and **Analyser**, in an intermediary position.

Schuler and Jackson (1987) argued in favour of a behavioural approach towards SHRM as a way of linking firm strategies with desired employee behaviours; HR practices should be aligned with the prevailing strategic focus of the organization using the strategic options outlined by Porter (1985) of cost leadership, quality, or innovation (see Chapter 3). Their argument is that performance will improve if HR policies and practices are aligned to strategic focus because employees will be encouraged to behave in ways that support the overarching strategic direction of the organization. For instance, a strategy of innovation will require behaviours focused around creativity, cooperation, risk taking, and tolerance of ambiguity, which they argue can be fostered through HR techniques such as selecting highly skilled staff, appraisals focusing on individual and group performance, broad career paths, high levels of discretion, and tolerance for failure.

On the other hand, a cost-reduction strategy will require predictable behaviours, a short-term focus, concern for quantity rather than quality, and low risk-taking, which can be achieved through HR policies focused on concern for results, use of flexible working practices, little attention to training and development, tightly defined jobs, and work simplification. A strategy of quality enhancement tends to require a high concern for quality, low risk-taking, high commitment to organizational goals, and long- to medium-term focus, fostered by HR practices that encompass fixed job descriptions, high focus on empowerment, concern for feedback, job security, and training and development (Schuler and Jackson, 1987).

This model represents an important contribution to debates around SHRM, but there are a number of drawbacks. First, it does not account for the fact that in large, complex organizations, there will be different groups of employees, and it is perhaps overly simplistic to expect that the same behaviours will be appropriate for all. Equally, the model is predicated on the assumption that there is one, clearly defined organizational strategy with which HR policies can be aligned, which may well not be the case, either because the strategy is not clearly articulated or because there are multiple strategies being pursued (see Chapter 3).

Researchers within the contingency perspective have argued that there are two forms of fit, or alignment, that are relevant: **vertical fit**, or the linkage between HRM and corporate strategy, and **horizontal fit**, or the interlinkages between the various elements of the HR strategy (Truss and Gratton, 1994; Gratton and Truss, 2003; Ericksen and Dyer, 2005). Wright and Snell (1998) suggest that flexibility to enable the reconfiguration and redeployment of resources is also a desirable organizational feature, and that approaches that enable both a degree of fit and the option of flexibility are the most desirable. Fit, they argue, relates to the link between HR and corporate strategy at a particular point in time, whereas flexibility can be regarded as a long-term organizational characteristic, and the two are therefore not incompatible. However, as Purcell (1999) argues, there is little agreement about which HR policies, in particular, should be linked and not much evidence about the link with performance.

 Key Concepts

Vertical fit refers to the relationship between HR strategy and corporate strategy, whilst **horizontal fit** refers to the relationship between individual HR policy areas.

5.5.1 Critiques of the contingency approach

Contingency approaches to SHRM have been criticized on a number of counts:

- There is little empirical evidence to support the idea that matching HR practices to business strategy leads to positive outcomes (Truss and Gratton, 1994; Huselid, 1995).
- The concept of 'fit' implies rigidity and inflexibility that could be incommensurate with positive outcomes (Lengnick-Hall and Lengnick-Hall, 1990). It is also not clear which contextual aspects may be most important and relevant for HRM in terms of creating a 'fit' (Boxall and Purcell, 2008; Marchington and Wilkinson, 2008).

- Matching HR and business strategies implies that all organizations have an articulated strategy with which HR approaches can be matched, which is frequently not the case (Boxall, 1991; Purcell, 1999).

- There are a variety of ways in which HRM and strategy can be linked, and the best-fit approach implies that corporate strategy precedes HR strategy. However, as Golden and Ramanujam (1985) argue, this may not necessarily be the case, and an integrative linkage where they are developed together may be more appropriate.

- There are different perspectives on strategy (see Chapter 3) and the best-fit approach is commensurate with only one of these, the 'classical' approach (Truss and Gratton, 1994; Purcell, 1999).

- The role of human agency needs to be taken into consideration; Monks and McMackin (2001) note that a multi-level perspective can reveal the processes by which HR systems are constructed, shedding light on the role of group, divisional, and strategic business units in the construction of the HR system. The negotiation and interpretation that takes place in the development of HR strategies at these varying levels militates against the emergence of a coherent system.

- A disconnect between intended HR strategy and implemented HR strategy is to be expected. Building on Mintzberg's seminal (1978) work on strategy (see Chapter 3), Dyer (1985) argues that it is necessary to distinguish between planned or intended HR strategy, and implemented or experienced HRM. Since both corporate and HR strategy may be emergent, this raises questions about the possibility of creating strong linkages between the two. In light of the evidence of a gap between what is planned and what is implemented (Gratton et al, 1999), Gratton and Truss (2003) propose a three-dimensional model of HR strategy that juxtaposes vertical and horizontal integration, together with an 'action' dimension that evaluates the extent to which intended policy is put into practice (see Chapter 7).

- Organizations are complex and comprise different employee groups. In some cases, these may require different HR approaches and strategies. The best-fit model does not account for these (Boxall, 1991; Truss and Gratton, 1994).

- Contingencies do not of themselves determine the approach that should be taken towards HRM; managers make strategic choices in light of the circumstances in which they find themselves, and therefore issues around the nature of decision making, bounded rationality, and politics come into play (Leopold et al, 2005).

 Critical Reflection

Contingency theorists argue that the context within which SHRM takes place is an important influencing factor. Thinking about an organization known to you, what factors within and outside the organization do you think would be relevant to consider when developing a strategic approach to HRM?

Conclusion

In this chapter, we have begun to consider the domain of SHRM and have traced the origins of the topic back to its roots within industrial relations and personnel management. We have focused on two opposing views of what marks out an SHRM approach as being successful, the universalist, or best-practice approach, and the contingency, or best-fit approach, and we have evaluated the strengths and weaknesses of both of these. As Marchington and Grugulis (2000: 1116) note:

> There are several reasons why the 'HRM as best fit versus best practice' question is so difficult to answer. First, organizations are dynamic and complex, and typically operate in multiple product markets, whereas contingency models rely on examining links betwen two sets of static variables. . . . In addition, similar HR techniques may be perceived in quite dissimilar ways by employees in different situations. Second, empirical research is dogged by problems of causality and prescription/description.

Ultimately, there are useful elements to both views; as Boxall and Purcell (2008) argue, it is helpful to differentiate between the surface level and the underpinning layers of SHRM. At the surface level, where we are concerned primarily with HR policies and practices, there is certainly merit in trying to adopt best-practice approaches, for example, to use generally advocated approaches to interviewing. However, there is also an underpinning layer, where the focus is more on the particularities of the organization, on examining how the overarching approach to SHRM contributes to organizational success, and it is here that the contingency framework may be most usefully applied. We continue to explore these issues over the next few chapters.

In the next chapter, we consider the contribution made to debates around SHRM by the resource-based view of the firm and the new institutionalist perspectives.

 ## Summary

- Significant interest in SHRM first arose during the 1980s.
- There are various definitions of SHRM, but they tend to suggest that it is a holistic approach to managing people geared towards helping achieve organizational objectives.
- Contingency approaches suggest that SHRM should 'fit' with organizational strategies and other organizational factors.
- Universalist approaches suggest that there are SHRM 'best practices' that all organizations should adopt.
- Research evidence on the efficacy of either approach is equivocal.
- There is some agreement that SHRM systems should include elements of best practice at the level of HR activities, and elements of best fit at the strategic level.

 ## Review questions

1. If you were an HR Director charged with developing an HR strategy for your organization, would you be considering a universalist or contingent approach to designing the HR system, and why?

2. What do you think are the key contextual variables that influence HR strategy? Which are the most important and why?

3. For you, what are the key distinguishing features of a strategic as opposed to a non-strategic approach to managing people?

End-of-chapter case study   Specsavers: developing HR's strategic role

(Based on an interview with Mark Moorton, International HR Director, Specsavers Ltd)

Specsavers is an international, family owned and run business based in Guernsey, the Channel Islands, providing eyecare and hearing services. The business employs around 20,000 staff worldwide, most of whom work in the Specsavers stores, which are run as joint ventures rather than franchises. In addition to the stores, the group also includes manufacturing sites for lens production and coating, most of which, like its stores, are based in the UK and Ireland, although manufacturing also takes place in Hungary and Australia.

The company pursues a strategy of active growth and now has a network of over 1,500 stores worldwide. Due to its ownership structure, Specsavers still has a family-based, paternalistic feel to its culture.

SHRM is a relatively new concept within the company. Prior to 2008, the HR function was small and largely operated in a reactive way responding to the needs of the line. In 2008, a Group HR Director was recruited, tasked with moving the function towards a more strategic role. The function is now structured with HR business partners working alongside line managers, and two small centres of expertise in recruitment, development and resourcing, and reward.

The development of an HR strategy has been a relatively recent undertaking for the organization and has focused on the core areas of performance management, reward, and recruitment. The international HR function is even more recent, and one focus has been how to develop an overarching strategic framework worldwide, whilst also allowing for flexibility at the national level to ensure that policies and practices fit with local needs.

The HR challenges faced by the company vary between countries, and the HR team work hard to ensure that solutions are consistent, whilst not necessary identical, across locations. For instance, whilst in the UK, performance review is linked with pay, the process being launched in the Netherlands and Finland is based around behaviours and competencies. A job family system is being introduced to the Netherlands as this fits well within the culture, although this is not used in other countries.

At the heart of the HR agenda are the company's core vision and values which have developed from a situation where they varied between countries to one where there is a consistent message around the world identifying what is unique about Specsavers. HR strategy development has been embedded in the business planning cycle, so that senior HR managers are involved from the outset in setting the overall business strategy.

In developing its approach to HR, Specsavers has considered some of the generic frameworks and models for structuring the HR function and developing an HR strategy, but has not found them to be helpful, as there is little fit between these and the company's unique ownership structure and the way the stores are set up. The approach has very much been to establish a high-level framework and set of aims, and then to allow local flexiblity in how to achieve these.

The success of the HR operation is evaluated through customer feedback, alongside the more traditional quantitative measures such as turnover, salary levels, and attendance. A strong emphasis is placed on personal relationships and the need to talk to people face-to-face to get their views. The idea of developing shared service HR call centres is not one that would fit well with the culture at Specsavers.

Case study questions

1. What do you see as being the key challenges faced by Specsavers in developing an international HR strategy?

2. How can the interests of the company overall be balanced with those of different country locations?

Further reading

Boxall, P. and Purcell, J. (2008) *Strategy and Human Resource Management*, 2nd edn. Basingstoke: Palgrave Macmillan.
An extremely thorough and incisive overview of the topic of SHRM.

Huselid, M. (1995) The impact of human resource management practices on turnover, productivity and corporate financial performance. *Academy of Management Journal*, 38(3), pp. 635–672.
A seminal article in the field of SHRM.

Marchington, M. and Grugulis, I. (2000) 'Best Practice' human resource management: perfect opportunity or dangerous illusion? *International Journal of Human Resource Management*, 11, pp. 1104–1124.
A very helpful review of the issues raised by the best practices approach to SHRM.

 For additional material on the content of this chapter please visit the supporting Online Resource Centre www.oxfordtextbooks.co.uk/orc/truss.

6 Resource-based and institutional perspectives on SHRM

 Learning Objectives

By the end of this chapter you should be able to:

- Define the resource-based view (RBV) of the firm and explain its core elements.
- Analyse the usefulness and limitations of the RBV as a framework for theorizing in SHRM.
- Appreciate the contribution made by new institutionalist and resource-dependence perspectives to extending the RBV.
- Critically evaluate theoretical frameworks that seek to explain the importance of HRM to organizational success.

 Key Concepts

Resource-based view of the firm
New institutionalism
Resource-dependency theory

6.1 Introduction

For many years, the field of SHRM was criticized for being atheoretical (Wright et al, 2001). In particular, it was argued, the literature was dominated by a mixture of empirical studies that could not demonstrate causality, and prescriptions for practice that were not founded in evidence (Guest, 1997). A common complaint was the absence of any theoretical foundation to support the suggestion that SHRM can impact significantly on organizational performance. We will look in more detail at the broader issue of the HRM–performance linkage in Chapter 8, but here we are going to examine how the application of one theoretical framework in particular, the resource-based view (RBV), led to a shift in research and thinking in the SHRM domain. We are also going to examine how debates have moved on beyond the RBV to incorporate ideas drawn from new institutionalism and resource-dependence theory to shed more detailed and nuanced light on how SHRM 'works'. First, however, it is important to gain an understanding of the origins of the RBV and of its underlying propositions.

6.2 Origins of the RBV of the firm

A central concern within the field of corporate strategy has been to generate theories that can help to explain why, how, and under what circumstances firms are able to achieve consistently superior levels of performance (Foss, 1996). We discuss this in more depth in Chapter 3. Many theorists working in this area have focused on the relationship between the firm and its environment, and have sought to examine how a firm can be positioned in relation to its competitors and in relation to customer demands in such a way that the firm outperforms others (Porter, 1980). In this body of work, relatively little attention has been paid to the question of what actually happens *inside* the firm or how leaders and managers can impact on performance through the way they manage their resources. However, an alternative perspective, the RBV, approached the question of how to create and sustain competitive advantage from precisely this angle.

The origins of the RBV have been attributed to the economist Edith Penrose (Kor and Mahony, 2004; Boxall and Purcell, 2008). In her book published in 1959, *The Theory of the Growth of the Firm*, Penrose made the point that existing theories could not adequately explain the way in which firms grow over time. Considering the firm in terms of its internal resources, rather than purely its products or its relationship with the external environment, shifts the focus of strategic decision making to the question of how firms can best capitalize on and develop their resource base in order to secure long-term survival and advantage (Barney, 1995). The argument was that whilst some resources are necessary for a firm to undertake its activities, others could help mark out the firm from its competitors and thus help to create sustained competitive advantage over time (Penrose, 1959; Barney, 1991). These ideas became popular within the strategy field during the 1980s and 1990s.

The RBV is based firstly on the idea that firms can have varying types and levels of resources available to them ('resource heterogeneity') and, secondly, on the notion that resources cannot necessarily be easily traded, and therefore this resource heterogeneity may persist over time (Wernerfelt, 1984). This implies that competition within an industry may be primarily reliant on the deployment of **internal** resources, and therefore throws into focus the importance of management and leadership (Conner, 1991).

Sirmon et al (2007: 2273) provide the following definition of the RBV:

Resource management is the comprehensive process of structuring the firm's resource portfolio, bundling the resources to build capabilities, and leveraging those capabilities with the purpose of creating and maintaining value for customers and owners.

 Critical Reflection

Undertake an internet search for Edith Penrose and read some more about her contribution to thinking in economics and strategy. What do you consider to be her most original ideas and how are they relevant for SHRM in theory and in practice? What are some of their limitations?

6.2.1 **Definitions within the RBV**

The RBV can be a complex idea to understand, partly because the terms associated with it have a very precise meaning.

6.2.1.1 **Resources**

Internal firm resources lie at the heart of the RBV. They have been defined as:

> . . . all assets, capabilities, organizational processes, firm attributes, information, knowledge, etc. controlled by a firm that enable the firm to conceive of and implement strategies that improve its efficiency and effectiveness (Barney, 1991: 101).

Resources can either be fully owned by the firm, such as buildings or land that it owns outright, or 'tied semipermanently to the firm' (Wernerfelt, 1984: 172), for example, resources available through subcontractors or suppliers. This would include 'all of the financial, physical, human and organizational assets used by a firm to develop, manufacture and deliver products or services to its customers' (Barney, 1995: 50).

Resources fall into three categories:

- **Physical capital resources**: including plant and machinery, land, location, access to raw materials.
- **Human capital resources**: the knowledge, skills, and abilities of the workforce and their relationships.
- **Organizational capital resources**: such as organizational systems and processes, planning, and structures.

  (Becker, 1964; Williamson, 1975; Tomer, 1987; Barney, 1991).

Some aspects of physical, human, and organizational capital may constitute strategically relevant resources, whilst others may be neutral in terms of value-creation, and some may actively prevent the firm from achieving its goals (Barney, 1991). However, an important point to note is that proponents of the RBV argue that resources are not evenly distributed amongst firms in the same industry, which is a key reason why resources can be so important in terms of sustained competitive advantage.

6.2.1.2 **Sustained competitive advantage**

The core rationale of the RBV is to identify the factors that will lead to sustained competitive advantage for a firm. As Barney (1991: 102) explains:

> A firm is said to have *sustained* competitive advantage when it is implementing a value creating strategy not simultaneously being implemented by any current or potential competitors *and* when these other firms are unable to duplicate the benefits of this strategy.

This means that firms will need to have an advantage over both current and potential future competitors. Barney (1991) argues that a competitive advantage is regarded as sustained only when it persists after competitors have abandoned efforts to copy the successful firm. Of course, circumstances change over time and what constitutes 'success' in one period is subject to redefinition and there is always the risk that resources may become disadvantageous.

6.2.1.3 The four attributes of resources

In order to help secure sustained competitive advantage, firm resources need to have four attributes. Other types of resources may be necessary for the firm to function, but only those that meet these four criteria can be classified as 'resources' from an RBV perspective:

1. **Valuable:** resources must be valuable in the sense that they help a firm exploit opportunities or neutralize threats in the environment; for example, resources that help a firm improve its efficiency or effectiveness. Over time, changes in customer tastes, the nature of the industry, and technological advances can mean that some resources lose their value, and so one task is the constant re-evaluation of the alignment between resources and value.

2. **Rare:** resources must be hard to come by for other organizations. If many competing firms all have the same resource, even if it is valuable, then they all have the potential to create advantage in the same way. Resources that are readily available may be important to a firm's survival but can only contribute to sustained competitive advantage if they are rare.

3. **Imperfect imitability:** it must be difficult for other firms to copy the resources. There are three reasons why resources can be imperfectly imitable. The first is 'unique historical conditions', in other words, firms develop through a unique trajectory over time to form their own identities and characteristics so that resources they accrue will not necessarily be easily imitated by others. One example of this would be organizational culture. The second is 'causal ambiguity', i.e. it may not be readily understood how a firm's resources are linked with its sustained competitive advantage, making it hard for others to copy. The third is 'social complexity', i.e. a resource may be a complex social phenomenon, such as interpersonal relations or reputation, and therefore hard to replicate.

4. **Non-substitutable:** it must not be possible to replace the resource with a substitute of some kind to achieve a similar advantage.

(Lippman and Rumelt, 1982; Reed and DeFillippi, 1990; Barney, 1991; 1995; Conner, 1991; Boxall and Purcell, 2008).

Where resources meet all four of these conditions, then they can be a source of sustained competitive advantage, provided the organization is able to exploit them (Barney, 1995). The effective management of resources enables organizations to develop new ideas and ways of working so that it can keep evolving in response to changes in the environment (Penrose, 1959; Kor and Mahoney, 2004). Resources can exist at varying levels of complexity, from the most basic resource such as individual capabilities, which are then aggregated into, for example, organizational culture, and again into the creation of organizational reputation (Conner, 1991).

Despite its appeal, the RBV is not without its critics. We explore the criticisms that have been levied against the RBV in section 6.5. First, however, we examine how the RBV has been applied in the field of SHRM.

Key Concept

The **resource-based view** of the firm is based on the premise that firms can achieve sustained competitive advantage if they secure and effectively deploy resources that are not available to, or imitable by, their competitors.

 Case study 6.1   Delta Airlines

Reflecting on what it means to be an HR manager in the 21st century, Wright and Snell (2005) outline three future challenges that HR specialists must address:

1. Value creation: do HR managers sufficiently understand the business environment that is calling into question the business model currently adopted by most firms?
2. Value delivery: do HR managers know how to demonstrate alignment of HR activities with business issues?
3. Value guardianship: how does the HR profession understand its role as guardian of the organization's strategic capability, people, and values?

Delta Airlines had a reputation for excellent service, a family atmosphere, and attracting talented individuals. During the early 1980s, increased competition came from low-cost entrants to the market, compounded by globalization and changing information technologies during the 1990s, which led to severe price competition. Delta expanded by purchasing Pan Am's European routes and undertook a strategic change called Leadership 7.5, in an effort to reduce costs. This led to the redundancy of large numbers of staff and the recruitment of lower-paid contract workers, which returned Delta to profitability. Writing in 2005, Wright and Snell reflected that when firms are faced with the need to cut costs, they need to weigh up carefully the impact on the talent base. Where firms focus too heavily on short-term value, they risk cutting too deeply into their strategic capability and eroding their capacity to compete in the long term. The HR function has an ongoing responsibility to ensure that a firm adheres to its core values.
    Citing the case of Delta Airlines, Wright and Snell note:

> We seek to be business partners, but if we take the shortcut by sacrificing our values and integrity for a 'seat at the table', we may actually end up playing a significant role in the demise of our organizations. Instead, HR leaders require the vision and courage to integrate the different value systems in an organization for its long-term viability. . . . HR leaders must be the guardians of our ethical and moral integrity (Wright and Snell, 2005: 181).

Source

Adapted from Wright and Snell (2005: 177–181).

Activity

1. What are the key factors to weigh up when considering the balance between employing costly but talented staff, on the one hand, and lower-skilled but lower-paid staff, on the other?
2. How can HR professionals help their organizations to make these kinds of decisions?

6.3 Application of the RBV to SHRM

It has been widely acknowledged that the RBV has become the dominant theoretical framework within the SHRM field (Boxall and Purcell, 2008; Marchington and Wilkinson, 2008). In particular, commentators seeking to understand how HRM impacts on organizational performance have turned to the RBV as a way of explaining how the process works, with a US-based group of researchers led by Patrick Wright being particularly influential (Wright and McMahan, 1992; Wright et al, 1994; 2001). The basic argument is that HRM impacts on performance because a firm's HR meet the RBV criteria for a 'resource', and therefore the role of SHRM is to deploy those resources effectively in such a way that sustained competitive advantage accrues to the firm. As Wright et al (2001: 702) argue: 'growing acceptance of intenal resources as sources of competitive advantage brought legitimacy to HR's assertion that people are strategically important to firm success'. Delery and Shaw (2001) have argued that the RBV has a number of advantages as a framework for understanding SHRM; for instance, it emphasizes the role of HR in securing firm competitive advantage and acknowledges the complexity of the HR system.

However, the RBV has been applied to SHRM in a number of different ways, depending on the perceived locus of sustained competitive advantage.

6.3.1 Human capital advantage

Wright et al (1994) define HR as: 'the pool of human capital under a firm's control in a direct employment relationship' (p. 304). Thus, employees themselves, the human capital pool, constitute the source of advantage. All firms need a certain level and quality of human capital in order to operate; those that recruit and effectively deploy people with a high calibre of skills and capabilities, it is argued, are more likely to secure sustained competitive advantage (Boxall, 1996; 1998).

Wright et al (1994) suggest that it is individuals' knowledge, skills, and abilities, together with their behaviour, that constitute the potential source of advantage. They go on to show how HR meet the RBV criteria for resources:

- **Valuable:** research has shown that employees with high levels of skill are those that bring the most value to the firm.
- **Rare:** highly skilled people are rare; given that they are not evenly distributed throughout the workforce, it is argued that people with high levels of skill will not be available to all employers.
- **Inimitable:** firms differ in the way they manage people and therefore, even if similar skills are available across firms, there will be differences in terms of the way people deploy these skills due to these different management practices.
- **Non-substitutable:** HR cannot realistically be substituted in any way.

Whilst Wright et al (1994) argue that it is the entire workforce that should be taken into consideration, since some advantage also accrues through the network of interrelationships between employees and with the outside world, Lepak and Snell (1999b) suggest that advantage is most likely to accrue to a firm only through its 'core' employees. For example, a management consultancy firm may well regard its consultants as 'core' employees primarily responsible for creating business for the firm, whereas its administrative staff may be essential to the smooth running of the operation but not be responsible for wealth creation. They make the point that different HR management approaches may be required for these different groups, with greater investment required for those who create sustained competitive advantage. It may be particularly important to reward, retain, and motivate this group and seek to create a longer-term 'relational' contract with them. For a pharmaceutical firm, this group might comprise skilled researchers, or highly qualified medical consultants in the case of a hospital. They term this approach the 'HR architecture' model, whereby different HRM approaches are deemed suitable for different groups of workers.

Although the HR architecture model enables organizations to think about the nature of their workforce, a note of caution does perhaps need to be sounded. For instance, this approach does not take into account broader factors, such as employment law and the need for equality, or the role that might be played by trade unions or other representative bodies. Equally, as Boxall and Purcell (2008) point out, differentiating too much between segments of the workforce could damage firm social capital and undermine the sense of community and fairness.

6.3.2 Advantage through core competencies and capabilities

Some have argued that it is particular aspects of employees individually and collectively that constitute the 'resource'. For example, Hamel and Prahalad (1993; 1996) focus on the concept of 'core competencies', which are defined as bundles of skills and technologies that are unique to the firm and arise out of the collective learning of employees and units. They argue that where firms are able to capitalize on their collective skills, then they will achieve sustained competitive advantage. Thus, it is the firm's ability to learn faster and better than its rivals that counts (Boxall, 1996: 65).

Leonard (1998) refers to the importance of the firm's 'core capabilities' that underpin an organization's products and services. Her work emphasizes the interconnected nature of core capabilities; the potential benefits of technical systems can only be realized through an appropriately skilled and motivated workforce. The inherent danger, however, is that, over time, core capabilities can become simply enablers or, at worst, 'core rigidities' and barriers to success (Leonard, 1998: 30). Leonard makes a useful distinction between three kinds of capability:

- **Core capabilities,** which are superior and cannot be easily imitated.
- **Supplemental capabilities,** which add value to the core capabilities but can be easily copied.
- **Enabling capabilities,** which are necessary conditions to be in a particular industry.

    (Boxall and Purcell, 2008: 97)

Wright et al (2001) point out that a focus on core competencies and capabilities can provide a bridge between the strategy and HRM fields through the emphasis placed on people as a source of sustained competitive advantage. This builds on the work of Kamoche (1996) who makes the link between the core competencies of employees and companies' core products and services. The role of the HR system is in creating an environment where these competencies can be deployed effectively.

6.3.3 Social capital advantage

In addition to human capital, working relationships that arise between groups and individual employees give rise to another form of capital, social capital (Nahapiet and Ghoshal, 1998). The quality of these interpersonal and intergroup relationships can also constitute a source of advantage to the firm (Swart and Kinnie, 2003). When human capital and social capital operate synergistically, this can be a distinctive source of sustained competitive advantage (Boxall and Purcell, 2008). Cabrera and Cabrera (2005) extend the notion of social capital to argue that a key factor in corporate success is based on knowledge sharing and suggest that one HR role is the creation of policies and practices that foster effective knowledge creation and sharing within the firm.

6.3.4 Human process advantage

Boxall and Purcell (2008) argue that HR processes or practices can in their own right be a source of sustained competitive advantage. Wright et al (1994:304) define HR practices as: 'the organizational activities directed at managing the pool of human capital and ensuring that the capital is employed towards the fulfilment of organizational goals'.

However, this is rarely true of **formal** HR policies as they are easily replicable by others and do not provide a basis for advantage (Wright et al, 1994; Mueller, 1996). Equally, there may well be important gaps between policy rhetoric and experienced reality that serve to undermine the best of intentions (Gratton et al, 1999). Boxall and Purcell (2008: 97–98) suggest that HR 'table stakes' are the minimum HR policies and practices required to operate in a particular industry. Inevitably, they suggest, any firm will have a combination of HR practices very similar to those of other comparable organizations, and some that are dissimilar. Boxall (1996) explains that human process advantage rests on the organization's ability to configure HR systems, policies, and processes in a holistic way that fosters an environment of cooperation, learning, and innovation. The rarity of the HR system and its value to the firm therefore rests on the complexity of this overarching system, rather than being dependent on the individual policies.

Bowen and Ostroff (2004) suggest that there are two important factors. Process factors, i.e. how the HR system is designed and administered, and content factors, which are the policies and practices themselves. The combination of these process and content factors, where they create a 'strong situation' with consistent messages being given to employees, should create an organizational climate where employees will be willing to display appropriate attitudes and behaviours that foster performance.

6.3.5 Human systems advantage

Wright et al (2001) argue that competitive advantage accrues through the alignment of people's skills and motivation with organizational systems, structures, and processes, rather than simply from employing the right people. They suggest that the RBV should be considered holistically and that core competencies comprise a mixture of human capital, social capital, and organizational capital, i.e. the processes and technologies at the organization's disposal. According to this view, HR's 'effects are more encompassing in that they help weave those skills and behaviors within the broader fabric of organizational processes, systems and, ultimately, competencies' (Wright et al 2001: 710). Thus, the RBV can be applied to the field of SHRM by providing a rationale for considering the impact of SHR processes and practices on individuals, their interrelationships, organizational knowledge stocks and flows, core competencies and, ultimately, performance.

6.3.6 Summary

As we have seen, the RBV has been welcomed by those writing on the subject of SHRM for providing a much-needed theoretical framework (Boxall, 1996). This has been applied in different ways, with some commentators arguing that it is employees and their knowledge, skills, and abilities that constitute the resource, and others arguing that it is the HR system that may meet the resource criteria. The overall consensus, however, seems to be that the advantage accruing to organizations through their human capital needs to be considered holistically in terms of not only people themselves but also their interconnections with one another and with the broader internal and external environment, and in terms of the way that they are managed through the HR system. The RBV has been widely cited in a range of empirical studies focused on SHRM and its link with performance; we explore these further in Chapter 8.

 Critical Reflection

Take the example of a chain of successful supermarkets. You can find some examples on the internet. What do you consider to be their resource base? Which of these resources would you consider to be core, supplemental, and enabling? In relation to their workforce, how would you categorize the source of their sustained competitive advantage through people?

6.4 Critiques of the RBV

Despite the enthusiasm with which the RBV has been greeted in the HRM community, a note of caution has been sounded.

At a fundamental level, Priem and Butler (2001) argue that the RBV does not currently constitute a theory and they question the extent of its explanatory and predictive power. In other words, can the RBV really explain how firms work or predict which firms will do better than others over time? Commentators have also noted that the RBV does not take sufficient account of the external environment, which will have a significant impact on all aspects of a firm's functioning (Foss, 1996; Oliver, 1997). For example, levels of profitability cannot always be determined by the deployment of internal resources; factors outside the control of an individual firm, such as the actions of competitors or customer demands, will also be highly significant. Equally, as Boxall and Purcell (2008) note, the RBV does not take account of the benefits that might accrue to an organization due to industry clustering in terms of potential labour supply and networking opportunities. Priem and Butler (2001) crucially point out that the value of resources within the RBV is actually determined externally to the firm, rather than internally as proponents claim, since it is changes in the environment that serve to alter the value of resources, rather than any change in the way they are managed internally.

Also, given the very precise definition of what constitutes a resource, it may be very difficult to identify resources that fit all the criteria all the time. One example of this is the notion of causal ambiguity; if one characteristic of a resource is that it is impossible to know how it helps to create advantage, then how can an organization manage that resource effectively (Priem and Butler, 2001)? Another example is that it is not clear what the term 'sustainable' competitive advantage means in practice, and therefore it is difficult to test empirically.

Others have noted that organizations within one industry will always need some degree of commonality in order to compete (DiMaggio and Powell, 1983). The RBV does not allow an exploration of the shifting patterns of necessary versus value-creating resources over time (Boxall and Purcell, 2008). As Oliver (1997) has indicated, the RBV also does not take into consideration the impact of external industry or societal pressures that may drive firms in the same industry towards similar solutions to managerial dilemmas.

We also have to ask the question whether the RBV can be applied to all kinds of organizations and all kinds of circumstance (Paauwe and Boselie, 2003). Since the foundation of the RBV is to provide an explanation for why some firms outperform others through resource deployment, it is hard to see how it can apply to public sector or third sector organizations, for example. Small firms may be more focused on survival than on becoming leaders (Priem and Butler, 2001). Deephouse (1999) has also made the point that firms that offer significantly different products or services may fail to meet customer expectations by diverging widely from what is on offer elsewhere, and so difference may not always be a source of advantage.

Finally, a number of commentators have noted the relative dearth of empirical studies that seek to test out the propositions inherent in the RBV except at the most generalized level (Boxall and Purcell, 2008). Priem and Butler (2001) further comment that the RBV does not contain any inherent prescription that would be useful for practitioners, whilst Paauwe and Boselie (2003) state that the RBV contains no real explanation as to the processes by which resources are translated into a source of sustained competitive advantage.

Overall, it would seem that there are some important limitations to the RBV that suggest that its adoption as a theoretical framework to drive research and understanding may well be restricted. It is certainly true that the RBV has made an important contribution at a conceptual level in terms of providing a rationale for explaining why HRM can contribute to firm performance. However, the dearth of empirical studies, together with concerns about its status as a theory, lack of predictive power, and the problems inherent in operationalizing the RBV, have led researchers to seek to develop alternative frameworks that build on and extend the RBV in important ways.

 Case study 6.2 Nuclear Decommissioning Authority (NDA)

The NDA was created in the UK in 2005 with the task of overseeing the decommissioning of nuclear waste by contracting with specialist companies. Although it only employs around 300 staff, it has an annual budget of £2.2 billion, most of which is spent through contracts with Site Licence Companies who carry out the decommissioning work. The NDA's objectives are to develop waste solutions and eliminate site hazards, ensure the highest standards of safety, security and environmental management, build an effective and world-class industry, gain full support from stakeholders, and make best use of assets. The NDA is therefore dependent on both its own employees and those of its contractors, and attracting and retaining talented staff is vital. However, jobs may involve moving to remote areas of the UK, and there is some public prejudice against nuclear power that could deter new recruits. The NDA's HR strategy involves retaining and re-skilling staff through specialist training, direct sponsorship of university students, an industry-wide nuclear graduate scheme with 2 years of professional development, and the promotion of postgraduate research. In addition, the company seeks to encourage more GCSE science students. The NDA has a set of values which include always acting safely and responsibly, building talent and teams, being open and transparent, challenging the company and its contractors, confronting problems, delivering what NDA promises, and learning from experience.

Due to the nature of the work it undertakes, the NDA needs employees who are skilled, flexible, able to work in teams, and who willing learn continuously. Each employee has a personal development plan and clear objectives linked with the company's overall objectives, outlining pathways to professional accreditation where possible. The NDA also focuses on helping employees achieve an effective work–life balance and invests in employee training and welfare.

Source

http://www.thetimes100.co.uk.

Activity

What does the RBV of the firm reveal about the NDA's workforce and approach to HR strategy?

6.5 Extending the RBV

Bearing in mind the limitations of the RBV, researchers have explored how other theoretical frameworks and models might potentially be grafted on to provide a better explanation of how SHRM contributes to performance.

6.5.1 New institutionalist perspectives

A core criticism of the RBV is that it overlooks the importance of factors external to the firm, most particularly the potential impact on SHRM of societal-level factors. It has been argued, for instance, that current conceptualizations of SHRM are anglocentric and do not account for differences that may arise between countries (Paauwe, 2004). For instance, best-practice models such as that of Pfeffer (see Chapter 5) contain HR approaches that are already very common in countries such as the Netherlands but relatively uncommon in the UK (Boselie et al, 2001). Boselie et al (2003) show that in the Rhineland countries of Europe, institutions and stakeholders like trade unions and works councils play a key role in shaping HR policy and practice to a far greater extent than in the US and UK.

An influential group of researchers based in the Netherlands has explored how new institutionalist theory can be combined with the RBV to create a more nuanced framework for understanding SHRM (Boselie et al, 2001; 2003; Paauwe and Boselie, 2003; 2005; Paauwe, 2004).

Proponents of the new institutionalist perspective argue that it is important to take account of the fact that organizations are embedded in a wider social and institutional environment. In consequence, management practices frequently reflect the rules, norms, and structures prevalent in their societal setting (Oliver, 1997). The argument is that organizations within one type of setting will tend towards similar solutions to managerial dilemmas due to pressures exerted from the environment, creating a situation where organizations in the same industry tend to become increasingly similar over time. This stands in contrast with the RBV, which would suggest that firms tend towards different solutions (Oliver, 1997).

DiMaggio and Powell's influential paper (1983) identified three mechanisms by which organizations are pushed towards similarity or isomorphism:

- **Coercive:** institutions such as governments, trade unions, works councils, and employment legislative frameworks tend to drive organizations to adopt comparable policies and practices for managing people within one national setting. One example of this would be the UK minimum wage, which specifies the lowest hourly rate that organizations are permitted to pay. These can also operate at the international level, for instance, through the International Labour Organization (ILO) conventions on the prevention of child labour or European directives such as the Working Time Directive. Organizations are obliged to conform with such legislative requirements which limits the scope of their choices.

- **Mimetic:** organizations tend to copy the strategies and practices of competitors as one way of dealing with uncertainty. Another powerful influence here is professional consultancy firms advocating particular kinds of solutions.

- **Normative:** these mechanisms are associated with professional and group norms arising out of associations such as the Chartered Institute of Personnel and Development in the UK and the professional education for HR practitioners that they advocate. Equally, other professional groups, such as accountants and lawyers, have their own norms and expectations which will impact on the way in which they are managed.

The RBV and the institutionalist framework are therefore based on different assumptions about the behaviour of firms and individuals. 'Institutional theory assumes that individuals are motivated to comply with external social pressures whereas the resource-based view assumes that individuals are motivated to optimize available economic choices' (Oliver, 1997: 700). Researchers seeking to extend the underlying principles of the RBV have sought to combine these two approaches by suggesting that firms are subject to external forces that will tend to foster similar approaches, and the key therefore is to find ways of managing these constraints to develop unique solutions that are difficult for competitors to copy (Paauwe and Boselie, 2003).

This perspective represents an important contribution to the debate. Further research is needed to explore how this framework can be applied in practice and how the components can be operationalized.

 Key Concept

New institutionalism is based on the idea that external pressures on organizations will exert a homogenizing effect, leading to similar solutions being adopted by firms in the same industry.

6.5.2 **Resource dependency approaches**

Some researchers have noted that whilst the RBV tends to assume that organizations have a completely free choice in how to deploy their resources and the new institutionalist framework suggests that constraints over choice exist at the societal and national level, neither approach has taken account of the influence that organizations within a firm's immediate network can exert.

For example, Kinnie et al (2005b) argue that all organizations are situated within a network of other organizations, which may be clients, suppliers, collaborators, or competitors, and that a firm's 'freedom to develop HR policies may be severely restricted by the actions of other more dominant members who are able to exercise power in the network' (p. 1004). Drawing on the relational approach (Granovetter, 1995), Kinnie and colleagues argue that the structure of networks, together with the nature of relationships within them and the way they evolve through time, are all significant in terms of understanding how individual firms within the network make choices. Their research suggests that patterns of relationships within networks can be either coercive or collaborative. Where they are collaborative, there is extensive interaction between firms, leading to a sharing of skills and expertise and raised levels of social capital. Where networks are coercive, then the tendency is for some firms to set demands about who they work with and how, and thereby pressure the HR systems of other network members in terms of recruitment and deployment of staff.

Similarly, others have highlighted the permeable boundary between organizations in the case of franchise firms in the automotive sector. Here, the products of one car manufacturer are sold by car retailers on a franchise basis. The manufacturers determine the design and layout of the car showrooms, the branding of the franchise, and also factors such as the uniforms worn by staff in the dealerships, as well as the selection of general manager within the franchise, even though these general managers are employed and paid by the franchise (Kelliher et al, 2004; Truss, 2004).

Thus, whilst the RBV has emphasized the role of internal resources in achieving advantage, this has neglected the influence that interorganizational relationships can have on firm-level decisions.

 Key Concept

Resource dependency theory argues that firms are dependent on others in their network for important resources, and that the nature of the dependency relationship will impact on the leeway available to the firm to choose its own solutions to managerial dilemmas.

6.5.3 **The complex RBV**

Another perspective that has been put forward is based on complexity theory. Colbert (2004) argues that complexity theory can be combined with the RBV to create a living-systems theoretical framework that can be used to analyse and understand SHRM. Complexity science encompasses theories of complex adaptive systems (CASs) 'characterized by networks of relationships that are independent, interdependent and layered' (p. 349). Thus, CASs feature numerous independent interactions between the system elements, so that each pushes the system towards a new configuration, like twisting a kaleidoscope. There are two features of CASs: (1) they have a large number of interacting elements or agents; (2) they generate emergent patterns due to the interaction between elements of the system. Thus, the system evolves and adapts over time within its environment. Examples of CASs include ant colonies, brains, political parties, and corporations. When a firm is regarded as a CAS, this brings to the fore the importance of self-organization, downplaying the role that managers can play in influencing and determining strategic direction. CASs evolve through time and their steps cannot be retraced; they are inherently unpredictable (Colbert, 2004: 350; Truss and Gill, 2005).

The contribution of complexity theory to the field of SHRM arises through combining its propositions with those of the RBV, Colbert argues. The RBV provides a framework articulating the importance of higher-order objectives, such as unleashing creative potential and developing capabilities. The complexity perspective highlights the point that interactions between agents are critical to the way that the HR system evolves through time in a self-organizing way. Some suggested implications for the HR system arising out of this are shown in Table 6.1.

Table 6.1 Implications of complexity theory for HRM

Principle	HR application
Distribute being: living systems are distributed over a wide number of small units	Eradicate boundaries and foster interdepartmental and interorganizational assignments and movement
Control from bottom up: everything is connected, so therefore governance arises from interdependent local acts	Democratize the workplace, feed information to all levels, and encourage participation
Cultivate increasing returns: any actions that alter the environment, such as using a skill or an idea, create positive feedback leading to increasing returns	Deliberately link reputation, image, and internal identity using consistent models and language. Ensure high levels of training and development
Grow by chunking: complex systems grow, they are not created	Encourage local innovation and build learning capacity; foster knowledge exchange across units
Maximize the fringes: organizational fringes have most interaction with the environment and therefore can speed up adaptation	Encourage debate and experimentation
Honour your errors: there will inevitably be errors in the process of adaptation	Encourage reflective practice through reward systems
Pursue multiple goals: a trade-off is needed between exploiting a known path to success and diverting energy to new paths	Tolerate multiple aims and examine the impact of the HR system on all stakeholders

Source: adapted from Colbert (2004: 354).

Colbert's paper makes interesting reading and extends our understanding of the nature and purpose of SHRM in important ways. However, the paper does not make it clear how the suggested model may be tested, or whether the proposals for best practice would be applicable to all settings.

 ## Conclusion

In this chapter we have looked in some detail at the RBV and its contribution to SHRM. The RBV provides a much-needed boost to theorizing in SHRM, most particularly because it creates a framework for explaining how and why SHRM contributes to organizational performance by homing in on the importance of managing internal firm resources for sustained competitive advantage. However, a number of shortcomings have been identified with the RBV in terms of its status as a theory, the testability of its underlying propositions, and its implications for practice. In response to these concerns, various other theoretical approaches have been grafted on to the RBV in order to increase its explanatory power. However, none of these is entirely satisfactory either, since they simply 'add on' additional theories without addressing the fundamental shortcomings of the resource-based perspective. Overall, then, the conclusion is that more work is needed to fully understand how SHRM contributes to organizational performance. We examine this issue in more depth in Chapter 8. In the next chapter, we focus on HR strategy.

 ## Summary

- The RBV of the firm was first popularized by the economist Edith Penrose and applied in the field of strategy before being adopted in SHRM.
- The RBV is based on the idea that firms secure competitive advantage through their internal resources, rather than through the way they position themselves in relation to their external environment.
- Resources meet four criteria: inimitability, value, rarity, and non-substitutability.
- The RBV has become the most popular theoretical framework in the SHRM field.
- However, there are limitations in its applicability both to strategy and to SHRM.
- Various approaches have been 'grafted on' to the RBV, such as new institutionalism, resource dependency theory, and complexity theory, in an effort to create a more holistic framework.

 ## Review questions

1. Outline the four criteria for resources within the RBV. Give two examples of each criterion.
2. What do you consider to be the main contribution of the RBV in its application to the field of SHRM? To what extent does the RBV represent an advance on the best-fit, best-practice approaches outlined in Chapter 5?
3. What are the shortcomings of the RBV?
4. To what extent do some of the ideas proposed for extending the RBV help to move towards a fundamental framework for understanding SHRM?
5. If you were an HR Director, what lessons would you take away from the RBV that could be applied in the workplace?

End-of-chapter case study   Standard Chartered Bank: a strengths-based approach to HRM

(Based on an interview with Dr Tim Miller, Director, Property, Research and Assurance and Chairman, Standard Chartered, Korea)

Standard Chartered is a long-established international bank with headquarters in the UK, dating back to the mid-19th century. The bank has 75,000 employees; just 4% of these are located in Europe and the Americas, with the remainder concentrated in Asia, Africa, and the Middle East. It is one of the top 20 companies on the London FTSE and operates through its Wholesale Banking and Consumer Banking divisions.

Although Standard Chartered has performed consistently well through the global financial crisis, a significant challenge facing the bank is the changing nature of the regulatory environment for financial institutions, coupled with ongoing market volatility. Conversely, the bank's strong international reach creates opportunities to grow into newly developing areas. In terms of people, the rising global demand for talent has meant that the need to attract, recruit, retain, and manage talented individuals remains a core focus.

HR strategy is global, with a 'one bank' culture strongly supported at Board level. This is founded on the belief that consistency across the company is essential to ensure alignment of HR processes and practices in support of the culture. For example, a single employee database is maintained, and the underlying approach to managing people is the same everywhere, whilst allowing for local variation to meet legal requirements. One example is that in the United Arab Emirates, there is a requirement that a certain percentage of employees should be Emiratees. The company's HR strategy is developed centrally, but each business is expected to align this with the particular needs of its division. Thus, there is a universal approach that is also contingent upon business needs.

The company's five core values are Courageous, Responsive, International, Creative, and Trustworthy. The values are an integral part of the bank's culture and ways of working. In addition to performance objectives, all employees have values objectives relating to how they will demonstrate the values in their role every day. Managers and employees then have detailed conversations about the extent to which they have lived the bank's values at their objective setting meeting, and during twice-yearly formal performance assessments, as well as through ongoing feedback. The bank's approach to variable compensation also takes into account how an employee demonstrates the bank's values.

One key feature of the HR strategy is that it is strengths-based, i.e. people are recruited and developed in line with their personal strengths, rather than fitting people into roles. Talent very much lies at the heart of the bank's HR agenda; ongoing development is critical for even the strongest performer and recruitment is based on identifying individuals with the recurrent patterns of thought, feeling, and behaviour associated with success on the job, as well as cultural fit.

Aligned with this, the bank focuses strongly on employee engagement and has used the Gallup 'Q12' engagement index for many years. Each team, of which there are between 6,000 and 7,000 within the bank, is given its own personal scorecard based on this process and is expected to develop a plan for improvement for the following year, working with the team's HR manager. A key aim is to create an environment where people are encouraged to give of their best and deploy their discretionary effort for the benefit of the company. The combination of a focus on talent and on core values creates a culture where people feel their views matter, and where they are able to spend their working day doing what they do best, which the bank feels is important for individual wellbeing, engagement, and performance.

Case study questions

1. Why do you think Standard Chartered has weathered the financial storm better than many others in the industry?

2. What dilemmas does a strengths-based approach to HR bring to the HR department?

Further reading

Barney, J. (2001) Is the resource-based view a useful perspective for strategic management research? Yes. *Academy of Management Review,* 26, pp. 41–56.

Paauwe, J. (2004) *HRM and Firm Performance.* Oxford: Oxford University Press.
This book represents an important contribution to our knowledge and understanding of the field of SHRM and its potential links with performance.

Priem, R. and Butler, J (2001) Is the resource-based view a useful perspective for strategic management research? *Academy of Management Review,* 26(1), pp. 22–40.
This pair of articles provides a fascinating insight into the debates and controversies surrounding the RBV.

Wright, P., Dunford, B. and Snell, S. (2001) Human resources and the resource based view of the firm. *Journal of Management,* 27, pp. 701–721.
Very useful overview of the RBV field and its application to SHRM.

 For additional material on the content of this chapter please visit the supporting Online Resource Centre www.oxfordtextbooks.co.uk/orc/truss.

7 HR strategy

Learning Objectives

By the end of this chapter you should be able to:

- Define 'HR strategy'.
- Explain several different approaches that can be used to develop an HR strategy.
- Participate in the development of an HR strategy.
- Demonstrate awareness of the content domains of an HR strategy.
- Critically evaluate an organization's HR strategy in light of underlying theories.
- Explain the process, content, and implementation issues of an HR strategy.

Key Concepts

HR strategy
HR strategy content
HR architecture
HR strategy process
Devolution

7.1 Introduction

One question that is frequently asked by HR professionals is 'What is a good HR strategy?', and a second question is 'How do you go about developing one?' These would seem to be very important dilemmas facing senior HR professionals. However, although researchers have produced literally thousands of academic papers and articles on the topic of SHRM, there are far fewer devoted to HR strategy. This would appear to be an important omission, and we feel that it is impossible to write a book devoted to SHRM without considering this important topic.

In this chapter we examine HR strategy from the perspectives of content, process, and implementation. From a content perspective, we consider the range of choices available to HR professionals when developing an HR strategy, and examine the construct of the HR architecture. From a process perspective, we examine some of the propositions that have been put forward to explain the process by which HR strategies can be developed and the critical role that line managers play. Finally, we consider issues of implementation. This issue is also examined in Chapter 4, where we examine the role of the HR function.

7.2 What is an HR strategy?

Boxall and Purcell (2008) define HR strategy as a firm's pattern of strategic choices in labour management. Gratton and Truss (2003: 74) define people strategy as: 'a strategy, with its underpinning policies and processes, that an organization develops and implements for managing its people to optimal effect'. Whilst the former is essentially a descriptive statement, the latter is more normative and implies that the fundamental purpose of an HR strategy is to achieve certain organizational outcomes through the effective management of people.

It has been pointed out that, particularly in large, complex organizations, HR strategies are likely to be varied, with different approaches selected for different employee groups. Lepak and Snell (1999) refer to this as the 'HR architecture'. For example, a retail chain may well employ large numbers of part-time, casual staff paid low wages and with little opportunity for development or career advancement, alongside a management cadre offered relatively high salaries, generous benefits, and a career track. Thus, an organization's HR strategy may well contain different sub-strategies within an overarching framework.

When considering HR strategy, it is important to bear in mind that there are three linked areas: **HR strategy content**, which concerns the actual strategies that the organization adopts; **HR strategy process**, which refers to the process by which the HR strategy is developed; and **HR strategy implementation**, which means the way in which the strategy is enacted in practice in the organization, which will influence employees' actual experiences. As Bowen and Ostroff (2004: 206) point out: 'HRM content and process must be integrated effectively in order for prescriptive models of strategic HRM actually to link to firm performance.' Thus, it is only through enacted HR strategy that performance can be affected. We explore this issue further in Chapter 8.

Becker and Gerhart (1996) suggest that there are three levels to an HRM system:

- **System architecture**, which is the overarching HR strategy and guiding principles.
- **Policy alternatives**, which refers to choices available at the HR policy level.
- **Practices**, i.e. individual HR practices and implementation.

HR strategy choices therefore arise principally at the system architecture level, which would then be cascaded through policy and practice. Purcell (1989) has pointed out that strategic choice in HRM is a third-order strategy, following from first-order decisions such as the long-term direction of the firm, and second-order decisions at the divisional or business unit level, such as internal operating procedures.

 Key Concept

HR strategy refers to the strategy that an organization adopts for managing its people. Some firms do not have an HR strategy, but all will be driven by employment law to have appropriate policies in place for managing people. Organizations may have one overarching HR strategy and/or different strategies for managing different groups of employees. HR strategies may be explicit and documented, or implicit.

Case study 7.1 ThyssenKrupp Access HR vision statement

US company ThyssenKrupp manufactures home stair and wheelchair lifts. Its HR vision statement is as follows:

We believe in the dignity of every employee. All employees will be treated with fairness and respect, while being encouraged to think independently, trained, and then empowered to act with due authority. We foster an atmosphere of excellence in the area of human resources by providing service to employees at all levels in a professional and respectful manner. Employees are ThyssenKrupp Access' most valuable resource. Every action each employee takes helps determine our reputation, and the ideas, vision and strength they provide are the main driving force behind our success. Each employee will be encouraged to share his/her ideas, thoughts, and concerns to make ThyssenKrupp Access a better, more enjoyable place to work.

We believe in empowering our employees to succeed. We believe in creating a culture that values racial and cultural differences, as well as differences in abilities, attitudes, and aptitudes. For the Company to move forward we must maintain a human relations climate and environment that encourages and stimulates the employee, produces loyalty and commitment to the Company, and inspires employees at all levels to take calculated risks and perform at their highest level. We want all employees to achieve their personal goals and aspirations and achieve financial security for themselves and their families.

Source

http://www.tkaccess.com/join-our-team/joinourteam_hr_vision.aspx

 Critical Reflection

Imagine that you have been put in charge of developing an HR strategy or vision statement for a university. What elements would you want to see included and why? Which might be the most controversial?

7.3 HR strategy: content issues

HR strategy content refers to the nature of the HR strategy itself and its constituent elements. Inevitably, the content of any organization's HR strategy will be heavily influenced by a range of internal and external factors. Externally, issues discussed in Chapters 1 and 2 such as supply and demand within local labour markets, the prevailing economic climate, and demand for the organization's product and services will all influence HR strategy choices. In one study, Wright et al (2004) found that the business challenges most frequently cited by HR Directors as influencing their HR strategies were retention of staff, organizational growth, and globalization.

Internally, organizational structure and culture, geographical locations, technology, and staffing levels will all be significant influences on HR strategy (Truss and Gratton, 1994; Baron and Kreps, 1999; Monks and McMackin, 2001).

Case study 7.2   McDonald's mission statement

McDonald's brand mission is to 'be our customers' favorite place and way to eat'. Our worldwide operations have been aligned around a global strategy called the Plan to Win centering on the five basics of an exceptional customer experience—People, Products, Place, Price and Promotion. We are committed to improving our operations and enhancing our customers' experience.

Source

http://www.aboutmcdonalds.com/mcd/our_company/mcd_faq/student_research.html#1.

Activity

Considering McDonald's vision and overarching HR strategy statement, what do you think are the implications for HR policy in individual areas such as recruitment and selection, performance management, and rewards?

The degree to which an HR strategy should take account of these influencing factors and achieve vertical fit with corporate objectives, versus the degree to which best practice should be followed in the various HR domains, has been discussed in Chapter 5. It is perhaps helpful to think about this issue in relation to different levels of analysis, for example Becker and Gerhart's (1996) three HR systems levels:

- **HR system architecture:** this is the overarching strategy level which encompasses broad considerations of the overall HR strategic approach.
- **Policy alternatives:** at this level the focus is on determining individual HR policy within particular areas, such as reward management, recruitment, and selection.
- **Policy/practice:** at this level the focus is on the implementation of HR policies through organizational processes.

Therefore it may be the case that at the HR system architecture and policy alternatives levels, issues of strategic fit may be most significant. At the policy/practice level, concern with best pratice may come to the fore. Thus most HR strategies will be a blend of best practice approaches aligned with corporate objectives and taking into account the internal and external context. As Bowen and Ostroff (2004) note, there is no clear-cut evidence that any one particular HR strategy is appropriate for any specific corporate strategy, but rather a range of approaches can be effective.

Beyond this, common sense and research evidence suggest that it is important to achieve consistency, or horizontal alignment, within HR strategy. Baron and Kreps (1999) identify three different forms of consistency:

- **Single-employee consistency:** each individual employee's experiences of the HR system elements should be consistent.
- **Among-employee consistency:** treatment of different workers should be consistent.
- **Temporal consistency:** the HR philosophy and premises of the organization need to be consistent over time.

The authors identify five sets of reasons why consistency is beneficial:

- **Technical:** the benefits of certain HR approaches such as heavy investment in training and development accrue over time. There are also reduced administration costs associated with consistency.

- **Psychological:** through reinforcement, messages are perceived as more salient by employees.

- **Social:** consistency and congruence aid learning.

- **Recruitment:** consistency enables prospective employees to understand the type of employment on offer to avoid mismatching.

- **Distributive justice:** among-employee consistency defuses social comparisons and feelings of injustice.

Wright and Snell (1998) also refer to this notion of consistency or horizontal fit, and argue that both fit and flexibility are important within the HRM system. Fit exists at a point in time, whilst flexibility is a longer-term organizational characteristic. They suggest that the role of the HRM system is to promote fit with the demands of the competitive environment, together with simultaneous flexibility so that the organization, and the HR system, can adapt quickly to change. Flexibility can take two forms: **resource flexibility** and **coordination flexibility** (Sanchez, 1995). Resource flexibility refers to the extent to which a resource can be applied to a range of alternative uses, coordination flexibility refers to how firms can re-synthesize the strategy, reconfigure, and redeploy the resources. Flexibility gives the firm options in terms of its positioning in the competitive environment, referred to by Sanches as 'simultaneous loose–tight coupling' (1995: 138).

In addition to the requirement for flexibility, an HR strategy will need to take account of the fact that different employee groups may require different strategic approaches. For example, many firms rely on different employment modes including contracting, subcontracting, outsourcing, and agency workers, alongside permanent, full-time staff members (Lepak and Snell, 1999a; 2002). The way in which people are managed is likely to depend, at least in part, on two factors:

- The strategic value of their human capital, i.e. the potential to improve efficiency and effectiveness.

- The uniqueness of their human capital, i.e. the extent to which the human capital meets the resource criteria of the RBV (see Chapter 6). Human capital that is not readily available and not easily replicated is a potential source of competitive advantage.

These two factors, argue Lepak and Snell (1999a; 2002), give rise to four potential employment modes:

- **Commitment-based HR:** this is most likely to be used for core employees who are sufficiently valuable to be able to contribute to the firm's strategic objectives. This is most likely to include the firm's knowledge workers and to focus on developing long-term commitment to the firm. The focus is on employees' skills and competencies, with an emphasis on longer-term training and development. These workers are likely to be empowered and involved in decision making with a considerable degree of job security. Skill acquisition is likely to be rewarded through the reward system and appraisals.

- **Productivity-based HR:** this identifies human capital with strategic value but limited uniqueness. These employees are likely to make a significant contribution, but without unique skills. They are likely to be employed to carry out particular tasks. Here, employers are likely to pay the market-based wage and focus on performance. Firms are likely to recruit people who already have the skills they need and to focus more on short-term results, with pay focused on job performance and productivity.

- **Compliance-based HR:** where employees are neither of high strategic value nor unique, they are candidates for outsourcing. Short-term contractual arrangements may therefore be desirable. In contractual arrangements, the focus may be on ensuring compliance with the contract. Discretion would be limited, with a focus on rules and regulations.

- **Collaborative-based HR:** firms rely on alliances or partnerships for human capital that is unique but of insufficient strategic value to employ internally. The focus would be on sharing information and developing trust in a teamwork setting.

In an empirical study, Lepak and Snell (2002) found support for their model. In other words, organizations look at the value of human capital when making decisions about internal or external employment mode. Knowledge-based workers have the highest level of uniqueness, with contract workers the lowest. Thus, firms rely on contract workers to meet fairly generic needs or access widely available skills. Commitment-based HR is more likely to be deployed for knowledge-based employees, and the compliance-based configuration is most extensively used for employees in a contract mode. However, their study also brought to light some variations; for instance, they found that knowledge workers may be managed in different ways, which suggests that although the categorization is useful, it may not always reflect reality.

 Key Concept

HR architecture refers to the fact that organizations may have different sub-strategies for different employee groups. Taken together, these form an overarching HR architecture.

 Case study 7.3   HR vision for Irish bank First Active

First Active's HR mission statement reads as follows:
    'Our goal is to become the employer of choice in the financial services market in which we compete. To achieve this we will deliver:

For the Organisation:

- Demonstrated understanding of the business strategy and how 'our products' align with it
- Talented flow of people at all organisational levels, the raw material for our future growth
- Cost-effective HR service and lower pro rata costs than any competitor organisation
- Catalysts for change, continuous development, and learning throughout First Active

For Managers:

- Responsive and high-quality internal customer service
- A conduit for best-practice thinking in relation to managing people
- An expert support role when needed
- Strategies to help our line management partners retain their best performers

For Staff:

- The opportunity for personal development and growth: we will facilitate staff in building a successful career
- Ease of access to career development and personal counselling through a highly visible service
- A guarantee that key human resource issues are continually represented on the management agenda
- The provision of a positive work climate built on a culture of fairness

For Ourselves:

- The opportunity to work within a world-class HR function with clear performance targets and measurement
- A professional standard of excellence in everything we do
- The development of a high-performance team which leads by example in the effective management of staff'

Source

Mooney, P. (2001) *Turbo-Charging the HR Function.* Wimbledon: CIPD, pp. 12–13.

Mooney (2001) offers an additional model (see Fig. 7.1) for selecting an HR strategy depending on the industry within which the organization is operating. There are two criteria: the extent to which people are strategically important to the product or service offered, and the degree of profitability in the industry. This model has some similarity with the Lepak and Snell (1998) model, although the horizontal axis is concerned with profitability and thefore resources available to invest in the HRM system.

In summary, the literature offers us a number of different models that can be pursued in developing HR strategy content. Ensuring some congruence between HR strategy and corporate objectives has been advocated and makes sense intuitively, although, as we saw in Chapter 5, the notion of 'matching' HR and corporate strategy is far from straightforward at a practical level and raises conceptual and theoretical questions.

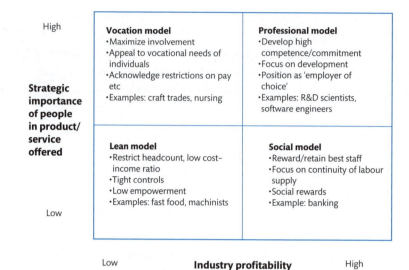

Figure 7.1 Mooney's HR strategy choice matrix.

Source: adapted from Mooney, P. (2001) *Turbo-Charging the HR Function.* Wimbledon: CIPD, p. 20.

 Key Concept

HR strategy content refers to the actual content of the HR strategy in terms of the statements it contains about how people should be managed in the organization and what the underlying purpose of the HR policies is.

 Critical Reflection

How do you think HR professionals can reconcile the potential need to differentiate their HR strategy for different employee groups, on the one hand, and the need for creating a consistent HR 'experience' for employees, on the other?

7.4 HR strategy: process issues

In addition to consideration of the actual content of the HR strategy, HR professionals also need to consider the process by which the strategy is developed. This involves addressing questions such as:

- Who should be involved in the process?
- How should the process work?

- What is the starting point?
- How innovative are we prepared to be?
- What form should the strategy take and when should it be reviewed?

Wright et al (2004) interviewed representatives from 20 large US companies about how they developed their HR strategies and, in their paper, outline the basic process involved in best-practice approaches to developing an HR strategy:

1. Scan the firm's external environment.
2. Identify the strategic business issues that need to be addressed.
3. Pinpoint people issues critical to the success of the business.
4. Develop a strategy to address the relevant issues, including connecting relevant metrics to the strategy.
5. Communicate the strategy.

   (Wright et al, 2004: 40)

In their research, they found that many companies did not scan the external environment or focus on business issues. In relation to the input of line managers, the companies reported the following:

- 18/20 companies said line managers were involved in some way in providing input into the HR strategy development process, although in many caes this was at an informal level.
- 5/20 companies said line managers were formally involved by serving on the team developing the HR strategy; in 13/20 cases there was no involvement of line managers.
- 15/20 firms communicated their HR strategies to the line, but only 9/20 sought formal approval from the line.

   (Wright et al, 2004: 41)

Building on the work of Golden and Ramanujam (1985), Wright and colleagues categorize firms depending on how they go about developing their HR strategies:

- **Business-driven:** five out of 20 firms aligned their HR function with the strategic needs of the business and had an in-depth knowledge of business needs. HR issues are fitted into the business.
- **Business-linked:** five firms were bound by an inside-out mindset but considered how their HR strategy impacted on business outcomes.
- **People-linked:** seven firms had clearly articulated their HR activities around people issues and outcomes but not business issues and outcomes.
- **HR-focused:** three firms started from what the HR function currently does, rather than from an understanding of how people outcomes link with the business needs.

   (Wright et al, 2004: 43–44)

Wright and colleagues argue that HR functions and HR strategies can add more value when they adopt an outside-in perspective on developing their strategies, in other words, they adopt a business-driven style. Similarly, Ulrich and Brockbank (2005b) show the importance of building a 'line of sight' between investors and customers through management and employees, to powerful HR practices.

However, as we saw in Chapter 3, the 'classic' perspective on strategy which assumes that it is possible to develop and articulate a rational strategy is just one of a range of possible perspectives. Strategies can be 'emergent' and therefore not clearly articulated, but rather develop over time through multiple incremental changes that can perhaps only be understood as a strategy with the benefit of hindsight. Research has, however, suggested that reliance on HR strategies 'emerging' may be damaging to organizational effectiveness (Tyson and Witcher, 1994; Grundy, 1998), creating a problematic tension for HR professionals.

Another key phase in the process is the identification of sources of competitive advantage (see also Chapter 6). Ulrich and Brockbank (2005b: 158–159) suggest there are 12 potential sources:

- Innovation: identifying new markets, developing new products or services.
- On-time delivery: strength in getting goods to customers quickly.
- Convenience: ease for customers.
- First-to-market: being ahead of the competition.
- Quality: offering better quality products or services.
- Cost: offering less expensive goods or services.
- Relationships: having good ongoing relationships with clients.
- Mergers, acquisitions, alliances: strength in identifying and integrating deals.
- Synergy: strength at sharing knowledge and experience across disparate business units.
- Branding: developing a strong identity.
- Distribution: dominating business channels.
- Service: providing excellent customer service.

HR professionals therefore need to ensure that they have developed a clear understanding of the basis upon which they compete within their market in order to inform HR strategy development.

The next step is to identify the desired outcomes of the HR strategy in the areas of cultural capabilities and employee behaviours (Ulrich and Brockbank, 2005b). Some examples of how organizations have described their cultures include 'restless creativity' (Unilever), 'teams passionate about winning' (AstraZeneca), and 'resourceful agility' (BAE Systems) (Ulrich and Brockbank, 2005b: 164). The final step is identifying the key HR practices that will lead to these. HR practices fall into four categories:

- Flow of people.
- Flow of performance management.
- Flow of information.
- Flow of work.

  (Ulrich and Brockbank, 2005b: 169)

Key Concept

HR strategy process refers to the process by which the HR strategy is developed. It includes such considerations as who is involved in developing the strategy, the way they work together, and the factors that are taken into consideration.

Bowen and Ostroff (2004) suggest that the HR strategy design process also needs to include consideration of how employees themselves will experience the strategy. They advocate the creation of a 'strong situation' whereby employees have a shared perception of HR policy and practice, thus creating an organizational climate conducive to high performance. Bowen and Ostroff identify three features of an HRM system that are necessary to create a strong situation and that need to be taken into account during the process of HR strategy development:

- **Distinctiveness:** where an organization's HR system is distinctive, then it captures people's attention. An HRM system can achieve this through being visible, easily understood, authoritative, and relevant.

- **Consistency:** for employees to make sense of the HRM system, its consistency is important. This can be achieved through sending clear messages about how the HRM system works, ensuring that HR policies are put into practice, consistency between espoused and inferred values, consistency amongst HR practices, and stability over time.

- **Consensus:** this occurs when there is agreement amongst employees about the way the HRM system works. This occurs when there is consensus among the principal HRM decision makers and the HRM system is perceived as fair.

Where these are in place, employees will experience low levels of variability in terms of their experience of HR strategy, leading to clear expectations about rewards and incentives, collective sense-making, and enhanced performance. Conversely, in weak situations, opinions will vary as to what the aims and objectives of the HRM system are and there will be a lack of consensus amongst staff about what is expected.

Decisions also need to be made concerning the speed at which firms adopt new HR strategies. Mirvis (1997) identifies four main approaches:

- **Leaders:** represent 11% of firms. They tend to be the first to adopt HR strategic approaches and are able to see connections between external environmental changes and internal HR strategies and approaches.

- **Fast Followers:** around 39% of firms. Fast Followers seek to be ahead of their competitors in the adoption of HR practices, but are more limited in their approach to innovation compared with Leaders.

- **Slow Followers:** accounting for a further 39%. They typically are less influenced by environmental changes and more hampered by company culture and cost in terms of adopting new HR practices. They tend to adopt certain approaches once they are common within their industry.

- **Laggards:** around 11% of firms. Laggards report substantial barriers to HR change and have difficulty getting HR taken seriously within their firms.

All of these models are based on the premise that a 'planned' approach is most desirable. However, as we have seen previously, planning may not always be feasible. In addition, Holbeche (2001: 92) identifies several further barriers to the development of planned HR strategies:

- Some HR teams prefer to work in an emergent way and wait until there is a clear business strategy.
- Some fear being criticized for moving ahead of the business strategy.
- The complexity of issues involved in creating an HR strategy may hamper development.
- Periods of change can undermine the link between corporate and HR strategy.

Thus, circumstances and attitudes can act as barriers to the development of planned HR strategies. Holbeche (2001) notes that where there is a planned and formalized HR strategy, senior managers tend to be more appreciative, but the evidence from other studies is that relatively few organizations achieve this in practice.

In summary, a general, common-sense consensus appears to be that the process of HR strategy development should reflect the external environment and business imperatives, and that attention needs to be paid to the creation of an overarching HR system that comprises mutually reinforcing policies and practices. Equally, though, the reality is that different approaches may be needed for different employee groups, and so the key task for the HR professional is identifying the most appropriate strategies for sub-groups of employees.

 Critical Reflection

In developing an HR strategy, some HR professionals deliberately choose to involve senior line managers whom they believe to be most critical of HR and its contribution, whilst others prefer to have a strategy development team comprising entirely HR professionals. What do you think are the advantages and disadvantages of these two approaches?

 Case study 7.4   HR strategies in the tourism industry

Most of Scotland's 950 visitor attractions are non-profit-making, but the notion that employees need to be managed strategically in the sector has become prevalent. Most stakeholders believe that softer values are most appropriate to the sector, with a focus on engaging staff in development programmes to enhance skills and foster a team spirit. However, the workforce in the sector is very diverse and this creates a dilemma. Political pressure has intensified to encourage the organizations to become less dependent on public funding and develop their commercial potential. Management has traditionally been weaker than in some other sectors. Surveys have highlighted a shortage of management and HR skills. The workforce involves not only paid staff but also large numbers of seasonal workers and, the biggest group, volunteers. Many volunteers do not expect to be managed and are often less interested in training than permanent staff, creating a challenge for line managers charged with trying to manage them effectively. HRM in this context may be more about getting the best out of people, without being overly prescriptive. Paradoxically, some organizations reported having more volunteers than they were able to manage, creating a further challenge.

Source

Human Resource Management, International Digest, 12(3), pp. 30–32, derived from Graham, M. and Lennon, J. (2002) The dilemma of operating a strategic approach to human resource management in the Scottish visitor attraction sector. *International Journal of Contemporary Hospitality Management*, 14(5), pp. 213–220.

Activity

How would you go about reconciling the different needs of volunteers as compared with salaried workers from an HR strategy perspective?

7.5 HR strategy: implementation issues

It would be true to say that a strategy at any level is only as good as its implementation. Research in Pakistan found that those organizations where the gap between intended and implemented HR strategies was the smallest were also the most highly performing (Khilji and Wang, 2006). However, it is almost inevitable that the HR strategy experienced by employees will not measure up in all respects to that which was intended.

Gratton and Truss (2003), in their 'three dimensional people strategy' model, bring together process and implementation issues. In a study of 4,500 employees in seven organizations over 10 years, they found that only 20% believed their HR department had a clear strategy guiding its activities and only 34% believed the HR function was competent at its job, suggesting that HR departments have some way to go in selling themselves to the rest of their organization. The three-dimensional model is intended as a framework to help HR professionals visualize how the links between corporate and HR strategy, between individual HR policy areas, and strategy implementation can work.

The model includes a vertical dimension, the link between HR strategy and business goals; a horizontal dimension, or link between individual HR policy areas; and an action dimension, or implementation. The authors argue that merely having a strategy in place is insufficient, but that implementation is vital. The action dimension has two components: employees' experiences of HR practices, and the behaviours and values of line managers whilst implementing the policies. For instance, body language can be critical here; the line manager who is clearly just 'going through the motions' of appraising employees will send negative signals to his or her staff about the importance of the process. The three dimensions when plotted in a matrix give rise to eight potential variations of HR strategy approach. Four of these variants are described as 'enacted', in other words, they are actually put into practice as intented. The remaining four are not enacted; the linkages between corporate and HR strategy and within HR policy domains remain at the rhetorical level. Figure 7.2 shows the 'actioned' dimensions of the Gratton and Truss (2003) model and Fig. 7.3 depicts the 'non-actioned' dimensions.

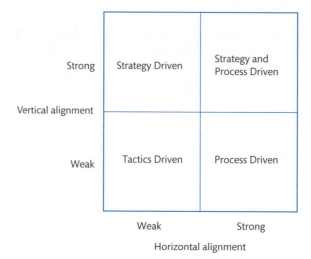

Figure 7.2 Gratton and Truss's three-dimensional people strategy: actioned dimensions.
Source: adapted from Gratton and Truss (2003: 77).

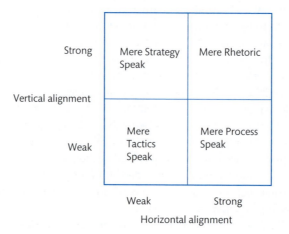

Figure 7.3 Gratton and Truss's three-dimensional people strategy: non-actioned dimensions.
Source: adapted from Gratton and Truss (2003: 77).

The eight variants are:

- **Mere Tactics Speak:** characterized by weak vertical and horizontal alignment and lack of implementation. This occurs where there is no people strategy or a very weak link between people strategy and corporate objectives. This is often found in small organizations.

- **Mere Process Speak:** characterized by strong horizontal alignment but weak vertical alignment and implementation. This is found in firms with a strong set of HR policies disconnected from the corporate strategy. This may occur where the HR Director is not closely integrated with the senior management team.

- **Mere Strategy Speak:** characterized by strong vertical alignment, weak horizontal alignment, and implementation. This occurs where there is clearly articulated HR strategy, but it is not translated into a coherent set of HR policies and there is weak implementation. This was found to occur during the early phase of a merger where the focus was on aligning the overarching HR strategy, but pulling all the various HR areas under this umbrella took some time.

- **Mere Rhetoric:** this occurs where there is a clearly articulated HR strategy that is strongly linked both vertically and horizontally, but it is not put into practice. This may happen due to lack of line management support for HR.

- **Tactics Driven:** featuring weak vertical and horizontal alignment but strong action. This is the traditional 'administrative' HR function where there is a focus on implementing discrete HR policies, but they lack connection with one another or with the overarching strategic direction of the organization.

- **Process Driven:** weak vertical alignment but strong horizontal alignment and action. This occurs where the HR team has strong process skills but lacks strategic focus.

- **Strategy Driven:** strong vertical alignment and action, but weak horizontal alignment. Here, HR strategy is seen as a line management responsibility and so there is a strong linkage with the overall direction of the organization but lack of systematic reinforcement through the entire HR system.

- **Strategy and Process Driven:** featuring strength along all three dimensions. This is the 'ideal type' HR strategy and consequently difficult to achieve and hard to sustain.

Therefore, according to both theories of HR strategy and normative models of best practice, most organizations should be striving towards the Strategy and Process Driven variant, where there are strong links between both corporate and HR strategies and between HR policy areas, and the strategy is also put into practice by line managers. Gratton and Truss (2003) suggest that the 'action' dimension can be strengthened through:

- Building a complete picture of relevant HR policies and indices such as staff surveys so that there is an accurate understanding.

- Taking bold actions: be prepared to make a stand to reinforce desired behaviours.

- Keeping the best: continuity in terms of the fundamental underpinnings of the HR strategy emerged as important in order to maintain an understanding of what the organization was trying to achieve.

- Focusing on 'doing': focus on a few key projects and initiatives, and ensure they are driven through the business, rather than trying to do too many disparate initiatives that are then not embedded.

7.5.1 The role of line managers

There is no doubt that the role played by line managers is fundamental to the successful implementation of HR strategies.

Key Concept

Devolution refers to HR professionals passing responsibility for HR tasks over to line managers. This can take various forms, varying from total devolution accompanied by the removal of the HR function entirely, to simply asking line managers to fill out relevant forms. It can apply across the full range of HR activity or just across certain areas, such as recruitment.

One of the key features of the shift towards HRM has been the increasing focus on the importance of line managers in the HRM cycle (Storey, 1992; Hope-Hailey et al, 1997). The relationship between line managers and the HR department has historically been problematic in many organizations, with line managers often feeling that HR are 'out of touch', unresponsive, and sometimes acting in conflict with business needs (Marchington and Wilkinson, 2008). The trend in many firms now is for HR to work more closely alongside line managers, and research evidence has shown that line managers are becoming more involved in HR work (Hope-Hailey et al, 1997; Sisson, 2001). Line managers play a pivotal role in determining the way in which employees experience HRM (Purcell and Hutchinson, 2007: 4): 'poorly designed or inadquate policies can be 'rescued' by good management behaviour in much the same way as 'good' HR practices can be negated by poor front line manager behaviour or weak leadership'.

The boundary between HR and the line is continually shifting, and there is no one accepted model of which activities should be undertaken by HR and which by line managers (Tamkin et al, 2006). In all probability, this will also vary at different organizational levels (Currie and Procter, 2001). Research by the CIPD in 2003 (Tamkin et al 2006) found that half of organizations report that recruitment and selection are shared between HR and the line, compared with one-third where line managers are in control; employee relations are shared in 40% of firms whilst in half HR takes the lead (Tamkin et al, 2006). However, expecting line managers to take on responsibility for HR can be problematic. Some of the issues are shown Table 7.1.

Table 7.1 Obstacles to line managers' taking responsibilities for HR

- Lack of skills or knowledge in HR.
- Lack of clarity on the part of line managers about what is expected of them.
- Lack of confidence.
- Lack of training provided to line managers.
- Reluctance to take on HR work or disdain towards it.
- Competing priorities and a focus on the short term on the part of line managers.
- Lack of time.
- Lack of reward for line managers relating to HR activities, leading them to focus on other areas such as the achievement of objectives.
- Inconsistent application of HR policy.
- Concern by some HR managers, for instance, about 'giving up' part of their role, fears over job security, and anxiety at lack of line manager capability.

Sources: Hope-Hailey et al (1997); McGovern et al (1997); Currie and Procter (2001); Sisson (2001); Guest and King (2004); Tamkin et al (2006); Marchington and Wilkinson (2008).

Hope-Hailey et al (1997) in their research on the HR function found that in many firms line managers were being given responsibililty for decision making in the HR domain, but that administrative work remained the responsibility of the HR department, leading, in some cases, to a weakened and fragmented role for HR. Overall, research into the division of tasks between the HR function and the line has concluded that the idea that people management is a clearly definable workload that can be easily devolved is not the case. Flood et al (1995) suggest that some companies are choosing to operate with no HR department at all. Here, HR is seen as fully the job of line managers. The advantages of such an approach are shown in Table 7.2.

Table 7.2 Advantages and disadvantages of devolution of responsibility for HR

Advantages	Disadvantages
• Low overheads	• Lack of synergy
• Flexibility	• Lack of structure
• Responsibility given to line managers	• Possible lack of time for line managers to devote to HR
• Possibility to tailor HR to needs of the line and employees	• Lack of uniformity
	• Inefficiencies
	• Arbitrariness

 Case study 7.5   Inchcape UK

At Inchcape UK, a large independent automotive retailer and distributor, the General Managers running each of the firm's 60 franchise operations had considerable autonomy in developing and implementing HR policy, with a very small central HR team responsible for providing advice, online support, and HR strategy. As a cost-driven business, the firm had taken the decision to run a very lean HR team and empower line managers with decision making. Inchcape was performing very well, but the HR Director began to be aware of inconsistencies in the application of HR processes and practices across the company. Whilst some GMs were very capable, there were instances of poorly managed appraisals, lack of training and development, and inconsistent pay reviews. With a shift in the firm towards an emphasis on the Inchcape culture, and away from the fragmented identities associated with the franchises, the HR Director decided that the central HR team needed strengthening and expanding, with more focus on uniform policies and practices.

Source

Adapted from Truss and Katz (2003).

Activity

Consider how you think organizations can manage the tension between devolving too much responsibility to line managers and not devolving enough.

Conclusion

In this chapter we have considered the issue of the development of an organizational HR strategy, taking into account content, process, and implementation issues. Whilst there is a broad consensus that the development of an HR strategy is a good thing, the notion inevitably rests on an acceptance of the classical view of strategy (see Chapter 3), with its inherent limitations. Nevertheless, in the practitioner community, most senior HR professionals will inevitably be called upon, or wish to develop, an HR strategy for their organization. We have therefore reviewed some of the major considerations that need to be borne in mind during this process. In particular, there are two points that are noteworthy. First, it is likely that, for most organizations, the HR strategy will differentiate at some level between employee groups. Strategies therefore need to be sufficiently flexible to cope with this variability, and HR professionals will need to bear in mind the importance of how to manage this variation in terms of how it is put into practice, communicated to staff, and complies with employment law. Second, the strategy will only succeed if it is implemented, and so consideration needs to be given to the role of line managers in this process.

Summary

- There are three key elements to bear in mind regarding HR strategy: content, process, and implementation.
- Intra-organizational differences suggest that many employers will need to vary their HR strategies for different employee groups.
- HR strategies are likely to contain elements of best practice and best fit.
- The development of an HR strategy should ideally involve a range of stakeholders and be geared towards securing positive organizational outcomes.
- The devolution of HR activities to line managers is an important aspect of implementation, but there are no clear guidelines as to which HR activities are best devolved, and practice varies considerably.
- Line managers may face a range of barriers in implementing HR policies.

Review questions

1. What are the three aspects of HR strategy that need to be borne in mind by the HR professional?
2. What are some of the most common reasons why line managers may struggle to cope with devolved HR and how can a balance be achieved?
3. What is meant by 'vertical alignment' and 'horizontal alignment' and how can they be achieved?
4. How important is it, when developing an HR strategy, that the strategy takes into account the organization's external environment and corporate objectives?
5. Who do you consider to be the most important stakeholders to include in the development of an HR strategy and why?

End-of-chapter case study   The Chartered Quality Institute (CQI): strengthening HR's role

(Based on an interview with Gillian Brookes, HR Manager)

The CQI is a charitable membership organization with the mission of placing quality at the heart of all organizations in order to benefit both business, industry, and society. Based in the UK, it currently employs 43 people at its London offices servicing around 25,000 members and certified auditors. The CQI has three strategic objectives: to raise the profile of quality, to raise levels of competence among quality professionals through learning and development, and to be an excellent organization.

Gillian Brookes joined the CQI in August 2009 as HR Manager and, on the basis of her discussions with line managers, soon became aware of some significant gaps in terms of HR provision that needed to be addressed. In particular, managers expressed their concern to her that the organization did not always make the best hiring decisions and there was no training available in recruitment and selection. Equally, from her own experience, Gillian was aware that job descriptions tended to be too verbose and not accurately reflect the content of jobs. To start to tackle these issues, Gillian first rewrote her own job description, making particular reference to the competencies and skills required, as well as the core job elements, and showed this to the Chief Executive alongside the original job description as an example of how it could be improved. Impressed with her work, the CEO was happy to let Gillian start work on a competency framework for the whole organization that could be used to underpin a raft of HR initiatives, including job descriptions, recruitment and selection, appraisals, training and development, succession planning, and performance management.

In order to develop an appropriate set of competencies, Gillian went back to the organization's five values: inspiring, innovating, caring, quality, and integrity. She was aware that few in the organization knew what the values were or how they might be relevant to them. Drawing on these, she developed a series of one-day workshops where she took everyone in the organization through the values one at a time to create a shared understanding, and began to generate awareness of what behaviours might be associated with each. These were then translated into four competency levels equating to the four principal job levels in the organization. Her next task will be to draw on these to rewrite all the job descriptions so that the linkage between the competencies and jobs is clear to everyone. Following on from this, her plan is to redesign the appraisal system, simplifying the currently onerous paperwork and aligning targets with the values and competencies. Equally, salaries have been highlighted in exit interviews as a source of dissatisfaction. Gillian plans to benchmark the CQI's salaries against those of comparable organizations, and also to align them to the four competency levels as part of a suite of interventions designed to make the organization more attractive to prospective employees and help improve retention rates. In the interim, as a short-term solution, Gillian is running workshops for line managers on effective recruitment and selection, and for all employees on effective appraisals linking individual objectives to the organization's three overarching strategic objectives.

As a member of the senior management team, Gillian is also working with colleagues to examine the interface between her planned HR developments and other organizational changes, such as improvements in the IT system and restructuring. One task is to draw these projects together under strategic themes in order to evaluate the organization's capability and capacity to handle the expected level of change required over the coming year.

Case study questions

1. What particular constraints do organizations in the not-for-profit sector face when developing and implementing a new HR strategy?

2. What do you think of Gillian's approach to the current dilemmas faced by CQI?

3. How could Gillian go about evaluating the success of her interventions?

Further reading

Gratton, L. and Truss, C. (2003) The three dimensional people strategy: putting human resources policies into action. *Academy of Management Executive*, 17(3), pp. 74–86.
This article was co-authored by one of the writers of this book. In the article, the authors outline their 3-D model and provide some examples from their 10-year study of HR strategies.

Ulrich, D. and Brockbank, W. (2005) *The HR Value Proposition*. Boston, MA: Harvard Business School Press.
David Ulrich has been named the world's leading HR 'guru' and has been enormously influential. It is therefore essential for the aspiring HR professional to read some of his work. This book brings together much of his recent thinking.

Wright, P., Scott, S., Peder, H. and Jacobsen, H. (2004) Current approaches to HR strategies: inside-out versus outside-in. *Human Resource Planning*, 27(4), pp. 35–47.
A very useful article on the process of developing an HR strategy with insights into the practices adopted in large US firms.

 For additional material on the content of this chapter please visit the supporting Online Resource Centre www.oxfordtextbooks.co.uk/orc/truss.

SHRM and performance

 Learning Objectives

By the end of this chapter you should be able to:

- Critically evaluate the claim that SHRM can impact on firm performance.
- Explain the significance of the 'black box' between HRM and performance outcomes.
- Be aware of the difference between possible HR outcomes at the individual, group, and organizational levels.
- Understand some of the theories that seek to explain why and how HRM impacts on organizational performance.
- Appreciate how organizations may go about measuring the outcomes of HRM and appreciate the complexities and difficulties involved.

 Key Concepts

High-performance work practices
The 'black box'
AMO model
HR Balanced Scorecard

8.1 Introduction

Since the field of SHRM first emerged, a central focus of concern has been to try to establish whether there is a link between SHRM and organizational performance. Indeed, examining this link was a key concern in the first influential publications in the area (Fombrun et al, 1984; Beer et al, 1985). Many studies have now been conducted around the world using increasingly sophisticated statistical techniques that have lent weight to the argument that, when carried out effectively, SHRM interventions can improve firm financial performance, raise levels of individual productivity, and even lead to positive societal-level outcomes (Arthur, 1994; MacDuffie, 1995; Patterson et al, 1997; Becker and Huselid, 1998; Collins and Smith, 2006). Some commentators have gone so far as to quantify the precise impact that adopting SHR practices can have:

> The magnitude of the returns for investments in high performance work practices is substantial. A 1% standard deviation increase in such practices is associated with a 7.05% decrease in

labour turnover and, on a per employee basis 27, 044 US$ more in sales and 18,641 US$ and 3,814 US$ more in market value and profits respectively. (Huselid, 1995: 667)

Studies have taken place not just in the UK and the US but around the world; research in Greece, France, Taiwan, and India has examined the link between high-performance work practices and organizational performance and found a positive relationship (Guerrero and Barraud-Didier, 2004; Katou and Budhwar, 2006; Shih et al, 2006; Som, 2008). Evidence has accumulated to the point where the Chartered Institute of Personnel and Development concluded some years ago that there is 'no room for doubt' that a clear link between people management and performance exists' (CIPD, 2001: 4). Other researchers, though, have been more cautious (Guest et al, 2003; Patterson et al, 2007; Gooderham et al, 2008). Guest (2011: 3) goes so far as to remark that 'after over two decades of extensive research, we are still unable to answer core questions about the relationship between human resource management and performance'.

 ## Key Concept

High-performance work practices refers to a bundle of HR practices that is expected to yield positive performance outcomes at the individual and organizational levels. In Chapter 5, we examined some of the ways in which these bundles have been conceptualized. However, although the concept is intuitively appealing, there is little consensus as to the precise practices that should be in the bundle, and the evidence as to their impact is mixed.

In this chapter, we build on the arguments presented in the preceding chapters to examine in more detail some of the research that has been conducted on the HRM–performance linkage. In particular, we outline the strengths and contributions made by some of the seminal studies that have taken place, but we also examine the drawbacks and limitations of research in the field.

In Chapters 5 and 6, we examined some of the main theoretical approaches that have been developed by researchers keen to find a rationale explaining why SHRM might be linked with performance outcomes at the level of the firm. For instance, the resource-based view, which we discussed in Chapter 6, has been used to argue that an organization's employees constitute a resource that enables the firm to secure sustained competitive advantage. Our intention here is to dig deeper into the SHRM–performance linkage in three areas. First, we examine some of the key findings arising out of research on the topic, differentiating between outcomes at the individual, unit, organizational, and financial performance levels. Second, we evaluate a range of theoretical frameworks that have been used to explain the mechanisms underpinning the HRM–performance linkage and explain the process by which interventions in the HRM arena should give rise to outcomes at the organizational level. Third, from a practical perspective, we explore some of the methodologies used by practitioners in an effort to evaluate and measure the contribution of the HR department to organizational performance.

Case study 8.1 Pace

Back in 2006, set-top box manufacturer Pace was under threat of bankruptcy; the company was losing £15 million on sales of £175 million. With debts of £30 million, the company was also experiencing a crisis of leadership. However, by 2009, the company was able to announce revenues of £1.1 billion and won the CIPD People Management Award. Employee numbers had risen from 600 to over 1,000. The change was spearheaded by new CEO Neil Gaydon and new HR Director Jill Ezard. When Jill was appointed, she found several underlying factors. Leadership was poor and so staff were demoralized. The hierarchical structure meant that communication was poor and decision making slow and unwieldy. The staff were not close enough to the customer to understand what they wanted. A complete overhaul was needed. First, Jill decided to restructure the workforce and create a stronger customer focus. Four of the existing eight management layers were removed and the previously separate sales and engineering staff were brought together in teams focused around the customer. Roadshows were held to explain to staff how the organization was going to work, and to start to embed cultural change with behaviours focused around customer focus, leadership, communication, teamwork, driving for results, and personal responsibility underpinned by the values of passion, integrity, accountability, innovation, and appreciation. These were all linked to the company's performance management scheme. Performance metrics were changed to focus on speed, margin, and quality, and rolled out across the entire workforce, from senior managers down. Staff surveys showed that employees felt positively about the changes, and levels of employee satisfaction also rose alongside improved financial performance.

Source

Churchard, C. (2010) In the top set. *People Management*, 8 April, pp. 18–21.

....

Activity

1. What do you think it was about the HR changes and the way they were implemented that contributed to improved performance?

2. Drawing on the example of Pace, what role can HR play in turning around a failing organization?

8.2 Findings of research on the impact of SHRM on performance

A very large number of studies have suggested that SHRM can impact on organizational performance. However, reviewing these reveals a broad array of performance outcomes that have been explored at the individual, unit, and organizational levels (see Table 8.1).

It is therefore important to bear in mind, when reading analyses of the impact of HRM on performance, that performance may be conceptualized in different ways. Many studies have focused not just on one set of outcomes, but on several. For example, Guthrie et al (2009) examined the impact of a set of high-performance work practices on individual-level behavioural outcomes such as absenteeism and turnover, and on productivity and labour costs, finding that high-performance work practices reduced turnover and absenteeism and raised levels of productivity. Gould-Williams (2007) found in a study of over 3,000 staff in 47 local authorities in England that

Table 8.1 Indicators of SHRM outcomes

Level	Measures	Examples
Individual	Attitudes, such as commitment or engagement	Applebaum et al (2000) found that investments in high-performance work practices were associated with increased levels of trust, job satisfaction, and commitment in a range of different industries.
	Behaviours, such as turnover and levels of absenteeism, or organizational citizenship behaviour	Guthrie et al (2009) in a study of 165 firms found that high-performance work practices improved attendance and retention.
	Performance	Wright et al (2003) studied over 5,000 employees in 50 business units and found that progressive HR practices led to higher levels of commitment and individual productivity.
Unit	Group or unit level performance	MacDuffie (1995) found that bundles of HR practices were associated with quality and productivity on automotive assembly lines.
Organizational	Organizational characteristics, such as agility and flexibility, organizational learning, innovation, and social climate	Youndt and Snell (2004) found that the design of HR practices impacted on levels of firm social capital. Collins and Smith (2006) found that HR impacted on organizational social climates and knowledge exchange and combination.
	Organizational performance, productivity, and quality	West et al (2002) found that HR practices in the areas of teamworking, training, and appraisal reduced levels of patient mortality in hospital.
Financial	Cost control, sustained competitive advantage, shareholder value, return on assets, stock price, and sales	Huselid (1995) in a study of 1,000 US companies found that investment in high-performance HR practices led to higher sales, profits, and shareholder value; Collins and Smith (2006) found that increasing commitment-based HR practices led to a 16.9% increase in sales from new products and services, and an 18.8% growth in sales overall in high-tech firms.

approaches to HRM that fostered a positive attitude towards the organization also led to raised levels of discretionary effort and motivation, reduced intent to quit, and lower stress levels.

One question that needs to be asked is, at what level can a causal relationship between SHRM and outcomes reasonably be measured, particularly since the application of HRM can vary significantly within organizations (Truss, 2001; Wright et al, 2003; Gerhart, 2005), and secondly whether notions of relevant outcomes will also vary between sectors (Harris et al, 2007).

In order to better understand the scope of the research, seven especially interesting or influential studies are described in more detail below.

8.2.1 **Huselid (1995)**

Mark Huselid was the first researcher who claimed to have established a causal link between high-performance work practices and performance. Through a survey of senior HR managers in almost 1,000 US firms, Huselid found that a one standard deviation increase in high-performance work practices yielded a 7.05% decrease in employee turnover, $27,044 increase in sales, $18,641 increase in market value, and $3,814 increase in profits per employee. He did not find evidence to support the argument that high levels of fit between HR policies, or fit between HR strategy and corporate strategy, impacted on performance (see Chapter 5). Huselid's study has been extremely influential. However, his methodology meant that there was only one survey respondent in each organization, and so it is difficult to be sure that their views are representative. The two factors that emerged through his analysis of data, 'employee skills and organizational structures', and 'employee motivation' lack internal consistency, and the data he obtained were cross-sectional, in other words, the outcomes were measured at the same time as the HR interventions.

8.2.2 **West et al (2002)**

Michael West and his team explored the HRM–performance link in the context of hospitals in the UK. The methodology used in the study was cross-sectional and involved a survey completed by the HR Directors (or their representatives) of 61 NHS Hospital Trusts. Statistical analysis showed a significant association between teamworking, appraisals, and training and levels of patient mortality. This study has been very widely cited due to the far-reaching implications of the argument in the paper that the way people are managed may influence mortality levels. However, the authors point out that their sample is small. Also, the time periods covered by the elements comprising the overall measure of mortality were not identical, which may have given rise to measurement error. Finally, and crucially, as the data collection was cross-sectional, in other words, it took place at one point in time, the authors point out that 'no causal inferences can be drawn from the analysis' (p. 1308).

8.2.3 **Purcell et al (2003)**

Purcell and colleagues examined approaches to HRM in 12 organizations longitudinally over 30 months through interviews and questionnaires with a range of respondents, as well as objective measures of performance, such as wastage or shrinkage in the case of a supermarket and the ratio between number of presentations to clients and products sold in the case of a bank. A particular focus of the study was to test out a theoretical framework that explained why HRM interventions would affect performance. The team used the 'AMO' model and argued that employees perform well when they are 'able' to do so, i.e. have the necessary knowledge and skills, have the 'motivation' to perform well, and are given the 'opportunity' to perform well in their jobs. Eleven HR policies and practices were identified as enablers of AMO, and the team argued that these HR processes give rise to positive attitudes such as job satisfaction and commitment, which, in turn, give rise to higher levels of performance.

The team found that higher performing organizations had a 'Big Idea', such as a clear set of values or mission, which was embedded, connected, enduring, collective, and measured throughout the organization. The research also highlighted the importance of the role of line managers in implementing and enacting HR policies; in particular, the findings showed that HR interventions in the areas of career opportunities, training, job design, communication, performance appraisal, and work–life balance impacted positively on outcomes such as commitment, satisfaction, and motivation. Purcell and colleagues concluded that there were positive associations between some HR policies and practices and performance, and that negative outcomes arose from poorly managed HR policies. They also noted that 'it was difficult to isolate the impact of policies and practices from other factors, such as technology or market fluctuations' (p. xi). This study has made an important contribution to our understanding of the HRM–performance link, most particularly through the application of the AMO model which provides a theoretical underpinning.

 Key Concept

The **AMO model** suggests that employees perform well when they have the necessary skills or ability to do so, the motivation to perform, and are given the opportunity to perform by their line managers. HR policies and practices can impact on AMO and thus give rise to higher levels of performance.

8.2.4 Gooderham et al (2008)

Gooderham and colleagues examined data from the 1999 Cranet HRM survey which took place in 16 European countries. A questionnaire was issued to the HR managers of firms with over 100 employees, resulting in a dataset comprising 3,281 firms. Performance was measured by asking respondents whether gross revenue for the past 3 years has been well in excess of costs. The study differentiated between two approaches to HRM: 'calculative', which focuses on assessing and rewarding performance, and 'collaborative', which involves strategies of communication or cooperation. They found that the calculative approaches to HRM, and not the collaborative approaches, were most closely associated with performance, but that even in these cases the associations were relatively modest. This runs contrary to the findings of other studies. Interestingly, they also found considerable variation by country, which suggests that studies need to take account of national setting (see Chapter 5). Overall, they conclude that 'while certain HR bundles do have an impact on performance, this should not be exaggerated' (p. 2053). There are several limitations to the study, including the relatively weak performance measure, lack of explanatory theoretical framework, and the fact that it is cross-sectional and relies on single respondents in each organization. Nevertheless, this study has made an important contribution to the debate by providing evidence that suggests that the HRM–performance link may be weak.

8.2.5 Nishii et al (2008)

In their study, Nishii and colleagues were concerned to gain a better understanding of the process by which HRM impacts on performance. They draw on attribution theory, which suggests that people have a deep-seated need to understand their environment, and so are driven to seek out the patterns that underpin their employer's approach to managing people. Five possible attributions are outlined: a focus on service quality; a focus on employee wellbeing; the wish to reduce costs; the desire to exploit employees; and, finally, the need to comply with trade unions. The authors argue that these attributions will affect employee commitment, satisfaction, citizenship behaviours, and customer satisfaction. Data were collected from multiple sources within a supermarket chain in the US, resulting in a dataset of 5,600 questionnaires, and objective performance data. The study found that employees' perceptions of the underlying purpose of HR policies and strategies varied, and that there was a disconnect between employee perceptions and management intentions. They suggest that congruence between intentions and experiences of HR practices may be associated with a stronger link between HR and performance. This study contributes to our understanding of the HRM–performance link by moving away from a reliance on the resource-based view and, instead, drawing on theories based on organizational psychology. However, questions are raised due to the fact that the researchers could not find empirical support for all of their five proposed attributions, and due to the uncertainties surrounding the drivers of the attributions.

8.2.6 **Collins and Smith (2006)**

Collins and Smith (2006) examined how a commitment-based approach to SHRM influences organizational social climate and knowledge sharing as well as firm performance in 143 high-tech companies in the US. Overall, they found that increasing commitment-based HR practices by one standard deviation resulted in a 16.9% increase in sales from new products and services and an 18.8% growth in sales. These impacts were found to be mediated by organizational social climate and knowledge exchange. This study adds to our knowledge of the HRM–performance linkage by focusing on one industry and one approach to SHRM. It moves away from the RBV in terms of explaining how the link works and, instead, suggests that HRM impacts on social climate and knowledge sharing which, in turn, affect performance. One drawback with this study is that data were collected on HR practices from senior HR managers and, as the study by Nishii et al (2008) suggests, there may be a gap between intended and experienced HRM. It is also not clear whether the proposed model would work in other contexts.

8.2.7 **Boselie et al (2003)**

Boselie and colleagues set out to examine the impact of government institutions on the HRM–performance link in organizations in the Netherlands, drawing on their new institutionalist framework (see Chapter 6). Data were collected from three sectors, health care, local government, and tourism by questionnaires completed by 132 HR managers. They found evidence that there are two distinct approaches to SHRM, a commitment-based approach and a control-based approach, and that a focus on the control-based approach was associated with reduced levels of absenteeism. They also found that in highly institutionalized contexts such as hospitals and local authorities, the impact of control HR systems on absence levels was weaker than in the less institutionalized context of tourism organizations. The authors argue that it is important to take account of the degree of institutionalization, which may differ between countries as well as industries, when examining the link between HRM and performance. However, the authors also note that their research was cross-sectional and they would have preferred to have carried out some in-depth case studies to explore the process of causality more deeply.

 Critical Reflection

Choose two of the articles referred to above and obtain copies of the entire text. Read both articles carefully and, for each, answer the following questions:

1. What theory is proposed to explain how HRM impacts on performance?
2. What measures of both HRM and performance outcomes are used?
3. What data were obtained and what methods were used?
4. What are the strengths and weaknesses of the study?
5. How could HR managers use the study in developing their own approach to SHRM?

Taken together, these seven studies represent a good cross-section of the extensive research that has taken place on the HRM–performance link. It is evident that the studies have adopted different methodologies and theoretical foundations, measure both HRM and performance in different ways, and the findings all tend to point towards a variety of different conclusions. The authors are all at pains to point out that their research has limitations. Overall, the conclusion would appear to be that there is *some* evidence of a link between HRM and performance, but that, at this stage, there is no conclusive proof.

8.3 Evaluation of HRM–performance research

In reading these and other studies examining the link between HRM and performance, it is important to bear in mind that the SHRM–performance literature is one that is beset with problems and controversies. Commentators have noted difficulties in at least six interrelated areas:

- **Defining SHRM.** What aspects or features should be included and why? In Chapter 5 we outlined some of the many ways in which SHRM has been conceptualized and argued that no clear agreement has been reached as to what constitutes 'best practice'. Studies have used widely different measures of high-performance work practices and reported significant variations in results (Marchington and Grugulis, 2000; Wright et al, 2001; Guest et al, 2004; Chang and Huang, 2005; Hesketh and Fleetwood, 2006). Although on paper the 'high commitment' approach is favoured, there is some research evidence that 'low road' or high control, cost minimization strategies may be more closely associated with performance (Wood and de Menezes, 1998; Orlitzky and Frenkel, 2005). We know little about which HR practices, specifically, might be more important than others, or under which circumstances (Patterson et al, 2007).

- **Rhetoric/reality gap.** Is it sufficient to measure intended HR strategies and policies when exploring the HRM–performance linkage? Research suggests that there is a significant gap between rhetoric and reality, with employees' HR experiences normally falling some way short of what is intended. Studies that rely on stated HR strategies may therefore be failing to measure what is actually happening in organizations (Truss, 2001; Gerhart, 2005; Kinnie et al, 2005a; Patterson et al, 2007; Nishii et al, 2008; Conway and Monks, 2009). The most recent trend is towards focusing on employees' experiences or perceptions of HR.

- **Specifying outcomes.** At what level should the outcomes of SHRM be measured? Should the focus be on firm financial performance, individual performance, or divisional/unit performance, for example? Are these outcomes relevant in all contexts? For example, a focus on firm financial performance will not be relevant for public or third sector organizations. Firm performance may be too far removed from the HRM/employee relationship and dependent on other factors (Purcell and Kinnie, 2007). Should the focus be on the individual level and, if so, should we be concerned with behavioural or attitudinal outcomes (Wright et al, 2001; 2003; Boxall and Purcell, 2008)? It is also the case that a focus on short-term financial outcomes may be at the expense of longer-term outcomes such as generating organizational sustainability and resilience over time. Practical issues have meant that important topics such as these have not yet been subject to empirical research.

- **Theoretical linkage.** Commentators have referred to the 'black box' between SHRM, on the one hand, and outcomes, on the other. Many feel that there is a lack of an appropriate theoretical framework for explaining why SHRM should be linked to performance at any level. Is the gap too great between high-level SHRM policy making, on the one hand, and the financial performance of the firm, on the other, for any meaningful conclusions to be drawn? And, significantly, on what theoretical grounds can we assert that there is a causal linkage? It is insufficient merely to observe that firms with particular approaches to SHRM perform better than others; without an explanatory framework, such an observation may be either a coincidence or masking other, underlying factors, and in fact causality may even be reversed, i.e. firms that perform better can afford to invest more in their SHRM processes (Guest, 2001; Hesketh and Fleetwood, 2006; Boxall and Purcell, 2008). A surprising number of studies have failed to provide any theoretical underpinning for their empirical research. Table 8.2 summarizes some of the main theories used to 'explain' the HRM–performance linkage and their limitations. In summary, no single theoretical framework has so far been able to provide an adequate explanation of the process by which HRM impacts on performance, but those that focus on the link between HRM interventions as experienced by employees and performance outcomes at the individual level are the most persuasive.

- **Methodology.** The majority of studies in the area have, for pragmatic reasons, used cross-sectional research designs that also rely on the views of one respondent in each organization. This creates a series of problems. For example, can one person's views on a firm's HR strategy and its financial performance be relied upon? How can collecting data at one point in time on both input factors, such as HR strategy, and output factors, such as performance, be valid? We would normally expect some kind of lag between an intervention and an outcome (Gerhart et al, 2000; Guest, 2001; Boselie et al, 2003; Wall and Wood, 2005). More worryingly, in a review of the literature, Wright et al (2005) found that a significant number of studies relied on performance data from an

Table 8.2 Summary of key theories on the HRM-performance link

Theory	Summary	Evaluation	Examples
Resource-based view	HRM can increase the quality of HR which constitutes a source of sustained competitive advantage.	The RBV is the most widely used theoretical framework in the field, but it is difficult to test empirically. Not all firms seek advantage, some are focused on survival. The RBV may not apply to public/third sector organizations and it does not constitute an adequate explanation of the processes by which HRM can raise performance levels. The RBV is relevant only at the level of the firm, rather than at the level of the individual employee.	See Chapter 6 for extended discussion
Social exchange theory	Where employees are treated well by their employer, this creates an expectation that this will be reciprocated through high levels of performance and loyalty.	There have been relatively few studies so far using this perspective, so evidence is limited. Social exchange theory can be used to examine outcomes at the individual level. However, more research is needed to explore which aspects of HRM may be most relevant.	Gould-Williams (2007)
Ability, motivation, opportunity theory (AMO)	People will perform well when they have the necessary skills and abilities, motivation, and opportunity to do so. HRM policies and practices can help bring about these circumstances.	Relatively few studies have used this approach so far. The AMO model is intuitively appealing and derived from sound theoretical roots. It can help to explain performance outcomes at the individual level, but more research is needed to examine the three core components in more detail.	Purcell et al (2003)
Job performance theory	Individuals' actions impact on the achievement of organizational goals in three ways: in-role behaviour, i.e. behaviour that is expected; extra-role behaviour, i.e. behaviour that is beyond the immediate requirements of the job; and dysfunctional behaviour aimed at harming the organization. HRM can impact on workers' attitudes which, in turn, will impact on these three aspects of behaviour and affect unit level performance.	This perspective is founded in organizational psychology and provides a promising avenue for future research by examining individual performance from a number of angles. It also suggests the mechanisms that may be relevant for linking individual and unit performance. More research is needed to explore the application of this approach.	Wright et al (2003)

Human capital theory and variations (e.g. intellectual capital, social capital)	HRM impacts on the knowledge, skills, and abilities of employees, the processes by which employees develop and combine knowledge, and the organizational climate, which combine to enhance performance outcomes.	Evidence is weak, e.g. Youndt and Snell (2004) found that HRM only explained 28% of variance in firm social capital. Also the theory does not explain precisely how these mechanisms work.	Swart and Kinnie (2003) Rodwell and Teo (2004) Youndt and Snell (2004) Kang and Snell (2009)
New institutionalism	Organizations in the same setting will be subject to various pressures to develop similar HR solutions and thus become increasingly homogeneous over time. These effects will mediate the relationship between HRM and performance.	New institutionalism underlines the importance of context and setting, which have been downplayed in the RBV. However, it cannot alone provide a theoretical basis for understanding how and why HRM might impact on organizational performance, which is why it has been combined by Boselie et al (2003) with the RBV. Like the RBV, this framework is relevant at the level of the firm, rather than the individual employee.	Boselie et al (2003)
Attribution theory	Employees make attributions about management's motivations in the HR practices they see implemented. There are five possible attributions: compliance with the union; employee wellbeing; exploiting employees; focus on service quality; focus on cost reduction. Those approaches associated with positive consequences for employees are likely to lead to higher levels of performance.	Only one study has used this approach, and support was found for only three of the possible attributions. However, the research found that there was a link between attributions and employee attitudes, and that employees respond to the same HR practices in different ways. The study has important implications for future research in the field.	Nishii et al (2008)

earlier period than was covered by the HR practices that were measured. Guest (2011) argues that the absence of longitudinal methodologies in the field casts doubt on many of the findings. He states that past performance is a far stronger predictor of current performance than is HRM.

- **Perspective.** Critical scholars have noted that studies on the SHRM–performance linkage are unitary in perspective and overemphasize financial performance at the expense of employee, ethical, or societal level outcomes (Paauwe, 2004). Some have argued that SHRM has been associated with efforts towards work intensification, decreasing job security, and other outcomes that are undesirable at the individual level (Marchington and Grugulis, 2000; Wright et al, 2003; Guerrero and Barraud-Didier, 2004; Harley and Hardy, 2004; Chang and Huang, 2005; Legge, 2005; Long, 2007; Boxall and Purcell, 2008). There is lack of agreement over whether data relating to HR practices should be collected from individual employees or from HR managers, and whose perspective is of most value and relevance (Guest, 2001; Hesketh and Fleetwood, 2006). Delbridge and Keenoy (2011: 800) refer to the 'moribund and limited nature of mainstream HRM' and the absence of theoretical critique or reference to alternative voices within studies of the HRM–performance linkage.

 Key Concept

The **black box** refers to the unknown processes that occur between HR interventions, on the one hand, and performance outcomes, on the other. One focus of research has been to find an appropriate theory to explain how this 'black box' works in order to better explain why and how HRM might impact on performance.

 Case study 8.2 Nick's Pizza and Pub

It is often the case that staff turnover is high in the catering industry (around 200%) due to uncomfortable working conditions, stress, and the fact that many employees are young people working part-time. This means that achieving high levels of motivation and performance can be hard. Nick's Pizza and Pub, based in Crystal Lake, Illinois, in the USA, has managed to buck this trend, achieving a manageable turnover rate of 20% and expanding its number of outlets. The company attributes its success to three key management practices. First, it has moved away from a 'command and control' style towards what it calls 'trust and track', where employees are told the reasons behind all the decisions that are made. Staff are encouraged to offer their own solutions for improving operations. Second, the company offers several levels of training that are voluntary, but those who choose to do more training receive an automatic pay rise, and those attaining the highest level train new employees. As employees move up the training levels, they wear different coloured hats so they are instantly recognizable. This system ensures that those who put in the most effort receive most rewards. Finally, Nick's has designated a 'safe area' in each outlet where employees can talk to managers and give them feedback. Employees are able to call managers at all levels into this safe area at any time and know that they will be listened to. Nick's feels that its approach to managing people places an emphasis on creating a great place to work and enhances customer service.

Source

Adapted from *Improving Employee Performance in 3 Simple Steps: A Restaurant Case Study*, posted by Greg McGuire, Halogen Software Talent Management and Employee Performance blog, 16 March 2011. http://www. halogensoftware.com/blog/improving-employee-performance-in-3-simple-steps-a-restaurant-case-study/.

Activity

What do the theories of SHRM outlined above tell us about why Nick's approach has been successful?

 ### Critical Reflection

Researchers have highlighted the difficulties of seeking conclusive evidence that HRM is linked to performance. For instance, if an organization is performing well, then any number of other factors, aside from the way in which people are managed, could be influential. Equally, causality could be reversed, in other words, it may be the case that high levels of organizational performance could enable a company to put in place sophisticated approaches to managing people. How do you think that researchers could go about addressing these complex issues?

8.4 The practicalities of measuring SHRM outcomes

Although academics debate the processes by which HRM may be linked with organizational outcomes, HR professionals are being regularly called upon by senior colleagues to provide management information relating to the contribution made by HR activities (Mooney, 2001). As Ulrich and Brockbank (2005b) note, being able to provide these kind of data is a core requirement for HR managers keen to to establish their credibility. However, the demands on HR managers today in terms of information are becoming ever more complex. Large organizations may require data such as return on investment (ROI), Balanced Scorecard evaluations of the HR department and HR activities, or benchmarking of HR policies and practices against other organizations (Marchington and Wilkinson, 2008). As Holbeche (2001: 51) notes: 'for many Human Resource practitioners, it's an act of faith that people management is a key factor in determining profitability. Whether that view is shared by management team colleagues is a different matter.'

8.4.1 HR data

One of the first issues is to determine what should be measured. Standard HR areas that are often measured by organizations tend to fall into the categories shown in Table 8.3.

A study in the US (Gates, 2004) found that the single most common HR metric used was turnover, used by 96% of organizations participating in his survey, followed by average compensation, 82%, average workforce age, 77%, diversity, 76%, compensation, 76%, seniority, 75%, and accident rate, 74%. However, there are a vast number of possible HR metrics, for example, Ulrich (1997b) identifies 52, and it is therefore difficult to know which might be the most important. A survey carried out in 2007 on behalf of the CIPD involving 787 organizations

Table 8.3 Domains of HR measurement

Employee attitudes	For instance, measuring levels of engagement through a staff survey, as well as satisfaction with the HR department and activities
Employee performance	These would include measures such as individual productivity and performance, for example, through annual appraisals and team performance
Employee behaviours	For instance, turnover and absenteeism
Health and safety measures	Including accident rates
Workforce profile and costs	E.g. competencies, talent, proportion of employees at particular grades, total workforce, salary costs, diversity statistics, talent pool
ROI in HR department	E.g. ratio of HR staff to employees, operational cost of the HR department
Cost and efficacy of HR activities	Such as number of applications per vacancy, training costs per employee, training satisfaction, speed of response to applicants
Customer outcomes	Such as customer satisfaction

Sources: Ulrich, 1997b; Holbeche, 2001; Mooney, 2001; Ulrich and Brockbank, 2005b; Boudreau and Ramstad, 2007; CIPD, 2007; Crail, 2007; Marchington and Wilkinson, 2008.

examined which outcome measures were most commonly used. Out of a range of 40 possible measures, none was used by more than 60% of respondents, reflecting the lack of consensus over what to evaluate.

Mooney (2001) suggests that factors for measurement can be evaluated on the basis of how easy or difficult the data are to obtain and their degree of relevance to business performance (see Fig. 8.1).

Although it would appear that data that are relatively easy to obtain and highly relevant (upper right-hand quadrant) will be the most helpful for the HR department, some caution must be exercised. A CIPD report (2009b) concluded that there is no one definitive way of measuring HR outcomes that will be relevant in all contexts, but rather that it is the process of measuring that is itself of greatest value as this will generate discussion about HR's contribution. However, for the HR professional it is important to be able to gather data that are 'relevant'. Mooney (2001) suggests that 'relevant' data are those that are most closely linked with

Low relevance Easy to obtain	High relevance Easy to obtain
Low relevance Difficult to obtain	High relevance Difficult to obtain

Figure 8.1 Mooney's HR data collection matrix.

overall business performance, such as labour turnover, performance reviews, training and development, adherence to budgets, health and safety, compliance with legislation and HR policy, and line manager satisfaction with HR performance.

Marchington and Wilkinson (2008) show how service-level agreements (SLAs) are becoming an increasingly common approach to evaluating HR's contribution. SLAs comprise a series of statements about the level of service that the HR function is expected to provide for the organization, for example, preparing job offer letters within 1 day or providing advice on disciplinary matters within 2 days. Shell is one firm that uses this approach (Sparrow et al, 2004: 165). Whilst SLAs can be useful in providing a clear statement of what is expected of the HR function, unless they are closely aligned with organizational goals, they may fail to serve a useful function.

Whilst many organizations collect internal measures of various kinds, benchmarking against comparator organizations is increasingly common. A study carried out by the CIPD in 2006 found that there are over 1,000 indices that have been used in benchmarking exercises. However, Marchington and Wilkinson (2008) point out that contextual variations can have a considerable impact on results; what is relevant in one sector may not be in another, and aggregate-level data can mask substantial differences. Employers therefore need to be sure that the benchmark organizations are relevant.

Two possible approaches that can be used by organizations to evaluate their HR contributions are reviewed below.

8.4.2 Boudreau and Ramstad's (2007) LAMP model

Boudreau and Ramstad (2007) show that, despite the advances in HR measurement, often these measures do not yield substantive, strategic change. The reason for this, they argue, is that 'many HR measures originate from a desire to justify the investments in HR processes or programs. Typically, HR seeks measurement not to improve decisions, but to increase the respect for (and potentially the investment in) the HR function and its services and activities' (p. 190). They compare this with the measures used by accounting departments, which focus on outcomes rather than on justifying the department's activities. Instead, they argue, HR's role should be on providing measures that senior managers can use to guide future decisions about the management and deployment of staff. They propose a four-component measurement system with the acronym LAMP: logic, analytics, measures, and process:

- **Logic:** the chosen measurement system should focus on the factors that are logically most relevant to performance. Starbucks measured the performance of its baristas in such a way as to capture issues of trust and discretion as these would impact most on customer service.

- **Analytics:** effective data analysis is important in order to interpret the data correctly. A simple correlation between two factors, such as staff satisfaction and customer satisfaction, does not necessarily signify a causal relationship. Customers could be more satisfied due to location, or more highly satisfied customers could lead to more satisfied staff. The more data that HR managers have at their disposal, the more important analysis becomes.

- **Measures:** should be of high quality and focus on what matters. Traditional HR measurements can be supplemented by linking to metrics collected in other areas of the organization, such as information systems and R&D. Over time, they recommend that organizations should shift their focus from measures focused on efficiency towards effectiveness and, finally, towards impact. For instance, employee turnover can vary in its significance depending on who is leaving and the context. In firms competing on the basis of quality, if turnover is high among well-qualified, highly trained and experienced employees, this will leave important talent gaps where the recruitment of suitably qualified replacements will take time. In firms competing on the basis of speed but not quality, then rapid recruitment of lower-skilled workers is important. The issues will need to be tackled differently, and so nuanced, context-specific measures are required.

- **Process:** measuring HR outcomes should be part of an overarching strategic change management process, and a key element of this is educating line managers to accept that HR measures are an important component of the change process.

(Boudreau and Ramstad, 2007: 187–206)

Global retailer Limited Brands adopted the LAMP approach to strengthen the link between business performance and HR processes. This involved an analysis of the critical success factors required for improving the overall performance of its shops, within which HR issues, such as staff deployment and core competencies, were integrated. Next, appropriate measures were developed, including the tracking of in-store customer and employee movements. One learning point that emerged was that customers were more likely to purchase an item if they entered the changing rooms; this was used to develop employee training and deployment programmes (Boudreau and Ramstad, 2007: 206-213).

8.4.3 The HR Balanced Scorecard

The Balanced Scorecard was developed in the 1990s by Bob Kaplan and David Norton as a methodology for linking strategic objectives with a range of performance outcomes from four perspectives (Kaplan and Norton, 1998):

- Customers
- Organizational learning and growth
- Internal business processes
- Financial performance

The concern was to move away from simplistic performance evaluations based purely on financial outcomes, and instead to consider performance from a more holistic perspective in terms of their contribution to the overarching aims of the organization. The Balanced Scorecard has been widely adopted internationally by organizations as diverse as Tesco, Kenya Red Cross, Veolia, AT&T, and BMW (http://www.balancedscorecard.org).

 Key Concept

The **Balanced Scorecard** was developed by Kaplan and Norton (1998) as a tool to help managers find holistic ways of measuring organizational performance.

The approach was extended into the HR domain by Becker et al (2001), who show the importance of the management of intangible assets to organizational performance outcomes. Their HR Scorecard rests on two core questions:

- How should strategy be implemented in the firm? How does the firm generate value?
- What performance measures capture this?

The answers to these two questions generate the insights needed to start to develop an HR measurement process that accounts for both leading indicators, i.e. those with a future-focus such as R&D cycle time, and lagging indicators, such as financial metrics, that focus on the past, for each of the four areas of the Balanced Scorecard. Becker et al (2001) identify four domains where decisions should be made:

- HR deliverables or outcomes, in order to identify how the HR system generates value in the firm.
- The high-performance work system elements that generate the deliverables, providing examples of what the deliverables should be for each system element.
- The elements of the HR system that need to align with one another to achieve the deliverables, which focus on the alignment of the HR system with strategy implementation.
- HR efficiency measures, differentiating between core (i.e. significant HR expenditure that makes no direct contribution to strategy implementation) and strategic metrics (i.e. those designed to produce the HR deliverables).

Becker and colleagues (2001: 75–76) argue that the benefits of the HR Scorecard include:

- It reinforces the distinction between HR doables and HR deliverables
- It enables you to control costs and create value
- It measures leading indicators (as opposed to lagging indicators)
- It assesses HR's contribution to strategy implementation and the bottom line
- It lets HR proccesionals effectively manage their strategic responsibilities
- It encourages flexibility and change.

One organization that has adopted the HR Balanced Scorecard is US-based car accessories manufacturer ABPS. ABPS has used commercially available HR Balanced Scorecard software to help it track progress in such areas as training, recruitment, culture, performance management, and HR expenditure in the wake of a complex merger. (See http://www.strategy2act. com/case_studies/proved_ways_to_measure_and_improve_performance_in_hr.html.)

8.4.4 Issues in HR measurement

Whilst approaches to measuring HR's contribution have become ever more sophisticated, it is important to bear in mind the constraints and complexities that this entails:

- Seeking to quantify HR's contribution places the emphasis on areas that can easily be measured, rather than what is necessarily most important.

- Service-level agreements can lead to an overemphasis on meeting the needs of other departments, and downplay longer-term HR strategic objectives.

- Relevant data may not be easy to obtain. Boudreau and Ramstad (2007) cite the example of turnover measures the greatest value is knowing why people are leaving and where they are going, which are rarely measured.

- The link between HR interventions and organizational performance is complex and multilayered; the collection of HR metrics risks oversimplifying the process and creating a misleading impression.

- Simply measuring outcomes does not lead to change or improvement.

- The relevance of different measures varies between industries and organizations. What is relevant in one context may be less so in another. Benchmarking may therefore not be as useful as managers believe.

- To be useful, HR measures need to focus on people outputs rather than HR processes.

Conclusion

In this chapter we have examined the issue of whether or not SHRM impacts on performance. Opinion on this subject is divided. Some commentators have argued that there is now ample evidence to suggest that effective HR practices will yield significant performance outcomes at both the individual and organizational levels. However, most have urged a degree of caution in asserting that there is a clear and causal link between the two, citing problems in terms of the way in which HRM and performance are specified and measured, the methodologies used in research studies, variations between sectors, and uncertainties surrounding the relevant theoretical framework. Yet, intuitively it makes sense that if people are managed effectively, their contribution will be greater, although there is as yet not enough evidence on exactly what 'effective' means in this context. Both HR managers and line managers have a role to play, and more research is needed on how line management and HR interact with one another to create a positive organizational performance climate.

Despite the reservations, it is clearly important for HR managers to be able to show how their strategies and policies yield beneficial outcomes for their organizations, or it will be difficult to argue for investment in the department. Several measures have been suggested and two more holistic methodologies for examining HR's contribution have been discussed.

Summary

- A great deal of research has been conducted to find out how HRM impacts on organizational performance.

- A large number of studies have concluded that there is a link between the two.

- Commentators have also argued that we need to be cautious in asserting that this link exists.

- There is lack of agreement over the best way to measure HR and over the theory that explains how the link might work.

- Various performance outcomes have been considered at the individual, unit, and organizational levels, but evidence is mixed.

- More research is needed that examines the HR–performance link using more sophisticated methodologies and in different settings.

- HR practitioners are, however, under pressure to measure the activities of the department and the outcomes of their policies and practices.
- There are a number of methodologies that practitioners can use, including the HR Balanced Scorecard.

 ## Review questions

1. Outline and evaluate some of the theoretical frameworks that have been used to explain the HRM–performance link.
2. Critically evaluate the research evidence on the HRM–performance link.
3. If you were to undertake research on how HRM impacts on performance, how would you go about this and why?
4. For an organization known to you, explain some of the HR metrics that could be used to evaluate HR's contribution.
5. How can HR professionals balance the short term vs the long term when considering the outcomes of HR interventions?

 End-of-chapter case study   Department for Work and Pensions (DWP): people strategy in the public sector

(Based on an interview with Joyce Henderson, People Insight Consultant)

The DWP is the UK's largest public service delivery department, employing over 100,000 people across the UK. The DWP is responsible for welfare and pension policy and exists to:

- Contribute towards fair, safe, and fulfilling lives, free from poverty
- Reduce welfare dependence and increase competitiveness
- Provide greater choice and personalization and higher quality service for customers.

The recession has raised significant challenges for the DWP, both in terms of its service delivery role, supporting people in returning to work and managing the benefits system, and in terms of the internal management and organization of the department. Costs had already been cut by £1.5 million between 2005 and 2008, and the department is now required to cut costs in a far more radical way as part of the government's programme to drive down the cost of delivering public services.

The DWP's business strategy is to transform the quality of customer service, drive up efficiency, and use each as a key means of achieving the other. Senior leaders believe that people management, building a positive work environment, and improving the skills of senior leaders are fundamental to achieving these, and so the HR department has a vital role to play during these challenging times.

To help the organization ensure it can deliver on its business objectives, the HR team has developed a people strategy based on four values:

- Respecting people
- Looking outwards
- Achieving the best
- Making a difference

The people strategy sets out how the DWP will support people in achieving the department's objectives and was developed by taking into account factors in the internal and external environment. Externally, critical factors included the prevailing economic climate and pressures on public spending, expected rising levels of worklessness, an ageing working population, and patterns of migration. Internally, it was important to take into account the need to improve leadership and management skills, increase diversity, build positive relations with the trade unions, and account for the changing skill requirements of the workforce. These factors, coupled with the DWP's business strategy, gave rise to a complex set of Key People Activities organized under five core headings:

- Designing and resourcing: including creating an affordable and sustainable organization, facilitating cross-boundary working, and retaining people with the right skills.
- Building current and future capability: particularly in order to enhance customer service.
- Increasing employee engagement: through using survey results to identify improvement areas and strengthen relationships with unions.
- Enabling change and new ways of working: through involvement and innovation.
- Enabling high performance: using HR policy to drive higher levels of performance.

These five areas were linked to the DWP's four values to create the DWP People Wheel, which shows how the HR strategy is configured to help the business achieve its goals. Progress in delivering on these is measured through an HR Scorecard, setting out key measures and targets under each section, showing HR enabling activity and outcomes. This is complemented by the DWP's overall Balanced Scorecard which captures a range of key people-related measures across the businesses and HR itself. Some specific targets include raising satisfaction levels with HR services to 70%, improving staff perceptions of leadership by 2%, raising engagement levels by 5%, and contributing 5,000 days of staff time to community initiatives.

Case study questions

1. The DWP is a large organization located on multiple sites and with many different types of employees. What difficulties do you think this poses for achieving HR strategic objectives and measuring them against target?

2. The after-effects of the recession create a significant challenge for the DWP as it seeks to raise service levels whilst simultaneously cutting costs on a very large scale. What do you think are the key principles for HR functions to bear in mind during times of retrenchment?

 Further reading

Boudreau, J. and Ramstad, P. (2007) *Beyond HR: The New Science of Human Capital.* Boston, MA: Harvard Business School Press.
This book aimed at HR practitioners provides guidance and case studies on how to evaluate the outcomes of HRM.

Delbridge, R. and Keenoy, T. (2011) Beyond managerialism? *International Journal of Human Resource Management,* 21(6), pp. 799–817.
This article is written from a critical HRM perspective and sets debates about the link between HRM and performance within a broader socio-economic perspective.

Gooderham, P., Parry, E. and Ringdal, K. (2008) The impact of bundles of strategic human resource management pratices on the performance of European firms. *International Journal of Human Resource Management*, 19(11), pp. 2041–2056.

The authors present findings from across Europe on the possible link between HRM and performance, comprising one of the most extensive datasets on the topic.

Patterson, M., Rick, J., Wood, S., Carroll, C., Balain, S. and Booth, A. (2007) *Review of the Validity and Reliability of Measures of Human Resource Management*. Report for the National Co-ordinating Centre for Research Methodology and the National Co-ordinating Centre for NHS Service Delivery and Organisation R&D (NCCSDO). Report No. RM03/JH10/MP. Institute of Work Psychology, Sheffield University. August.

This lengthy report is a systematic literature review on the link between HRM and performance, and provides a comprehensive analysis of the literature, findings, and evidence.

 For additional material on the content of this chapter please visit the supporting Online Resource Centre www.oxfordtextbooks.co.uk/orc/truss.

Part 3

Strategic imperatives

9 SHRM and human resource development

 Learning Objectives

By the end of this chapter you should be able to:

- Explain the concept of human resource development (HRD).
- Appreciate the importance of human expertise and learning to competitive advantage.
- Understand the relationship between training and development, career development, and organization development.
- Understand the relationship between formal and informal learning.
- Appreciate the role of workplace learning.
- Critically evaluate an organization's approach to HRD.

Key Concepts

Training
Development
Learning/informal learning
Organization development
Career development
Human resource development
Strategic human resource development

9.1 Introduction

The purpose of human resource development (HRD) is to develop human expertise (Herling, 2001: 228). This is important because human expertise underpins organizational capabilities which represent what an organization does well and enables it to outperform its competitors (Levis, 2009). Examples of organizational capabilities include talent management, collaboration, and speed of change (Ulrich and Brockbank, 2005). In the case of Apple it is the firm's ability to innovate and 'produce yet more beautifully designed products' (Levis, 2009: 76). Human expertise is developed through learning which is why learning processes are vital to achieving and sustaining competitive advantage in an increasingly globalized context (Crouse et al, 2011). Learning processes can be discerned within organizations at three interrelated levels: the individual, group, and the organization (Chalofsky, 1992). Individual learning involves knowledge acquisition which provides employees with the necessary expertise (i.e. knowledge and skills or competencies) to improve their performance as well as their ability to adapt to change. Employees also need to understand how to unlearn old skills as well as master new ones (Ulrich and Brockbank, 2005) and how to reflect critically on their performance. Learning within groups involves knowledge sharing which underpins innovation and the creation of new knowledge (which is discussed in more detail in Chapter 13 on knowledge management). Organizational learning has two dimensions. First, there is learning at the system level (Dixon, 1992). This enables systemic changes to be made which improve an organization's ability to respond to changing external conditions. Second, there is collective learning which involves learning that is embedded in organizational routines (Prahalad and Hamel, 1990). Routines are the regular and predictable patterns of activity that individuals engage in as part of their daily work (Grant, 1991). Routines can be formal (e.g. using a machine in accordance with a safety manual) and informal (e.g. drawing upon experience to do something more effectively than existing procedure allows). Developing new routines is typically dependent on social interaction and the creation of new knowledge through knowledge sharing (this also illustrates the interconnectedness between the levels).

In globalized and technology-driven markets competitive advantage is often short-lived unless new capabilities based on new routines can be implemented. For instance, Google achieved competitive advantage between 1999 and 2001 because of its innovative and radically different approach to internet search (Levis, 2009). Since 2001 the firm has sustained competitive advantage by developing new products and services, such as Google Chrome and Gmail.

It can be seen from the above that HRD is concerned with change, learning, and improved performance. The latter in particular is made explicit in many definitions of HRD. For instance, Swanson (2001a) argues that HRD needs to be 'a process of developing and/or unleashing human expertise through organization development (OD) and personnel training and development (T&D) for the purpose of improving *performance*' (p. 304, emphasis added). The inclusion of OD as well as training and development (T&D) indicates that performance improvement is expected to be a feature of both the individual and the organization. Gilley and England (1989:5, cited in Swanson and Holton, 2001) make this distinction explicit by referring to performance improvement in 'the job, the individual and/or organisation' (p. 5). This is why Swanson (2001b) argues that two of the three principal theories that inform the theory and practice of HRD are psychology (understanding individual human behaviour) and systems thinking (viewing organizations holistically as open systems with inputs, processes, and outputs). The third theory Swanson (2001b) refers to is economics, which reflects the historical association of HRD with human capital theory which views employees as intangible assets that are critical to achieving and sustaining competitive advantage (Ghoshal and Moran, 2005). More recently, the emphasis has started to shift to intellectual capital which comprises human *and* social capital. The latter, which is discussed in Chapters 3 and 13, helps to explain the nature of both group and organizational learning. Social capital is 'the sum of actual and potential resources within, available through, and derived from the network of relationships possessed by an individual or social unit. Social capital thus comprises both the network and the assets that may be mobilised through that network' (Nahapiet and Ghoshal, 1998: 243). In effect social capital is about new knowledge that is created when individuals, who share a common interest, socially interact.

The principal learning process for the development of human capital has been formal learning. These are organized interventions 'provided by employers, within a specified period of time, to bring about the possibility of performance improvement and/or personal growth' (Nadler and Nadler, 1989: 4). Typically these include training courses and workshops, education courses, and on-the-job coaching and instruction. The shift of emphasis to intellectual capital has been accompanied by a growth of interest in workplace learning which encompasses formal *and* informal learning. There have always been examples of formal learning in the workplace in the form of on-the-job training which can be described as a process of knowledge replication and application (Grant, 2008). It often involves rote learning through guided practice training so that a series of repetitive actions are carried out in the correct sequence within a specified period of time and/or to a particular standard (e.g. assembly line production; call centre protocols). Other popular methods are coaching and mentoring. Whilst coaching can be focused on a narrow range of skills or activities, in a similar way to guided practice, it is also a popular method for developing manager competencies (e.g. the continuing popularity of executive coaching). Indeed, formal coaching strategies are being increasingly seen as a viable option for developing organizational capability (Ali et al, 2010). Mentoring is much more wide-ranging and flexible, and tends to be associated with management and/or career development. E-learning also falls into the category of formal learning, although the learner tends to have a much greater say in when and where such learning will take place. In contrast informal learning has been defined as learning that is 'tacit and integrated with work activities' (Marsick, 2003: 389). Examples include observation, trail and error, reflection, and feedback from others (Crouse et al, 2011). The tacit nature of informal learning means that it also includes incidental learning whereby learning occurs as a by-product of another activity, such as a meeting or briefing, and the individual remains unaware that learning has occurred (Mankin, 2009). It is now generally accepted that most learning in the workplace occurs informally on the job or outside the workplace rather than in the classroom (Marsick, 2006).

 Key Concepts

Training involves planned instruction in a particular skill or practice and is intended to result in changed behaviour in the workplace leading to improved performance.

Development is much broader than training and usually has a longer-term focus. It is concerned with the enhancement of an individual's personal portfolio of competencies to meet future career plans.

Whilst surveys indicate that the level of classroom-based training has been declining in recent years, it is still unclear whether informal learning opportunities have really overtaken traditional approaches to training and development. It is difficult to measure the impact of informal learning on individual and organizational performance. Informal learning can be haphazard and offer no guarantees that outcomes will be favourable for the organization (Marsick and Volpe, 1999). Consequently being able to leverage informal learning, such that any new knowledge or skills that emerge in the workplace do actually support organizational goals, is probably the single most important challenge facing HRD professionals today. What is clearly understood is that informal learning often occurs in collaborative settings where social interaction takes place on a regular basis; for example, in both formal and informal groups. Formal groups can include section-teams, departments, and project teams, while informal groups are typically social networks or communities of practice (see Chapter 13 for a more detailed explanation of these two concepts). The major advantage of informal learning is that it helps employees cope with situations and problems that arise daily as they carry out their work (Vries and Lukosch, 2009). Informal learning also helps professionals to acquire the expertise and skills needed to develop their careers (Billet, 2001). Whilst it is easier to manage and control, and evaluate, formal learning, it lacks the flexibility and immediacy that is offered by informal learning. It is also less suited to handling the implications of the speed of changes taking place in the external environment of many organizations (Vries and Lukosch, 2009).

The strategic dimension of HRD lies in the fact that strategy provides the context for the development of intangible assets, by setting out how they are expected to help the organization accomplish its goals (Kaplan and Norton, 2004). This means that HRD strategy, policies, processes, and practices must be strategically aligned with the business strategy. For example, if a firm is seeking to gain competitive advantage through the innovation of new products the following HRD initiatives may be needed: specialist induction, sponsorship of postgraduate qualifications for research and development personnel, financial support for attendance at conferences. This strategic dimension can be influenced by a wide range of external or environmental factors such as those discussed in Chapters 1 and 2 (e.g. globalization, demographics, technology). In many respects these are similar to several of those discussed by Porter (2008) in relation to the competitive forces that shape an organization's strategy: competitors; industry growth rate; technology and innovation; and, government influence. All four have implications for the development of an organization's core capabilities, but it is the last that will be discussed in more detail in this section.

Competition in today's business world is increasingly global and organizations need to develop capabilities that reflect what an organization can do better than its competitors (Grant, 1991). The recent financial crisis has made these markets less predictable (Magnus, 2011). This has serious implications for growth forecasts. Most firms will continue to seek long-term growth, yet a narrow focus on growth is a principal cause of poor strategic decision making (Porter, 2008). However, HRD professionals need to be able to predict future HRD requirements based on such forecasts. This is particularly important because core competencies can take a long time to develop (Prahalad and Hamel, 1990). As highlighted above, learning is critical to innovation and, in turn, innovation is critical to competitive advantage (Porter, 1990). To date, Asian economies such as Japan, China, and Taiwan have been better at innovation based on incremental changes in existing technologies, while Western economies such as the US and Europe have been better at innovation based on radically new products and processes (Magnus, 2011). In terms of government influence there is a growing divergence between the two principal business models in today's global markets: China's state-controlled economic model versus the US version of free-market capitalism (Kaletsky, 2010). There is unlikely to be any agreement on a wide range of economic and political differences between the US and China in the foreseeable future (Rachman, 2010). Meanwhile global markets continue to be characterized by a wide range of regional and local differences in national policies and legislation that can influence an organization's strategy: health and safety; environment; corporate governance; employment law; and so on.

The nature of organizational HRD is influenced by national policies for vocational education and training (NVET). NVET policies are a government's strategic response to the long-term skills needs of a nation's human capital. It is beyond the scope of this chapter to detail the full range of national policies; however, the OUP website contains many topical examples which you may wish to read (see www.oxfordtextbooks.co.uk/orc/truss). Presently there is considerable debate about the role of higher education. This is being driven by the global shift from an industrial to a post-industrial knowledge economy. In developed and emerging economies there is a rising demand for workers with higher-level skills (see also Chapter 10 on talent management and Chapter 13 on knowledge management). This situation is becoming even more fluid with the emergence of a new global marketplace for higher education that is challenging the traditional dominance of Western universities (Wildavsky, 2010). For instance, growing numbers of students from countries such as Japan, South Korea, Vietnam, Thailand, and Indonesia are now studying at Chinese universities (Jacques, 2009) rather than travelling to countries such as the US and UK, while in India, leading technology firms are developing corporate universities to complement existing government-funded higher education provision (Mankin, 2009). Over the last decade the concept of national human resource development (NHRD) has emerged as an alternative term for NVET. Although the nature and purpose of HRD at national level differs from one country to another it is possible to discern five emerging models of NHRD: centralized, transitional, government-initiated, decentralized/free market, and small nation (Cho and McLean, 2004). These are summarized in Table 9.1 along with examples. The nature of NHRD will influence, to varying and constantly changing degrees, the nature of HRD in individual organizations.

Organizations need to recruit employees who have received a level of education appropriate to the job. Education courses have also been a popular feature of HRD practice; for instance, professional development programmes for the Chartered Institute of Personnel and Development (CIPD) and Chartered Institute of Marketing (CIM), and general management qualifications such as the MBA. Thus good quality education provision illustrates the importance of NHRD provision to the development of human capital in organizations. The development of the theory and practice in developing economies is going to have another impact. To date, the discourse on HRD has been dominated by Anglo-American perspectives (Wang et al, 2010). As new business models emerge in Asia and higher education becomes less reliant on Western perspectives, new approaches to the theory and practice of HRD are likely to emerge.

9.2 The theory and practice of HRD: formal and informal learning

It is now recognized that there is a wide range of theories relevant to HRD (Lincoln and Lynham, 2011). However, the origins of HRD lie in a narrow focus on training which can be traced back to the development of post-war approaches to the training and development of employees. The first training model emerged in the US just after World War II. This was

Table 9.1 National HRD in a selection of countries

Category	Description
Centralized	Central government is responsible for the provision of education and training (a top-down approach). China provides a good example of this approach.
Transitional	This reflects a situation in which the responsibility for NHRD is in transition from a centralized to a decentralized model. India provides a good example of this approach.
Government-initiated	NHRD initiatives are initiated by government. The UK and Australia provide good examples of this approach.
Decentralized/free-market	Vocational education and training are the responsibility of the private sector with indirect support from government. The US provides a good example of this approach.
Small-nation	Small nations need to cooperate and share resources through regional initiatives. The Pacific Islands provide a good example of this approach.

Sources: adapted from Cho and Mclean (2004) and Mankin (2009). Please note that each of the above examples is discussed in more detail on the OUP website for this textbook (www.oxfordtextbooks.co.uk/orc/truss).

the ADDIE training model—analysis, design, development, implementation, and evaluation (Allen, 2006). This evolved into a generic model that has been modified numerous times. The simplest and perhaps most popular version is the systematic training cycle which comprises four stages: the identification of training and development needs followed by the design, delivery, and evaluation of the training and development intervention (whether it is a short coaching session, a day-long workshop, or a longer classroom-based course). The model has been principally associated with formal learning (especially training). Although it has been criticized for being too mechanistic and inflexible, it has actually proven to be a robust and reliable model when used properly by professionals (Mankin, 2009).

The most common starting point for formal learning is the identification of training needs. Typically, training needs are determined by the line manager and/or employee and may often involve a negotiation between these two parties. Unfortunately, line managers often fail to identify their own training needs effectively as well as those of their employees. For instance, in a study of Danish firms by Brandl et al (2009) it was found that while 'the managers in the study show considerably greater interest in improving how they handle "motivating others" and "staff well-being", activities such as "team building", "handling conflicts" and "coaching" are seen as less important' (p. 204). Put simply, managers may know *what* needs to be addressed but they don't always appreciate *how* this can be achieved. Why should this be? It is not uncommon for line managers to be promoted to a management role not because they have displayed evidence of the ability to manage people but rather because they are believed to possess relevant professional or technical skills or experience (CIPD, 2010h). Consequently, developing managers continues to be one of the principal concerns of organizations (see Case study 9.1 below).

 Case study 9.1   Developing managers in Haier

Haier is one of China's leading firms with an annual turnover of over $15 billion. It has over 240 subsidiary companies and employs over 50,000 people. The company has a significant home market share in the following product ranges: refrigerators, refrigerating cabinets, air conditioners, and washing machines. The company has been successful at penetrating markets in Europe and the US and is following in the footsteps of firms such as Hyundai and Samsung, which initially focused on making products cheaply and efficiently before moving on to become more innovative and producing recognized global brands associated with product innovation. However, Haier is presently weighed down by the low-brow image of its products.

The published aims of the HR function are to support the firm's strategic objective of globalization and to develop talent. The latter is being achieved through the adherence to a particular management style that was first implemented in 1986 and is now regarded as being the cornerstone of the firm's successful growth and expansion. Referred to as the 'OEC Approach', this management style is aimed at maintaining a comprehensive control over all company functions. The purpose of the OEC Approach is to achieve each day's plan, evaluate that plan, and improve upon those daily accomplishments 1% better than the day before. This approach has been supported by formal management development programmes designed to produce versatile managers. For instance, every senior manager based in China attends a series of Saturday morning sessions at the firm's training centre in Qingdao where real work problems are discussed in teams of six to eight and potential solutions debated. During the week, managers experiment with these solutions on-the-job and report back to their team colleagues at a later Saturday morning session.

Sources

Van Agtmael (2008); Smith (2008); Bahl (2010); McGregor (2010); Tappin and Cave (2010); FT (2011); Haier (2011a; 2011b).

....

Activity

What might be the advantages and disadvantages of adopting Haier's approach to management development? Develop your answer by finding out more about the firm and other examples of management development initiatives.

Formal learning interventions tend to be designed using psychological perspectives on learning. These focus on human behaviour and human cognition. Behavioural learning theory focuses on behavioural outcomes as a result of a learning process (i.e. the purpose of learning is to produce specific, prescribed behaviours). From this perspective learning is portrayed as 'a mechanistic and involuntary process over which learners can exert little control' (Starbuck and Hedberg, 2001: 330). Skills training through coaching, guided practice, and instruction are typical examples of the application of this learning theory in an organizational context. Cognitive theory is technically about how we think (Jarvis, 2006), how we process information (Billet, 2004), and involves the development of representations or mental models of the world around us (Bowden and Marton, 2004). Understanding is achieved through reading, listening, and writing, often in conjunction with observation or doing something (e.g. learning a new skill; learning how a piece of machinery works). Consequently, learning occurs when we make a change in how we think and act, no matter how small the change (Billet, 2004).

Experiential learning theory sits in the cognitive camp of theories and helps us understand how an individual learns something. This includes learning both explicit knowledge *and* practical knowledge. Learning is defined in terms of a cyclical and continuous process (Kolb, 1984) whereby individuals learn from experience (often from deliberate experimentation or trial and error; or from making a mistake while doing something else). This theory has proven very popular with HRD professionals when designing formal learning interventions (Mankin, 2009). Experiential learning can be traced back to the work of Dewey (1916) who argued that everyone is able to learn from experience. He argued that the starting point for learning was a real-world problem or situation which acts as a catalyst for inquiry and reflection. This stage is followed by three further stages comprising: reflection, ideas generation, and application and testing (in real situations). Kolb (1984) based his experiential learning cycle, which is often referred to as the Kolb cycle, on Dewey's four stages. The four stages in the Kolb cycle are: having a concrete experience which is personal and immediate (this corresponds to Dewey's empirical situation); observation and reflection (reviewing the concrete experience); abstract conceptualization (drawing conclusions and generalizing about concepts and theories); and active experimentation (testing new concepts or concepts in new situations).

Although Kolb identified four learning styles associated with the experiential cycle, it is the Honey and Mumford (1992) learning styles typology that has been popularized and favoured by HRD professionals. Learning styles, sometimes referred to as learning preferences, explain how information is organized and processed (i.e. how we prefer to **think** about something). Unlike Kolb, who focused on learning behaviour, Honey and Mumford decided to focus on general management behaviour as they believed managers rarely think about learning behaviour (Yorks, 2005). Honey and Mumford (1992) also identified four learning styles: activist; reflector; theorist; pragmatist. Each one is associated with one of the four stages in the experiential learning cycle as follows: activist (having a concrete experience); reflector (observation and reflection); theorist (abstract conceptualization); and pragmatist (active experimentation).

However, to better understand informal learning in the workplace it is necessary to appreciate what may be termed sociological perspectives on learning. These complement psychological perspectives. From a sociological perspective learning is deeply influenced by the social context within which it occurs (Reynolds et al, 2002). Learning is **situated** in a real-life or work setting and is a social activity which 'allows people to hold learning conversations, where they solve problems, tell **stories** and share insights, from hunches and feelings to analysis and well-researched ideas' (Sallis and Jones, 2002: 96). The focus is on learning through collaboration, termed 'social participation' by Wenger (1998). Although proponents of this perspective, such as Lave and Wenger (1991), are highly critical of formal, traditional approaches to learning which focus on the acquisition of explicit knowledge, the reality is that in practice psychological and sociological perspectives are intertwined: an individual generates ideas and then these are generalized (i.e. shared) across the organization (Ulrich et al, 2009).

Key Concept

Informal learning is learning 'that is predominantly unstructured, experiential and non-institutionalised' (Marsick and Volpe, 1999: 4). This means that it is based on learning from experience, is embedded in the organizational context, is oriented to a focus on action, and governed by non-routine conditions (Watkins and Marsick, 1992).

9.3 The theory and practice of HRD: career development and organization development

As well as training and development HRD is associated with career development and OD (McLagan, 1989). It is important to differentiate between career management and career development. Career development tends to be associated with professionals such as accountants, lawyers, HR professionals, teachers, and doctors, with the objective of a career development initiative being 'the professionalization of individuals and their personal well-being, as well as the prosperity of the organization they are part of' (Palade, 2010: 125). Armstrong (2006) describes career management in terms of a process by which an individual's professional development is planned in accordance with organizational needs. This perspective does not reflect the role of individuals in shaping their career in accordance with their personal needs and aspirations (i.e. wellbeing). The long-term perspective of career development means that the concept is closely associated with the concept of lifelong learning (Mankin, 2009). Whilst lifelong learning is usually seen as a fairly recent concept, it is highlighted as a principal goal of HRD in Craig's (1976) definition of HRD. The other learning process associated with career development is reflective learning.

This is often referred to as reflective practice which is about how 'individuals think about [a] situation and then act upon it, either conforming or innovating upon it' (Jarvis, 2006: 10). Reflective learning is about enhancing self-awareness and this is a vital requirement for career development (McCarthy and Garavan, 1999). Jarvis's notion of 'innovating' is very important to adult learners. Adults already possess well-developed cognitive frameworks (also referred to as mental models or constructs) and therefore they are not necessarily just interested in accumulating more knowledge but rather in understanding how any new ideas will help them get what they want (Ulrich and Brockbank, 2005). However, for reflective learning to be effective, individuals need to discuss their needs in open dialogue with their managers (van de Ven, 2007). This again illustrates the importance of social learning. Whilst many HRD professionals tend to have little or limited involvement in career development, the recent global crisis has almost certainly prompted many individuals to pause and evaluate their career progress to date (Wagner, 2010), which means that career development may demand more attention from HRD professionals.

OD 'is the process of systematically unleashing human expertise to implement organisational change for the purpose of improving performance' (Swanson, 2001b: 260). OD initiatives are planned, organization-wide, managed from the top, and intended to improve organizational performance (Beckhard, 1969). They tend to be long-range projects (French, 1969) that are focused on an organization's problem-solving capabilities (Hall, 1976). As with career development many HRD professionals tend to have little or limited involvement in OD. This is understandable given that the responsibility for OD has never been associated with a single function. Arguably, all functions have a vested interest in OD. However, as a counter-argument OD is inextricably linked with change and as the introduction to the chapter explained change is also a feature of individual and group learning. Consequently, 'learning and change processes are part of each other. Change is a learning process and learning is a change process' (Beckhard and Pritchard, 1992, cited in Swanson, 2001: 286). The recent growth of interest in knowledge management has highlighted the importance of organizational learning (Grant, 2008). Consequently, OD becomes an important tool for the deployment and development of organizational learning processes (Argyris, 1999). This can help to address problems such as organizational fatigue where deeply embedded routines inhibit performance. As Levis (2006) observes, 'complacency is always a danger for successful companies, thinking that they have little left to learn' (p. 364).

Figure 9.1 sets out the principal elements of HRD as discussed so far in this chapter.

In practical terms much of the work of HRD professionals still continues to be focused on formal learning, whether it is delivered on-the-job or off-the-job. Arguably, training remains a process of knowledge acquisition (Grant, 2008) that is 'one of the most pervasive methods for enhancing the productivity of individuals and communicating organisational goals to personnel' (Galanou and Priporas, 2009: 222). However, successful off-the-job training is dependent on the transfer of learning from the 'classroom' to the workplace. The clearer the link between the skills being taught and the skills needed to do the job competently, the greater the likelihood that learning is integrated into work processes and systems (Leimbach, 2010). Unfortunately, the transfer of learning is often inhibited by a wide range of factors; for instance, lack of peer support; lack of line manager interest; attending a training course that

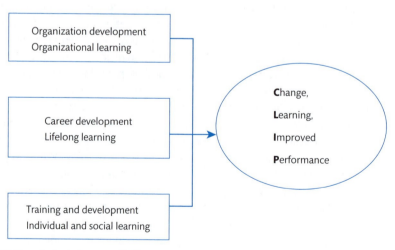

Figure 9.1 The principal elements of HRD.

Source: adapted from Mankin (2009).

is not directly relevant to the employee's role. This is perhaps one of the reasons why informal learning can be so powerful. Whilst it is typically unintentional, opportunistic, and unstructured, and occurs in the absence of a trainer (Eraut, 2004), it is usually directly relevant to the job in hand. The next section will discuss the strategic options for the implementation of formal and informal learning.

9.4 Strategic options for HRD

It has been recognized for some time by theorists and professionals that HRD should be 'positioned to act strategically throughout the organisation' (Marsick and Watkins, 1994: 355). Yet in many organizations it is difficult to discern a strategic approach to HRD. This seems odd given that the relationship between organizational capabilities and competitive advantage highlights the importance of developing human expertise. Today much emphasis is placed on the knowledge economy and the knowledge organization; yet much of the focus on knowledge management has been on information technology rather than human beings (this is discussed in Chapter 13). It is perhaps the continued association of HRD with training and the operational nature of much training practice that have fuelled this situation. It is also part of a wider issue: the credibility of HR professionals. The aim of this section is to discuss the SHRD options available to HRD professionals (see Fig. 9.2). As shall be seen, each option contains much that can be described as operational practice. However, the strategic dimension is the way in which these options are blended together in order to support business strategy.

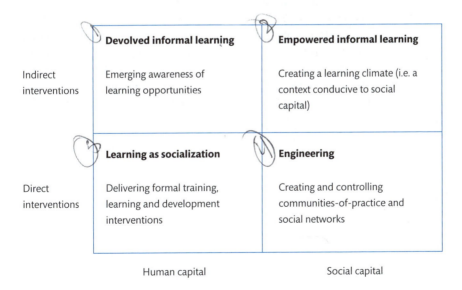

Figure 9.2 SHRD choices.

Source: adapted from Mankin (2009).

9.4.1 **Learning as socialization**

Learning as socialization reflects traditional approaches to the development of human capital. The focus is on formal learning interventions such as training courses, coaching sessions, and education programmes where primary responsibility is with the HRD professional as a 'training expert' and much of the training takes place off-the-job. This strategy is heavily reliant on the transfer of learning from the 'classroom' to the workplace.

Transfer of learning will be influenced by the extent to which an organization's learning climate supports change and the use of new skills (Leimbach, 2010). Typically these formal interventions are used to maximize the ability of employees to meet performance targets and standards. However, they are also designed to ensure employee conformance to organizational values and beliefs. Some organizations will go to great lengths to achieve this; for instance, the international shoe retailer Zappos:

> . . . employs a strategy to weed out workers who don't believe the Zappos mantra (which boils down to providing service that awes customers). Zappos doesn't wait until an employee has worked for the company for years—even months—before testing their loyalty. Instead, after a four-week training session, employees are given the 'Offer': If you quit today, we will pay you for the amount of time you've worked, plus we will offer you a $1000 bonus. Some people—about 10 per cent—take the money and run. The remaining 90 per cent, the ones who believe in Zappos, stay on. Zappos has some of the highest employee retention rates and positive ratings across the industry (Meyer, 2010: 56).

This strategic option also includes formal initiatives that support career development and lifelong learning.

For several years now some of the world's best known brands have been setting up corporate universities to cater for training and educational courses that fall within this strategic choice. Often multimillion dollar campuses have been built (see Case study 9.2 below). Examples of corporate universities include: Motorola University, Disney Institute, Harley-Davidson University, Intel University, and McDonald's Hamburger University (Mankin, 2009). The decision to set up a corporate university can sometimes transform an organization's approach to training and development. However, in many cases it is simply a rebranding of an existing centralized training and development centre or equivalent (e.g. learning centre) that offers a range of formal interventions delivered at the centre or over an intranet or the internet.

 Case study 9.2   Infosys Technologies

Infosys began life as a very small start-up business in 1981 but expanded rapidly to become one of India's leading firms and is now a global organization. The firm's principal HRD challenge is the retention of talent. The average employee age is just 26 and the firm has a reputation for recruiting the best qualified graduates (typically 1% of applicants). Learning through training has been one of the contributors to the firm's success. Infosys currently spends $180 million on training per annum including a 16-week programme for new recruits. It has invested in a 337-acre campus built at a cost of over $120 million. The Infosys Centre is now one of the largest training facilities in the world, with facilities to train 13,500 candidates every quarter and accommodation for 10,000 candidates and training personnel. It is, in effect, a corporate university (and is referred to as 'Infosys U' on the company website) which offers a range of courses including leadership development programmes which enable talented employees to progress quickly up the management hierarchy. As the firm has scaled up its training resources it has increasingly relied on technology for the delivery; for instance, providing case studies online that help employees better understand client needs. As part of the firm's learning strategy the Infosys Leadership Institute trains executives and develops managers through instructor-led training programmes as well as e-learning programmes. There is also the 'Campus Connect' programme which aims to align the curriculum of engineering institutions across India with industry requirements. The firm provides advice on learning and development to its customers on issues ranging from training needs analysis to e-learning. Particular emphasis is placed on integrating traditional training methods with modern ways of learning and performance management. The latter reflects the performance orientation of HRD discussed earlier in the chapter. In May 2011 Infosys Technologies won the 12th Annual Corporate University (CorpU) XChange award in the Excellence and Innovation category for its 'Campus Connect' programme. The CorpU awards are an independent evaluation of corporate learning and talent programmes which recognize corporate and government learning organizations that have improved both business and employee performance.

Sources

Nilekani (2008); Smith (2008); Cho and McLean (2009); Kumar (2009); Bahl (2010); Capelli et al (2010); CNN (2011); Infosys (2011); http://www.indiainfoline.com/Markets/News/Infosys-Technologies-wins-12th-Annual-Corporate-University-CorpU-Xchange-Awards-2011/5151352591 (accessed 12 June 2011).

Activity

What might be the drivers for investing in a corporate university? Develop your answer by finding out more about the company and other examples of corporate university or large-scale training centres. The challenge is how this type of learning can be blended with other strategic options that focus on the development of informal learning.

9.4.2 Devolved informal learning

Devolved informal learning is predicated on the trend in recent years for the devolvement of the responsibility for learning to individuals (managers and employees). Their ability to understand the essentials of learning and development (e.g. how individuals learn; how individuals can learn differently; how individuals can use reflection to improve their personal learning) is supported by a mix of formal interventions designed and delivered by HRD professionals (e.g. training workshops on learning styles and reflective practice; e-learning courses that encourage self-managed learning; coaching sessions to help line managers develop facilitation skills). The role of the line manager is critical in this process (Beattie, 2006). Studies have shown that the more managers are trained in how to support and coach, the more likely it is that employees use new skills in the workplace (Leimbach, 2010). However, managers need to better understand the conditions that trigger informal learning and how learning opportunities can be enhanced for employees (Ellinger, 2005). This knowledge can be developed through greater interaction between line manager and employees in the form of improved communications and the exchange of information sufficient for getting the job done (van der Heijden et al, 2009). In turn, social interaction with colleagues and an appreciation of the value of learning needs to be encouraged by line managers (Doornbos et al, 2004). Specific methods such as micro-training can be used to leverage informal learning in a devolved context (Vries and Lukosch, 2009). Micro-training involves short sessions of 15–20 minutes that can refresh or improve individual knowledge through collaborative problem-solving in the workplace (Vries and Lukosch, 2009). Rather than an HRD professional acting as a trainer, this role can be delegated to an appropriately skilled employee within a work team. This strategic choice is also associated with an emphasis on lifelong learning and career development (e.g. formal and informal mentoring; informal career counselling from peers).

9.4.3 Empowered informal learning

Empowered informal learning is focused on developing the potential offered by social capital and this requires a very different approach to the first two options which focus on human capital. It requires that strategic alignment between HRD and business strategy is achieved through the development of an organizational learning climate that nurtures social capital (e.g. informal networks, communities of practice). This builds on the Marquardt and Engel (1993) definition of HRD which specifically refers to learning climate, as well as the argument by Watkins and Cervero (2000) that 'there is some evidence in the larger field of human resource development that a focus on the learning of individuals is less significant than a focus on the organisation as a context for learning' (p. 193). Primary responsibility for HRD interventions in this strategic option is held by line managers in partnership with employees. The role of the HRD professional is concerned with strategies for nurturing the learning climate, not necessarily getting directly involved in the design, implementation, delivery, and review of individual HRD initiatives and interventions. This strategic option is predicated on the argument that if the context is right then the specifics will take care of themselves. Managers need to shed a control-oriented mindset and place their trust in the ability of their team members. However, not only are organizations inherently unstable but also fostering a learning climate within which social capital is dominant requires high levels of trust between managers and employees. In many organizations this remains an aspiration rather than a reality. Mentoring is ideally suited to a long-term change in management attitude and thus can have a dramatic effect on organizational learning climate (Chalmers Mill, 2010; Emelo, 2010). Empowered informal learning can also be encouraged in a variety of ways. For instance, through line managers delegating more responsibility and more challenging tasks (van der Heijden et al, 2009). Helping employees to develop social networks is also important (Mankin, 2009). This strategic option requires an OD focus by HRD professionals. It is diametrically opposed to the next option.

9.4.4 Engineering of learning

Engineering of learning is focused on OD interventions that are intended to develop social capital. This strategic approach reflects a managerial control mode (Alvesson and Kärreman, 2001) where managers interpret learning 'as a vehicle for manipulating employees and persuading them to adopt organisation aims' (Slotte et al, 2004: 482). Whilst it is possible to exercise a high level of control over direct interventions designed to develop human capital, the situation is very different with social capital which has been shown to be most successful when allowed to emerge within the workplace (Mankin, 2009). Social capital is about the development of communities, whether they are physical or virtual, collocated or dispersed. However, as Alvesson and Kärreman (2001) observe:

> Community is difficult to accomplish or control for management. It is basically an organic, social quality, associated with background, long-term commitments, downplayed hierarchy and considerable space also for non-instrumental virtues in a social context. The corporate form is typically not a setting that encourages community formation, but tends to work against it, at least on the level of the whole organisation (p. 1006).

For this reason empowered informal learning is the preferred choice for leveraging social capital (although there is no guarantee that social capital will always work in the organization's favour).

As can be seen from the above, the emergence of informal learning as a form of workplace learning enables HRD professionals to craft a more varied and innovative approach to SHRD. However, there is still a wide range of barriers to and facilitators of workplace learning which need to be considered. These are shown in Table 9.2.

 Critical Reflection

There has been much debate about the difference between performance and humanist perspectives on HRD. What do these two terms mean? How might these two perspectives influence your understanding of the theory of HRD and SHRD?

Developing a strategic approach to HRD also entails strategy-makers engaging in reflective learning and asking themselves challenging questions about the way in which business strategy has been formulated. For instance, asking themselves questions about the efficacy of the decisions made: Did they have enough information? Did they have the right information and, if not, why not? Have they involved all the right people in the decision-making processes? What have they learnt about themselves? Do they have gaps in their knowledge? Persuading strategy-makers to do this is perhaps a challenge too far for many HRD professionals.

Lastly, there is one aspect of HRD practice that still tends to be neglected: evaluation. Whilst the focus of evaluation has been moving from training interventions to the return on investment in human capital (Fitz-enz, 2009) it is still the case that few firms fully evaluate the impact of employee learning on work performance (Griffin, 2010). This is so in developed as well as developing economies. In China, for instance, management development has been evolving through a process of trial and error and 'although efforts in improving the process can be observed, such as decentralized MD policy making, this process has yet to be effective in addressing the overall problem of shortage of management skills. A major reason is that the policies to date lack accountability requirements, evaluation mechanisms, and defined implementation processes' (Wang et al, 2009: 216). In contrast, countries such as Singapore are 'requiring more results based evidence that HRD investments are paying off. [Consequently], HRD professionals will need to equip themselves with updated knowledge of human capital measurements and the use of effective evaluation models' (Osman-Gani and Chan, 2009: 64). Evaluation is needed not only to demonstrate the effectiveness of HRD but also because 'HR professionals would benefit from a more detailed understanding of employee perspectives on HR practices than currently exists' (Atkinson and Hall, 2011: 101).

Table 9.2 The barriers to and facilitators of workplace learning

Characteristics of workplace learning	Barriers	Facilitators
Integrated with work and daily routines	Time constraints; lack of access to challenging work; lack of access to learning resources and computers; lack of expert guidance; low importance attached to learning; low motivation; lack of management commitment to learning; poor learning climate; lack of incentives	Autonomy should be encouraged and work pressures minimized; development of an appropriate learning climate; line managers demonstrating commitment to learning (role model); presence of informal coaches; using multiple learning methods and increasing the resources that support learning
Responding to internal or external triggers	Poor understanding of learning; silo mentality which prevents effective communications and decision making across work groups; cynical attitude; perception that there is too much to learn	Donald Schön (1983) referred to non-routine 'surprises' as triggers of reflective learning; in a similar vein Jarvis (2006) refers to a 'disjuncture' which is when an individual is not sure how to act. Educating line managers and employees to recognize these triggers is important
Not highly conscious	Lack of self-awareness	Individuals need to consciously interpret what has happened
Often haphazard and influenced by change	Learning is not cost effective	Assess intended and unintended consequences
An induction process of reflection and action	Individuals constrained by existing mental models; prior unsuccessful learning experiences; fear of failure	Individuals need to externalize rather than suppress individual and group failures, and examine alternative solutions; experimentation/trial and error should be encouraged

Table 9.2 (*continued*)

Characteristics of workplace learning	Barriers	Facilitators
Linked to learning by others	Lack of collegiate availability; inconvenient	Encourage collaboration between colleagues; being open-minded and willing to listen to others; evaluate learning through discussion with others; engage in the constructive discussion of problems and concerns; create a deeper awareness of isolated and shared relationships; externalize potential barriers to learning

Source: adapted from the following sources: Marsick and Volpe, 1999; Lohman, 2009; Sostrin, 2009; van der Heijden et al, 2009; Crouse et al, 2011.

 ## Conclusion

The purpose of HRD is to develop human expertise and as a consequence it is concerned with change, learning, and improved performance. Human expertise underpins organizational capabilities which represent what an organization does well and enables it to outperform its competitors. Such expertise is regarded as an intangible asset which is often referred to as an organization's intellectual capital (which embraces both human and social capital). The principal learning process for the development of human capital has been formal learning in the form of training courses and work-based instructional techniques such as coaching and guided practice. The shift of emphasis to intellectual capital has been accompanied by a growth of interest in workplace learning which encompasses formal *and* informal learning. Whilst surveys indicate that the level of classroom-based training has been declining in recent years, it is still unclear whether informal learning opportunities have really overtaken traditional approaches to training and development. This is because it is difficult to measure the impact of informal learning on individual and organizational performance. The strategic dimension of HRD lay in the fact that strategy provides the context for the development of intangible assets, by setting out how they are expected to help the organization accomplish its goals. This means that HRD strategy, policies, processes, and practices must be strategically aligned with the business strategy.

 ## Summary

In this chapter we have examined the theory and practice of HRD and discussed strategic choices available to organizations. These strategic choices are based on the extent to which they are based on direct or indirect interventions and the extent to which they impact on human capital or social capital. Intuitively it makes sense that organizations adopt a mix or blend of choices. The following is a summary of the key points:

- HRD is important for developing the human expertise which underpins the organizational capabilities that support competitive advantage.
- Training is one aspect of HRD yet remains the principal focus for many HRD professionals.
- HRD also encompasses workplace learning and informal learning; career development and lifelong learning; and OD and organizational learning.
- A strategic approach to HRD is dependent on a coherent set of HRD policies and practices that are strategically aligned.
- A strategic approach to HRD is also depdendent on the existance of an appropriate learning climate (within which individual, group, and organizational learning are processes that are embedded).
- New perspectives on HRD are now emerging from Asia and these are likely to challenge the long tradition of Anglo-American perpsectives.

 ## Review questions

1. How can you best define and explain the concept of HRD?
2. How is HRD different from the concept of training?
3. What are the three conditions for SHRD?
4. What are the four strategic choices that make up SHRD?
5. Why is national HRD important?

 ## End-of-chapter case study   Toyota: a Japanese approach to HRD

Toyota, valued at $188 billion, or £98 billion, is the world's biggest car maker. The potential key competitors of the future are likely to be from South Korea, China, and India where companies such as Hyundai, Kia, and Tata are making cheap cars of a good quality. Toyota has been able to combine product quality and reliability with low pricing, fuel efficiency, and good design, although its reputation as a quality brand has been badly shaken due to the recall of millions of cars to correct faults. This has exposed the company to criticisms it has not previously had to handle. Traditionally, it has been successful at aligning its operational activities with strategic goals. The company is driven by what it terms the 'Toyota Way' rather than by cost reduction (which characterizes many Asian and Far Eastern manufacturing companies). The 'Toyota Way' has been evolving since the company was originally founded in 1926. It is all about the learning climate of the company and emphasizes mutual trust and respect for everyone involved in and with the business. Toyota is regarded as one of the most efficient companies in the world because of the Toyota Production System (TPS) based on lean production and *kaizen* (continuous improvement) principles. These are at the heart of its approach to business strategy. The approach adopted by Toyota has resulted in the institutionalization of lean manufacturing skills and *kaizen*. The company places great emphasis on teamwork that reflects a learning climate characterized by collaboration, cooperation, and trust. The company believes that teams are better at solving problems, and that people learn from each other.

In terms of its approach to HRD the principal emphasis is on training. The HR function itself is viewed as playing a key leadership approach in the company's improvement processes and has a coordination role when it comes to training. The training and development team is part of a broader 'Human System' which focuses on development, recruitment, and retention. The aim of the 'Human System' model is to make everyone a member of the Toyota learning climate. In the US a corporate university (University of Toyota) has been created to provide training and consultancy on Toyota's business practices, particularly lean manufacturing. The principal strength of the company has always been its approach to on-the-job training, although this has become increasingly supplemented with classroom training (although the latter was not greatly appreciated in the past). The company prefers the term on-the-job development because it is felt to be broader than training. This approach includes methods such as job rotation which reflects this broader development. Team leaders are trained as facilitators and instructors and do most of this classroom training. It is a requirement that anyone in this role has production experience. The increase in classroom training reflects the influence of globalization on the company. Employees are able to identify personal training opportunities which are referred to as 'self-initiated development'. The training of general managers involves learning about business planning and policy, Toyota Business Practices, and several other related issues. Most of this is handled by the Toyota Institute in Japan, although job rotation is also a characteristic of this level.

Toyota has always stressed the importance of recruiting people who not only have the capacity to learn but also possess the motivation and desire to do so. The company is always trying to find ways to improve the training methods it uses because people are trained without slowing down the line. This is a challenging situation for anyone new to the job. This is because the TPS is so interconnected that to slow down one part affects the whole system. Standardized instruction methods are used across the company. Recently, the company has been trying to drive down costs and there are concerns that this is harming its long-standing reputation for quality.

Sources

Ulrich, D. and Brockbank, W. (2005) *The HR Value Proposition*. Boston, MA: Harvard Business School Press.

The Times, 7 August 2006, p. 35.

Bryan, L.L. and Joyce, C.I. (2007) *Mobilising Minds: Creating Wealth from Talent in the 21st-Century Organisation*. New York, NY: McGraw-Hill.

Liker, J.K. and Meier, D.P. (2007) *Toyota Talent: Developing Your People the Toyota Way*. New York, NY: McGraw-Hill.

Morgan, M., Levitt, R.E. and Malek, W. (2007) *Executing Your Strategy: How to Break it Down and Get it Done*. Boston, MA: Harvard Business School Press.

Liker, J.K. and Hoseus, M. (2008) *Toyota Learning Climate: The Heart and Soul of the Toyota Way*. New York, NY: McGraw-Hill (written in collaboration with the Center for Quality People and Organizations).

The Times, 1 March 2008, p. 73.

Cappelli, P., Singh, H., Singh, J. and Useem, M. (2010) *The India Way*. Boston, MA: Harvard Business Press.

http://www.bbc.co.uk/news/business-11593952 (accessed 6 January 2011).

http://www.guardian.co.uk/business/toyota (accessed 6 January 2011).

http://www.toyota.eu/ (accessed 7 Januray 2011).

Liker, J. and Ogden, T.N. (2011) *Toyota Under Fire: Lessons for Turning Crisis into Opportunity*. New York, NY: McGraw-Hill.

Case study questions

1. How would you describe Toyota's approach to HRD and what do you think are the principal advantages and disadvantages?

2. To what extent do HRD activities appear to be vertically and horizontally aligned?

3. How can Toyota best tackle its recently damaged reputation for quality?

Further reading

Fitz-enz, J. (2009) *The ROI of Human Capital: Measuring the Economic Value of Employee Performance.* New York, NY: AMACOM.
This article will introduce you to one of the principal financial measures used for the evaluation of training.

Garavan, T.N. (2007) A strategic perspective on human resource development. *Advances in Developing Human Resources,* 9 (1), pp. 11–30.
An excellent article for enhancing your understanding of SHRD.

Jarvis, P. (2006) *Towards a Comprehensive Theory of Human Learning.* Abingdon: Routledge.
This is by one of the best academics on the subject and is ideal if you want to improve your understanding of learning theory.

Mankin, D.P. (2009) *Strategic Human Resource Development.* Oxford: Oxford University Press.
This textbook provides comprehensive coverage of HRD and SHRD and includes a wide range of international examples.

Yang, B. and Wang, X. (2009) Successes and challenges of developing human capital in the People's Republic of China. *Human Resource Development International,* 12 (1), pp. 3–9.
This article provides an insight into one of the world's leading developing economies.

 For additional material on the content of this chapter please visit the supporting Online Resource Centre www.oxfordtextbooks.co.uk/orc/truss.

10 SHRM and talent management

 Learning Objectives

By the end of this chapter you should be able to:

- Define and explain the concept of talent management.
- Appreciate the relationship between human capital management and talent management.
- Understand the differences between HRD and talent management.
- Appreciate the role of the HR function in the acquisition, development, and retention of an organization's talent.
- Analyse an organization's approach to talent management.

 Key Concepts

Human resource development (HRD)
Human capital
Employer branding
Talent management
Talent development

10.1 Introduction

A survey of HRM managers in Western countries has found that they consider talent management to be one of the most important challenges facing organizations in today's globalized economy (Sumardi et al, 2010). Global demand for talent is becoming increasingly competitive (Wildavsky, 2010) as a result of changing markets, changing demographics, and the demand for highly skilled employees (Schuler et al, 2011). The rapid growth of Asian economies such as China and India is fuelling this global demand for talent. For instance, in 2008 the city of Shanghai in China was short of over a million finance professionals (Bahl, 2010). There is also a shortage of management talent in China (Cooke, 2011). More Asian firms are using talent management than their UK counterparts (CIPD, 2010d).This trend is likely to gain even greater momentum as emerging economies acquire more advanced technologies in order to speed up their economic development and reduce their reliance on relatively low-skilled employees (Magnus, 2011). But what exactly do we mean when referring to the concept of talent? Talent is one of those concepts we intuitively understand but which we find difficult to define. For instance, talent has been defined in the field of HRD as 'the innate, genetically coded predispositions that create natural strengths and abilities within any individual' (Gilley et al, 2003: 8–9) and is different from skills, which are 'tools, techniques, and procedures that can be learned through instruction or experience' (ibid: 10). This definition of talent is a rather technical or 'scientific' explanation which is unlikely to gain legitimacy within many organizational settings. There is also a danger that talent will be treated like an abstract commodity with a single definition (Garrow and Hirsh, 2008). Not only is talent context-dependent but also, as Ulrich and Ulrich (2010) argue, the study of talent 'has evolved from a focus on employee competence (*ability* to do the work) to employee commitment (*willingness* to do the work)' (p. 43). This broadening of the concept of talent is captured in Table 10.1 in the section on the role of HR and strategic HRM.

The origins of talent management can be traced back to the 1990s (Madhanya and Shann, 2010), and, more specifically, to a study published by McKinsey in 1997 entitled *War for Talent* which 'identified recruitment as the number one concern for business leaders' (Caplan, 2011: 1). Initially the focus of talent management was on addressing skills shortages at senior management level, but broader alternative perspectives have emerged which encompass the assessment, deployment, and development of key employees (Caplan, 2011). This raises the question of the relationship between talent management and HRD. HRD focuses on all employees while talent management focuses on 'key employees' or 'top talent'. Top talent can be defined as 'employees who routinely exceed expectations while exhibiting the right behaviours and are agile in learning and approach. These are people who customers pay a premium to do business with and others strive to work with' (Morgan and Jardin, 2010: 24). The principal characteristics of talent management are that it is strategically aligned; tends to be exclusive (i.e. focuses on executives and employees perceived as critical to competitive advantage); has both an internal focus (e.g. appointing from the internal labour market, induction, training and development) and external focus (e.g. hiring from external labour markets); builds on succession planning and career development; and can be measured using a mix of qualitative and quantitative metrics.

 Key Concept

Human resource development encompasses a range of organizational practices that focus on learning: training, learning, and development; workplace learning; career development and lifelong learning; organization development; organizational knowledge and learning. Please see Chapter 9 for a detailed explanation of the concept.

However, talent is a context-dependent concept and this is why it is important to consider talent management's relationship to human capital management. Human capital management traditionally underpins strategic HRM and focuses on the development of employee competence in the form of employees' skill, knowledge, and ability. The leveraging of human capital is critical in building the 'dynamic capabilities' that secure an organization's competitive advantage (Teece et al, 1997). Dynamic capabilities are a firm's 'ability to integrate, build and reconfigure internal and external competences to address rapidly changing environments' (ibid: 516). Human capital theory enables managers to distinguish between generic skills, which are transferable and therefore of equal value to all firms but do not contribute to competitive advantage, and firm-specific skills, which provide value only to a specific firm but underpin competitive advantage (Barney and Clark, 2007).

Adopting an RBV perspective means that firms should be very selective with the employees they decide to train and develop (Carmeli and Weisberg, 2006: 202). Talent management can provide criteria for making this type of decision for training and development as well as other HR practices such as recruitment and retention. However, organizations first need to define talent and this is where competencies can be useful. Competencies are being used in assessment centres and development centres 'for identifying, developing, and promoting talented individuals' (Haldar, 2009: 173). The next issue that needs to be considered is the efficacy of decision-making processes. In multinationals the complexities of global business can have a significant impact on management decision-making processes (Harvey et al, 2009). There is an implicit assumption that organizations recognize talent. Senior managers may appreciate the competitive value of talented employees, but they are often less effective in utilizing this resource (Bryan and Joyce, 2007). Bias and subjectivity as well as bounded rationality can impact on decision making, and whilst competencies can help if used effectively, this can only ever achieve their minimization rather than their complete elimination. As Hutton (2010) cautions: 'the distribution of reward and position does not correspond to talent, effort and virtue' (p. 272). It would be naive to believe that problems associated with other organizational processes and practices, such as bias and halo effect, are not a characteristic also of talent management processes and practices.

Some definitions actually make the interrelationship between talent management and human capital management much more explicit. Talent management is 'the process through which employers anticipate and meet their needs for *human capital*. Getting the right people with the right skills into the right jobs . . . is the basic people management challenge in any organisation' (Capelli, 2008: 1, emphasis added). In turn, human capital 'is the value of the knowledge and *talent* which is embodied in people who make up the organisation, representing its know-how, the capacities, the knowledge, talent, competence, attitude, intellectual agility, creativity, and others' (Santos-Rodrigues et al, 2010: 55, emphasis added). While Hall's (2008) definition of human capital management could also be used as a definition of talent management: 'It is a system for enabling the business to meet its short-term and long-term business objectives by improving the performance of those in *critical roles*' (p. 24, emphasis added). These definitions suggest that human capital management and talent management are interchangeable and this goes well beyond a blurring of the boundaries between the two concepts.

As already indicated above, the BRIC countries (i.e. Brazil, Russia, India, and China) are most representative of the challenges encountered when managing talent globally (CIPD, 2010b). For instance, demand for experienced people in China is 'extremely high and poaching seems common' (Story, 2010: 111). Yet it is now apparent that India's IT sector has been incredibly successful because the importance of acquiring and developing talent has been recognized (Cho and McLean, 2009). This trend also reflects the growth in indigenous approaches to business strategy that were highlighted in Chapter 3. For instance, there is an increasing emphasis on the relationship between new HR practices and intangible assets in countries such as India (Madhanya and Shann, 2010) which are uniquely Asian in character. With the emergence of global brands in India and China the role of employer brand in the acquisition and retention of talent is becoming increasingly important to these firms, and the days of expatriates dominating the management structure of Western subsidiaries in Asian countries is rapidly disappearing as the competition from indigenous managers grows. The importance of brand has been understood for some time. Brand adds value to an organization. For instance, the Marriott name adds value because it inspires consumer confidence in its product and services (Ulrich et al, 2009). Global branding enabled premium pricing for products such as Nokia in the 1990s (Steinbock, 2010) and Apple in the first decade of the 21st century (Levis, 2006). Employer brand is a more recent concept. It has been important to multinationals for at least the last decade and is now regarded as an essential element in building and sustaining a firm's reputation (Martin and Groen-In't-Woud, 2011). An employer brand has an appeal to potential applicants and existing employees in the same way that a company brand appeals to potential and existing consumers.

 Key Concept

The concept of **human capital** is underpinned by economic-based theory (e.g. Becker, 1964; 1975) and can be defined as 'the development of personal knowledge, skills, and abilities' of individual employees (Lesser and Cohen, 2004: 3). Human capital 'possesses organisation-specific knowledge [and] is an invaluable asset that has the potential to produce a competitive advantage and sustain it. Hence, firms should be very selective with the employees they decide to train and develop' (Carmeli and Weisberg, 2006: 202). This is why the concept of human capital is closely associated with the resource-based view of strategy (see Chapter 6).

10.2 The strategic dimension of talent management

Talent management is still an evolving concept that has captured the imagination of academics, HR professionals, managers, and other organizational stakeholders. Although there is a lack of consensus on a definition of talent management, along with concerns that current theory and practice lack coherence and focus (Caplan, 2011), there is a broad agreement that the concept should be treated as a strategic imperative (Ulrich et al, 2009; Madhanya and Shann, 2010). This perspective is predicated on the argument that organizations need effective processes and practices for talent management in order to achieve their business objectives (Capelli, 2008). As Morgan and Jardin (2010) observe:

> The demand for strategy-based talent management has never been greater. Senior management, boards of directors, analysts, and investors often factor a company's talent management maturity and the quality of its workforce into the valuation equation. Considering that staff costs including salaries and benefits comprise a very large percentage of most companies'

overall spending, it is vitally important to run talent management like a business in order to drive maximum return on investment in people (p. 23).

But how can organizations ensure that talent management is vertically aligned with business strategy? One way is to ensure that the talent management strategy is focused on developing the organizational capabilities that sustain competitive advantage; as long as managers understand what the organization's capabilities are and how they can be leveraged.

Talent management strategy, practices, and processes can help create a high-performing organization that can survive and prosper in a rapidly changing business environment (Caplan, 2011: 1). However, it is no surprise that talent management has been described as 'a critical and difficult task' (Madhanya and Shann, 2010: 44). Tappin and Cave (2010) describe companies that have successful talent management strategies as being 'talent-magnet companies'. Such companies 'make it a critical objective to attract the top 1 per cent of the best people globally and structure their business to ensure they provide attractive and stimulating routes for that talent' (p. 74). Leading firms with well-established brands fall into this category. Mergers and acquisitions offer another potential solution to satisfying the demand for talent. For instance, the acquisition of IBM Consulting by Lenovo enabled the Russian firm to 'absorb a cadre of globally trained managers into its organisation' (Kelly, 2008: 77).

 Critical Reflection

Identify an organization that has published a detailed commitment to talent management. To what extent does this commitment appear to conform to the prevailing perspectives on the theory and practice of talent management?

10.3 The role of HR and SHRM

The processes and practices associated with talent management highlight the extent to which the concept is inextricably linked with the role of HR and SHRM. They range from the acquisition and integration of new workers to the development and retention of current workers (Madhanya and Shann, 2010), as well as reward, succession planning, and career development. In particular, training and development is critical to the development of competencies (Schuler et al, 2011). These are fairly traditional HRM activities (Sumardi et al, 2010), but as argued above they do need to be aligned with business strategy, both vertically and horizontally, and the failure to achieve this is a common problem in many organizations. Arguably, a holistic approach to talent management is needed as this has the potential to support strategic alignment or, as the CIPD argues, a better 'joining up' of 'HR practices and the processes behind a clear business and personal set of goals' (CIPD, 2006: 1). However, in developing a talent management strategy, organizations need to implement more innovative and creative HR practices. As the CIPD observes:

... organisations are currently innovating around their talent strategies and, in particular, around their talent development opportunities. Such creative practices seem to come to the fore in challenging circumstances and when organisations and individuals have their backs to the wall. The real challenge for organisations is to retain this energy and momentum around new ideas and creativity on a day-to-day basis and make this part of 'business as usual'. (CIPD, 2010c: 9)

Adopting greater internal labour market flexibility is consistent with the RBV perspective (Sparrow et al, 2011). This strategic perspective was highlighted in the Introduction (and is discussed in more detail in Chapter 3). To remain competitive organizations need to develop the internal labour market in a more imaginative way and managers need to learn to think more creatively and carefully before automatically going to the external marketplace (CIPD, 2010). As well as drawing upon increasingly competitive external labour markets, larger firms with a much more diverse workforce, particularly multinationals, are ideally placed to create talent market-places from which senior managers can appoint key employees (i.e. top talent) to permanent and part-time posts (Bryan and Joyce, 2007). It is also more cost effective than searching for the required talent from outside. 'Many of these searches for competent managerial talent require the service of head-hunters and their services are usually costly' (Sumardi et al, 2010: 181).

Internal talent marketplaces build on the more traditional approach of succession planning. Succession planning has always been viewed as a facet of HR planning and its predecessor, manpower planning. HR planning is about predicting how many and what kind of employees will be required in the future and if implemented effectively will result in 'the right people doing the right things in the right place at precisely the right time' (Graham and Bennett, 1992: 172). However, HR planning encompasses all employees and therefore the more selective focus of succession planning is better suited to meeting the needs of talent management. A detailed discussion of HR planning is beyond the scope of this chapter, so please refer to the list of recommended further reading at the end of this chapter if you wish to find out more about this topic. Succession planning has tended to focus on senior management positions (Beardwell, 2007). It also assumes that the external environment is relatively stable, which is no longer the case (McDonnell and Collings, 2011) as discussed in Chapter 1. Consequently, new methods for mapping the talent requirements of an organization need to be devised by HR professionals. These new methods must be able to accommodate both organizational and individual aspirations. This also highlights the importance of retention. Retaining talented employees is seen as a more viable, longer-term solution to addressing global skill shortages than an over-reliance on recruitment from external labour markets. But there are inevitably risks attached to such a strategy. These risks centre on the balancing of interests between internal development and external recruitment, and between the interests of employees and those of the organization (Capelli, 2008). This will necessitate the design and implementation of career development initiatives that have substance and go beyond the facile platitudes that can characterize annual performance appraisal discussions. 'Top talent' will need and expect an organization to make an investment in their personal development; which is also in the interests of the organization.

Table 10.1 differentiates between processes and practices that are directly or indirectly associated with HRM. This linkage, or perhaps intertwining is a better term, is also evident in definitions of talent management within HRM literature. For instance, Ulrich et al (2009) argue that talent management 'focuses on competency requirements and how individuals

Table 10.1 Talent management processes and practices associated with talent management

Processes and practices directly associated with HRM/HRD	Processes and practices indirectly associated with HRM/HRD
• Succession-planning, career development, and promotion	• Developing employee loyalty
• Recruitment and/or retention	• Teamwork, collaboration, and knowledge sharing
• Reward	• Risk management
• Training and development/learning and development—developing competence	• Organization development
• Management and leadership development	• Developing and/or nurturing a supportive culture
• Performance management	• Knowledge management, innovation, R&D
• Employer branding: developing employee motivation, commitment, and engagement	
• Developing high-performance/high-performance work systems	
• Diversity	

enter and move up, across, or out of the organisation' (p. 109). Sparrow et al (2010) highlight the knowledge management implications of talent management; while Ulrich and Ulrich (2010) suggest that talent should be seen as an important intangible asset or capability alongside leadership, innovation, skill, and vision (Ulrich and Ulrich, 2010). Diversity is also an important consideration in today's global markets. In particular:

> Talent management and diversity need to be interlinked. Diversity should be threaded through all talent management activities and strategies to ensure that organisations make the best use of the talent and skills of all their employees in ways that are aligned to business objectives (CIPD, 2010a: 1).

A survey carried out on behalf of the CIPD (CIPD, 2010d) suggests that only 22% of organizations do not attempt to integrate diversity and talent management. Reasons for this include cultural differences, inadequate levels of investment, and the mindset of line managers. This last point is an interesting one as it reflects the extent to which practices are not embedded as routines within an organization's culture.

Performance management is seen as a key element in talent management, although studies reveal that in countries like China there are a wide range of performance management practices being used (Cooke, 2011). The evolution of HRM practices in emerging economies might suggest that the processes and practices shown in Table 10.1 may be little more than a rebranding or repackaging of existing HRM practices and processes that have previously failed to secure strategic credibility for the HR profession. Previously, panaceas have included not only human capital management but also high-performance work systems, employee commitment, and employee engagement. It is important to avoid overhyping the concept of talent management. This recycling of Western approaches in Asia is likely to be countered over time by the emergence of new indigenous business models. However, the concept of employer branding has the potential to provide an effective (holistic) framework for the alignment of SHRM and business strategy.

 Key Concept

Employer branding is 'the practice of developing, differentiating and leveraging an organisation's brand message to its current and future workforce in a manner meaningful to them . . . [and] is aimed at motivating and securing employees' alignment with the vision and values of the company' (Price, 2004: 263).

Ulrich et al (2009) argue that the 1990's HR role of 'employee champion' now needs to be split into two new roles: 'employee advocate' and 'human capital developer'. The latter role 'focuses on how employees prepare for the future . . . [human capital developers and] build the future workforce' (ibid: 104). This new role embraces processes and activities that fall within the remit of HRM (e.g. HR planning, recruitment, reward) and HRD (e.g. induction, management induction). For instance, the Indian company Infosys Technologies has a human capital planning process that 'builds out twenty months in advance and includes special leadership development programs to pull front-line workers into the management ranks' (Capelli, 2008: 202). This emphasis on forward planning demonstrates why HR strategy and human capital management need to be fully integrated. Ulrich et al (2009) posit a similar argument for talent management: 'HR professionals should ensure that the company's means of talent management and organisational capabilities are aligned with strategy, integrated with each other, and working effectively and efficiently' (p. 109). However, this does require the combination of the 'human capital developer' with that of business or strategic partner if there is to be effective strategic alignment. In terms of the HR function's role in supporting talent management, the CIPD proposes a range of initiatives (see Table 10.2).

One of the reasons why talent management may prove problematic for HR is that the credibility of HR professionals is under attack: 'Many CEOs are scathing about the HR profession' (Tappin and Cave, 2010: 72). This is an issue touched upon in earlier chapters. However, it does have important implications for the perceived role of HR. Some of the criticisms are harsh but on further reflection may be accurate. There is still a sense that many organizations still employ relatively traditional practices that are more reflective of personnel management than HRM.

The acquisition of talent needs to be supported by HRD processes and practices such as induction and socialization, and management development. Often there is an imbalance between hiring and developing in favour of the former. For instance, Western multinationals have tended to rely on hiring talent from local labour markets (e.g. in Asia) rather than investing more on talent development (Kelly, 2008). There is a danger that HRD processes and practices are not properly aligned with business strategy. Yet, if Kelly's criticism is to be addressed, it is important

Table 10.2 How the HR function can support talent management

Country context	• Gather intelligence in order to understand what is happening in a particular country and how talent can help
	• Research the external labour market and the legal context as these may affect an organization's ability to manage talent effectively
	• Think about the role of learning and development
Cultural awareness	• Learn about other cultures so that managers properly understand a particular country and its customs
	• Promote and embrace diversity
Market awareness	• Recognize and understand the differences in consumer needs and expectations across global markets
	• Understand the ways in which low- and middle-income countries use talent differently
Internationalization of talent	• Use international postings and assignments to equip managers with necessary skills
	• Develop management and leadership skills
Legal awareness	• Understand local legislation and the impact this can have on how a business is managed

Source: CIPD (2010b).

for talent development to be viewed as a strategic approach (Morgan and Jardin, 2010: 24). As Chapter 9 explains, SHRD encompasses individual and organizational development which is inextricably linked with the cultivation of a supportive, learning-oriented culture within which change is embraced. Given that talent management embraces both individual and organizational development (OD), particularly in response to changing and complex operating environments, the creation and maintenance of a supportive, people-oriented culture is crucial to talent management. HRD and OD are interrelated concepts that can be differentiated in theory but much less so in practice (Mankin, 2009). Consequently, both HR and OD professionals have 'a great opportunity to solidify their standing as strategic business partners who drive sustainable high performance at both the organizational and individual levels. If they make the right moves, they can get out in front and literally skate to where the talent management puck is headed' (Morgan and Jardin, 2010: 29). The sporting metaphor may be rather clumsy, but it does capture the action-orientation of these concepts.

In terms of individual development, Sumardi et al (2010) highlight the importance of coaching and mentoring for developing top talent. These are important drivers of devolved informal learning whereby the HRD professional has an indirect impact on developing employees and is more concerned with interventions that develop the skills of managers and support the nurturing of an appropriate learning culture (Mankin, 2009). A study of Singapore Airlines shows that when a firm 'has good people in the first place, investment in training and retraining can yield outstanding results' (Heracleous et al, 2006: 152).

Implicit in individual- and organization-level initiatives is the adoption of a facilitation role by HR professionals, and this requires support from HRD practioners:

> As facilitators, HR professionals are attuned to the processes of macro and micro change. At the micro level, they facilitate team meetings and planning sessions. At the macro level, they facilitate large-scale change. . . . As facilitators, HR professionals can help negotiate not only what should be changed but how to go about making the desired change happen. In daily interactions, HR professionals should have an agenda for how the culmination of diverse activities keeps the organisation moving toward a longer-term success (Ulrich et al, 2009: 106).

 ## Case study 10.1   Talent management in Africa

Company South Africa (CSA) is the pseudonym given by academic researchers to a large company involved in the country's ten principal airports. To date there has been a lack of such studies on South African firms, so this study makes an important contribution to the field of talent management. Over a period of 14 years CSA has been transformed from a fragmented and poorly performing commercial enterprise into one that has a focused strategy and is making a profit. Like many other organizations in Africa (and beyond) it has been experiencing skills shortages. Indeed, 'Skills shortages have become a feature of many African countries . . . [and] competition to attract and retain human capital in the form of talented individuals and the ability to retain them have become a major competitive consideration even when compared to other competitive dimensions such as capital, strategy and even research and development. It is becoming clear that as competition for critical talent heats up, organizations must somehow rethink the strategies they take to retain and attract talent' (Ngozwana and Rugimbana, 2011: 1524–1525). The study involved a survey of managers and employees working for CSA. Managers 'responded very positively to talent management questions relating to issues such as creating tools/processes for talent conversations, developing competency frameworks, determining workforce vulnerabilities and identifying critical jobs' (p. 1527). However, there was a discrepancy with responses from employees. The majority of employees responded less positively. Various concerns were highlighted, including the fact that the organization's mission and purpose did not make them feel that their job was important; they felt that their opinions did not appear to matter to management and that the supervisor did not seem to care about them as persons. They also felt they did not receive any recognition or reward for performing well in their jobs. These concerns are important as they reveal weaknesses at the core of the strategy and effort to implement talent management and employee engagement at CSA' (ibid).

Source

Ngozwana, K. and Rugimbana, R. (2011) Assessment of talent retention strategies: the case of a large South African company (CSA). *African Journal of Business Management*, 5(5), pp. 1524–1527.

Activity

1. What does this case study tell us about other HR strategies, policies, and processes that need to be in place to support a talent management strategy?

2. Apart from skills shortages, what other external factors are likely to be impacting on African firms?

The above quote highlights the centrality of change to HRD processes and practices as well as the importance of informal learning in the workplace (see Chapter 9). The latter can be particularly cost effective and an important factor in times of recession (CIPD, 2010c).

Talent management has brought back into focus the role of career development, an often neglected aspect of HRD theory and practice. The CIPD suggests that organizations should 'help employees to develop a long-term career plan and highlight all the possible progression and development opportunities that could be achieved within your organisation' (CIPD, 2010c: 8). Traditionally career development initiatives have been associated with career development, a concept that has had an indifferent history in recent years. Yet Madhanya and Shann (2010) highlight the importance of employee loyalty to talent management and development, suggesting that building loyalty through employer branding 'can be used as a long term strategy for talent management in any organisation irrespective of size' (p. 47). This differs from the normal HR emphasis on commitment and engagement. Indeed, employee loyalty is often dismissed as a redundant concept in today's global economy. Ultimately talent management has an important development dimension (see Case study 10.2 below).

In a study of attrition rates in the Malaysian service sector, Ho et al (2010) provide an Asian perspective on a range of 'push' and 'pull' factors that have implications for talent management. Push factors exert pressure on an employee to withdraw their labour and look elsewhere for employment. Arguably, this is a fact of life. However, a study by Lehmann (2009)

 Case study 10.2 Perspectives on talent management

Judith Germain, Managing Director of Dynamic Transitions UK, comments: 'Managing talent effectively involves blending the needs for individual talent management with the requirement to develop the entire talent pool in a way that improves the overall standing of the business. Real talent management draws on the ability to make employees more wilfully independent, as well as being able to harness the talents of maverick employees and leaders. Mavericks need particular attention because passion without good intent in the workplace can rapidly become destructive. . . . Traditional talent management techniques and HR initiatives thrive on the organisation's ability and willingness to seek a homogenous response to the company's stated goals. The hope is that an efficient organisation ensues and that litigation around discrimination are reduced or eradicated. Whilst a laudable goal, all too often it can lead to an uninspiring status quo where where challenge is discouraged and top performers feel stifled.'

Source

Germain, J. (2010) How to drive your troublesome talent forward to success. *British Journal of Administrative Management*, Spring, 70, p. 18.

Chris Bones, Principal, Henley Management College, comments that: 'Talent development can only take place successfully if an organisation understands the capabilities it needs to ensure that it can deliver its strategy, understands how best these can be identified and, where gaps exist, how they can be closed. Any organisation needs a wide range of talents to succeed, not just those associated with leadership at the top, and the challenge for professionals in the field is to think through how to define these and how to develop them in those who already work for them, as well as those who may join in the future.'

Source

Cited in CIPD (2006: 2).

At Google, 'We believe we have created a work environment that attracts exceptional people. We know that people value meaning in their work; they want to be involved with things that are important and that are going to make a difference. . . . Talented people are attracted to Google because we empower them to change the world.'

Source

Google Founders' Letter and Owners Manual (2004). Cited in Tappin, S. and Cave, A. (2008) *The Secrets of CEOs*. London: Nichloas Brealey Publishing, pp. 214–215.

Activity

1. To what extent do each of these examples reflect current thinking on talent management?

2. What might be the principal HR implications of each of these statements?

shows that Malaysian firms 'are not very conducive to motivating and retaining talented knowledge workers' (pp. 162–163). In terms of pull factors, these are the 'external conditions that attract employees away from their work, usually to another job, career or employer' (Ho et al, 2010: 19). Lehman (2009) notes from survey data that the primary reason why employees leave is because of management style.

Table 10.3, which is based on a wider range of sources, illustrates how these push and pull factors are not necessarily unique to Asia. There are lessons here for Western firms as well.

However, in countries such as Malaysia and Thailand employees find it difficult to accept changes which manifests as a barrier to the implementation of new HR practices, particularly when these practices are Western in origin (Lehmann, 2009). This is why it is important for Asian firms to develop indigenous HR practices (Mankin, 2009). Indigenous HR practices that focus on issues such as developing employee commitment are still in their infancy in many Asian countries. For instance, in China high employee turnover is prevalent in SMEs which are characterized by low levels of employee commitment and loyalty (Yang and Wang, 2009). The internalization of SMEs means that this type of organization increasingly needs to develop a talent management strategy (Scullion and Collins, 2011). However, in countries such as India the low quality of HR professionals is acting as a barrier to the development of effective HR practices (Rao and Varghese, 2009). This illustrates the extent to which effective talent management practices are reliant on a competent HR function.

10.4 Evaluating the effectiveness of talent management

At the heart of the debate on talent management is the issue of evaluation. However, this has been handled poorly in the past. For instance, human capital evaluation has long been neglected

Table10.3 Push and pull factors of talent management

Push factors	HR response
Poor quality work–life balance	• Provision of flexible working arrangements (time and/or location) • Avoid overloading employees with too much work (e.g. requiring them to stay back after working hours or work on weekends)
Co-workers' relationships (poor social relationships that have negative impact on employee motivation and commitment)	• Develop a culture that promotes learning and trust • Design and incorporate teamwork for task accomplishment • Create a supportive environment so that employees feel as if they are part of a close-knit organization (approximating family ties)
Work stressors (poor working conditions)	• Encourage managers to provide detailed job specifications, procedures, and standards in order to reduce any confusion about the nature and purpose of job roles • Ensure appropriate staffing levels • Provide stress management programmes
Management style (treating employees how they like without fear of repercussions; employees seeking to escape incompetent management)	• Implementing effective management and leadership development programmes • Developing managers as facilitators • Developing leadership skills that are not dependent on position power • Promoting coaching and mentoring • Focus on effective task delegation and empowerment so that employee confidence is developed • Design and implement a performance appraisal system that is fair and not vulnerable to manager bias
Social norms and hierarchies (seniority is a prevalent practice and decision-making processes are top-down; dissatisfaction with lack of career opportunities)	• Moving away from traditional social norms in which subordinate roles do not disagree with the decisions made by senior roles • Redesigning traditional top-down decision-making processes and empowering knowledge workers to make their own decisions • Providing career development opportunities for talented employees

(continued)

Table10.3 *(continued)*

Pull factors	HR response
Terms and conditions of employment (pay, work–life balance, job security)	• Offering competitive compensation schemes • Offering greater job security • Promoting and nurturing employee engagement
Organizational vision and values (tangible and meaningful)	• Promoting values such as trust that are tangible and not simply rhetoric • Developing employer brand • Ensuring HR practices are fully aligned with the firm's business strategy
Stimulating work	• Offering work that is more stimulating and rewarding for the employee • Tapping into employee creativity • Providing varied job tasks • Encouraging job enrichment and job rotation
Promotional opportunities	• Provide clear promotional criteria • Develop transparent career paths • Provide employees with opportunities to learn skills and procedures for career development • Encourage training and lifelong learning

Sources: Lehman, 2009; Davies and Kourdi, 2010; Ho et al, 2010; Vaiman, 2010; Berger and Berger, 2011; Caplan, 2011.

as part of business reporting (CIPD, 2007), while the evaluation of training and development has been handled in a highly inconsistent manner (Mankin, 2009). Evaluation is crucial if decision making is to be fully informed (CIPD, 2007). Measuring the effectiveness of talent should involve the calculation of return on investment (ROI), but only if the data can be validated (Hall, 2008). This does reflect a 'hard' approach to HRM particularly when Hall adds: 'Performance improvements require a clearly defined aim and a disciplined system for delivering that aim' (ibid: 163). There is growing indication that the Asia region evaluates learning and development projects more thoroughly than in the West, with more than one-third of firms measuring expected outcomes, more than half linking learning and talent development with key performance indicators, and about one-fifth conducting ROI and cost–benefit analysis as well as other softer dimensions (CIPD, 2010d: 2). Over twice as many Indian firms have metrics for talent management than their US equivalents (Capelli et al, 2010).

To date there has not been a great deal written about measuring the effectiveness of talent management strategies, and this may well reflect the poor track record of evaluating HRD initiatives, particularly in the UK and Europe, as suggested above. This is despite the existence of a wide a range of strategic- and operational-level measurement systems. Research carried out on behalf of the CIPD shows that 'where the effectiveness of talent management practices is evaluated, the most popular forms of evaluation tend to be feedback—both from line managers (63%) and the employees involved in the initiatives (53%)' (CIPD, 2010d: 7). As Ulrich et al (2009) argue in relation to competence and commitment of talented employees:

> Leaders can assess the extent to which their organisation regularly attracts and keeps top talent and the extent to which that talent is fully applied for optimal performance. . . . Competence of employees can be tracked by assessing the percentage of employees who have the skills to do their job today and in the future, by benchmarking current employees against competitors, and by productivity measures that track employee output per unit of employee input. . . . Leaders can track commitment through retention of the top employees . . . [and] through employee attitude surveys done frequently as pulse checks and by direct observation as executives intuitively sense the engagement level of employees (pp. 38–39).

The problem with these and similar proposals is that they do not offer leaders, managers, and professionals anything new. The history of training and development is littered with such methods and yet evaluation remains the Achilles' heel of HR functions. There also tends to be too much emphasis on efficiency and not enough on effectiveness. This is because it is far easier to identify metrics for efficiency. Data on effectiveness tend to be more qualitative (and therefore more subjective) and difficult to capture accurately. For instance, how do you ensure consistency in executive intuition such that employees are treated fairly and equitably?

Ultimately, Western firms need to address two challenges. The first is the growing competition for talent from Asia's emerging economies. The second is aptly captured by Capelli (2008):

> Talent management practices, especially in the United States, fall into two equally dysfunctional camps. The first and most common is to do nothing—making no attempt to anticipate your needs and developing no plans for addressing them. This reactive approach, which effectively relies on outside hiring, has begun to fail now that the surplus of management talent has eroded. The second strategy, which is common among older companies, relies on complex bureaucratic models of forecasting and succession planning from the 1950s (p. 2).

It is not surprising that the concept of talent management continues to occupy the attention of theorists and professionals.

 ## Conclusion

Talent management is considered to be one of the most important challenges facing organizations in today's globalized economy. Global demand for talent has become increasingly competitive. Initially the focus of talent management was on addressing skills shortages at senior management level, but broader alternative perspectives have since emerged which encompass the assessment, deployment, and development of key employees. It is this focus on key employees that differentiates talent management from the broader concept of HRD which embraces all employees. As with HRD the theory and practice of talent management should be treated as a strategic imperative. The processes and practices associated with talent management highlight the extent to which the concept is inextricably linked with the role of HR and SHRM. They range from the acquisition and integration of new workers to the development and retention of current workers; Table 10.2 listed these in more detail. To date there has not been a great deal written about measuring the effectiveness of talent management strategies and this is an area where the HR function could make an important contribution.

Summary

The chapter has discussed a range of issues surrounding the concept of talent management, including:

- How talent management can be defined.
- The relationship between talent management and human capital management.
- The relationship between talent management and HRD.
- The relationship between talent management and SHRM.
- The challenges facing the effective implementation of talent management in global markets.
- The potential role of the HR function in managing and developing talent.
- The importance of measuring the effectiveness of talent management processes and practices.

 Review questions

1. How can you best define the concept of talent management?
2. Which HRM processes are most commonly associated with talent management?
3. Why has talent management emerged as such an important topic?
4. What are the principal differences between human capital management and talent management?
5. What are the principal push and pull factors associated with talent management?

 End-of-chapter case study   The role of HR in developing organizational capabilities in Nokia

Nokia is Finland's best known company and its area of business reflects Finland's position as one of the world's leading ICT specialist countries. Finland has been particularly adept at exploiting the internet for e-commerce, having one of the highest internet connection rates globally. The economy is underpinned by a well educated and trained workforce. Since the mid-1990s adult education and training has become an increasingly important feature of national policy and is available in over one thousand institutions, although the majority of adult learning takes place within organizations in the form of training provision or workplace learning. Finland has been able to realize the benefits of a knowledge-based economy, achieving excellent levels of productivity, innovation, and competitiveness. National Vocational Education and Training has been heavily influenced by the EU commitment to the development of a learning society and competence-based training. Training practice in Finnish organizations has been regarded as being quite innovative, drawing upon a wide range of learning and development interventions including the implementation of new types of training course, the facilitation of workplace learning, and the utilization of organizational intranets

In 1999 Nokia appointed a new head of HR, Hallstein Moerk, who set out to design a global approach to HRM. The first step involved putting in place some new basic HR tools and systems (e.g. global recruitment and performance management systems). The second step was to improve and maximize employee commitment and engagement through a focus on development, recognition, and employee wellbeing. The third step was to begin the improvement of organizational capabilities which entailed a great deal of time and effort. In the past Nokia was renowned for its ability to be innovative and flexible and now needs to be even more so as global competition increases, industry boundaries blur, and the pace of change becomes more intense.

This means that as the company moves forward there will need to be increasing emphasis on finding new ways of working. The HR function is playing an important role in this process. For instance, there is a shift in emphasis from traditional training courses to action learning settings (e.g. Nokia's global leadership development programme): 'Nokians have discovered that learning comes from action, experiences, new jobs, living in a new country, and participating in action learning settings.' There is also an emphasis today on HR processes and practices that attract talent worldwide to ensure diversity, the improvement of creativity and innovation, and the enhancement of consumer satisfaction with Nokia's products and services. The company has been seeking to improve retention of talented employees through the improvement of management skills and teamwork.

These changes have paralleled the firm's decision to divest its non-core activities, such as paper, rubber, footwear, chemicals, and cables, in order to focus on its core business of telecommunications. In February 2011 the company announced its new strategic direction, broadly covering the following areas:

- Plans for a broad strategic partnership with Microsoft to build a new global mobile ecosystem with Windows Phone serving as Nokia's primary smartphone platform.
- A renewed approach to capture volume and value growth to connect 'the next billion' to the internet in developing growth markets.
- Focused investments in next-generation disruptive technologies.
- A new leadership team and organizational structure with a clear focus on speed, results, and accountability.

The firm's continued growth reflects its investment in research and development as well as its acquisitions and divestments. Currently, it is the world's largest manufacturer of phones and a globally recognized brand.

Sources

Wetherly, P. and Otter, D. (2008) *The Business Environment: Themes and Issues*. Oxford: Oxford University Press.
Mankin, D.P. (2009) *Human Resource Development*. Oxford: Oxford University Press.
Steinbock, D. (2010) *Winning Across Global Markets: How Nokia Creates Strategic Advantage in a Fast-Changing World*. San Francisco, CA: Jossey-Bass. http://investors.nokia.com/phoenix.zhtml?c=107224&p=irol-newsArticle&ID=1527949&highlight= (accessed 11 March 2011).

Case study questions

1. In terms of talent management, to what extent is it possible to discern both vertical and horizontal strategic alignment in this case study?

2. In what ways could the role of the HR function be changed in order to provide better support for Nokia's talent management strategy?

3. What might be the principal barriers to implement any changes identified in answering the second question?

Further reading

Caplan, J. (2011) *The Value of Talent: Promoting Talent Management Across the Organisation*. London: Kogan Page.
This is a very good text which is written in a straightforward manner.

Garrow, V. and Hirsh, W. (2008) Talent management: issues of focus and fit. *Public Personnel Management*, 37(4), pp. 389–402.
This article provides some useful insights into the meaning and purpose of talent management from a strategic perspective.

Lehmann, S. (2009) Motivating talents in Thai and Malaysian service firms. *Human Resource Development International*, 12(2), pp. 155–170.
This article provides a very good insight into some of the challenges facing Asian firms.

Scullion, H. and Collings, D.G. (2011) Global talent management: introduction. In H. Scullion and D.G. Collings (eds) *Global Talent Management*. Abingdon: Routledge.
This is an excellent new text on the concept of talent management. It is slim but packed full of topical chapters.

Vaiman, V. (2010) *Talent Management of Knowledge Workers*. Basingstoke: Palgrave Macmillan.
This book focuses on a particular type of employee: the knowledge worker. It can also be read in conjunction with Chapter 13 on knowledge management.

 For additional material on the content of this chapter please visit the supporting Online Resource Centre www.oxfordtextbooks.co.uk/orc/truss.

11 SHRM and employment relations

 Learning Objectives

By the end of this chapter you should be able to:

- Explain the fundamentals of the employment relationship and the implications for SHRM.
- Critically evaluate the choices open to organizations in their approach to managing employment relations and understand the factors likely to influence these choices.
- Identify the various sources of legal regulation in employment relations and critically evaluate the ways in which employers may respond to regulation.
- Understand the significance of employee voice and the various mechanisms for enabling voice.

 Key Concepts

Perspectives on employment relations
Choices in managing employment relations
Voluntarism and interventionism
Employee voice

11.1 Introduction

This chapter is divided into four main sections. It starts with an introduction to the field of employment relations and discusses how it relates to SHRM. At the outset a number of definitions will be presented and key concepts introduced. The second section is concerned with examining the choices open to managers in the way in which they manage employment relations and will also examine the kinds of factors likely to influence these choices. Third, the chapter considers the legal regulation of the employment relationship. Whilst space does not permit examination of the detail of regulation, the chapter will explore the sources of regulation (national and international) and discuss how employers may wish to respond and what the consequences of such choices may be. Finally, in this chapter we examine the notion of employee voice. We examine the different means by which it may be expressed and some of the challenges associated with implementation.

11.2 Employment relations

Employment relations can be defined as 'the study of the regulation of the employment rela-tionship between employer and employee, both collectively and individually' (Rose, 2008: 9). This is similar to how the term 'industrial relations' has been defined more recently (see, for example, Edwards, 2003), but employment relations has been used here to stress the inclu-sion of individual as well as collectively determined relations. The employment relationship is in essence the deal that is struck between the employee and the employer to govern paid employment and which is likely to be the subject of ongoing renegotiation as the needs and circumstances of the parties to the relationship change. This is at the heart of SHRM since it defines the nature and character of the relationship that an organization has with its employees.

At one level the employment relationship is an economic transaction, where the employer purchases time and skills from the employee for some pre-agreed level of remuneration. However, the nature of the employment relationship is more complex, in that the employee provides an ability to work, rather than work per se, and as a result there is a need for a means to establish how much and what work is done and how this is determined (Edwards, 2003; 2010). Whilst the economic basis of the relationship is clearly important, ongoing employ-ment relationships will also often involve some form of social exchange (Blau, 1964), where obligations are generated through a series of transactions between two parties over time (Emerson, 1976), but where there is no prior agreement between the parties about how these obligations will be discharged (Molm et al, 1999).

Furthermore the employment relationship is not usually confined to a simple, single transac-tion. Instead the employment relationship is normally ongoing and as a result has a dynamic quality. What both the employer and the employee seek from the relationship is likely to change over time and needs to be seen in the light of the external and internal context changes examined in Chapters 1 and 2. In contemporary organizations employers may seek more than time and skills from their employees; they may be looking for flexibility in the way in which they use labour, for loyalty, and for the willingness to go the extra mile in order to meet customer demands, and therefore require something different from the relationship. Employees may seek job and income security, but they may also be looking for a degree of satisfaction from interesting and/or meaningful work, the opportunity for progression and development, and the flexibility to balance the demands of work with other aspects of their life. The ongoing nature of the employment relationship means that it needs to have some form of mechanism for change.

 Critical Reflection

Think about what is being 'bought' and 'sold' in the employment relationship.
- How easy is it to specify these things in the terms of the contract of employment?
- What might be the implications for SHRM?

The study of employment relations has traditionally focused on the rules and rule-making processes governing the employment relationship (Clegg, 1979). The rules governing the employment relationship may exist in a variety of forms and may be both formal and informal. They may be found, for example, in the following:

- Contracts of employment (including any appendages such as an Employee Handbook).
- Collective agreements made between the employer and a recognized trade union.
- Legislation and statutory instruments.
- Common law.
- Custom and practice.[1]

 Critical Reflection

- Think about a workplace you are familiar with and identify the informal, unwritten rules which have become established through custom and practice.
- How might managers go about trying to change these rules?

11.2.1 Perspectives on the employment relationship

There are a number of ways of understanding the basis of the employment relationship. In a seminal work Alan Fox (1966) distinguished between what he termed the unitary and the pluralistic perspectives on employment relations. Below we examine each briefly and consider what they mean for understanding the conduct and development of the employment relationship.

- **Unitary:** under this perspective the employer and the employee are seen to have common interests. Harmony, not conflict, is seen as a natural state of affairs in the employment relationship. Where conflict does occur it is seen to be as a result of miscommunication or as the work of troublemakers.

- **Pluralistic:** under this perspective, conflict in the employment relationship is seen as inevitable, since the parties are seen to have differing interests. Both parties are seen as seeking to maximize their own interests—employers might want higher productivity and reduced costs, whereas employees might want higher wages in return for their labour. In this perspective the approach for employers is to attempt to manage conflict, rather than to avoid or suppress it.

Table 11.1 summarizes the assumptions underpinning each perspective and how each perspective views the nature of conflict, the way to resolve it, and the role trade unions can play.

In essence these perspectives rest on very different assumptions about the nature of the employment relationship. Accordingly, the employer adopting a unitary perspective is likely to

---

[1]Custom and practice represents informal norms and expectations of behaviour in a workplace which are not written down and are subject to tacit rather than formal agreement.

Table 11.1 Perspectives on employee relations

	Unitary	Pluralistic
Assumptions	Integrated groups. Common values, interests, and objectives	Coalescence of sectional groups. Different values, interests, and objectives
Nature of conflict	Single (managerial) authority and loyalty structure. Irrational	Competing authorities and loyalty structures. Inevitable and rational
Resolution of conflict	Coercion	Compromise and agreement
Role of trade unions	Intrusion from outside. Only accepted (if forced) in economic relations	Legitimate. Integral to work organization. Accepted role in economic and managerial relations

Source: adapted from Salamon, M. (2000) *Industrial Relations Theory and Practice*, 4th edn. London: FT Prentice Hall.

take a non-union stance, since managerial prerogative is seen as legitimate and rational. However, the employer may put in place other mechanisms for employee voice (see below for further discussion), since it may be recognized that employees can usefully contribute knowledge and ideas to organizational decision making. The employer adopting a pluralistic perspective is likely to be interested in allowing employee interests to be heard, since it is believed that multiple and conflicting interests exist and, as such, trade unions or other representative bodies are seen as important mechanisms in reaching a compromise. These perspectives are ways of understanding the employment relationship and do not translate into a managerial approach per se. However, an understanding of these perspectives can help us both to understand what is informing an approach adopted by an employer and to interpret such actions.

 Critical Reflection

Identify an industrial dispute currently being reported in the media. What perspective do you think is being taken?

11.3 Choice in managing employment relations

In this section we examine the choices open to managers in the approaches they adopt to managing employment relations and explore some of the factors that influence these choices. This discussion should be seen in the context of Strategic Management and HR strategy outlined in Chapters 5 to 8. Employers have a number of options open to them in the way in which they conduct employment relations. Whilst historically much research attention has been paid to the activities of trade unions, managers have considerable opportunity to shape employment relations and in more recent years managers, not trade unions, have been responsible for initiating major change in employment relations (Kochan, 2000).

If managers are viewed as agents of capital then it may be assumed that they are concerned with minimizing costs and maximizing efficiency and profits (Sisson and Marginson, 2003); however, the concern here is how they choose to go about achieving those goals. There have been a number of attempts to categorize the approaches that managers can take (e.g. Fox, 1974; Purcell, 1981; 1987; McLoughlin and Gourley, 1992; Kitay and Marchington, 1996). Essentially, these are built around key areas of policy and practice that managers may make choices about in managing employment relations.

 Key Concept

Choice in managing employment relations includes areas such as:

- The degree of formalization in the relationship.
- The extent to which the relationship will be based on trust.
- The overall approach to the conduct of the relationship—driven by a desire to be cooperative, or the preparedness to be adversarial to bring about change.
- Whether or not to recognize a trade union for collective bargaining purposes.
- Whether/how to combine individual and collective approaches to employment relations.

The degree of formalization concerns the extent to which rules and regulations are developed to govern the conduct of the employment relationship. They may include rules concerned with the economic aspects of employment relationship (substantive) and the behaviour of the parties involved in the employment relationship (procedural). On the one hand, a high degree of formalization allows managers to control and regulate but, on the other, may limit organizational flexibility and inhibit their ability to utilize employees' creative capability as a resource.

Choices about how the relationship will be conducted will influence the activities of managers on a day-to-day basis, as well as those involved in formalized processes and negotiations. An employer might choose to pursue cooperative relations, or alternatively they might opt for more conflictual or adversarial relations (Kitay and Marchington, 1996). Pursuing a cooperative approach will usually mean that the employer is taking a longer-term view and that they may in some circumstances be prepared to make concessions or deal with matters in a different way in order to reach an agreement and preserve the quality of the relationship they have with their employees or a representative trade union (see QinetiQ case study at the end of the chapter). Whilst in most circumstances cooperation is likely be preferable to conflictual or adversarial relations, there may be circumstances where employers are prepared to take a conflictual approach if they feel that there are certain goals that need to be achieved in order to bring about organizational change. Employers also need to consider the extent to which they wish to pursue relations based on high or low trust. To pursue a high-trust approach is, however, not a simple choice since trust takes effort to build and can sometimes be destroyed by careless actions or lack of forethought (Dietz et al, 2010). However, research shows that there are many benefits to be gained by developing trust (Dirks and Ferrin, 2001), and as a result investing in and protecting trust relations with employees may reap significant benefits for the organization.

Finally, employers need to make choices about the extent to which they wish or are prepared to deal with relations through a trade union acting as a collective representation of employees' interests. Employers may pursue a union recognition strategy, a union substitution, or avoidance strategy (Beaumont, 1987). Some employers see considerable benefits to be gained from operating with trade unions, and taking a collective approach may not necessarily exclude pursuing an individual approach also. Those adopting a union substitution approach may seek to provide themselves the benefits, such as improved pay and conditions and fair treatment, which employees may gain through the trade union. In practice, though, employers may not have a free choice in this respect, since in many countries there are legal provisions that require employers to recognize a trade union for bargaining purposes, if certain conditions are fulfilled. In the UK the Employment Relations Act 1999 requires employers with more than 20 workers to recognize a trade union where the trade union can demonstrate that following a secret ballot it has the support of 40% of those working in the bargaining unit, as well as the majority of those voting. Alternatively, they will have to demonstrate that more than 50% of the workers in the unit are members of the union. However, in spite of these legislative provisions some employers remain resolutely non-union. One of the best-documented examples of this is McDonald's which has pursued a non-union approach throughout its global expansion (see, for example, Royle, 1998; 2005; 2006). In response to a question about working with trade unions on 'Make Up Your Own Mind', a website set up by the company to provide information about McDonald's food, business, people, and practices, the following answer was given

The company does not currently work with any trade union. While McDonald's is not anti-trade union, it believes that the company has sufficient methods of engaging with employees without the need to involve a third party. It believes in good, open dialogue between employees and the company, and works with employees and franchisees to make sure this happens both in restaurants and within the organization as a whole (http://www.makeupyourownmind.co.uk/question-search?key=trade+unions#question3).

 Critical Reflection

Identify what you think are the main advantages and disadvantages for employers of working with a trade union.

In Fig. 11.1 we present a three-dimensional typology of managerial approaches to employment relations developed by Kitay and Marchington (1996). The dimensions are based on the degree to which managers are proactive/reactive in managing employment relations; the

MANAGEMENT STRATEGY

	Proactive		Reactive	

EMPLOYEE ORGANIZATION

NATURE OF MANAGEMENT–EMPLOYEE INTERACTION

	Cooperative	Adversarial	Cooperative	Adversarial
Non-union	Early and extensive communication with employees. Use of consultation if it exists. Planned change	Management formulates plans early, informs employees of changes late	Ad hoc unilateral management action, without pre-planning. Frequent resort to communication retrospectively	Ad hoc unilateral management action. Little or no information provided by management. Change imposed on employees
Inactive unions	Early and extensive communication with employees. Consultation with full-time union officials	Management formulates plans early, informs individual employees and union officials late	Ad hoc management action with late involvement of union officials and employees	Ad hoc unilateral management action. Little or no information provided by management. Frequent resort to third party to resolve impasses
Active unions	Integrative bargaining with workplace union representatives plus communication with employees. Active involvement of unions	Management formulates plans early, distributive bargaining with workplace union representatives late	Amicable joint problem solving on a short-term basis with workplace union representatives	Classic conflictual relations. Information given under duress. Change effected/resisted through exercise of power

Figure 11.1 Typology of change in workplace industrial relations.

Source: Kitay, J. and Marchington, M. (1996) A review and critique of industrial relations typologies. *Human Relations*, 49, pp. 1263–1290.

nature of the management–employee interaction (from cooperative to adversarial); and employee organization (non-union, inactive unions, and active unions). They take proactive to be the extent to which there is alignment between the business objectives and the approach adopted to employee relations (McLoughlin and Gourley, 1992); internal consistency across the range of employee relations policies; and a clearly articulated approach to employee relations.

Whilst it is acknowledged that employers can take an active role in shaping employment relations, it also needs to be recognized that managers will face constraints and as such decisions need to be considered in the context in which they are made. For example, the business system may impose legal and/or institutional constraints on the way in which the employer operates. This may present additional challenges for multinationals that operate across countries that have different business systems. In addition, factors such as nature of the business, the organization's strategy, the economic context, and history are likely to influence the approach managers adopt.

The strategy adopted and the role employees play in the delivery of the strategy may influence the extent to which an employer prefers to adopt a conflictual or cooperative approach. For example, for a service business that competes on the basis of quality and where front-line employees play an important role in determining quality of service delivered (e.g. hospitality, airlines, health care), a cooperative approach may be preferable to a conflictual approach, since poor quality employment relations may be reflected in employee behaviour which could jeopardize quality of service. These decisions also need to be in line with the wider HR strategy adopted, as discussed in Chapter 7.

The nature of the business activity undertaken may also have an influence. For example, an employer may wish to avoid a conflictual approach where the costs associated with any industrial action could be high and have implications for the future of the organization. In other circumstances employers may feel that the risks associated with a protracted and/or acrimonious dispute are a price worth paying, especially when the issue at stake relates to desired organizational change. Equally, history may play a role here. It could, for example, be difficult (and risky) for an employer who has historically recognized a trade union for collective bargaining purposes to decide to take a more unitary stance, especially if trade union membership is high in the organization. Organizations that operate in the public or voluntary sector may have different considerations here. For example, in the public sector there may be other agendas, since governments may use their role as an employer to engineer wider public policy and societal goals (Masters et al, 2008). Furthermore, in recent years the New Public Management ideology, with a focus on performance, has become more influential in the management of public services in many countries (Hood, 2005). Equally, in the voluntary sector decisions about approaches to employment relations may be influenced by the organization's mission or ethos (Cooke, 2004b).

The wider economic context may play a role in influencing employment relations, since it is likely to have an impact on the level of pay increases. This impact may be felt on individual agreements, before collective agreements, since given the annual basis on which collective bargaining processes tend to operate, there may be some time lag before this comes into play. For example, the European Foundation for the Improvement of Living and Working Conditions reported that the economic crisis in Europe from mid-2008 had little immediate effect on collectively agreed pay increases, since they had largely been negotiated before the downturn took hold. However, the effect was more noticeable in 2009, where lower pay increases were the norm.

However, it is always important to remember that the employment relationship is, under most circumstances, an ongoing, dynamic relationship and both employers and employees or their representatives need to consider the long-term implications of any actions they take. In employment relations as in many relationships, we have to live with our past.

 Critical Reflection

Consider the potential costs and benefits for an employer associated with both a cooperative and a conflictual approach. You should reflect on both the long and the short term.

11.4 **Legal regulation**

Historically, employment relations in the UK have been characterized by a tradition of voluntarism, with an absence of significant legal regulation governing the employment relationship. However, from the 1980s onwards there has been a growing framework of legislative provisions concerning the conduct of employers, employees, and their representatives (for a discussion see CIPD, 2011). In this chapter we do not have space to consider the detailed content of the legislation. However, we will briefly examine the sources of legal regulation at national, regional, and international levels and consider how employers may respond to these provisions.

 Key Concepts

Voluntarism can be described as an approach where the state seeks to minimize its role in regulating employment relations, since this is seen to be the business of the employer and the employee.
Interventionism is where the state seeks to regulate employment relations through legislation, government policy, and/or its role as an employer.

At national level we have seen legislation enacted in recent years concerning, for example, parental leave, equal treatment of part-time workers, protection for 'whistle blowers', flexible working, minimum wages, and working time. Regional-level regulation stemming from bodies such as the European Union may also be important. For example, the last two areas in the above list were put in place as a result of the UK's obligations under the Social Chapter of the EU. Here, countries agree to overarching regulation of the employment relationship, in order to protect labour standards and to take terms and conditions of employment out of the competitive equation to some degree. The intention here is to prevent employers who are willing to use exploitative practices from thereby gaining a competitive advantage over employers who seek to provide fair terms and conditions of employment. Regulation seeks to avoid so-called social dumping, where unequal standards distort competition for investment in favour of countries with lower labour standards and consequently inhibits the integration of social policy across the EU. The EU, it is argued, is unique amongst world economic groupings in that it combines a market-building agenda with a social agenda that includes emerging transnational industrial relations arrangements (European Commission, 2008). It is also argued by the European Commission that the EU has been at least in part responsible for achieving increasing convergence in European industrial relations. It argues that, together with a consensus around a common set of values and standards in relation to the conduct of industrial relation, the EU has encouraged convergence and the establishment of EU-wide objectives for member states, through social dialogue and the exercise of its regulatory powers (European Commission, 2008).

At international level the International Labour Organization (ILO) based in Geneva is perhaps one of the most influential organizations in attempting to regulate global labour standards. The ILO issues conventions, which are legally binding international treaties, and recommendations, which are non-binding guidelines for member states. Countries that choose to sign up to ILO treaties then take on the responsibility to ensure that local mechanisms are in place in order to ensure that they fulfil their obligations as a signatory to the convention (see case study below). The ILO Declaration on Fundamental Rights at Work covers four areas and is deemed to be a central plank of what is considered decent work. These areas are:

- Freedom of association and the right to collective bargaining.
- The elimination of forced and compulsory labour.
- The elimination of discrimination in the workplace.
- The abolition of child labour.

 Case study 11.1 Freedom of Association

In 2008 the ILO Committee on the Freedom of Association requested the government of Mauritius to review its Public Gathering Act, since Mauritius has ratified the Freedom of Association and Protection of the Right to Organise Convention and the Right to Organise and Collective Bargaining Convention. This followed a complaint presented to the ILO by the National Trade Unions Confederation (NTUC), the Mauritius Labour Congress (MLC), and the Mauritius Trade Union Congress (MTUC), supported by the International Trade Union Confederation (ITUC). They alleged that the government used repressive measures against the trade union movement, including criminal prosecutions, in violation of the right to strike and engage in protest.

Source

International Labour Office, *351st Report of the Committee on Freedom of Association*, 19 November 2008.

Activity

1. Consider why countries choose to sign up to ILO treaties.
2. How can the ILO ensure countries fulfil their obligations under these treaties?

When faced with these various layers of regulation employers may respond in a number of different ways. First, they may choose to embrace the spirit of the legislation and possibly go beyond the actual legal obligations. They may choose to comply with legislation at the basic level. In other words, they may choose to fulfil the letter but not necessarily the spirit of the law. Alternatively, employers might choose to disregard the legislation and deal with consequences if they are forced to do so.

In the UK many large employers have opted to go beyond their legal obligations under the 'right to request' flexible working legislation by making the opportunity to request flexible working open to all employees, not just parents and carers provided for under the legislation (Nadeem and Metcalf, 2007). Decisions made about responses to regulation are of strategic importance to the organization, since there are both risks and potential benefits associated with the different approaches. At one level, compliance is likely to result in associated cost since it may be necessary to put new policies and procedures in place. Where an employer chooses to embrace the sentiment behind the legislation it may be because they support the principle (for example, it is considered morally wrong not to ensure a safe working environment is provided), or it may be because they believe that there will be some business benefits from this approach (high safety standards will reduce potentially costly workplace accidents and sickness absence). Furthermore an employer who has a reputation for embracing both the spirit and the letter of the law may be seen as a responsible employer and this may enhance their position in the labour market, allowing them to be more effective in the recruitment and retention of high-calibre talent. They may also reap benefits gained from perceptions of justice on the part of the employee. For well-known employers, being in the public eye for poor employment practice or through press reports of tribunal cases may harm their reputation not only as an employer but also as an organization to do business with. Many organizations make public statements about their values, and if these are to be credible, the organization must be seen to be living those values in the way in which they interact with their employees.

At international level there may be strong incentives for states to comply with international labour standards. Being a signatory to the ILO Declaration on Fundamental Rights at Work and being seen to enforce these obligations may be a way in which a country can improve its attractiveness for inward investment. A multinational company, for example, may only wish to locate itself in a country where minimum labour standards are adhered to for corporate social responsibility (CSR) reasons and/or to protect itself from the negative consequences of adverse publicity if its labour standards are found to be wanting.

Other sources of regulation may be by agreement. For example, large multinational employers who work with trade unions may opt to sign a Global Framework Agreement (GFA) with a Global Union Federation (GUF). Through this type of agreement the employer commits to adhering to a set of minimum labour standards, wherever they operate in the world, irrespective of the local-level regulation in place. GUFs are federations of trade unions and so the local trade union can play a role in monitoring employment practice and ensuring that the agreed standards are maintained. For some employers a major advantage of a GFA is that there is local-level monitoring. A number of companies have struggled to monitor their labour standards throughout the supply chain and setting up a central team to monitor this may have only limited success.

11.5 Employee voice

In this section we explore the notion of employee voice. We examine definitions, the different forms that voice may take, and what employer and employee motivations might be for participating in mechanisms for allowing employee voice to be expressed. Finally we examine some of the wider implications associated with implementing mechanisms for employee voice in organizations.

The term 'employee voice' refers to circumstances where employees are given the opportunity to have some input into organizational decision making. Voice has been the language increasingly adopted by academics and practitioners in recent years (Wilkinson et al, 2004). However, we also see terms such as industrial democracy, employee participation, and employee involvement used and we will examine the differences between them here.

Key Concept

In essence, the notion of **employee voice** is concerned with allowing employees to put forward their ideas and views and have these taken into account when organizational decisions are made. What is important here is that the ability to influence the outcome of organizational decisions is accorded to those who, under traditional hierarchies, would not normally have the opportunity to do so (Wagner, 1994).

Freeman and Medoff (1984) who originally coined the 'voice' term used it to relate to both consensual and conflictual forms of voice. Consensual voice describes circumstances where an employee might contribute to improving organizational performance through contributing ideas and suggestions. Conflictual forms of voice describe a mechanism where employees can channel discontent. In this context there are two potential elements of voice: grievance processes and opportunities for input into organizational decision making (McCabe and Lewin, 1992). Other writers have distinguished between employee participation and involvement (Hyman and Mason, 1995).

- **Participation** relates to employee rights to have their interests represented in organizational decision making.
- **Involvement** refers to management-led practices where employee input is seen to assist in the achievement of organizational objectives.

Employee involvement represents a situation similar to consensual voice and is often implemented at the level of task decisions, allowing individuals or work groups to contribute. Employee participation is similar to conflictual voice, but may go beyond the channeling of discontent by establishing the representation of employee interests in the decision-making process. This normally takes place through some form of collective representation, and non-union firms may deliberately set up representative mechanisms for the purposes of employee voice. In many European countries mechanisms for employee participation start from the premise that employees have a right to be informed about and participate in decisions that affect their working lives, consistent with a democratic society. As Towers (1997) remarks:

> Industrial democracy can be regarded as an extension of political democracy. If citizens have a fundamental right to be included in the making of decisions which affects their interests, they have an equally fundamental right to be part of the rule-making processes which regulate their working lives.

Examples of consensual voice or employee involvement include briefing groups (downward communications), teamworking, quality circles, continuous improvement groups, and employee suggestion schemes (upward communication). Examples of conflictual voice or employee participation include joint consultation committees, works councils, and employee surveys. Table 11.2 compares employee involvement and participation according to a number of dimensions.

Table 11.2 A comparison of employee involvement and employee participation

Employee involvement	Employee participation
Management inspired and controlled	Government or workforce inspired; some control delegated to workforce
Geared to stimulating individual employee contributions under strong market conditions	Aims to harness collective employee inputs through market regulation
Directed to responsibilities of individual employees	Collective representation
Management structures flatter, but hierarchies undisturbed	Management hierarchy chain broken
Employees often passive recipients	Employee representatives actively involved
Tends to be task based	Decision making at higher organizational levels
Assumes common interests between employer and employees	Plurality of interests recognized and machinery for their resolution provided
Aims to concentrate strategic influence among management	Aims to distribute strategic influence beyond management

Source: Hyman, J. and Mason, B. (1995) *Managing Employee Involvement and Participation*. London: Sage Publications.

From a strategic point of view it is important to consider both of these mechanisms. Consensual voice or employee involvement may be important since employees can be a valuable resource in improving organizational decisions as a result of the detailed and sometimes unique knowledge about the operation of organizational systems and process that they possess through the daily conduct of their jobs. For instance, in a customer service environment it may be that employees who have frequent and regular contact with customers are best placed to understand what contributes to customer satisfaction. According to the unitary perspective discussed earlier, employees would be expected to be willing to share their ideas and suggestions if they saw this as a means of contributing to organizational success. However, if we adopt a pluralistic perspective, then conflictual voice and/or employee participation also becomes important. Where conflict is seen as integral to the employment relationship, employers who wish to actively manage conflict would be advised to identify a mechanism for the expression of interests so attempts can be made to resolve conflict. Furthermore, the opportunity to express grievance may influence the way in which an employee responds to his or her employer and may impact on workforce retention. As Hirshman (1970) has observed, where employees are dissatisfied with their organization and there is no opportunity for voice, exit may be their response.

In practice the presence of employee voice in an organization can be examined in a number of ways (Wilkinson et al, 2004) including:

- The existence of mechanisms to facilitate employee voice (Folger, 1977).
- A climate that encourages employees to put forward their ideas and opinions.
- The extent to which voice is associated with influence, i.e. do employee ideas and opinions really have an impact on the outcome of decisions?

These are important distinctions, since the simple existence of systems or procedures will not ensure that they are utilized or that they are effective in allowing employees to influence decisions. Only if these two are achieved will any benefits from voice be realized. Employee perceptions of the opportunity to put forward their views and to have these taken into account in the decision-making process, rather than simply the existence of voice mechanisms, are important in influencing behaviour. There is evidence that employee perceptions of voice have a positive effect on employee outcomes such as organizational commitment (Farndale et al, 2011) and employee engagement (see Chapter 12 for a discussion). Perceptions of voice lead to beliefs about being able to influence decisions and provide recognition to employees that their views are respected by the organization. Voice can contribute to perceptions of fairness both in relation to the outcome of decisions and in relation to the process of decision making (Folger and Konovsky, 1989). Voice may also have a positive impact on the employee-line manager relationship because the employee may feel valued by the line manager who has given him/her the opportunity to influence decisions and which may in turn contribute to improved organizational commitment (Korsgaard et al, 1995).

In Europe, through the European Charter of Fundamental Rights, there has been legislative support for employee voice introduced in the form of the Information and Consultation Regulations 2004. These regulations make provision for employees to be given information and to be consulted about major changes affecting their workplace. The areas covered can be broadly divided into issues concerning the economic context, implications for employment, and/or the organization of work (Storey, 2005). Although initially only covering large employers (150+), since 2008 the regulations cover all organizations with at least 50 employees. Furthermore, for companies in the EU with employees in two or more member states, the European Works Councils Directive requires a European Works Council to be established for information and consultation purposes. The intention here was to curb the power of multinational corporations (MNCs) in one country making decisions that would have implications for employees elsewhere without them having an opportunity to be involved in the decisions.

11.5.1 Implementing employee voice

It needs to be recognized that when mechanisms for employee voice are implemented, irrespective of the form, there are likely to be a number of issues that arise which may need management attention if the implementation is to be successful.

- **Power:** the intention of voice, irrespective of the form, involves some degree of power sharing and redistribution. Sharing power inevitably involves some curtailment of managerial prerogative. It is important to be aware where in the organization this is most likely to be felt. There may be resentment amongst those who are to share their power, especially if they were not involved in the thinking behind and the development of the initiative. Hence, almost by definition, voice is unlikely to be effective if it is imposed on an organization. Salamon (2000) argues that where the existing distribution of power is unequal, there needs to be real commitment to allow employees to influence decisions.

- **Openness:** for benefits to be gained, employee voice needs to operate in an atmosphere of genuine openness and communication.
- **Pro-active stance:** for example, if employee concerns are raised via a voice mechanism set up and sanctioned by the organization, this places some degree of obligation on managers to respond.

A further positive outcome may be that it encourages all employees to think about the organization and what factors influence its success and sustainability.

 ## Conclusion

This chapter has presented a brief overview of employment relations. Employment relations is a large field and has been the subject of much academic study. This chapter has necessarily been selective about what has been included. We have examined those aspects that have strategic importance and which relate to SHRM more generally. We have overviewed the nature of the employment relationship and examined the different perspectives and the choices in managerial approaches. We have explored the sources of legal regulation that global organizations may encounter. We have examined the notion of employee voice, including why and how it might be implemented.

 ## Summary

- Employment relations is at the heart of SHRM since it defines the nature and character of the relationship an organization has with its employees.
- The employment relationship differs from other economic relations in so far as it is indeterminate and ongoing.
- The unitary and pluralistic perspectives represent very different sets of assumptions about the employment relationship. The unitary assumes common interests and a single source of authority, whereas the pluralistic assumes differing interests and therefore the need to reach a compromise.
- Managers may be faced with choices about the approach to employment relations (formality, trust base, character) and whether to recognize one or more trade unions. However, such choices may be influenced by the nature of the business, the strategy adopted, history, the business system, and the economic context.
- Legal regulation of the employment relationship takes place at national, regional, and international levels. Employers may consider whether to embrace the spirit and/or the letter of the law.
- Employee voice may take the form of employee involvement and/or employee participation. Employee involvement tends be individual and task-based and assumes common interests. Participation is normally based on collective representation and aims to allow employee interests to influence higher-level organizational decisions.

 ## Review questions

1. Describe the nature of the employment relationship. In what ways does it differ from other economic relationships?

2. What are the different perspectives on employment relations and what are the main assumptions they are based on?

3. Identify the main things managers need to make choices about in their approaches to employment relations. What might influence these choices?

4. What are the various sources of legal regulation governing the employment relationship and what benefits might be gained from compliance?

5. Explain what is meant by employee voice and the main motivations for establishing mechanisms for voice in the workplace.

 End-of-chapter case study   QinetiQ and Prospect: working together for a sustainable future?

The case study is based on interviews held with Andy Brierley, Group HR Director, QinetiQ, and David Luxton, National Negotiator, Prospect.

QinetiQ is a major provider of technical advice to customers in the global aerospace, defence, and security markets. The company was founded in July 2001 from the former Defence Evaluation and Research Agency and was subsequently privatized in 2006. A significant part of its business is concerned with providing advice to government departments in the UK and the US (e.g. defence, intelligence, and security departments).[1] As a result of significant cuts in government spending, the company is facing a tough trading environment. In November 2009 a new CEO was appointed with the brief of 'putting the business back on its feet'.

In the region of 80% of the 6,300 staff employed in the UK are technical specialists and scientists. The terms and conditions of employment for these staff are determined by collective bargaining between QinetiQ and the trade union Prospect.[2] Approximately 40% of eligible staff are members of Prospect. Prospect has been recognized from the outset as a continuation of the existing arrangement with the Ministry of Defence. Both parties indicated that their relationship had generally been constructive and worked well. However, they had had to deal with some difficult issues over the years and there had been some tough negotiations.

Certain terms and conditions of employment operate on a two-tier basis. Staff who transferred into QinetiQ from the civil service have superior terms relating to redundancy, pensions, and annual leave compared to those who have joined the company since 2001.[3] At the time of the case study, approximately 50% of staff were on pre-2001 and 50% on post-2001 terms and conditions.

In the light of the financial pressures the company faced,[4] the management team felt they were faced with a 'burning platform' and there was a need to take radical action to cut costs across the board, including the costs of employment. The new CEO felt the existing redundancy terms were not sustainable. These arrangements provided 8 weeks' pay for every year of service for those on pre-2001 contracts and 4 weeks' pay for those on post-2001 terms. Based on previous redundancy exercises, the company estimated that it took in the region of 3 years for any savings to be realized. They proposed that the existing arrangements be cut by 50% for both groups of staff, together with a 1.25% pay increase for 2009.

1 For more detail on the company go to http://www.qinetiq.com.
2 For more detail on the trade union go to http://www.Prospect.org.uk.
3 The Transfer of Undertakings (Protection of Employment) Regulations give employees protection when their employer changes as a result of a transfer of undertakings.
4 Group profit warnings were issued in late 2009 and early 2010.

A meeting was called with senior Prospect officials to explain the position and enter into negotiations.[5] Andy Brierley, the Group HR Director, commented, 'We wanted to be honest and open with employees and with the trade unions', and indicated that they were prepared to invest the time to reach a negotiated settlement. QinetiQ wanted to avoid imposing changes and the costs and upset caused by any industrial action. Following a confidentiality agreement, QinetiQ shared detailed financial information with the trade unions to provide support for its proposals.

A period of intense negotiations followed, with 'a fair amount of huffing and bluffing on both sides'. This included the company giving Prospect 6 months' notice of their intention to withdraw from collective agreements and derecognize the trade union for bargaining purposes. The union was taken aback by this action, but as David Luxton, the Prospect National Negotiator, reported, after careful reflection they decided the best response was to re-engage with QinetiQ, in order to attempt to secure the best deal for their members. He commented, 'We could have walked away and called for industrial action, but there was no agreement and even harsher changes could have been forced through'. This action forced the pace of negotiations and after modeling on a number of different cost bases a way forward was proposed. This involved linking the proposed change to redundancy payments to two pay increases—a slightly improved 1.5% for 2009 (which had still not been settled) and a further 2% from July 2010.[6]

Once this agreement had been reached, the next challenge was to convince the membership to vote for it, and both parties undertook a series of communications to this effect. David Luxton commented that the membership were aware of the worsening financial position and that this time they found a more receptive mood than when redundancy terms had been changed 3 years earlier. There was an understanding that some concession was needed in exchange for longer-term job security. A ballot was held and 75% voted in favour of accepting the agreement. The agreement was formally signed at the end of June 2010.

Postscript

Over the next 3 months QinetiQ announced approximately 800 redundancies.

A new recognition agreement was signed on 30 September 2010.

5 QinetiQ recognizes three other trade unions (Unite, Public and Commercial Services Union (PCS), and the GMB). Prospect acts as the chair of the trade union side of the negotiation and consultation committee and led on these negotiations.
6 Andy Brierley indicated a 0% increase would have been a closer reflection of the market.

Case study questions

1. Do you think the concessions made in order to reach an agreement were worthwhile in the longer term? What might have been alternative courses of action?

2. Consider the relative advantages and disadvantages for both parties of linking issues in negotiations. Was the linking of pay rises to reduced redundancy payments a good outcome in this case?

Further reading

Blyton, P., Bacon, N., Fiorito, J. and Heery, E. (2008) *The Sage Handbook of Industrial Relations*. London: Sage Publications.

This handbook is a collection of essays on aspects of employment relations, written by some of the leading writers and researchers in the field.

Hyman, J. and Mason, B. (1995) *Managing Employee Involvement and Participation*. London: Sage Publications.

This book draws together the debates on employee involvement and participation and includes useful data on implementation.

Kersley, B.A.C., Forth, J., Bryson, A., Bewley, H., Dix, G. and Oxenbridge, S. (2006) *Inside the Workplace: Findings from the 2004 Workplace Employment Relations Survey*. London: Routledge.

This book reports the findings on employment relations practice from a large survey of UK employers.

Kitay, J. and Marchington, M. (1996) A review and critique of workplace industrial relations typologies. *Human Relations*, 49(10), pp. 1263.

This article overviews and critiques the various attempts at categorizing managment approaches to employment relations.

http://www.eurofound.eu

This website provides data on employment relations matters across the EU.

http://www.ilo.org

The International Labour Organization website provides detail on the work of the ILO and on global labour standards.

 For additional material on the content of this chapter please access the OUP website www.oxfordtextbooks.co.uk/orc/truss.

12 Employee engagement

 Learning Outcomes

By the end of this chapter you should be able to:

- Explain several definitions of employee engagement and clarify the major facets of engagement.
- Critically evaluate how engagement differs from other, similar constructs.
- Outline some of the key drivers of employee engagement, according to recent research.
- Understand the processes by which engagement leads to a range of outcomes for individuals and employers.
- Appreciate the role that the HR professional can play in managing employee engagement.

 Key Concepts

Engagement strategies
Employee engagement
Engagement consequences
Engagement antecedents

12.1 Introduction

Employee engagement has become something of an international phenomenon over the past few years, driven, on the one hand, by the growing focus within the academic community on positive psychology and, on the other, by the ever-present quest for organizations to find better and more effective ways of motivating staff towards higher performance levels. The UK's Chartered Institute of Personnel and Development (CIPD) has commissioned several research studies on the topic (Truss et al, 2006; Gatenby et al, 2009a; Alfes et al, 2010a), and concluded that engagement is now so important that it has named it as one of the ten required 'professional areas' for HR managers. The UK government also commissioned a nationwide review of the evidence base for employee engagement in 2009 (MacLeod and Clarke, 2009), which asserted that:

If employee engagement and the principles that lie behind it were more widely understood, if good practice was more widely shared, if the potential that resides in the country's workforce was more fully unleashed, we could see a step change in workplace performance and in employee well-being, for the considerable benefit of UK plc (p. 3).

Many consultancy firms around the world have developed their own survey instruments to measure levels of employee engagement and all correlate high levels of engagement with positive outcomes such as performance, low levels of turnover, high levels of employer advocacy, and positive individual wellbeing. The MacLeod Review makes a strong 'business case' for employers to invest in strategies to raise engagement levels; for example, it reports on a number of research studies which showed that:

- Engaged organizations grow profits three times faster than their competitors, reduce turnover by 87%, and improve performance by 20%.

- Organizations with high levels of engagement improved operating income by 19.2% over 12 months, whilst those with low engagement experienced a 32.7% decline.

- Over 12 months, firms with high engagement scores showed a 13.7% improvement in net income growth, whilst those with low engagement saw growth decline by 3.8%.

- Firms scoring in the top half of an engagement index had 27% higher profitability than those in the bottom half.

- Highly engaged employees take on average 2.7 days of sick leave per year compared with 6.2 for disengaged employees.

(MacLeod and Clarke, 2009: 36–37)

The UK's Cabinet Office, responsible for developing policy across the Civil Service, has focused its energies on the development of an employee engagement evaluation survey in order to be able to track trends in engagement levels across the entire Civil Service (http://www.civilservice.gov.uk). In 2011, the UK's coalition government commissioned a second MacLeod Review to build on the findings of the first.

However, from an academic perspective, employee engagement is still very much in its infancy. Its origins can be traced back to a seminal paper by William Kahn, published as recently as 1990 in the *Academy of Management Journal*. In that paper, Kahn set out what he regarded as the distinguishing features of engagement as compared with other, similar and related, constructs. In the next section, we examine Kahn's definition of engagement in more detail, alongside those put forward by other researchers. We then explore the factors that have been described as the drivers of high levels of employee engagement, and those that have been referred to as the outcomes or consequences of engagement. We also discuss throughout some of the tensions and unresolved questions that persist around engagement, as well as the potential importance of engagement for HR professionals.

12.2 What is employee engagement?

Writing in 1990, Kahn defines employee engagement as 'the harnessing of organization members' selves to their work roles; in engagement, people employ and express themselves physically, cognitively, and emotionally during role performances' (p. 694). For Kahn, engagement implies the authentic expression of self at work, whereby individuals invest emotional, cognitive, and physical energy into the performance of their role, and experiences positive connections with those around them. Kahn's research involved a qualitative study of architects and summer camp workers in the US. At the architect's firm, a senior architect experiencing high levels of engagement described how she invested her energy into the project she was working on, thought hard about her work, and was emotionally attuned to the needs of her team, whilst also focusing on producing high-quality work (p. 701). At the opposite extreme, Kahn found that disengagement was characterized by the withdrawal of the person's preferred self, 'a lack of connections, physical, cognitive and emotional absence, and passive, incomplete role performances' (p. 701). He found that disengaged employees kept their preferred selves hidden and were uninvolved in their work, sometimes keeping back their views and opinions, leading to lower levels of performance. He also noted that levels of engagement tend to fluctuate for individuals throughout the working day depending on factors such as person–role fit and the extent to which people felt comfortable with the roles they were asked to perform. The core of Kahn's conceptualization of engagement is that it represents the extent to which employees are psychologically present during the conduct of their work. As Rich et al (2010: 619) conclude, engagement refers to the allocation of personal resources to job performance and the intensity and persistence with which those resources are applied.

Kahn's conceptualization of engagement has been operationalized by other researchers in the field. May et al (2004) developed Kahn's core ideas into a three-component measure of engagement comprising cognitive, emotional, and physical dimensions. However, the researchers experienced problems in trying to separate these dimensions into three distinct facets from a statistical perspective, an issue that emerged in a later replication of their work (Truss et al, 2006), suggesting that more research was needed to develop a fully robust measure. Building on this, researchers within the Kingston Employee Engagement Consortium have defined engagement as 'being positively present during the performance of work by willingly contributing intellectual effort, and experiencing both positive emotions and meaningful connections with others' (Alfes et al, 2010a: 5). According to this view, engagement has three facets:

- Intellectual engagement, or the propensity to think hard about work tasks.
- Affective engagement, or experiencing positive emotions in relation to work, such as enthusiasm.
- Social engagement, or discussing work-related improvements with colleagues.
  (Rees et al, 2009; Soane et al, 2010)

Whilst the intellectual and affective dimensions map onto May et al's (2004) original cognitive and emotional facets, the Kingston team found the third, physical, aspect of the May et al study more problematic, since the questions used to capture this suggested that working long hours and taking work home were features of engagement. Reverting to Kahn's original conceptualization (1990), their view was that engagement does not necessarily equate to overworking, but rather the intellectual effort that people make, the emotions they experience, and the quality of interpersonal interactions taking place around work and in relation to work (Gatenby et al, 2009a; 2009b; Rees et al, 2009; Soane et al, 2009; 2010; Alfes et al, 2010a). Kahn describes in his paper how one facet of engagement is demonstrated when workers readily become involved in discussions with colleagues or clients over how to improve the way that work is done, or how to ensure the project is completed on time, and it is this aspect of engagement that has been measured and tested within the Kingston study. The Kingston research is still at an early stage, and so it is too soon to say whether this operationalization of the engagement construct will become established.

Rich et al (2010) have also built on Kahn's work to develop a measure of engagement comprising three sets of factors that had originally been used to measure other constructs. Physical engagement was captured by a modified measure of work intensity (Brown and Leigh, 1996), emotional engagement was measured through the notion of 'core affect' comprising pleasantness and enthusiasm (Russell and Barrett, 1999), and cognitive engagement was measured through a set of questions that captured attention and absorption (Rothbard, 2001). There is evidence that this measure of engagement works well, but the authors argue that further research is needed.

Another group of researchers based in the Netherlands has developed the Utrecht Work Engagement Scale (UWES), arguably the best established and most widely adopted measure of engagement. According to their definition, engagement comprises three facets: vigour, or work-related energy and mental resilience; dedication, or being highly involved in work, feeling that work has significance, and pride in work; and absorption in the task, or the extent to which employees are fully focused on and engrossed in their work, which combine to create the state of engagement (Schaufeli et al, 2002; Schaufeli and Bakker, 2004).

> . . . work engagement is a positive, fulfilling and work-related state of mind that consists of vigor, dedication and absorption (Bakker and Xanthopoulou, 2008: 1562).

Again, though, there are statistical problems associated with the scale which have not been fully resolved (Shimazu et al, 2008), and it has also been argued that the measure includes items that tap into what might more properly be regarded as the drivers of engagement rather than engagement itself (Rich et al, 2010).

Whilst most commentators see engagement as a distinctive construct in its own right, Maslach and Leiter (2008) have argued that engagement can be regarded as the antipode of burnout and have measured it through the Maslach Burnout Inventory (MBI), originally developed to measure psychological burnout (Leiter and Maslach, 2005):

Burnout		**Engagement**
Exhaustion	->	Energy
Cynicism	->	Involvement
Inefficacy	->	Efficacy

However, as Schaufeli and Bakker (2004) note, it is not clear whether the opposite of burnout is the absence of burnout, rather than the presence of engagement, which can perhaps more properly be regarded as a separate state. One study found that there is simply a moderately negative correlation between burnout and engagement (Schaufeli and Bakker, 2004); hence it is probable that burnout and engagement are not polar opposites, but rather different constructs.

The lack of agreement over what, precisely, engagement is is exemplified by the fact that MacLeod and Clarke (2009: 8) found over 50 different definitions of engagement. One fundamental confusion is over whether engagement is a state experienced by the individual (as conceptualized within the academic literature) or something 'done to' employees by their organizations (as frequently described by practitioners). For example, MacLeod and Clarke (2009: 9) in their government report on engagement define it as:

> ... a workplace approach designed to ensure that employees are committed to their organisation's goals and values, motivated to contribute to organisational success, and are able at the same time to enhance their own sense of wellbeing.

Within the practitioner domain, just about every consultancy firm has its own measure of engagement and an impressive comparative database. One of the most well-known and commonly used is the Gallup Organisation's Workplace Audit of engagement (Harter et al, 2002). However, the set of items that comprise the audit has been regarded by academic commentators as capturing 'engagement conditions' that might affect levels of engagement, rather than engagement itself as a distinctive variable (Little and Little, 2006; Bakker and Schaufeli, 2008; Macey and Schneider, 2008).

Perhaps the easiest way of reconciling the broad difference between academic definitions and measures, on the one hand, and practitioner perspectives, on the other, is to suggest that researchers regard engagement as a state experienced by individuals in relation to their work, whilst practitioners in general use the term 'engagement' as a form of shorthand for 'engagement strategies' that are workplace interventions designed to raise levels of engagement. The two may therefore be complementary.

 Key Concept

Engagement strategies are workplace approaches used by employers with the aim of raising levels of employee engagement.

A further complication is introduced by Saks (2006). Whilst most agree that engagement concerns the relationship between an individual and his or her work, Saks (2006) has asked whether someone can also be engaged with their employer as a whole. However, the consensus at the moment is that engagement relates specifically to the feelings, cognitions, and behaviours that individuals experience and enact in relation to their specific job.

What are reported engagement levels for the working population? It is perhaps not surprising, in light of the variety of ways in which engagement can be measured, that estimates vary substantially:

- The Corporate Leadership Council (CLC) found that around one-quarter of the workforce are strongly engaged in those organizations where engagement levels are highest (CLC, 2004).
- Towers Perrin (2007) found that 12% of public sector staff are highly engaged and 22% are disengaged.
- Johnson (2004) found that around half of US employees are either not fully engaged or disengaged.
- Seijts and Crim (2006) found that 14% of all employees worldwide are highly engaged.

- Truss et al (2006) found that 35% of UK employees are strongly engaged.

(MacLeod and Clarke, 2009)

Inconsistencies in the reported figures can be attributed not only to different definitions and measures of engagement, but also to different statistical techniques and approaches used to analyse and interpret the data.

In summary, research in employee engagement is still in its infancy. There is no single agreed definition or way of measuring engagement, although researchers are tackling this issue with enthusiasm (Macey and Schneider, 2008). Definitions and measures developed by consultancy firms may be helpful since they can often provide extensive benchmarking data, but they need to be treated with a degree of caution since there is often a considerable gap between commercially available measures of engagement and academic thinking and research on the topic.

 ## Key Concept

The term **employee engagement** has been used in a variety of ways and there is no single agreed definition or measure. However, there is a consensus that engagement is a state experienced by individuals in relation to their work that involves investing intellectual energy into thinking about the task, physical energy and absorption in the task, and positive emotional energy and enthusiasm in relation to task fulfilment. It has also been variously proposed that engagement includes a social dimension and positive connections with others, or that it incorporates long working hours, but there is as yet no general agreement about this.

 ## Case study 12.1   Nampak Plastics UK

(Based on an interview with Eric Collins, Managing Director)

South-Africa-based Nampak Group is an international supplier of packaging products with an annual turnover of £1.6 billion. Its UK division, Nampak Plastics, is the leading supplier of plastic bottles to the dairy industry and has eight sites across the country employing 650 members of staff, most of whom are manual workers. Although the company had historically been a very strong performer, the new Chief Executive, Eric Collins, felt that the traditional top-down, centralized decision-making culture of the organization was likely to create problems for the company's future growth and impede efforts to increase employee engagement. Along with the company's newly appointed Organisational Development Director, he worked to demonstrate the business case of transforming the firm's way of operating to the senior management team. The company's new engagement model comprised three elements:

- Effective: ensuring that communcation was clear and that people were kept informed and empowered to make decisions.
- Satisfied: the working environment should be safe, be fair, and provide opportunities for growth.
- Motivated: people should be recognized for their contribution and given clear goals and the autonomy to pursue them.

These three elements were founded on a new set of values comprising openness and honesty, willingness to challenge, effective communication, participation, and respect. Eric Collins personally toured all the company's sites, inviting staff to air their concerns directly with him. Local problem-solving teams were developed to encourage staff to come up with solutions themselves, with public rewards given to the teams coming up with the best ideas. A regular newsletter was introduced to keep staff informed, and managers were put through additional training to encourage them to develop a more open and consultative style. The company also introduced an extensive social responsibility programme and performance review process to enable everyone to have feedback on their performance and set objectives. Nampak believes that these initiatives have boosted productivity, innovation, and turnover as well as staff morale, even in the face of the recent need to close down one of the company's sites. Eighty per cent of staff in a recent survey said that Nampak was a good place to work, and the company is now shortlisted for an Employee Engagement prize.

Activity

Bearing in mind the experiences at Nampak, what do you think the particular employee engagement challenges of employing a predominantly manual workforce might be?

12.3 Comparing employee engagement with other constructs

In order to gain a better understanding of engagement, it is worth considering how it compares with and differs from other, related constructs.

- **Job satisfaction:** job satisfaction has been referred to as a state of personal fulfilment in relation to one's job, comprising satisfaction with both extrinsic factors, such as pay and working conditions, and intrinsic factors relating to the job itself (Little and Little, 2006). The difference between job satisfaction and engagement is, firstly, that engagement is a multidimensional construct comprising not just feelings but also cognitions and behaviours and, secondly, that engagement implies not merely satiation but also activation (Macey and Schneider, 2008).

- **Commitment:** three forms of commitment have been identified: continuance commitment, or a willingness to remain with the organization; affective commitment, or feelings of emotional attachment towards the employer; and normative commitment, or the belief that staying with the employer is the right thing to do (Allen and Meyer, 1990). Commonalities have been found between affective commitment and emotional or affective engagement. However, as Saks (2006) notes, commitment is simply attitudinal, whereas engagement has additional dimensions.

- **Job involvement or flow:** job involvement suggests a psychological identification with one's work and cognitive preoccupation (May et al, 2004; Little and Little, 2006), whereas flow is absorption in work tasks such that time seems to fly by (Csikszentmihalyi, 1990). There are clear commonalities with these two constructs and aspects of engagement; Rich et al's (2010) study included a measure of absorption with work as one of the dimensions of engagement. However, flow or involvement captures just one aspect of engagement and does not reflect the behavioural or attitudinal elements. May et al (2004) argue that involvement arises from a cognitive judgement about the extent to which someone's job is able to meet his or her needs, and Saks (2006) notes that flow is a momentary occurrence whereas engagement is a longer-term and more holistic involvement in work performance.

- **Organizational citizenship behaviour (OCB):** OCB refers to extra-role activities, such as helping others or going beyond the call of duty, that employees may perform in relation to their work (Bateman and Organ, 1983). However, as Saks (2006) notes, engagement is concerned with someone's attitudes, feelings, and behaviours specifically in relation to their formal work role and may be associated with OCB but not directly comparable. It would be reasonable to suppose that an engaged employee would be more likely to perform OCB than would a disengaged employee, which is in fact what Rich et al (2010) found.

Overall, research has shown that engagement is sufficiently different from other, related constructs that it can legitimately be regarded as a construct in its own right. However, it is important to bear in mind the fact that more theoretical and empirical research is needed in order to clarify further the core dimensions of engagement.

 Critical Reflection

Employee engagement has gained enormous popularity amongst HR professionals and senior line managers in recent years. However, some have argued that engagement is little more than a 'fad'. What do you think? Is employee engagement a distinctive construct in its own right, a passing trend, or just too similar to other constructs to be taken seriously in its own right?

12.4 The outcomes and consequences of engagement

Considerable research effort has been dedicated to finding out how engagement affects a range of possible outcomes at the individual, unit, and organizational levels. MacLeod and Clarke (2009) draw on their research to argue unequivocally that engagement is associated with higher performance, higher profitability and productivity, lower levels of intention to quit, improved individual health and wellbeing, and lower levels of sickness absence. Seeking to raise engagement levels is, they argue, sound business sense, as engaged employees will contribute more to the bottom line than will disengaged staff. This perspective is supported by a growing body of academic research that has come to the same conclusion (Harter et al, 2002; Bakker and Schaufeli, 2008; Rich et al, 2010). Table 12.1 summarizes the key research findings in relation to engagement outcomes.

Overall, the research to date has yielded overwhelmingly positive findings. The one excep-tion to this is the work of Halbesleben et al (2009) who found that engaged employees experi-ence higher levels of work–family conflict because they enact more helping behaviours in the workplace, leading to personal resource drain. Similarly, Truss et al (2010) suggested that

Table 12.1 Research findings on the outcomes of high levels of employee engagement

Outcome	Evidence
Improved individual health and wellbeing	Several studies have shown that engaged employees enjoy significantly higher levels of wellbeing than their disengaged colleagues (Schaufeli and Bakker, 2004; Bakker et al, 2008; Alfes et al, 2010a). Soane et al (2010) found in a study of 2,194 employees in two organizations that highly engaged workers had higher levels of wellbeing.
Reduced sickness absence	Harter et al's (2002) meta-analysis of data from 23,910 business units from Gallup found that engaged employees took on average 2.7 sick days a year compared with 6.2 for the disengaged.
Reduced turnover	Alfes et al (2010a) in a study of 5,300 employees in eight organizations found that highly engaged staff are significantly more likely to want to stay with their employer.
Higher levels of individual productivity and performance	Wellins et al (2005) found in a study of US Fortune 100 companies that quality errors were significantly higher for poorly engaged teams.
Higher levels of organizational citizenship behaviour	Rich et al (2010) found in a study involving 245 fire fighters that highly engaged workers were more likely to be helpful and courteous.
Higher levels of corporate performance	Towers Perrin-ISR (2006) in a study of 664,000 employees from 50 companies found that those with a highly engaged workforce improved operating income by 19.2% over 12 months compared with those with low scores which saw a 32.7% decline over the same period. Gallup (2006) examined growth rates of 89 firms and found that those with top quartile engagement scores were 2.6 times those with below-average engagement scores.
Higher levels of customer service	PricewaterhouseCoopers (MacLeod and Clarke, 2009: 38) found a strong association between high levels of staff engagement and client satisfaction. Fleming et al (2005) found in a study of 1,979 business units in 10 companies that units scoring above median on both employee and customer engagement were on average 3.4 times more effective financially than units in the bottom half of both measures.
Higher levels of innovation	Worrall and Cooper (2007) found a significant link between engagement and innovation. Alfes et al (2010a) found that highly engaged workers also display significantly higher levels of innovative work behaviour.
Higher levels of commitment, organizational advocacy, and job satisfaction	Truss et al (2006) in a study of 2,000 working-age adults in the UK found that those with high levels of engagement are also more satisfied with their work, more likely to advocate their employer, and more committed.

Source: MacLeod and Clarke (2009: 37–39).

those employees who are both very strongly and very frequently engaged are at higher risk of burnout than other groups, and Shantz et al (2010) found that women with dependent children and who are highly engaged are more likely to experience burnout than either men with or without children or women without children. At the organizational level, Rees et al (2009) have argued that employee engagement could be associated with work intensification and the manipulation of workers' attitudes and emotions.

At present, insufficient studies have been conducted to be sure about the potentially negative risks of high levels of engagement, but it is perhaps worth bearing in mind the point that engagement may well not be uniformly positive for everyone.

 Key Concept

Engagement consequences are the outcomes that arise from high levels of employee engagement, both for individuals and for employers. Most research has suggested that engagement is uniformly positive for individuals and for employers.

12.5 The drivers or antecedents of engagement

A key concern for both academics and practitioners has been to identify the factors that drive up engagement levels and considerable research has been conducted on this issue. Figure 12.1 depicts the key influencing factors.

As Fig. 12.1 shows, research has suggested that the factors influencing engagement occur at several levels. First, there are factors concerned with the individual, such as demographic

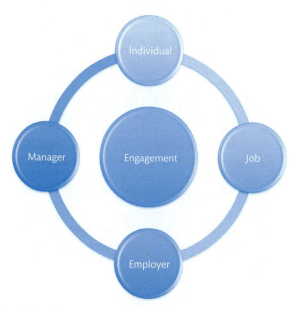

Figure 12.1 Key factors influencing engagement levels.

variables and personality traits; second, there are job-related factors including person–job fit and job design. The third set of factors, and arguably the area that has received most attention, is concerned with line manager behaviour, and the fourth set occurs at the level of the employer or organization overall. We consider each of these in turn; again, the fact that different definitions and measures of engagement have been used in the various studies needs to be borne in mind as this makes interpreting the findings more complex.

12.5.1 Individual-level variables

Some studies have explored the extent to which demographic factors affect engagement. For example, it has been found that women are significantly more likely to be engaged with their work than are men (Johnson, 2004; Truss et al, 2006) and that older employees are more engaged than younger employees.

Other researchers have looked at the possible link between engagement and personality. Macey and Schneider (2008) conclude that engagement may well be at least partly due to personal disposition, and include personality traits such as proactivity and conscientiousness as probable relevant features.

Rich et al (2010) suggest that core self-evaluation, or self-confidence in one's abilities, can be an important precursor of engagement. Building on Kahn (1990), they argue that those with high core self-evaluation tend to have more confidence in their own ability to influence events around them (agency), as well as being more positive and well-adjusted than others. These individuals are therefore more likely to be psychologically available to be engaged with their work.

Robinson (2006) has suggested that variation in people's perceptions of experiences and events may be important. Thus, faced with the same set of employment circumstances, employees will tend to respond in a variety of ways depending on their personality and cognitive schema. However, there has to date been insufficient research on the possible link between personality and engagement to be sure exactly how the relationship might work.

Another potential influence on engagement levels is emotional experiences (May et al, 2004). Events at work will cause a variety of emotional responses and it has been suggested that where an individual experiences negative emotions due to work-related incidents, this can have a depressive effect on engagement (Kular et al, 2008). Rewarding interpersonal relationships at work, whether with co-workers or customers, can serve to enhance engagement by increasing an individual's sense of meaningfulness (Kahn, 1990; May et al, 2004). Equally, it has been argued that ensuring a working environment that generates positive emotions through involvement and pride will enhance engagement (Robinson, 2006). Positive emotions at work have also been linked with higher levels of wellbeing (Robinson, 2006). This can be viewed through the lens of affective events theory (Weiss and Cropanzano, 1996), which suggests that individuals' emotional responses to work events influence their behaviour.

12.5.2 Job-related variables

Most researchers agree that the nature of the task that people are asked to do is important for engagement (Macey and Schneider, 2008). Kahn (1990) argues that levels of engagement are dependent on three interconnected factors. First, the extent to which someone finds their work personally meaningful, second, whether they believe that being engaged is psychologically safe and they are unlikely to suffer any negative consequences as a result of being engaged, and, third, the extent to which the individual is physically and psychologically available to be engaged with their work. This has been replicated in other studies (Rich et al, 2010; Soane et al, 2010).

Person–job fit, or the extent to which someone feels that they are well-suited to their job and have all the relevant skills and abilities to perform it effectively, has also emerged as important for engagement (Alfes et al, 2010a; Soane et al, 2010).

12.5.3 Line manager behaviour

A number of researchers have shown that an individual's experiences of work in relation to their line manager are critical for engagement. In particular, the degree of trust that employees feel towards their manager is important (Macey and Schneider, 2008; Soane et al, 2010). This can be linked back to Kahn's (1990) work and his point that psychological safety is important for engagement. If people feel that they work for a manager whose behaviour is predictable and supportive, then they are more likely to feel able to invest themselves in their work through engagement (Rich et al, 2010). Similarly, Truss et al (2006) found that employees who had experienced bullying or harassment were the least engaged.

12.5.4 Employer/organizational factors

A number of studies have explored the extent to which factors at the organizational level can be significant for engagement. Truss et al (2006) found that voice and involvement were major influences on engagement. Rich et al (2010) found that value congruence, or the extent to which there was a match between an individual's personal values and those required by the organization, also impacted on engagement levels. This is because value congruence raises levels of meaningfulness of work and increases the alignment between the role required by the organization and the individual's preferred self-image. In another study, Bakker and Xanthopoulou (2008) found that there are spillover effects for engagement between colleagues. Colleagues who interact frequently with one another influence each other's levels of engagement. This is an important and interesting point to note about the social dimension of engagement.

Overall, the research evidence suggests that factors at a number of levels can impact on engagement levels. One concern within the academic literature has been to find a theoretical rationale that can help explain how the engagement cycle of antecedents, engagement, and consequences works. The most popular theoretical framework has been social exchange theory. According to this view, employees develop a reciprocal relationship of trust and commitment with their employer provided that certain rules of exchange are followed (Cropanzano and Mitchell, 2005). Thus, employees who receive economic or socio-emotional benefits from their employer are more likely to feel obliged to respond in kind through engagement with their work (Saks, 2006). Employees are attuned to particular signals sent by their employer concerning how much they are valued and respected, such as the way they are treated by their line manager, employee voice and involvement, HR policy and practice, the jobs they are asked to do, the support they receive, and perceptions of the organization's senior managers. Viewed through a lens of social exchange theory, employees are more likely to be engaged with their work when perceptions of these organizational factors are positive. Equally, violation of these is likely to lead to disengagement and other negative consequences.

Employers have adopted a number of strategies in an effort to raise and maintain levels of employee engagement, focusing in particular on communication, personal and organizational development, leadership, and involvement. For instance, several organizations, including Amey plc and Birmingham City Council, have introduced 'Engagement Champions' into the business, who receive special training in the overarching engagement strategy of the firm and are tasked with organizing meetings and events around engagement. Lewisham Council has strengthened its employee suggestion scheme by ensuring that all suggestions are accompanied by a 'business case' and it has also invested in its in-house coaching and mentoring programme. At the Co-operative, the focus has been on the role of line managers in terms of fostering diversity and encouraging fairness, empathy, and flexibility in their management style. The company has also encouraged managers to focus on the recognition of employees and to adopt a 'strengths-based' approach to managing. Mace Group has emphasized corporate social responsibility as part of its strategy to raise engagement levels by fostering strong links with the local community and encouraging employees to volunteer. Mace believes that this, together with the company's focus on person–job fit, the creation of interesting projects, and management development, has served to foster high levels of engagement.

 Key Concept

Engagement antecedents are those factors that impact on levels of engagement. Research has shown that factors at the individual, job, line manager, and organizational levels can all influence engagement. In general, the consensus is that positive experiences at work will raise engagement levels, whilst negative experiences will depress them.

 Case study 12.2 Birmingham City Council

(Based on an interview with Raffaela Goodby, Employee Engagement Manager)

Birmingham City Council is the largest local authority in Europe with over 53,000 employees at over 600 locations across Birmingham. The council needed to undergo a radical transformation in order to keep its workforce motivated and engaged and also to increase efficiency and save costs, and launched the BEST programme to help raise levels of engagement. BEST (Belief, Excellence, Success, Trust) was aimed at helping focus employees on working effectively, collaborating across units, and on meeting the needs of local residents. It was felt that the programme would be most successful through adopting a bottom-up approach that involved staff but at the same time had clear leadership and political support from the top. All employees from the most senior to the most junior attend a 2-hour BEST workshop to enable them to think about how they can contribute at a personal level and at a team level to making improvements in the organization. The workshops involve a self-evaluation tool and the opportunity to work together to develop new ideas and initiatives. To date, over 6,000 new ideas have emerged from the workshops. Workshop leaders receive training from the engagement team on how to ensure they run well and achieve their objectives. On average, BEST teams have developed 2.7 actions that have directly led to an improvement in council services.

Alongside the workshops, other events and initiatives help to reinforce the values. For example, key messages from the Chief Executive and team successes are posted on YouTube, there are monthly awards ceremonies, and regular 'Dragon's Den' events based on the popular UK TV series which enable employees to pitch for up to £1,000 of funding to support new ideas.

The council has won numerous awards for its BEST programme, and feedback from employees suggests that they have enjoyed participating in the scheme and also feel that performance levels have been raised.

Source

http://www.birminghambest.co.uk/.

Activity

Why do you think the BEST programme has been so successful? What are the challenges?

12.6 Implications for HR professionals

In light of the growing body of academic evidence and practitioner enthusiasm, it would appear reasonable to conclude that many HR professionals will be called upon to evaluate levels of employee engagement and to develop and implement strategies to improve engagement. From an HR perspective, what are the important considerations?

- There is as yet no single agreed measure of employee engagement. Those used by practitioners generally differ substantially from those developed by academics. Many of those currently in use have merit and present impressive credentials, particularly in terms of available benchmarking data. However, careful consideration needs to be given as to which measure to use in any particular organization. Relevant factors include the purpose for which the survey will be used, organizational setting, climate and culture, senior management attitudes and willingness to invest in engagement strategies, employee availability to particpate in surveys, the importance of having benchmarking data, and the amount of time and other resources available to conduct the survey. In particular, the definition and precise questions used to determine levels of engagement need to be looked at in light of the discussion in this chapter on the meaning of engagement.

- Employee engagement is regarded by many organizations as one of the central planks in their HR or people strategy. HR professionals therefore have to think about how any strategies they develop for enhancing engagement link in with other areas of their people strategy and support their overall corporate objectives. There is considerable scope for HR interventions such as the performance management system, rewards, appraisals, training and organizational development, employee involvement, and corporate social responsibility to help create a climate conducive to high levels of engagement.

- Social exchange theory tells us that employees will respond positively and become more engaged in a climate of trust, openness, and reciprocity, and the line manager has a key role to play. HR professionals therefore need to consider whether their line managers have the requisite skills and knowledge to create an engaging work environment.

● Engagement is emotional as well as cognitive and behavioural, and so HR professionals will be required to consider engagement strategies holistically in terms of their likely impact on employees.

 Critical Reflection

Go to the UK government's Business Link website http://www.businesslink.gov.uk and find the pages in the Employment and Skills section that refer to employee engagement. Read some of the guidance for employers on raising engagement levels and watch some of the videos. What is your evaluation of the advice that is given to employers?

 ## Conclusion

In this chapter, our focus has been on the growing area of employee engagement. As we have seen, there is no one accepted definition and measure of engagement, and academic research has lagged behind practitioner interest. However, several more robust measures of engagement are now starting to emerge, and there is a growing consensus that engagement is a psychological state that involves the energetic emotional, behavioural, and cognitive investment of self into one's work role. There is agreement that it is sufficiently different from other, related constructs to now be considered a valid construct in its own right. Practitioners are particularly enthusiastic about engagement in light of the wealth of evidence that engaged employees perform better, take less sick leave, are less likely to quit, are more innovative, more likely to 'talk up' their organization, and help out others more than do their disengaged colleagues. It has also been found that engagement has beneficial outcomes for individuals as well in terms of improved health and wellbeing.

There is much that organizations can do to drive up levels of engagement, and studies have shown that factors at the individual, line manager, job, and organizational levels are all significant.

Summary

- Employee engagement is a multifaceted affective, behavioural, and cognitive construct.
- There is no accepted definition and measure of engagement, and academic research has lagged behind practitioner interest in the topic.
- However, it is generally agreed amongst researchers that engagement is characterized by positive emotions, intellectual focus, and energetic behaviour directed towards task performance. It has also been suggested that positive social connections are a feature of engagement.
- Research evidence shows that engagement is associated with a range of positive outcomes for both individuals and organizations.
- There is much that the HR professional can do to improve engagement levels.

Review questions

1. Why do you think that employee engagement has gained such popularity with practitioners over recent years?

2. What do you see as distinctive about engagement as compared with other constructs?

3. What are the most important factors to consider when designing an employee engagement strategy?

4. Do you think there are any downsides to employee engagement? Why?

5. To what extent do you think that the confusion over the precise meaning of engagement matters to HRM professionals, and how should they respond?

 End-of-chapter case study   Employee engagement at Mace Group

Mace is an international consultancy and construction company with a £700+ million turnover in 2009, employing 2,900 people, and operating across 49 countries. The Group's core business is programme and project management, construction delivery, quantity surveying, and facilities management, but it is truly multidisciplinary, with services spanning the entire property life cycle. Mace has been involved in some leading construction projects, including the London Eye, the London Bridge Shard, the Venetian Macau, and the Jumeirah Beach development in Dubai. In order to inspire its highly creative and well-educated workforce, Mace regards employee engagement as paramount. In addition to measuring employee engagement through its own annual staff survey, the company has also participated in the Kingston Employee Engagement Consortium in order to benchmark its engagement levels against those of other member organizations and to be part of an academic research project. Survey results showed that engagement levels were high across the company, and this has been attributed to the stimulating and varied work undertaken by employees. However, it also emerged that certain groups of employees, particularly those involved with high-pressure project deadlines, were allowing their work–life balance to suffer. Another factor that emerged was that Mace employees scored lower on the social engagement dimension of the Kingston Job Engagement Inventory, in other words, there was scope to raise the extent to which employees shared ideas and knowledge. The findings also showed that Mace managers could benefit from a more consistent approach to management development, that the company's approach to corporate social responsibility could be enhanced, and that the appraisal process could be improved.

Based on the survey findings as well as her broader reading, Engagement Manager Alex Michael has developed a specific engagement model for Mace, which identifies the key drivers of engagement and aspires to achieve the following:

- Professional recruitment: ensuring that prospective employees fit with the organization's culture and values.

- Interesting work: jobs are designed to be stimulating and intrinsically rewarding both in terms of the high-profile nature of the projects and by providing employees with varied opportunities around the world and in all aspects of property design and development.

- Training and development: the company offers a broad range of training and development for all staff, including sponsorship to gain professional qualifications.

- Communication: the company regularly shares information with employees through a variety of electronic and face-to-face media, as well as inviting employee participation through blogs, meetings, appraisals, and groups.

- Corporate social responsibility: Mace emphasizes the importance of being a responsible member of the community as well as recognizing, rewarding, and supporting staff through an employee assistance programme, extra 'Mace days' holidays, health checks, and increased pension contributions. The company also introduced new initiatives such as a payroll giving scheme, partnerships with local schools, and a volunteering day for members of staff, as part of a broader corporate responsibility strategy.

this type of work are often referred to as knowledge workers and their expertise (i.e. personal experience and knowledge) is viewed as a potential source of competitive advantage (see Chapter 3). Organizations in emerging economies such as China recognize the importance of knowledge work, innovation, and the newest technologies to the future development of their national economies (Magnus, 2011). Yet it is India rather than China that is making more progress in terms of entrepreneurship and cutting-edge technologies, with firms such as Infosys Technologies and Wipro leading the way (Bahl, 2010). Consequently, managing knowledge workers is now viewed as one of the core capabilities in many organizations (Pasher and Ronen, 2011). Organizations have been using various knowledge management (KM) strategies, policies, and practices to leverage this expertise. Whilst most, if not all, organizations involve some form of knowledge work, there are certain types of organization that can be described as knowledge intensive firms (KIFs). These include accountancy firms, management consultancies, and advertising agencies (Alvesson, 2004).

KM strategies tend to be associated with innovation (Almeida et al, 2005), which has been identified as an important determinant of successful business performance (Morgan et al, 2007). Innovation represents *new* knowledge and the principal KM process that supports the creation of new knowledge is **knowledge sharing** (Mankin, 2009). Although the concept of knowledge sharing has been defined in several different ways (see section 13.3 below) it can be viewed as a process that enables existing ideas and perspectives to be used in new ways. Knowledge sharing tends to be both more complex and more critical in larger organizations such as multinationals (Mundra et al, 2011) where organizations need to incorporate local cultural factors in any KM strategy (Jelavic, 2010). It is not surprising therefore that much of the literature on the topic is written from a multinational perspective. In contrast, little attention has been given to KM processes in small businesses (Bracci and Vagnoni, 2011).

Kaplan and Norton (2004) observe that 'there is no greater waste than a good idea used only once' (p. 301):

Ideas breed new ideas, and shared knowledge stays with the giver while it enriches the receiver. The potential for new ideas arising from the stock of knowledge in any firm is practically limitless—particularly if the people in the firm are given opportunities to think, to learn, and to talk with one another (Davenport and Prusak, 2000: 17).

This is pertinent to developing as well as developed economies. For instance, as India's economy grows and it starts to lose its low-cost position, the principal challenge facing indigenous companies will be moving away from strategies based on imitation to strategies based on the development of innovative products (Kumar et al, 2009). For firms such as Apple and Sony, continuous product innovation is critical (Levis, 2009).

Whilst there have been opportunities for HR professionals to get involved with KM processes, many firms with a KM strategy have tended to emphasize the role of computer specialists in developing and supporting formal technology-based systems for managing knowledge assets (such as databases and intranets). Consequently, the role of face-to-face collaboration is not always prioritized by managers (Mankin, 2009). Whilst collaboration does not need to be face-to-face, research shows that it continues to be more effective than online or virtual forms such as discussion boards, blogs, and wikis. This is partly due to the fact that individuals tend to trust people they know well and work with closely. These high levels of trust are essential for maximizing the effectiveness of collaboration and inherent knowledge sharing processes (Käser and Miles, 2001). Of course, this situation may change in the future as younger generations, who have a more intuitive understanding of technology, enter the labour market (although there is still no guarantee that this will be more effective than face-to-face sharing). A particular problem facing many organizations is that trust not only is an elusive concept but also can take a long time to mature. Such long-term perspectives are often at odds with the short-term goals of organizations. A further complication is that a great deal of knowledge work occurs informally as a result of individuals participating in informal groups such as social networks and communities of practice. Both of these emerge and evolve within work settings as a result of a shared interest, although social networks comprise weaker ties between individual members and tend to span organizational boundaries. Neither is under the direct control of managers, who may not even be aware that these informal groups exist.

 Key Concept

Communities of practice involve 'A group of people who have a particular activity in common, and as a consequence have some common knowledge, a sense of community identity, and some element of overlapping values' (Hislop, 2009: 167). They are different from social networks, which tend to span organizational boundaries and involve a much looser form of affiliation. An example of a community of practice might be a sub-group of academics within a large department who share a common research interest.

As discussed below, much of the uncertainty that surrounds knowledge work and knowledge workers is a result of the fact that knowledge is a problematic concept. It can be used as a term to represent the mundane aspects of everyday practices or the complexities of abstract thinking (Kalling and Styhre, 2003). The aim of this chapter is to give you a basic grounding in the concepts of knowledge and knowledge management so that you are able to appreciate some of the challenges facing organizations in the private, non-profit, and public sectors. The first section introduces you to the different ways in which knowledge and, in turn, organizational knowledge can be defined and understood. This lays the foundation for subsequent coverage on KM, the importance of knowledge sharing processes to the creation of new knowledge, and the implications of KM for SHRM, including the role of the HR function in the management and development of intellectual capital.

13.2 Knowledge

Although the concept of knowledge lacks a universal definition it is often explained by distinguishing between 'explicit' and 'tacit' knowledge (Mankin, 2009). Explicit knowledge is formal, abstract, or theoretical knowledge which relies on an individual's conceptual skills and cognitive abilities. It includes scientific knowledge, which has enjoyed a privileged status within Western culture (Lam, 2000) in contrast to Eastern culture which has tended to focus on tacit knowledge (Jelavic, 2010). Explicit knowledge can be stored in books, documents, diagrams, graphs, pictures, and computer drives (O'Dell and Hubert, 2011). Many organizations have centralized repositories (usually computerized) which can be accessed by individual organizational members who need to know more about a particular subject (e.g. products, processes, services). This is referred to as a **codification** strategy (i.e. knowledge is encoded in the different types of media listed above and can then be acquired by anyone accessing those media). In contrast, tacit knowledge can be defined as practical skills or expertise that accrue over time and reside within the individual (Polanyi, 1962; 1967). Indeed, it is so deeply embedded within an individual's experience, judgement, and intuition (Ahmed et al, 2002) that Spender (1996) describes it as **automatic** knowledge. It is for this reason that Polanyi famously observed: 'we can know more than we can tell' (1967: 4). For instance, in a study of pizza parlours, employees struggled to explain how to hand-toss a pizza, thus demonstrating the tacit nature of the process (Epple et al, 1996). Tacit knowledge is important because it has the potential to deliver competitive advantage: it is difficult for competitors to imitate, in contrast to explicit knowledge which is relatively easy to replicate (Mankin, 2009). It is important to appreciate that while it is possible to distinguish conceptually between explicit and tacit knowledge, they are not necessarily separate and discrete in practice (Lam, 2000).

Knowledge has also been defined in terms of its relationship to information and data (Dalkir, 2011). From this perspective data are the basic building blocks for information and knowledge. Data comprise numbers, words, and images. Information is created when data are interpreted in some way (e.g. sales figures are collated and presented in a document). In turn, information becomes knowledge when it is used in a meaningful way (e.g. collated sales figures are used to analyse and predict trends). O'Dell and Hubert (2011) refer to this as information-in-action. Marchand (1998) summarizes the relationship between information and knowledge in the following way:

> . . . it is important that the role of information use and sharing in a company should not be overlooked . . . information is the means or vehicle that companies employ to express, convey and share knowledge retained among their people. Thus, a company's capabilities to manage information provide the means through which knowledge development and management are possible (p. 267).

Often the boundary between information and knowledge blurs and this is why information is sometimes described as explicit knowledge. However, the relationship between information and tacit knowledge is markedly different as tacit knowledge is about practical expertise or know-how, which is almost impossible to convert or translate into explicit knowledge or information: it is difficult, if not impossible, to describe insights, wisdom, or intuitive knowing in information terms. Hence, 'It is the combination of people and information resources that will deliver superior performance and competitive advantage' (Hinton, 2006b: 10).

 Key Concept

Knowledge is a complex, multifaceted, and ambiguous concept that is difficult to define. In organizational settings it is often defined in terms of its relationship to information and data.

The term 'organizational knowledge' is often used to describe the knowledge that is held in the human minds, groups, and structures within an organization (e.g. routines, procedures, databases) as well as the potential new knowledge that can be created by individuals and groups when they interact with each other. Over time, organizational knowledge represents 'the set of collective understandings embedded in a firm' (Tsoukas and Vladimirou, 2005: 126). These collective understandings guide individuals and can change as new ways of working are created. Consequently, organizational knowledge is dependent on human action or activity in the workplace (i.e. engaging in work practices). An example of how collective understandings develop over time is illustrated by Orr (1990) who showed that photocopier engineers solved problems by sharing stories with each other rather than referring to the copier manual.

13.3 Knowledge management

The principal purpose of a KM strategy is to leverage organizational knowledge in order to achieve and/or sustain competitive advantage (Mankin, 2009). However, there are different perspectives on how this can best be achieved. Broadly speaking, these can be described as:

- Managing knowledge (i.e. direct control).
- Nurturing knowledge (i.e. indirect control).

These are not necessarily mutually exclusive or incompatible (Mankin, 2009). For instance, Barney and Clark (2007) refer to HR's role in 'nurturing', 'developing', and 'managing' an organization's HR resources and there is no reason why this should not be the case with knowledge assets. However, differences of opinion abound in the literature on KM. For instance, Von Krogh et al (2000) argue that the managing knowledge perspective, with its emphasis on information and information systems, 'represents a constricting paradigm rather than a transformative one' (p. 26). The authors prefer the term 'enabling'. In support of this perspective Alvesson and Kärreman (2001) argue that the use of the word 'management' in KM implies the control of processes that may be inherently uncontrollable. This is because managers can be unaware of how much knowledge is shared informally. Arguably, there is a need for a more **balanced** approach that combines perspectives (Swart et al, 2003).

 Key Concept

Knowledge management is 'the deliberate and systematic coordination of an organisation's people, technology, processes, and organisational structure in order to add value through reuse and innovation' (Dalkir, 2011: 4).

What is clear is that KM processes are important for innovation of new products and services. There is also increasing evidence that innovation is a particular feature of inter-firm networks (De Man et al, 2008). This highlights the need to consider the HR and KM implications of acquisitions and mergers, and strategic alliances. A good example of the latter is the collaboration of Nike and Apple to design and manufacture the Nike + iPod training system so that people can use their iPod while running (Fung et al, 2007). The joint creation of new forms of know-how (i.e. tacit knowledge) is one of several factors that can determine the success, or failure, of mergers and acquisitions (Larsson et al, 2004). However, a major concern of many Western managers is the way in which intellectual property right is being ignored by many of the indigenous firms in developing economies. For instance, there are widespread violations in China which help to keep costs down for the country's manufacturing sector (Harney, 2008). As Midler (2009) observes:

> American business leaders . . . have pushed for increased intellectual property protection in China [to counter] the most prevalent form of counterfeiting—factories took an original product from a customer and then reinvented the product so that it looked every bit like the real thing, but was in fact a rip-off (pp. 116–117).

In this way counterfeit products help to sustain China's competitive advantage through low costs. That said, inter-firm collaboration involving knowledge transfer between foreign multinationals and Chinese enterprises is seen as a highly effective strategy for establishing a foothold in China's burgeoning markets (Nie and Xin, 2009).

While state-owned enterprises in China have access to state funds for underpinning long-term development, this is not necessarily the case in other developing economies. For instance, in Brazil the government has been encouraging investment in science and technology (Barros, 2009), yet indigenous companies have been relatively unwilling to do so because their 'ability to divert resources into R&D ventures is often constrained by a lack of access to capital and a risk aversion borne of years of coping with significant instability' (Amann, 2009: 202).

When reading about the topic it is easy to become confused, as terms describing KM processes such as knowledge creation, knowledge sharing, and knowledge transfer are often used interchangeably, or alternatives are preferred (e.g. knowledge exchange instead of knowledge sharing). This actually reflects the extent to which the three processes are interlinked, with knowledge creation occurring as a result of both knowledge sharing and knowledge transfer. Knowledge sharing tends to be associated with what is happening *within* groups and networks, while knowledge transfer is associated with what is happening *between* groups and networks (e.g. across-company and inter-company collaboration). Knowledge transfer is often used in relation to multinationals where a particular challenge is finding ways to create connections between globally dispersed sources of knowledge (Doz et al, 2001). As supply chains become increasingly fragmented, larger firms are relying on SMEs to provide specialist products and services and universities to carry out R&D. Consequently, knowledge needs to flow effectively throughout the supply chain regardless of how many organizations comprise that chain.

As indicated above, populist approaches to KM tend to involve strategies that attempt to directly control knowledge processes, strategies that involve indirect control and focus on nurturing a culture that promotes knowledge processes, and strategies that are a combination of the first two. Hislop (2005; 2009) refers to two principal perspectives that underpin KM strategies: the 'objectivist' and 'practice-based' perspectives. Each of these is underpinned by a different interpretation of knowledge, and these differences are shown in Table 13.1.

Table 13.1 Summary of the objectivist and practice-based perspectives

Objectivist (direct control)	Practice-based (indirect control)
Knowledge is explicit and objective (e.g. facts and figures) and often treated as if it were an object that exists independently of human thought (referred to as the reification of knowledge). It has been described as **conscious** knowledge because we have an awareness of its existence and are able to articulate it.	**Knowledge is tacit and subjective** (e.g. perceptions, innate skills). It tends to be highly personal, context specific, difficult to express in words, and therefore not easy to share with others. It is inextricably linked with action (i.e. a work practice such as teaching, accountancy, law, engineering, or R&D). Consequently, knowledge can be contested (i.e. is the subject of continuous, ongoing debates and exchanges).
Tacit knowledge can be converted into explicit knowledge and stored (i.e. codified). In principle, this makes knowledge relatively easy to transmit to others (e.g. books, websites, newspapers).	**Tacit and explicit knowledge are two dimensions of knowledge** rather than two different types of knowledge (i.e. they are inseparable). They interact as individuals engage in their work practice. Consequently, it is not possible to totally disembody knowledge from people and the actions (practices) they are engaged in.
Individual cognition is emphasized (i.e. knowledge is held by individual minds). Consequently, KM processes are dependent on cognitive learning theory (i.e. psychological theories of learning).	**Cognition is no longer located solely within the individual mind** but also needs to be understood as a complex social phenomenon: knowledge is situated within and distributed across groups (especially informal groups or communities and social networks). Consequently, sociological theories of learning are emphasized.
Knowledge is underpinned by human capital theory: individuals are treated as a resource.	**Knowledge is underpinned by social capital theory:** employees and their network of relationships are viewed as assets.

Sources: Spender, 1996; Von Krogh, 1998; Baumard, 1999; Von Krogh et al, 2000; Patriotta, 2003; Seiler, 2004; Hislop, 2005; 2009; Mankin, 2009; Daud and Yusoff, 2010; Jashapara, 2010; Dalkir, 2011; O'Dell and Hubert, 2011; Mertens et al, 2011; Wilde, 2011; unpublished PhD thesis by David Mankin.

As can be seen from Table 13.1, an appreciation of human and social capital theories (see Chapters 9 and 10) informs our understanding of KM. Managers and HR professionals need to understand the differences between human *and* social capital, and the implications each form of capital have for SHRM. Both contribute to an organization's intellectual capital and it is this term that is often used when discussing an organization's intangible assets. However, it should be noted that social capital is particularly important in SMEs (Daud and Yusoff, 2010).

 Critical Reflection

The above discussion has highlighted two different perspectives on how knowledge can be defined and, in turn, how knowledge can be managed. Assess the validity of the arguments presented in this chapter. What are the implications for different stakeholders, such as HR, managers, and employees, of these different perspectives?

Case study 13.1   Innovation and competitive advantage in Apple

Apple was founded by Steve Jobs in 1976. He was replaced as the firm's CEO in 1985 but returned to the position in 1997 to save the company at a time when it looked doomed. One of Apple's distinctive capabilities is the ability to innovate and produce yet more beautifully designed, elegant, and easy-to-use products. This has given the company a tremendous competitive advantage in markets including design, publishing, and education. This strategy has been the brainchild of Steve Jobs who rejected traditional incremental approaches to innovation and instead focused on designing individual products such as the iPod, iPhone, and iPad to the highest possible standard. In effect he reinvented the firm as a consumer-electronics business which moved into the mobile-phone industry. He was extremely successful at combining technical know-how with new concepts, such as the shift to the digital downloading of music. Steve Jobs believed in having a product-oriented culture and employing highly skilled people. In effect, he believed in hiring the best and most committed people; those who are prepared to work unsocial hours in order to get the best product.

Apple's strategy has resulted in customers who are passionate about Apple products and who are prepared to pay a premium price for what they believe to be great products. As a consequence, Apple has been described as the most innovative company in the world. Yet the launch of the iPad met with much criticism from ICT experts who argued that the product would stifle innovation by competitors. Concerns were raised over the fact that the iPad is based on a closed system for iPhones: it can only run one program at a time and any applications must be approved by Apple. This is contrary to the traditional business model for PCs which can multitask several programs produced by a range of firms. In June 2011 Steve Jobs announced the launch of iCloud, a free service which is designed to replace the home PC as the central hub and storage facility for individual users.

Sources

Business Week (2004) http://www.businessweek.com/bwdaily/dnflash/oct2004/nf20041012_4018_db083.htm (accessed 12 June 2011).

The Economist (2007) http://www.economist.com/node/9302662 (accessed 12 June 2011).

Levis, K. (2009) *Winners and Losers: Creators and Casualties of the Age of the Internet.* London: Atlantic Books.

The Guardian (2010) http://www.guardian.co.uk/technology/2010/feb/01/apple-ipad-choke-innovation (accessed 13 June 2011).

Apple innovation (2011) http://appleinnovation.blogspot.com/ (accessed 13 June 2011).

Activity

What are the potential strengths and weaknesses of Apple's innovation strategy from a KM perspective?

13.4 Knowledge sharing

As indicated above, there are several perspectives on the concept of knowledge sharing (as well as knowledge transfer and, in turn, knowledge creation). There is no doubt that explicit knowledge is easier to share. In contrast, tacit knowledge is often described as being **sticky** (Brown and Duguid, 1998) because it is context specific. This can act as a barrier to knowledge sharing **between** groups and result in a 'wheels-being-reinvented' syndrome, with previous mistakes being repeated and new misunderstandings being created (Bartholomew, 2008). A range of barriers and facilitators of knowledge sharing is shown in Table 13.2.

In terms of appreciating the benefits of an effective knowledge-sharing strategy, look at Nokia, Finland's leading multinational. The company not only collaborates with a global network of leading universities but also uses customers' ideas to drive innovation (Steinbock, 2010). Another example is the Mittal Group's Knowledge Management Programme:

> By benchmarking the best in the Mittal Group, valuable knowledge transfer with respect to cost reduction occurred daily between managers. By pooling global expertise on a regular basis, the Mittal Group was able to share and implement best practice, technical knowledge, and target setting more quickly and efficiently than its competitors. The process of knowledge sharing occurred on various levels in the company and was coordinated at the corporate level (Kumar et al, 2009: 56).

This quote illustrates why it is important to link KM and HRM strategies in order to achieve both efficiency (cost reductions) and effectiveness (performance improvements). Coordination 'at the corporate level' implies the vertical alignment with business strategy. Significantly, the Mittal Group was India's first global business.

13.5 SHRM and KM

The first priority of the HR function is to help managers address the people and organizational issues necessary to achieve an organization's strategic objectives (Hall, 2008). As part of this process, the HR function has to consider how best to tackle the strategic and operational

Table 13.2 Knowledge sharing: barriers and facilitators

Barriers to knowledge sharing	Facilitators of knowledge sharing
Knowledge hoarding ('knowledge is power' syndrome)	Sympathetic organizational culture
Lack of social spaces (see end-of-chapter case study)	Shared physical location (face-to-face contact in shared offices or social spaces such as canteen, staff rooms, etc.)
Fear (of failure or loss of status if the knowledge generated resulted in actions detrimental to the organization. Do not assume that all knowledge is necessarily in the best interests of the organization)	Subordination of individual goals and associated actions to collectively defined and collectively enacted goals
Silo mentality (stickiness of knowledge)	Strong working relationships (regular contact; cooperation and collaboration; individuals motivated by communal norms; high levels of trust)
Perceived inequality in status	Status similarity

Source: Mankin (2009).

HR implications of any KM strategy. This involves careful consideration of how best to leverage an organization's HR:

> The ultimate quest should be for the HR function to provide the firm with resources *that provide value, are rare, and cannot be easily imitated* by other organisations. This quest entails developing employees who are skilled and motivated to deliver high quality products and services, and managing the culture of the organisation to encourage teamwork and trust. It also requires that HR functions focus more attention on developing coherent systems of HR practices that support these aims (Barney and Clark, 2007: 141, emphasis in original).

This reference to 'coherent systems of HR practices' highlights the importance of both vertical and horizontal strategic alignment, including the relationship between the strategic and operational aspects of HRM. Swart et al (2003) identify the following HR practices and processes as critical to managing what they term 'knowledge-intensive situations' (p, 2):

- Attracting, developing, rewarding, and retaining human capital.
- Recognizing the importance of social capital.
- Building network management skills.

All of these are focused on the maintenance and/or improvement of performance. However, this is difficult to achieve unless an organization's culture fosters teamwork and trust. Studies show that an organizational culture that supports innovation and KM is crucial (Donate and Guadamillas, 2010).

Knowledge sharing is unlikely to happen where employees distrust each other (Lesser and Prusak, 2004). In order to build trust amongst employees Levin et al (2004: 40) recommend that line managers should:

- Create a common understanding of how the business works (i.e. nurture the context).
- Demonstrate trust-building behaviours (i.e. act as role models).
- Bring people together (i.e. create physical and virtual spaces where knowledge sharing can take place).

The HR function needs to understand how it can support these recommendations without resorting to a best-practice approach:

> Rarely can something that has worked well in one location and in one situation be applied directly to another. The solution often disappoints (Collinson and Parcell, 2004: 6).

As explained in Chapter 10 on talent management, the resource-based view, also described as a knowledge-based view, requires the HR function to identify the nature of an organization's intellectual capital and then to put in place specific HR strategies, policies, and practices that maximize the benefits of this form of capital. By definition, intellectual capital is unique to an organization, as levels of human and social capital vary from organization to organization (Mankin, 2007). To date, the theory and practice of SHRM have tended to focus on the role of human capital. The role of social capital has tended to be ignored by both theorists and professionals. The tendency to focus on human capital only is rather disappointing given the potential for HR professionals to support line managers in the building of knowledge networks and the creation of learning opportunities which can secure the benefits of social capital (Stewart and Tansley, 2002).

Although this situation is changing there is still much progress to be made. A CIPD research report concluded that HR professionals need to consider the impact of HR practices on *all* forms of capital and not solely human capital (Kinnie et al, 2006). In order to do so, HR professionals need to be closely involved in the development of strategic plans. A particular problem is the extent to which HR professionals, as well as managers, struggle to grasp the practical implications of social capital. The informal relationships that comprise social capital are often invisible or at least only partially understood by managers (Cross et al, 2002: 26). Informal relationships tend to be mistrusted by management as fragile and susceptible to loss as people leave (Stacey, 2001). The challenge facing managers is captured aptly by Beaumont and Hunter (2002), who warn that if the knowledge of employees is to be exploited effectively, managers need to develop a much better understanding of how employees interact socially with each other and how new knowledge is created. Pfeffer and Sutton (1999) refer to this as the 'knowledge-doing' problem, reflecting the comments above about the embodied nature of knowledge. A study in India has highlighted the importance of social capital to knowledge-sharing processes and KM strategies (Vashisth et al, 2010).

The 'knowledge-doing' problem is arguably best addressed through a KM strategy predicated on 'management-by-facilitation' (Mankin, 2009) which is consistent with the **enabling** approach advocated by Von Krogh et al (2000). This is in contrast to an 'engineering' strategy which attempts to control the creation and development of informal groups, such as communities of practices, through financial incentives (e.g. performance-related pay, bonus schemes), thus limiting the role of the HR function to the implementation of reward policy (Mankin, 2007; 2009). This is similar to the distinction made by Brewer and Brewer (2010) who suggest that there can exist 'exploitative HRM' and 'explorative HRM' strategies:

> The exploitative HRM strategy, with greater emphasis on explicit knowledge, tends to result in information technology (IT) solutions to KM whereas an explorative HRM strategy, placing a greater emphasis on tacit knowledge, tends to result in increased knowledge transfer, increased innovation, and organizational learning (p. 331).

A few studies have been published that also highlight the role of formal training, learning, and development interventions; for instance, formal training of community leaders (O'Dell and Hubert, 2011). Unfortunately, these often miss the point about social capital: it is a form of capital that is far less constant than human capital; it emerges and changes over time and is very difficult to control.

It is possible to empathize with management attempts to control informal groups given that:

> They rely on serendipity rather than design. In large firms, multiple informal networks may form on related topics but never integrate into a single network. People who may have knowledge or skills of great value to the network may not join the network either because they are part of other informal networks or simply because they fail to discover that the networks even exists (Bryan and Joyce, 2007: 173).

There are no formally published rules or procedures governing activities in an informal context. Behaviour is guided by a tacit understanding between members. This is why formal networks are fundamentally and conceptually different from the informal social networks, and therein lies the problem with an 'engineering' approach. Whilst it may be argued that

Table 13.3 HR implications for different KM strategies

Management-as-control (direct control)	Management-as-facilitation (indirect control)
The HR function has a limited input to strategic management of the organization: treated as a secondary, reactive function. Associated with low levels of credibility.	The HR function tends to have more input to strategic management: treated as a primary, often pro-active function. Associated with a strategic business partner role.
Standardized performance appraisal based on human capital theory: employees are viewed as a resource. Performance and training, rather than development, are emphasized.	Performance appraisal acknowledges the contribution of both human and social capital. Employees tend to be viewed as an asset. There is much more emphasis on devolved responsibility for development (e.g. individuals taking responsibility for exploiting social networks and contacts to enhance career progression).
Formal induction and training interventions that focus on socialization and employability (i.e. developing transferable skills which will benefit the organization).	A blend of formal and informal learning opportunities that enable individuals to develop their employability for the benefit of themselves as well as the organization. Formal interventions often focus on workplace learning (e.g. mentoring and coaching). Informal learning is focused on shared work practice and situated in communities and social networks.
Reward and recognition schemes based on individual performance.	Team-based reward and recognition schemes. An emphasis on collaboration.
Retention of knowledge workers through reward incentives (e.g. bonuses, performance-related pay) and development incentives (e.g. sponsorship for academic and professional qualifications such as MBA).	Retention of knowledge workers through flexible working and other practices that facilitate an effective work–life balance.
Standardized work practices, routines, and procedures. An emphasis on employee consultation and limited involvement.	A blend of standardized and informal work practices and routines. An emphasis on decision making through employee participation or more extensive employee involvement.

Source: adapted and developed from Mankin (2009).

reward plays an important role there needs to be a combination of traditional and innovative mechanisms for rewarding knowledge sharing (Singh and Soltani, 2010). Table 13.3 sets out the principal implications for the HR function of the two contrasting perspectives on KM strategies (i.e. management-as-control versus management-as-facilitation).

A key challenge for HR professionals generally is to find ways to leverage organizational knowledge. Making the case for global innovation in multinationals is one way the professional can take the lead and add value to the organization, although this is a difficult and challenging task that will require changes in mindsets, processes, and structures (*People Management*, 12 October 2006, pp. 32–34).

A coherent set of HR practices can be used to motivate employees, build their commitment to the organization, and encourage innovation in the workplace. These practices need to be evaluated given the resource implications shown in Table 13.4. However, a recurring weakness has been the relative lack of evaluation strategies for measuring the effectiveness of HR systems (Mankin, 2009). This, in turn, creates a problem for measuring the effectiveness of the KM strategy and the HR function's contribution to that strategy. Stewart (2002) is quite scathing in his criticism of most KM systems because they either ignore tacit knowledge or do 'a lousy job of getting at it' (p. 125). This problem has also been highlighted by the CIPD which has published very useful practical guidance on how to improve evaluation processes (CIPD, 2009a). The reason why this is so important is summarized by Barney and Clark (2007):

> Knowing the economic value of the firm's human resources is a necessary pre-condition before any HR executive can begin to manage the function strategically (p. 135).

Interestingly survey data reveal that firms in India are already adopting more sophisticated measurement systems than their US counterparts (Cappelli et al, 2010).

A further consideration is the involvement of the line manager in these processes. Managers are pivotal to effective KM strategies (Mertens et al, 2011). They play an important role in fostering innovation through knowledge sharing (Pasher and Ronen, 2011). Consequently, HR professionals need to build on existing relationships and work in participation with this stakeholder group.

Table 13.4 Resource implications for HR practices that support KM

HR implications	Resource implications
Learning and development: training and education of employees to better understand KM processes, including the role of social capital and knowledge sharing processes. Training and developing employees in specific competencies that support innovation and creativity, continuous improvement, and reflective practice (e.g. project management, problem-solving skills, understanding how to learn).	**Substantial investment is likely to be needed** (HRD budget; indirect costs such as staff cover, loss of productivity while employees are being trained).
Organization design and development: supporting culture change where necessary in order to encourage knowledge sharing (critical to this is building trust; encouraging managers and employees to review the effectiveness of KM processes and to critically reflect on their own contribution to this process). The change process can be achieved through direct and indirect HR interventions (e.g. facilitating project teams set up to spearhead the change process; helping line managers and knowledge workers to support each other and colleagues in coaching). Ensuring the organization is structured in such a way that core capabilities can be maximized. Identifying which aspects of the organization need to be outsourced.	**High direct and indirect costs** (HRD budget; loss of productivity; feasibility assessments which may involve external consultants; restructuring costs).

Table13.4 *(continued)*

HR implications	Resource implications
Communications policy: highly effective communication systems need to involve upward as well as downward communications. Barriers to knowledge sharing across the organization need to be addressed.	**Medium to high direct costs** (depending on the efficacy of existing policy).
Reward and retention strategy: incentives to retain knowledge workers and to encourage knowledge sharing rather than knowledge hoarding.	**Medium to high costs** (depending on an organization's reliance on knowledge workers). Line managers need to be supported in their attempts to motivate employees to utilize a KM system (e.g. inputting information onto a computer database, utilizing information processed by other employees).
Recruitment and selection: adopting a talent management approach; identifying core competencies, plus ongoing evaluation of these.	**Low to high direct and indirect costs** (depending on the state of internal and external labour markets).
Work design: process mapping initiatives to maximize the effectiveness of work design; allowing discretion to employees to carry out their own work design—especially core or knowledge workers).	**Medium to high direct and indirect costs** are likely if an organization needs to redesign work flows and job roles.

Sources: table produced by author (David Mankin) and supplemented by the following sources: Davenport and Prusak, 2000; Kaplan and Norton, 2004; Liu et al, 2006; Levis, 2009; Kanti Srikantaiah, 2010; Vaiman, 2010; Aktharsha and Anisa, 2011; Mertens et al, 2011; O'Dell and Hubert, 2011; Pasher and Ronen, 2011.

 Case study 13.2 Different perspectives on the rise of China and India

It is common knowledge that Chinese firms invest relatively little in their own product development capability. In contrast, India is gaining a reputation for innovation, although it is the ability of Indian companies to imitate Western products that still holds sway over the invention of indigenous products. As these two economies develop further it is likely that home-grown innovation will start to flourish. Indian companies, including Wipro, Tata, and Infosys, are continuing to invest in new products and services in order to be competitive in global markets. Both the Chinese and Indians were sufficiently astute to make the West help them develop their own research facilities as a condition for outsourcing production. China has also been acquiring Western firms and demanding the freedom to utilize the ideas that these firms have already developed. Indian firms, in sectors ranging from manufacturing to health care and financial services, are trying to develop new, indigenous products and services. However, one particular obstacle to this is the level of investment required for good quality R&D. China is presently the global leader in product piracy which is as an illegal form of knowledge transfer. As China needs to create some 8 million jobs each year, because of the numbers migrating from rural towns and villages to cities and economic development zones, it is likely that the current business model based on imitation is likely to be the bedrock of the country's economic development for some time to come. This highlights the extent to which it is easier to imitate than it is to innovate.

Sources

Engardio (2007); Hamm (2007); Perkowski (2008); Steinberg (2008); Jacques (2009); Kumar et al, (2009).

Activity

1. What are the potential HR implications for firms in China and India of current approaches to KM?

2. In what ways may Chinese and Indian firms have to change their approaches to KM in order to remain competitive?

 ## Conclusion

In an increasingly knowledge-based global economy, managing knowledge and knowledge workers is now viewed as one of the core capabilities in many organizations. Most organizations involve some form of knowledge work. However, there are certain types of organization that can be described as knowledge intensive firms (KIFs). To date, the concept of KM tends to be most closely associated with innovation. Whilst there have been opportunities for HR professionals to get involved with KM processes, many firms with a KM strategy have tended to emphasize the role of computer specialists in developing and supporting formal technology-based systems for managing knowledge assets. Consequently, the role of face-to-face collaboration is not always prioritized by managers. Whilst collaboration does not need to be face-to-face, research shows that it continues to be more effective than online or virtual forms such as discussion boards, blogs, and wikis. This is partly due to the fact that individuals tend to trust people they know well and work with closely. These high levels of trust are essential for maximizing the effectiveness of collaboration and inherent knowledge sharing processes. However, it is not yet proven which perspective on KM is the best approach and the reality is that organizations need to develop a KM strategy that blends different perspectives.

 ## Summary

The chapter has highlighted the following points:

- Knowledge is a problematic concept which lacks a universal definition. Consequently, more than one approach to the management of knowledge in organizations has emerged: objectivist, practice-based, and balanced perspectives.

- These perspectives are predicated on different interpretation of knowledge, although these interpretations tend to draw upon the seminal works of Polanyi who differentiated between tacit and explicit knowledge.

- The objectivist perspective has been underpinned by human capital theory and has stressed the role of the individual and individual cognition.

- The practice-based perspective has been underpinned by social capital theory and has stressed the role of informal groups, such as communities of practice and social networks. This perspective shifts the emphasis from the control of knowledge through compliance interventions to the nurturing of the context within which knowledge is created and shared.

- The balanced approach recognizes the need to combine the objectivist and practice-based perspectives in ways unique to an organization.

- In terms of understanding KM, knowledge sharing, and in particular face-to-face sharing, is a pivotal process and seen as being more effective than sharing in a virtual environment (Mankin and Cohen, 2004).
- SHRM has an important role in supporting and developing knowledge sharing processes. This can best be achieved through a combination of different practices. These have specific resource implications which need to be understood.

 ## Review questions

1. Why is it difficult to arrive at a universal definition of knowledge?
2. What is the relationship between knowledge, information, and data?
3. Define and explain the concept of knowledge sharing.
4. How can HR functions support the development of intellectual capital?
5. Why is KM important to innovation?

 ## End-of-chapter case study Innovation in Wipro

Wipro is one of India's leading technical services companies, ranked third behind Tata Consultancy Services (first) and Infosys Technologies (second). The company's revenues have increased from $400 million in 1999 to $5 billion in 2008. Today the company has over 80,000 employees, up from 14,000 in 2002. Wipro's values are captured in the 'Wipro Promise' which focuses on respecting people, integrity, innovation, and value for money. Azim Premji, executive chairman and founder of Wipro, has reportedly claimed that 'Customers love us most for our humbleness. I believe, as a company, we listen carefully and are willing to learn'. His long-term goal is to provide services for every aspect of corporate activity and for this reason the company has embarked on an acquisition strategy to compensate for any gaps in the company's existing provision. This has included acquiring firms in Australia, Portugal, and Finland. Wipro's strategic goals are categorized under the following headings: quality, financial, people, innovation, business development. Each business unit can choose its own sixth category. Goals are cascaded downwards and monthly progress reports are produced in each business unit. The company uses 360-degree feedback for the performance reviews of managers who then receive help from the HR function in compiling action plans which they communicate to their team. Innovation is included in every employee performance review and forms part of senior management's business performance scorecard.

Innovation is strategically important because the company needs to create new information technologies and solutions for customers. The latter is particularly attractive to the company as they help to enforce Wipro's importance to its clients. Wipro can offer both technology and business process solutions at a significantly lower cost than if the work was done by the client. Employees are encouraged to submit ideas that focus on technology to the company's seven-member Innovation Council via the employee website. The council reviews proposals, allocates funds, and sets up project teams. These teams can comprise between 5 and 40 people and will include the employee who made the original suggestion as long as he/she has the necessary expertise. Managers are also encouraged to spot emerging technologies.

The company also has Centres of Excellence where engineers and programmers can focus on emerging technologies. In 2006 the company had over 40 such centres which employed some 250 engineers and programmers. The typical lifespan of these centres is 12–18 months as it can take that long to develop a new practice and get it established with clients. The expertise developed by these teams is shared across the company through training programmes organized through the HR function.

Sources

Hamm, S. (2007) *Bangalore Tiger: How Indian Tech Upstart Wipro Is Rewriting the Rules of Global Competition*. New York, NY: McGraw-Hill.

Kumar, N., Mohapatra, P.K. and Chandrasekhar, S. (2009) *India's Global Powerhouses: How They Are Taking on the World*. Boston, MA: Harvard Business Press, p. 56.

Schuman, M. (2009) *The Miracle: The Epic Story of Asia's Quest for Wealth*. New York, NY: Harper Business.

Capelli, P., Singh, H., Singh, J. and Useem, M. (2010) *The India Way: How India's Top Business Leaders Are Revolutionizing Management*. Boston, MA: Harvard Business Press.

Mundra, N., Gulati, K. and Vashisth, R. (2011) Achieving competitive advantage through knowledge management and innovation: empirical evidences from the Indian IT sector. *IUP Journal of Knowledge Management*, 9(2), pp. 7–25.

Case study questions

1. What employee competencies are likely to underpin Wipro's focus on innovation?

2. What appears to be the company's approach to KM?

3. What role does the HR function play and how might this be improved?

 ## Further reading

Barney, J.B. and Clark, D.N. (2007) *Resource-Based Theory: Creating and Sustaining Competitive Advantage*. Oxford: Oxford University Press.
Basically this gives you just about everything you need to know about the resource-based view.

Bracci, E. and Vagnoni, E. (2011) Understanding small family business succession in a knowledge management perspective. *IUP Journal of Knowledge Management*, 9(1), pp. 7–36.
This article offers an insight into KM from a small business perspective.

Conway, S. and Steward, F. (2009) *Managing and Shaping Innovation*. Oxford: Oxford University Press.
This provides excellent coverage on innovation generally and contains several sections that discuss various KM implications.

Hislop, D. (2009) *Knowledge Management in Organisations*. Oxford: Oxford University Press.
This is an excellent text on all aspects of KM.

Lesser, E. and Prusak, L. (eds) (2004) *Creating Value with Knowledge: Insights from the IBM Institute for Business Value*. New York, NY: Oxford University Press.
Although slightly dated now there is still a wealth of information on different aspects of KM in this text which makes it well worth reading.

 For additional material on the content of this chapter please visit the supporting Online Resource Centre www.oxfordtextbooks.co.uk/orc/truss.

14 SHRM and corporate social responsibility

 Learning Objectives

By the end of this chapter you should be able to:

- Define and explain the concepts of business ethics and corporate social responsibility (CSR).
- Appreciate the implications of global trends for the ethical and socially responsible management of organizations.
- Critically analyse organizational approaches to business ethics and CSR using shareholder and stakeholder theories.
- Explain the ways in which the HR function can support CSR policies and initiatives.
- Critically evaluate the relationship between SHRM and CSR in a range of organizational contexts.

Key Concepts

Business ethics
Corporate social responsibility
Shareholder theory
Stakeholder theory

14.1 Introduction

The recession of 2008–10 illustrates the globalized nature of modern markets which are increasingly integrated in what Authers (2010) describes as 'a tight and deadly embrace' (p. 10). The recession was triggered by a housing crisis in the US, where warnings went unheeded about reckless lending in the form of subprime mortgages to low-income families (Cable, 2009). This acted as a catalyst for a worldwide domino effect with country after country suffering some form of financial meltdown. Even the more robust, developing economies such as China and India have not been immune from this crisis, although their continued growth does illustrate how the balance of power in the global economy is shifting away from the US. The crisis has brought into sharp focus the extent to which financial globalization also has social, health, and environmental implications. For instance, the distribution of the world's population is increasingly characterized by a process of urbanization: more and more people are migrating to urban areas (Friedman, 2008). This can be seen on a large scale in China and to a lesser extent in other Asian economies such as Vietnam and India. This process of urbanization brings with it a wide range of social, health, and environmental implications such as: the disintegration of traditional rural communities; the need for more housing, medical care, and education; the provision of food and basic supplies needed for daily living; and the degradation of the environment. China's demand for raw materials and energy has potentially significant implications for the global environment (Magnus, 2011). On the international stage China and India are closing ranks in order to oppose the environmental demands of developed nations (Bahl, 2010). Green groups in particular see globalization as a threat to the world environment and have long argued that global markets are characterized by the competitive exploitation of natural resources (Mankin, 2009). Whichever perspective you subscribe to there is little doubt that human economic activity is depleting the world's natural resources (Werther and Chandler, 2011). Kaletsky (2010) argues that the new post-2009 version of capitalism 'should encourage much clearer and more constructive thinking about the new incentives required for changes in technology and behaviour to reduce pollution . . . [and] promote investment in a new global energy infrastructure' (pp. 322-323).

In recent years a growing number of organizations have responded to these concerns by developing policies on how to manage their operations in an ethically and socially responsible manner. The concept of corporate social responsibility (CSR) has emerged to explain this 'new' approach, building on the existing and more narrowly focused concept of business ethics. This shift can be seen in a range of changing organizational priorities; for instance, sourcing more products ethically (e.g. the growing commitment to Fairtrade products), the implementation of diversity policies that go beyond the minimum requirements of equal opportunities legislation, the increased use of environmentally friendly manufacturing operations, and the increased use of recycled materials. Increasingly organizations have been developing strategies and policies for CSR (Zerk, 2011) and publicizing these to customers, suppliers, shareholders, and employees, as well as to other relevant stakeholders, such as national and regional governments. In effect, CSR has become central to many organizations' strategic activities (Coombs and Holladay, 2011). Yet this trend has not been driven solely by firms in developed economies. The Tata group in India has a long history of community-based initiatives (Mankin, 2009), while similar initiatives by Unilever India (Hindustan Lever) and Unilever Indonesia can be traced back to the 1950s and 1960s respectively (Urip, 2010).

However, there are two important issues. First, approaches to CSR vary from region to region across the globe (Ubias and Alas, 2010). Second, it is not always easy to determine the underlying reasons why organizations adopt and promote CSR. Is it because senior management are truly committed to helping the poor and/or the environment? Or is it simply because it makes good business sense? For instance, in China CSR has been promoted 'to counter international criticism of the country's labour and environmental practices' (Harney, 2008: 262). Certainly, support for CSR is not universal, with some business executives still indulging in socially irresponsible and unethical behaviour (Idowu and Papasolomou, 2007). It is perhaps ironic that recent research shows that CSR is an increasingly important issue in the international banking industry (Scholtens, 2009).

To date there has been limited coverage of the relationship between SHRM and CSR and this chapter is intended to help bridge this gap. The first part of the chapter considers the salient global trends impacting on ethical and socially responsible management. This is followed by an explanation of relevant concepts and a discussion on the relationship between business ethics and CSR. The chapter concludes with a discussion on the role of SHRM in supporting organizational strategies and policies for CSR. Although all types of organization operating in all sectors are affected by business ethics and CSR, the chapter pays particular attention to the private sector.

14.2 Global trends

Global trends are summarized in Table 14.1. The principal trends encompass demographics global poverty, and the environment. It is always difficult to make predictions about demographics, although Sachs (2008) does argue that the global population will stabilize by the middle of this century. The main implication for developed nations is the prospect of an older and more culturally diverse workforce (Mankin, 2009) in conjunction with higher levels of unemployment. This trend is likely to have more serious implications for developed rather than emerging and developing economies (Vettori, 2010). An issue closely related to demographics is the problem of global poverty (Collier, 2010). It has been claimed that under globalization the total number of people living in basic poverty actually grew in the early years of this century, from 2.5 to 2.7 billion (Saul, 2005). As Stiglitz (2007) observes:

> The world is in a race between economic growth and population growth, and so far population growth is winning. Even as the percentages of people living in poverty are falling, the absolute number is rising (p. 10).

In recent years there have been poor harvests in Europe and Russia, crop failures in countries such as India, droughts in countries such as Australia, and flooding in Pakistan. All of these have had a significant impact on living standards. Until recently little consideration has been given to the role of private sector corporations in alleviating poverty, although this is now starting to change as corporations and civil society organizations engage in more successful collaborations (Prahalad, 2009). In contrast, mercenary entrepreneurs in the US have moved in quickly to exploit the credit-hungry working poor of the country (Rivlin, 2010). This is consistent with Klein's (2008) argument that even natural disasters are now being viewed as market opportunities to be exploited, a trend she describes as 'disaster capitalism'.

We now live in what can be termed a disposable society (Mankin, 2009). It is often cheaper to buy a new product than to get the existing one repaired, while globally natural resources, such as oil, gas, iron ore, water, and timber, are being consumed at a faster rate than at any previous period. The US and China are the world's biggest polluters, with industrial smog and untreated sewage being two of the principal by-products of China's developing economy (Kynge, 2006). However, global regulation of environmental standards is fraught with political difficulties. It is proving very difficult to achieve greater cooperation between developed and developing economies over the management of natural resources and a reduction in carbon emissions (Collier, 2010). Hayton (2010) provides a vivid and sobering description of what is happening in Vietnam, one of Asia's rapidly emerging economies:

Table 14.1 Global trends

Demographics	• The world's population has doubled from 3 billion to over 6 billion since 1960 and is predicted to reach somewhere between 10 and 12 billion this century before subsiding
	• Falling birth rates in some countries (e.g. the US, Africa) and rising in others (e.g. India)
	• An older and more diverse workforce in developed countries
	• Higher levels of unemployment in developed countries
Global poverty	• The number of people living in poverty continues to grow
	• Africa is the poorest continent on the planet and the only one that has actually grown poorer over the last 30 years
	• Aid agencies have been lobbying for an end to European Union subsidies that penalize African exports and create food mountains
	• Rising food prices
Environment	• Increasing exploitation of natural resources, including illegal deforestation and overfishing
	• Poor governance in organizations
	• Weak or non-existent environmental legislation in some developing nations

Sources: based on Mankin (2009) plus additional sources: Nilekani, 2008; Brainard and Martinez-Diaz, 2009; Collier, 2010; Hayton, 2010; Segerlund, 2010; Vettori, 2011; Zerk, 2011.

As the world's 13th most populous country . . . it won't be long before it starts moving into the pollution big league. The population is growing and increasingly able to afford the consumer goods people in richer countries take for granted: motorbikes, televisions, refrigerators, air conditioners and the other accoutrements of modern living. The government is building electricity networks and power stations, manufacturers are building industrial plants, and the result is a rapid increase in the emissions of greenhouse gases and other pollutants. . . . Every province wants growth; few are willing to tell those responsible for pollution, over-exploitation of resources or environmental destruction to stop (pp. 179-180).

The growing energy crisis has come to symbolize global environmental concerns. Easily extractable oil supplies are declining, demand for natural gas is rising, and there are shortages of electric power in developing countries such as India and China (Mankin, 2009). Ultimately, it is consumer demand for cheap fuel, electronic gadgets, and the other trappings of a 21st-century lifestyle that lie at the heart of the energy crisis (Hofmeister, 2010). The 2010 'Gulf Spill' incident involving BP has also highlighted the environmental risks associated with new exploration techniques, such as deep-sea oil drilling, which are being developed by oil companies as they seek out new reserves of crude oil. As Bower (2009) observes, finding a balance between 'boom' (driven by cheap oil prices) and 'bust' (driven by high oil prices) has been elusive. Ultimately society has become too reliant on oil, natural gas, and coal, and the environment is paying the price (Maas, 2009).

14.3 Business ethics

 Key Concept

Business ethics is about 'the study of business situations, activities, and decisions where issues of right and wrong are addressed' (Crane and Matten, 2007: 5).

In terms of defining business ethics (see key concept box), Crane and Matten (2007) are referring to what is *morally* right or wrong rather than what is *legally* right or wrong. The latter encompasses what can be referred to as the 'dark' side of organizations (Mankin, 2009). Those activities described as being 'dark', such as fraud, bribery, discrimination, bullying, and harassment, are covered by legislation in developed economies, although the situation is far from clear-cut in some of the developing economies. Whatever part of the world, the reality is that there will always be some organizations that attempt to avoid even their legal responsibilities (Boxall and Purcell, 2008). There is also a 'grey' side to organizations, and those activities described as being 'grey' fall within the realm of business ethics (Mankin, 2009). This includes such things as the mark-up on organic food in supermarkets (Harford, 2007). Ultimately, society expects managers and professionals to behave ethically (Lantos, 2001).

 Critical Reflection

To what extent has modern thinking about business ethics been influenced by historical perspectives? Compare and contrast the salient views of two philosophers.

The notion that something is morally right or wrong suggests that ethical standards are universal. However, they are not. The economic values that tend to prevail in corporations are often different from the personal values that guide our behaviour in our private lives. Operating in culturally diverse environments adds further complications and this partly explains the emergence of the concept of 'localization' (see Chapter 1). However, firms have recognized for some time that business ethics is important because this has been seen by many consumers, pressure groups, the media, and corporate managers as being good for business (Crane and Matten, 2007). In turn, HR professionals are expected to behave ethically and to monitor behaviour in their organization (Mankin, 2009). However, cases such as Enron (see the end-of-chapter case study) highlight that the role of HR is often ineffectual in tackling both illegal and unethical actions by senior managers.

To ensure against unethical behaviour organizations need to develop self-regulatory practices that are based on clearly defined ethical guidelines (Dowling and Welch, 2004). These are typically referred to as codes of conduct which specify the way in which employees or members of an occupational group are expected to behave when carrying out their work responsibilities. However, the limitations of codes of conduct need to be recognized; for instance, they are not proof against problems such as workplace discrimination (Demuijnck, 2009); they are also self-regulating.

14.4 Corporate social responsibility

Corporate social responsibility is a problematic concept that defies a universal definition (Blowfield and Murray, 2008). It is also difficult to operationalize (Pedersen, 2006). Although there are no easy solutions to the design and implementation of CSR strategies and policies there is a recognition that CSR needs to be an integral part of business strategy (Porter and Kramer, 2006). However, it is often impossible to determine underlying corporate motives (Crane and Matten, 2007). Is a firm being altruistic or simply trying to maximize profits? Or is it simply making good business decisions? Does any of this matter? Arguably it does because it has become apparent in the developed world that there is a strong consumer demand for ethical and socially responsibly management of corporations across a range of sectors. In an era of high-visibility brands consumers want to be able to trust the actions of the firms behind the brand.

 Key Concept

Corporate social responsibility is the extent to which an organization is managed in an ethical and socially responsible manner in order to achieve sustainable competitive advantage.

CSR has an internal as well as an external focus, although it is the latter that tends to receive more media coverage. The external focus is about the impact of an organization's activities on communities, the environment, and external stakeholders such as customers and suppliers. The internal focus is about how an organization is managed and the impact this has on employees. This internal focus includes practices such as HRM, diversity management, health and safety, and environmental protection (Mankin, 2009). Because of the external focus and demands for greater transparency and accountability, leading businesses in countries such as the UK, France, and South Africa are being required to formally report on their CSR activities (Idowu and Papasolomou, 2007). However, the differentiation between internal and external offers a partial insight only. In terms of understanding the impact on organizations of CSR it is important to appreciate two particular theories: shareholder theory and stakeholder theory.

Shareholder and stakeholder theories reflect the tensions that exist between the two competing perspectives on globalization discussed in Chapter 1. Shareholder theory gives priority to profit maximization based on a corporation's legal obligations to generate shareholder

Key Concepts

Shareholder theory posits that the primary duty of a firm's managers is the maximization of shareholder wealth; and, therefore, the only social responsibility of business is shareholder maximization.

Stakeholder theory is a long-term strategic perspective which recognizes that stakeholders other than shareholders have a vested interest in firm performance. It is closely associated with an ethical approach to management.

wealth (Key, 1999). This is consistent with an economic perspective on globalization. Stakeholder theory looks beyond profit maximization and focuses on social and environmental values, based on a corporation's moral obligations to all those who have a stake in the business (Freeman, 2011). This reflects a social perspective on globalization. 'While stakeholder theory describes interactions with interest groups external to corporations, which may or may not lead to positive CSR results, an increasing number of corporations adhere to voluntary international guidelines' (Dobers, 2009: 187). However, this delineation between economic and social is an artificial one as economic decisions tend to have social consequences (Pedersen, 2006).

A CSR strategy underpinned by shareholder theory tends to encourage a short-term perspective. Zink (2005) cites several financial scandals involving US corporations that have been caused through the adoption of a short-term perspective: Enron (where losses and debts were hidden in various subsidiaries); World Com ($3.9 billion was wrongly accounted); and Adelphia Communication (which invented 500,000 subscribers). Shareholder theory is more controversial in the UK than the US because commercial practices in the UK are underpinned by the values of European capitalism which emphasize the need for clear codes of conduct at the highest levels in organizations (Hutton, 2003). This may be a contentious perspective but it does correspond to other differences between the US and the UK/Europe; for instance, in terms of the UK/Europe's renewed emphasis on the rights of employees following a tradition of employee participation and involvement which has been markedly stronger than in the US (Boxall and Purcell, 2008). This illustrates that cultural differences over how business should be conducted exist even when a common language is shared. Cooke and He (2010) highlight the importance of the shareholder perspective in China, although they refer to this as the efficiency model:

> Findings suggest that the Chinese textile and apparel firms are beginning to realize the importance of adopting CSR. This is in spite of the fact that many of the enterprises do not have a written CSR policy and that the majority of enterprises have not obtained CSR standards. The main reasons for firms to implement CSR practices are to enhance their reputation, improve customer satisfaction and reduce operating cost. In other words, a business case approach is adopted (p. 372).

In contrast, stakeholder theory enables an organization to adopt a longer-term perspective. Stakeholder theory looks beyond shareholder value to embrace a wide range of stakeholders.

It is being increasingly recognized that long-term sustainability relies not just on the share-holder but on all other stakeholders relevant to the organization (Zink, 2005). This perspective increasingly underpins organizational approaches to CSR (Burchell and Cook, 2006), as a successful CSR strategy involves a two-way relationship between business corporations, as well as other types of large organization, and the societies within which they interact (Werther and Chandler, 2011). Multinationals, in particular, interact with a wide range of societies across the globe both directly (e.g. subsidiaries are located in different countries) and indirectly (e.g. sourcing of raw materials). Consequently, organizations need to wrestle with a balancing act between economic, ethical, and social objectives (Lantos, 2001) which can today be quite wide-ranging:

> There is now a growing recognition of the equal importance of issues such as: the links between sustainability and innovation; the role of small and medium-sized enterprises; the importance of sustainability in strategic business development; the emergent significance of green consumer demands on firms; sustainable practices in particular industries; and how firms can utilise the opportunities that market-based environmental policies (such as 'cap and trade' limits on water usage, or greenhouse gas emissions) provide (Schaper, 2010: 8).

It has been argued also that stakeholder theory is more relevant to HRM (Cooke and He, 2010), although there is a lack of empirical evidence to support this claim apart from isolated studies. For instance, in a study of Asian firms Kim (2011) concludes that CSR activities can enhance employee commitment and satisfaction (essentially employee engagement, as discussed in Chapter 12).

 Case study 14.1   Nokia and CSR

Senior managers increasingly see themselves as caught between critics demanding higher levels of CSR and investors applying pressure in order to maximize short-term profits. Senior managers occasionally apply a strategic way to thinking about corporate responsibility and base any decisions on the values underpinning Nokia's code of conduct. As leaders of one of the biggest companies in its sector Nokia's senior managers believe that the best contribution they can make to the global community is to conduct their business in a responsible way. They believe that the most effective way of doing this is through ensuring relevant CSR policies are embedded in every aspect of the company's operations. Nokia's strategy for the promotion of CSR has encompassed pioneering efforts to accelerate economic growth in emerging economies, and supporting sustainable development in relation to environmental protection, energy efficiency, and climate change. One initiative in Africa is designed to bring mobile access to unconnected communities across that continent through micro-financing. The latter involves the provision of small loans to individuals who are too poor to secure a conventional loan from a bank. The cost of buying a phone is significant in many parts of the world. In July 2008 Nokia set up a pilot scheme in the Indian state of Andhra Pradesh, with SKS Microfinance, one of the fastest-growing micro-finance institutions in that country. Through this programme, SKS customers are offered loans that are repayable on a weekly basis. This removes the cash barrier to buying a phone. Previously they would have to pay upfront the equivalent of 30% to 50% of a typical monthly income. The company has also provided mobile phones as well as funds to assist relief efforts following an earthquake in the Sichuan province of China and the donation of funds to assist cyclone victims in Myanmar.

Sources

Steinbock, D. (2010) *Winning Across Global Markets: How Nokia Creates Strategic Advantage in a Fast-Changing World.* San Francisco, CA: Jossey-Bass.

Nokia (2009) *Nokia Corporate Responsibility Review.* Nokia, http://www.nokia.com/NOKIA_COM_1/Corporate_Responsibility/CR_report_2008/nokia_cr_report_2008.pdf (accessed 20 June 2010).

Activity

Shareholder theory has been criticized as an overly simplistic view given that business organizations have to satisfy the needs of stakeholders other than shareholders (Freeman et al, 2004). How valid is this statement? What are the alternative perspectives?

Crane and Matten (2007) argue that CSR encompasses four principal responsibilities, and these are shown in Table 14.2 which also includes information drawn from other sources. Other authors such as Blowfield and Murray (2008) offer a different taxonomy that includes: legal compliance, philanthropy and community investment; environmental management; sustainability; human rights; animal rights; workers' rights; corruption; and corporate governance.

The potential benefits of CSR are set out in Table 14.3 which draws upon Mankin (2009). Equally important to appreciate are the consequences of having a poor, ill-conceived, or indifferent approach to CSR and these are shown in Table 14.4. This table also acknowledges the implications of adopting a controversial cause which can divide public opinion. Lantos (2001) argues that it is wiser to avoid such causes (Lantos, 2001).

Table 14.2 CSR responsibilities

Economic	• Business corporations exist to make a profit for shareholders while providing other stakeholders with economic benefits such as fair-paying jobs for employees and good quality products for customers.
	• Other types of organization, such as local government, health, charities, need to adhere to economic and financial principles to ensure their continued existence.
Legal	• All organizations operate within the context of a legal framework which can reflect national, regional, and international legislation.
	• The emphasis is on compliance.
Ethical	• Organizations may not be legally required to operate in a particular way but may choose to do so because of some overriding moral obligation.
	• This is about doing something because it is **right** to do so.
Philanthropic	• This is where an organization exercises discretion to improve the quality of life of employees, local communities, and ultimately society in general.
	• This has been termed **altruistic** by Lantos (2002) and often manifests as organizations making significant charitable donations.

Sources: based on Mankin (2009) using additional sources: Lantos, 2002; Maycunich Gilley et al, 2003; Crane and Matten, 2007.

Table 14.3 The benefits of CSR

The organization	The employee	The consumer	Society
Improves and enhances company image and reputation	Increases employee trust in management	Consumers feel good about buying products from companies they trust	NGOs want to work with companies they trust
Attracts new customers	Attracts new employees	Consumers will talk positively to family, friends, and colleagues about the company	Alleviation of social ills
Increases customer satisfaction and builds longer-term customer relationships	Increases employee satisfaction, motivation, and morale		Development of the arts and sport through company sponsorship initiatives
Accumulation of customer goodwill	Improves employee retention		
Employee benefits result in higher productivity			
Limits government interference			
Sources of finance are more readily available			
Minimizes the likelihood and cost of fines and legal actions			

Source: Mankin (2009).

Table 14.4 The potential problems of a poor approach to CSR

The organization	The employee	The consumer	Society
Poor publicity—impacting on company image and reputation	Less commitment to the company	Views the CSR cause as a publicity stunt	Environmental degradation
Loss of customer goodwill	Lower levels of productivity	Takes custom elsewhere	Breakdown in community cohesion
Consumers boycott products and/or services, thereby reducing turnover		Makes derogatory remarks about the company to family, friends, and colleagues	
Increases the likelihood of fines and litigation, thereby adding to the costs of the business			

Source: Mankin (2009).

14.5 **SHRM and CSR**

The rise of CSR has significant implications for the strategic role of the HR function yet the HR profession in Europe has been relatively reluctant to engage with the concept (Preuss et al, 2009). This phenomenon is not restricted to Europe where 'best management' practices are well established. In China, where HR processes are still evolving, the majority of enterprises do not have a written CSR policy (Warner and Rowley, 2010). This apparent inability or unwillingness to get directly involved in CSR is curious if Hallin and Gustavsson (2009) are correct in arguing that management practices within the fields of HRM and CSR are actually merging. This would seem to suggest that the HR profession is ideally positioned to exploit CSR as a way of establishing itself in a business partner role (see Chapter 4). As discussed earlier in the chapter, CSR is being seen increasingly as a strategic priority and a potential source of competitive advantage.

CSR embraces a range of issues that are fundamental to projecting the image of a responsible employer; for instance, employee consultation, diversity, fair treatment, and work–life balance. These issues reflect the extent to which CSR is inextricably linked with corporate governance (as well as being dependent on effective HR policies). As Aras and Crowther (2010) argue, 'good governance is essential for good corporate performance' (p. 2). However, as the Enron case illustrates, HR professionals may lack the power and influence that is needed to ensure compliance with governance. Cases such as Enron also illustrate the importance of having an appropriate ethical context upon which to build and develop a CSR culture. Ethical context is defined by Valentine and Godkin (2009) as an environment 'both perceived and actual, that is established through ethical business practices and adherence to corporate guidelines' (p. 62). In principle, codes of conduct are a self-regulating product of an organization's ethical context.

In principle, HR departments are responsible for many of the policies and processes on which effective delivery of CSR initiatives depend; for example, recruitment, diversity, employee involvement, performance appraisal, training, and communications (CIPD, 2003a; 2009). As Table 14.5 highlights, the implications of HR policies for CSR are not that dissimilar to those for other organizational processes that involve the management of the employer–employee relationship. For instance, the drivers for developing employee engagement, which are discussed in detail in Chapter 12, include employee voice (being able to feed your views upwards), senior management communication and vision, a supportive work environment, and good line management style (Alfes et al, 2010a). These can all be found in the table. Therefore, if we accept that CSR policies and processes are inextricably linked with HRM policies and processes, it is reasonably evident how Hallin and Gustavsson (2009) arrived at their conclusion that the two fields are merging.

There appears to be a consensus that CSR needs to be embedded in an organization's culture if changes in manager and employee actions and attitudes are to be realized (see Case study 14.1). Again, there is nothing new or remarkable in this statement. Training, in particular, is a long-established organizational practice (and is discussed in more detail in Chapter 16), while socialization processes that focus on developing employee commitment are well understood. These practices and processes are particularly important given that employee buy-in to CSR is pivotal to the success of CSR strategies (Davies and Crane, 2010).

Table 14.5 The implications of HR policies for CSR

HR policy	Implications
Recruitment	• Human capital and talent management includes recruiting individuals who can demonstrate a commitment to socially responsible and ethical management
	• Utilize social networks and business links to identify potential recruits
Diversity and equal opportunities	• Treating employees fairly
	• Maintaining ethical standards in how the employer–employee relationship is managed
	• Developing and promoting social inclusion
Employee involvement and communications	• Employees need to understand the purpose of an organization's CSR strategy and policies
	• Employees need to trust senior management and believe in their commitment to CSR
	• Employee values need to be aligned with the organizational values that underpin the CSR strategy and policies
	• Employee voice needs to encouraged by managers—employees must be allowed to express their opinions
	• Developing employee volunteering
Performance management and appraisal	• Creating meaning in work so that employees are more engaged and committed
	• Ensuring employee wellbeing is monitored
Training and development	• Educating employees about an organization's ethical standards and code of conduct
	• Training to support culture change initiatives and help embed commitment to CSR
	• Embedding a commitment to CSR across all training programmes

Sources: CIPD, 2003a; 2003b; 2003c; 2009a; Liu et al, 2009; Mankin, 2009; Preuss et al, 2009; Valentine and Godkin, 2009; Cooke and He, 2010; Davies and Crane, 2010; Gupta, 2010; Paetzold, 2010.

A key aspect of organizations acting in a socially responsible manner is an investment in human capital (Zink, 2005). This is easier for organizations that have a surplus of resources to invest in this way (Pedersen, 2006). Consequently, the training and development of employees needs to be integrated with the CSR strategy (Mankin, 2009; Sukserm and Takahashi, 2010). Training can be focused specifically on CSR (e.g. induction training) or on helping employees in ways that reflect an organization's commitment to CSR (e.g. in the provision of training and education interventions to help employees manage personal financial debt). Indeed, training has been one way in which the leading supermarkets in the UK demonstrate their commitment to CSR (Comfort et al, 2005). Companies such as Alcan use training to back up the importance of their CSR strategy (Esty and Winston, 2006). Unfortunately, many managers are left untrained or poorly briefed on the implications of CSR.

Management and leadership development also has an important role to play in the development of CSR. Inspirational leadership is fundamental to the nurturing of employee commitment to CSR (CIPD, 2003c). This is because visible senior management commitment to CSR raises the credibility of socially responsible and ethical management (CIPD, 2009a). However, this does mean that 'HR professionals will need to learn more about what issues are most critical in determining whether employees have a positive view of the ethics of their organisational leaders' (Schramm, 2004, p. 176). This may seem relatively straightforward but HR professionals have often been accused of an insular perspective and a lack of commercial and/or strategic acumen (Mankin, 2009). This has implications for HR competencies and is discussed in more detail in Chapter 16.

The ultimate challenge facing organizations is to demonstrate that CSR policies have added value to the organization. However, depending on which perspective is adopted by senior management, added value will be defined differently. For those who choose to adopt a shareholder (or efficiency business model) perspective on CSR it is all about maximizing profits and shareholder dividends. Arguably, this is about being more efficient. For those who choose to adopt a stakeholder (or socially conscious) perspective it is about delivering on a wider range of fronts. Arguably, this is about being more effective. This places evaluation at the heart of the strategic process (e.g. the role of the Balanced Scorecard). In 2003 the CIPD published the findings of a survey of 1,000 employees in the UK that revealed that they saw a clear connection between responsible business practice and a positive impact on the bottom line (CIPD, 2003c). However, this finding must be treated with caution. Many organizations still lack effective evaluation processes at both strategic and operational levels, including those managed by the HR function (Mankin, 2009). This deficiency needs to be addressed if Liu et al (2009) are correct in arguing that:

> Firms are under increasing pressure not only to satisfy social claims directly related to employee welfare but also to prioritise and manage its responses to other stakeholder groups in ways that are meaningful to its employees. This requires companies to fine tune their CSR strategy (p. 196).

There have been some studies which suggest this issue can be addressed. For instance, Rettab et al (2009) found in a study of 280 firms based in Dubai that there is a positive association between CSR and financial performance. However, many other studies are still inconclusive (Cooke and He, 2010). Part of the problem is the lack of cohesion to a CSR strategy. Often CSR comprises little more than isolated initiatives (Bohdanowicz and Zientara, 2008) and there is no real sense that CSR is fully integrated, both vertically and horizontally, with business strategy. In contrast, the Scandinavian firm, Scandic Hotels, provides an example of how CSR can be embedded in an organization's business model such that it 'influences all corporate decisions and thereby conditions the company's efforts to improve both the working conditions of employees and the quality of life in local communities' (Bohdanowicz and Zientara, 2008: 155). As Werther and Chandler (2011) observe, effective evaluation of CSR is dependent on the existence of a 'triple bottom line' whereby evaluation spans financial, environmental, and social performance. This requires a transparent CSR audit whereby all relevant information is widely published (ibid).

Case study **14.2**   Samsung's strategies for tackling unethical behaviour

Samsung, the Korean IT firm, has a global reputation for innovative products. It has global assets of just under $300 billion and employs 160,000 people across 61 countries. The firm promotes the importance of CSR and business ethics. As part of its values it claims that operating in an ethical manner provides the foundation of the business and that everything the firm does is guided by a 'moral compass' that ensures fairness, respect for all stakeholders, and complete transparency in how the firm operates. Consequently, an important element of the firm's corporate culture is loyalty, with an emphasis on integrity and a can-do attitude. The company has emphasized integrity and corporate ethics as part of a global code of conduct which 'sets forth detailed behavioural guidelines and judgmental standards for Samsung Electronics' employees as members of a world leading company. The code of conduct includes elimination of nationality or gender discrimination, transparent disclosure of business information, customer information protection and partner collaboration. All of Samsung electronics employees will abide by this code of conduct in their relationship with their peers and customers' (Samsung *Sustainability Report 2009*, p. 13). The firm prohibits the acceptance of bribes or any personal profiteering. It has designed and implemented ways to educate existing employees and new recruits. It has also implemented what is regarded as a meticulous auditing system to ensure that unethical practices do not take place. Auditors monitor employees closely and punish any offenders (e.g. instant dismissal). The company also puts together various scenarios of bribery cases and lets employees discuss and decide on solutions during training. The firm has a formal training programme called the Anti-Corruption Education Programme. This type of training reflects Samsung's broader approach to the development of employees. Induction training lasts 27 days and most training programmes are focused on shaping employees' state of mind when working. Employees are proud of this culture although Samsung's definition of unethical behaviour is rather narrow, encompassing only the taking of bribes or personal profiteering from inside information.

Sources

Chang, S.-J. (2008) *Sony vs Samsung: The Inside Story of the Electronics Giants' Battle for Global Supremacy*. Singapore: John Wiley and Sons (Asia) Pte. Ltd.

Samsung (2011) http://www.samsung.com/uk/aboutsamsung/corporateprofile/valuesphilosophy.html (accessed 14 June 2011).

Samsung (2011) http://www.samsung.com/uk/aboutsamsung/corporateprofile/ourperformance/samsungprofile.html (accessed 14 June 2011).

Samsung (2011) *Sustainability Report 2009*. http://www.samsung.com/us/aboutsamsung/sustainability/sustainablemanagement/download/SamsungValueCode_ofConduct.pdf (accessed 14 June 2011).

Activity

1. What are the potential strengths and limitations of 'imposing' a global code of conduct across 61 countries?

2. Identify another global organization that has a published code of conduct. How does this compare with Samsung's code?

A final issue to consider is the fact that studies have tended to focus on large or multi-national organizations (Davies and Crane, 2010). In contrast, 'SMEs may well be doing CSR without knowing it or calling it CSR' (Moore et al, 2009: 174). This reflects the more informal way that SMEs tend to operate, which makes it less easy to discern the relationship between CSR and SHRM (Mankin, 2009).

Conclusion

This chapter has argued that financial globalization also has social, health, and environmental implications. For instance, the distribution of the world's population is increasingly characterized by a process of urbanization which brings with it a wide range of social, health, and environmental implications, such as: the disintegration of traditional rural communities; the need for more housing, medical care, and education; the provision of food and basic supplies needed for daily living; and the degradation of the environment. The size and scope of emerging economies in Asia, particularly China and India, have heightened the demand for raw materials and energy and this has potentially significant implications for the global environment. Green groups in particular see globalization as a threat to the world environment and have long argued that global markets are characterized by the competitive exploitation of natural resources. In recent years a growing number of organizations have responded to these concerns by developing policies on how to manage their operations in an ethically and socially responsible manner. The concept of CSR has emerged to explain this 'new' approach, building on the existing and more narrowly focused concept of business ethics. This shift can be seen in a range of changing organizational priorities, for instance: sourcing more products ethically (e.g. the growing commitment to Fairtrade products), the implementation of diversity policies that go beyond the minimum requirements of equal opportunities legislation, the increased use of environmentally friendly manufacturing operations, and the increased use of recycled materials. To date there has been limited coverage of the relationship between SHRM and CSR and this chapter is intended to help bridge this gap.

Summary

- Modern consumers of products and services are becoming increasingly sophisticated in their understanding of global trends, such as population growth, global poverty, and environmental degradation. This means that organizations, and particularly business corporations, need to manage their operations in ethically and socially responsible ways.

- Increasingly, CSR is being seen as a source of competitive advantage.

- CSR builds on the concept of business ethics and an organization's approach can be informed by one of two competing theories: shareholder theory or stakeholder theory.

- Not all organizations view CSR as a strategic issue although there is a growing consensus that it needs to be viewed as an integral component in the business strategy. This also means that the values underpinning CSR need to be embedded in the organizational culture.

- The HR function is ideally placed to play a key role in the design, implementation, promotion, and evaluation of CSR policies.

- SHRM needs to be vertically and horizontally integrated with an organization's CSR strategy.

Review questions

1. What does the concept of business ethics mean?

2. What is a code of conduct and how is it used by organizations and professional institutes?

3. Define and explain the concept of CSR.

4. What are the benefits for an organization of adopting a CSR policy?

5. What are the principal ways in which the HR function can support an organization's CSR policy?

 End-of-chapter case study   The Enron scandal

Enron, the Texan energy giant once hailed as a model for 21st-century companies, collapsed under massive debt in 2002. Its risk-taking, entrepreneurial culture that encouraged young, inexperienced fast-trackers to take significant risks was credited first with propelling the company into rapid growth, and then for causing its spectacular collapse. Was its HR department to blame? Who developed its corporate values, recruitment policy, and peformance processes? But, faced with a management board that condoned the subversion of corporate ethics, HR's hands were tied. Should it have tried harder to act on behalf of the workforce?

Enron was created in the mid-1980s from the merger of two companies involved in operating natural gas pipelines. Over a 10-year period from 1989 the company's sales increased from $4.6 billion to $40.1 billion. Enron was hailed at this time as leading the way in forward-looking HR practice that fostered an entrepreneurial culture where employees were encouraged to take risks and build their careers. Internal recruitment was supported through the HR department's up-to-date internal database of CVs that made it easy to move around inside the company, with some moving jobs two or three times a year. What this also meant was that some young and inexperienced staff were given significant responsibility and authority with little auditing or checking. Corporate ethics were also high on the agenda with a 61-page booklet explaining Enron's values and principles which were displayed prominently around the firm.

The Enron scandal was characterized by greed and arrogance. Senior executives were involved in breaking the law through a series of complicated financial deceptions. The company's accounts were manufactured to conceal substantial financial losses. Over a period of several years senior managers took large bonuses from poorly performing subsidiaries and exploited flaws in the financial reporting systems. Enron exploited the political influence it had built up over a number of years, gained from making political donations, to remove government restrictions on how it operated its business. This then enabled the company to engage in further illegal and unethical but lucrative practices (e.g. creating an artificial energy shortage to drive up electricity prices and therefore boost profits). Amnesty International even set up an investigation into the company for allegedly allowing its private police to attack villagers in India who objected to the building of a power station because of its impact on the local environment and community.

Enron is a classic example of the difference between rhetoric and reality. The company published an annual CSR report which set out various targets, such as reducing greenhouse gas emissions and making pledges about putting a range of CSR issues at the core of its operations. Diversity was promoted. It was named the 'most innovative' company by the US *Fortune* magazine for five consecutive years from the mid-1990s and won several prestigious awards, although it seemed that the allocation of these was not policed. One example was that the Chief Executive took the decision that expense claims would be processed without checking in order to save time and focus on performance. The erosion of ethics took place gradually over time, and it became easy for staff to turn a blind eye to poor practices. What was managed very carefully, however, was individual performance through a process that became known as 'rank and yank'. Jeffrey Skilling, the Chief Executive, decided that every 6 months the bottom 10% of performers were to be eliminated regardless of individual performance, with predictable effects on morale and behaviour. This led to a dog-eat-dog system that focused exclusively on the individual's ability to add value to the bottom line. Some managers lied and altered the records of colleagues; others used the whistle-blowing system to submit negative views about people they wanted removed and to save themselves. Successful executives were rewarded with company stock options, which meant that they had every incentive to keep the share price high at any cost. One issue that emerged clearly from the Enron situation was that reliance purely on numbers in evaluating performance, rather than a more rounded Balanced Scorecard approach, did not work.

As Enron collapsed, so did its pension scheme, taking with it the pensions of thousands of employees whose whole pension fund was in the company scheme. It emerged that the fund's trustees acted more in the interests of the company than in those of its pension holders, for example, when employees were banned from selling their stock in the weeks before bankruptcy.

Although Enron was able to fool a wide range of stakeholders (e.g. investors, employees, customers, suppliers) it was unable to continue fooling the market. The company ran out of cash to keep unprofitable subsidiaries afloat and filed for bankruptcy protection in December 2001, provoking allegations of fraud and corruption. In the previous year the CEO of Enron, Jeffrey Skilling, had sold his stock options in the company for $270 million. Inside the firm, key executives had questioned the way the firm was being run for some time. However, in the minority, they were actively discouraged, ignored, or punished by the senior management team and by a culture that had simply stopped seeing that there was anything wrong. The HR department had not successfully put in place an independent scheme whereby complaints and doubts could be freely expressed.

Sources

Lewis, 2002; Bakan, 2004; Kay, 2004; Wheen, 2004; Ulrich and Brockbank, 2005; Wolf, 2005; Bower, 2009; Schuman, 2009; Zerk, 2011.

Case study questions

1. Do you think that similar issues could arise in other kinds of organizations, for instance, SMEs or public sector organizations?

2. What can HR departments in firms like Enron do to ensure that something similar does not happen again?

3. What are the problems faced by HR professionals working in firms where they suspect widespread malpractice? What would you advise they do?

Further reading

Blowfield, M. and Murray, A. (2008) *Corporate Social Responsibility: A Critical Introduction*. Oxford: Oxford University Press.
This is an excellent textbook on the topic of CSR, and is usefully read in conjunction with Crane and Matten (2007).

Crane, A. and Matten, D. (2007) *Business Ethics*. Oxford: Oxford University Press.
This is an excellent textbook on the topic of business ethics and the implications for a range of stakeholders.

Fisher, C. (2005) HRD attitudes: or the roles and ethical stances of human resource developers. *Human Resource Development International*, 8(2), pp. 239–255.
This article challenges the notion that HR is inherently good and discusses the implications of having to make moral choices.

Pedersen, E.R. (2006) Making corporate social responsibility (CSR) operable: how companies translate stakeholder dialogue into practice. *Business and Society Review*, 111(2), pp. 137–163.
An interesting article that focuses on the practical implications of CSR.

Steinbeck, D. (2010) *Winning Across Global Markets: How Nokia Creates Strategic Advantage in a Fast-Changing World*. San Francisco, CA: Jossey-Bass.
This provides an in-depth case analysis of one of the world's leading companies which enables you to place its approach to CSR within the context of its history, culture, and business strategy. It is a fascinating read.

 For additional material on the content of this chapter please visit the supporting Online Resource Centre www.oxfordtextbooks.co.uk/orc/truss.

15 SHRM and the management of change

 ## Learning Objectives

By the end of this chapter you should be able to:

- Appreciate the importance of the effective management of change as a core HR skill.
- Explain the principal approaches to understanding the process of change.
- Critically evaluate several models of change management.
- Analyse the phases of a change programme.
- Reflect on how individual responses to change can be affected by change programme design.
- Outline some of the main ways in which the HR function can contribute to change and reflect critically on the best approach to adopt in a given set of circumstances.

 ## Key Concepts

Organizational change
Transformational change
Incremental change
Punctuated equilibrium
Change management
Planned change
Change agency
Transition curve or coping cycle

15.1 Introduction

There is general agreement that the rate and pace of change facing organizations are greater now than they have ever been (Bamford and Daniel, 2005; By, 2005; Holbeche, 2006). External factors such as those we looked at in Chapters 1 and 2, coupled with internal drives to increase efficiency, raise productivity, and develop more effective ways of working, are leading organizations to reappraise their strategies, structures, and processes, all of which require implementing and managing change (Leppitt, 2006a).

Yet, with failure rates for major change programmes running at around 70% (Balogun and Hope-Hailey, 2004), there is clearly a long way to go in terms of the effectiveness of change management practices within many organizations.

Managing organizational change has been heralded as one of the most critical roles that the HR department can play in organizations today (Ulrich and Brockbank, 2005b). Yet, all the evidence suggests that many HR departments are not involved in any depth in leading or managing change, and that HR professionals often lack critical change management skills and expertise. Equally, it has been argued, there is little agreement as to the best way for change programmes to be managed, and there has been dispute amongst critics and theorists as to how to conceptualize change (Bamford and Daniel, 2005).

In this chapter we explore the nature and meaning of change management. In particular, we focus on 'planned' approaches to change where change is regarded as a project that requires managing and also discuss 'emergent' perspectives on change (Kitchen and Daly, 2002; Bamford and Daniel, 2005). 'Organizational development' (OD) approaches, where change is regarded more holistically as an organizational characteristic that can be nurtured, is explored in Chapter 9. HR professionals are very likely to become involved in both OD and change management during their careers, as reflected in Crail's (2007) finding that HR professionals in 93 out of 114 organizations had been involved with managing some aspect of change (see also Chapter 4).

We examine several change management models and frameworks in order to give an overview of the main approaches to managing change, and explain the principal stages of planned change programmes, as well as the impact of change on individuals. We then move on to consider aspects of change management in which HR departments may have most involvement, including managing individual-level change, communication, and designing HRM practices in support of change.

15.2 Understanding change

Change is an essential and inevitable feature of organizational life. Just as all biological organisms evolve and develop through time, organizations, which are human systems, are subject to change. Some of these changes will be deliberate and planned by organizational leaders, whilst others will arise through environmental pressures beyond their control; for example, the global economic downturn is forcing many organizations to restructure and make workers redundant, whilst others have not been able to survive. The British high street has lost many well-known names, including the chainstores Woolworths, The Pier, and Zavvi, and large-scale changes are taking place across the public sector (Bamford and Daniel, 2005). Change can therefore affect entire economies and industries, as well as individual organizations.

Change management is effectively the implementation of corporate strategy (Leppitt, 2006a), yet there is considerable evidence that there is a lack of change management capacity and capability within organizations generally (Balogun and Hope-Hailey, 2004; Bamford and Daniel, 2005). The consequences of this for the ongoing success of organizations are critical.

Within the literature on change management there is discussion about what the term itself actually means. For instance, it has been defined as 'a comprehensive, collaborative and planned process of solving problems through altering foundational assumptions and beliefs of individuals in order to improve work content, structures and relationships in organisations' (Rusaw, 2007: 349), or as 'the process of continually renewing an organization's direction, structure and capabilities to serve the ever-changing needs of external and internal customers' (Moran and Brightman, 2001: 111). Common to most definitions is a sense that change management is a process of organizational renewal that takes place over time. Where there is disagreement is over whether change is something that is 'done to' or 'happens to' an organization.

The **rational planning** perspective on change suggests that change is a process that can be actively 'managed' by organizational members (Stewart and Kringas, 2003; Burnes, 2004). Within this perspective, the role of 'change agent' becomes important.

Change can be **transformational**, at the one extreme, and require a complete rethink of what an organization does and what it stands for. However, at the other extreme, it can also be small-scale and **incremental** (Burnes, 2004), for instance, restructuring just one department, upskilling part of the workforce, or changing some internal processes (By, 2005).

 Key Concepts

Transformational change: a wide-reaching and fundamental change of an organization's strategy, culture, and structure.

   Incremental change: small-scale change affecting only part of what an organization does, such as introducing a new technology or restructuring a department.

   Punctuated equilibrium: periods of incremental change interspersed with transformational change.

Some examples of what an organization can seek to change are:

- Its strategy, core mission, and objectives.
- The products or services it offers.
- Its processes, or the way it works.
- Its values, culture, or shared beliefs.
- The outcomes of the way that people work, or its performance.
- Its location (including internationalization).
- The way it is structured and organizes its activities.
- The technology it uses.

Of course, it is not always easy to classify change in this way. The notion of **punctuated equilibrium** suggests that, for many organizations, periods of more minor incremental change are interspersed with periods of step-change over time (By, 2005). Balogun and Hope-Hailey (2004) argue that although some are of the view that change can always be managed incrementally, others argue that periods of incremental change may lead to organizational inertia with relatively little challenge to the status quo, creating a situation where more fundamental change is needed to avert a crisis.

However, change is not always regarded as a process that can be actively managed. The **emergent** or **processual** approach regards change as an integral part of 'organizing' which cannot be managed in a planned fashion (Bamford and Daniel, 2005). We now look in more detail at both perspectives.

 Critical Reflection

Look on the internet at the websites of some large corporations and find their 'corporate history' pages. Looking at the way these firms have developed over time, can you identify moments of transformational change, incremental change, and punctuated equilibrium? What was happening to the firm and in its environment at the time the changes were happening?

15.3 Models of planned change

The majority of models of change management are founded on the notion that change can be viewed as an active, planned activity that requires management (Bamford and Daniel, 2005). This is also predicated upon the assumption that an organization can move from one stable state to another (By, 2005). Broadly speaking, models of planned change can be classified as either 'analytical' or 'best-practice'. Whilst best-practice models suggest that there is a recipe that can be learned for managing change successfully, analytical models seek to provide a framework to help explain the process of managing a change programme. It is interesting to note that Crail's (2007) study of HR managers found that just four out of 106 respondents said their organization used a recognized model of change management, and he suggests that this might be one of the reasons why change programmes so often fail to meet their objectives. Equally, it has to be recognized that change is inherently a difficult, messy, and often unpredictable process, and that whilst planning is essential, there will inevitably be factors that emerge that could not have been foreseen.

 Key Concepts

Planned change is an approach to managing change that assumes that change is an activity that can be managed and organized and led by senior managers.

   Change agency is the practice of leading and managing change. A change agent is a person or group of people within an organization tasked with managing change.

15.3.1 **Best-practice models**

It would be difficult to find another area of management practice that has spawned so many 'how-to' papers and books as organizational change. One study found as many as one million articles (Fernandez and Rainey, 2006). Each commentator has their own preferred approach to managing change, and most advocate a certain number of steps that should be gone through in order to achieve success.

Although best-practice approaches such as these have attracted an avid following, they have been criticized for adopting a unitary, managerialist, and functionalist view of organizations that side-steps the complex reality of organizational life (By, 2005). Leppitt (2006a) notes that, in contrast to best-practice models, contingency-based perspectives suggest that formulae cannot be universally applied since all contexts are different; consequently, the focus should be on aligning the change process to the organizational situation at hand: 'the likelihood of developing a generic model capable of universal adoption is a 'chimera' and less value than looking for alignment with business strategy' (p. 135).

15.3.2 **Analytical models**

Theorists have devoted considerable attention to developing models that can help to understand how change comes about and is managed within a planned perspective (By, 2005). Whilst models such as these suggest that change management programmes should proceed through various phases, they do not prescribe specific actions that should be taken. Rather, the assumption is that the change programme should be designed to fit with contextual features.

15.3.2.1 **Lewin's model**

One of the original analytical frameworks for understanding the change process is that of Lewin (1951), which is still widely cited (Burnes, 2004). Lewin argued that change comprises three stages: unfreezing the status quo and discarding old ways of working; moving; and then refreezing. This was recently reframed by Balogun and Hope-Hailey (2004) as their unfreeze–move–sustain model, and by other researchers who have developed their own four- or eight-phase models (Bullock and Batten, 1985; Cummins and Huse, 1989). However, as Balogun and Hope-Hailey (2004) note, the pace of change in most organizations today is such that change is a constant state that requires managing, the 'acceleration trap' (Zaugg and Thom, 2003: 200), that leaves little or no time for recovery in between. Lewin's approach may be most applicable to small-scale incremental change where there is broad agreement amongst all stakeholders as to what needs changing and the ideal outcomes (By, 2005). In instances where there is disagreement about what the purpose or outcome of the change should be, or where the change is complex and long term, then it may be less relevant (Bamford and Daniel, 2005). Political perspectives on understanding organizations would suggest that consensus is rare and that change inevitably involves internal challenges.

15.3.2.2 **The Change Kaleidoscope**

Balogun and Hope-Hailey's (2004) Change Kaleidoscope model is founded on the notion that change needs to be context specific (Pettigrew et al, 2001). The approach to change that is chosen should be based on a thorough analysis of the context within which the change is taking place, and on a series of decisions around the way in which the change is to be managed. Failure to analyse the context sufficiently, they argue, will lead to inappropriate decisions and increase the likelihood that the change will not succeed. 'Best-practice' approaches to change should therefore be viewed with caution.

The Change Kaleidoscope model divides context into eight core segments (Fig. 15.1):

- Power: who are the powerful stakeholders in relation to the change? This could, for instance, include senior managers, unions, employees, and customers.

- Time: how much time is available to effect the change? Is it a crisis, or is more time available? If there is more time, then this increases the range of options.

- Scope: what is the extent of change in terms of breadth, how much of the organization is affected, depth, and how far-reaching the change is?

- Preservation: what are the critical things that need to be maintained in the organization through the change process and beyond? For instance, what are the experience and capability of middle managers?

- Diversity: how diverse is the organization in terms of demographics, location, functions, and so on, and how will this impact on the change design?

Figure 15.1   The Change Kaleidoscope.

- Capability: how capable and experienced is the organization at managing change? If line managers are inexperienced, then expertise from outside may be needed.
- Capacity: how much capacity in terms of time, resources, and people does the organization have to devote to the change to make it succeed?
- Readiness: what is the attitude of those affected by the change? How ready and willing are they to change?

Based on the results of this analysis, they argue that those leading the change need to make key decisions in the areas of:

- Change path: is the change to be incremental or transformational?
- Change start point: is the change to be driven top-down by senior managers, or bottom-up through employee suggestions? In practice, most managed change programmes are top-down.
- Change style: style refers to the extent to which the change is coercive or directive versus participative and collaborative. Decisions need to be made during the design of the change process about how much input will come from employees and how this will be managed.
- Change target: the target of change can be either outputs, or performance objectives; behaviours, or changing the way that people work; values, or changing the core organizational values; or some combination of these.
- Change levers: change levers are those interventions that are deployed in supporting the management of change, and these can include, for instance, routines and rituals, organizational structures, control systems, and power structures.
- Change roles: this concerns who will be responsible for managing the change. This could be a team of people, an external consultant, or a delegated change agent such as an HR manager.

Leppitt (2006a) comments that the Kaleidoscope model recognizes the impossibility of mapping all contextual variables with any one best-practice approach, and acknowledges the need to account for a wide range of situations. What the model cannot do is prescribe which approach should be adopted in any given set of circumstances; the interpretation of the contextual analysis, and decisions about how to implement the change, are in the hands of the change agents.

 Critical Reflection

The Change Kaleidoscope model can be applied to any change. Think of a change you either are planning or have recently been through in your personal life, such as a house move or change of job. What were the key contextual variables and how did you go about managing the change process? What does the application of the Kaleidoscope model tell you about how effectively you managed the change?

15.4 Emergent and processual change

Whilst many have focused on how change can be actively planned and managed, other commentators have noted that change often either emerges in an unplanned, non-linear way due to changes in the external environment, or develops bottom-up as people, perhaps unconsciously, change the way they work over time (Bamford and Daniel, 2005). Change is thus seen as an open-ended process of adaptation and learning, with a focus on organizations becoming open systems ready and able to change should the need arise (By, 2005). Rather than focusing on change as a programme to be managed, the emergent approach suggests that organizations need to enhance their general readiness for change through, for instance, regularly scanning the environment and fostering a culture of knowledge sharing. It has been argued that emergent approaches to change are more appropriate where it is not possible to determine what the outcome of the change should be, a feature common in rapidly changing environments (Bamford and Daniel, 2005).

Emergent approaches to change have commonalities with the OD approach, which is discussed further in Chapter 9. For example, Pettigrew and Whipp (1993) argue that change is multifaceted and complex with no clear start or finish point, characterized by differing perspectives and political struggles, rather than linear, rational, and manageable (Burnes, 2004).

15.5 HR professionals and change management

It has long been argued that, for an HR department to be operating at a strategic level, it needs to play a role in helping to lead and manage change (see Chapter 4). Ulrich (1997c; Ulrich and Brockbank, 2005b) in particular has argued strongly that HR should act as 'changemaker' or 'change agent'. A change agent has been defined broadly as an individual or group 'responsible for leading . . . change' (Balogun and Hope-Hailey, 2004: 49). Doorewaard and Benschop (2002) point out that it has been argued that the success or failure of change programmes may rest on HR's contribution in helping employees mobilize their efforts towards change.

There is a strong likelihood that HR professionals will be called upon to help manage change at some stage in their career. Crail (2007) found in his study of 114 UK organizations that 83% had undertaken a change initiative during the past 24 months, and that HR professionals in 93 of the organizations were involved in managing change at some level, whilst only 4% reported not being involved in change at all. Most were involved at early stages during the design and planning of change, undertaking tasks concerned with communication, implementation, and dealing with employees' information needs. Despite this finding, the consensus within the literature overall is that HR's involvement in the change process in many organizations is in practice very limited and often reactive rather than leading (Ogilvie and Stork, 2003; Antila, 2006).

Alfes et al (2010b), based on a detailed study of HR roles in change programmes in two public sector organizations in the UK, provide a model that shows how HR professionals may be either proactive or reactive in terms of managing both the content and the process of organizational change (Fig. 15.2).

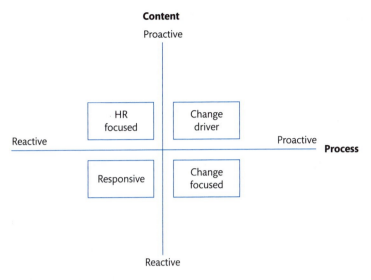

Figure 15.2 Alfes et al (2010b) model of HR roles in managing change.

This distinction between involvement in the **process** of change as opposed to the actual **content** of change programmes is helpful in understanding what HR's role might be. From a processual perspective, the model draws on Hayes' (2006: 54–59) six steps in managing a change process:

- Recognition of the need for change: early recognition that change needs to happen.
- Start of the change process: designing the change process, allocation of tasks.
- Diagnosis: this stage involves understanding the present state and identifying desirable future outcomes.
- Preparing and planning for implementation: choosing the appropriate change strategy.
- Implementation.
- Review: measuring the outcomes against the original plan.

From a content perspective, the model draws on Thornhill et al's (2000) seven domains of HRM practice that can be deployed in support of change:

- Cultural change, which can be influenced through values, beliefs, and learned behaviours.
- Recruitment, to ensure that the workforce has the required competencies.
- Performance management, to align individual and organizational goals.
- HR development, in order to develop appropriate skill sets.
- Reward management, to reward appropriate behaviours and competencies.
- Management of employee relations, to ensure a positive relationship with representative bodies such as trade unions.
- Downsizing, if necessary; HR's role here is to manage the process legally and fairly, and to minimize the impact on the remaining workforce.

Thus, the Alfes et al (2010b) model of HR roles in managing change reveals the distinction between involvement in the change process as opposed to the actual content of the change. Both are important.

The scope and scale of change programmes with which HR practitioners may become involved varies across the full spectrum, ranging from small-scale change within individual departments to mergers and acquisitions. The case study below provides an insight into how HR helped manage the merger between DHL and Exel in 2005.

 Case study 15.1   HR's role in managing a merger

HL Logistics, part of Deutsche Post World Net, acquired Exel in December 2005, creating the world's largest logistics company. Eleven thousand staff from Exel joined DHL's 30,000 workforce. The integration programme posed a significant management challenge, and the aim was to achieve integration quickly and smoothly. For HR, this meant focusing on the new management structure, organizational design, dealing with staff retention, and harmonizing policies and procedures.

A dedicated integration team was set up to manage the process. The focus was on open and honest communication, with initiatives such as a staff helpline and meetings. Within 6 weeks, 260 first and second line manager positions had been scoped and managers from both companies put through an assessment centre. Although there were redundancies, the final management distribution was 50:50 across the two firms, and employee numbers have since increased by about 25,000. The talent management programme from DHL's parent company, Deutch Post World Net, was used across the company, measuring individual performance against eight competencies. Seven company values were developed. Although the plan was that the integration would take 3 years, after only 18 months the programme was 90% complete and the company managed to retain most of its customers.

Source

Martindale, N. (2007) Delivering major change. *Personnel Today*, 27 November, pp. 30–31.

Activity

The DHL/Excel HR team was involved in both the process and the content of the changes arising out of the merger. In the context of a merger, what do you see as the key challenges faced by merging HR departments that are involved in either of these aspects of change?

15.5.1 HR's dilemmas

Although HR departments are under pressure from line managers to help with the management of change programmes, this may place HR managers in situations that cause them to experience role conflict (Francis, 2003). We discussed this in general terms in relation to the role of the HR department in Chapter 4, but it is also worth thinking about in relation to HR's specific role in managing change programmes. For example, involvement in managing change may create conflicts between HR professionals' ethical code and their role as 'organizational conscience', on the one hand, and the needs of senior line managers to impose change in response to economic imperatives, on the other (Caldwell, 2003; Wright and Snell,

2005). Legge, writing in 1978, and Ogilvie and Stork (2003) note that it is often easier for HR managers to play the role of 'conformist innovator', helping line managers design and implement change programmes, rather than 'deviant innovator', questioning and challenging line managers to explore more radical and innovative solutions.

Doorewaard and Benschop (2002) argue that organizations are inherently complex and ambiguous, and that the rational development and implementation of managerial policies is insufficient to ensure success. This is exacerbated by the fact that managing change is inherently a political process (Bamford and Daniel, 2005). The focus on HR's role in managing planned change is built on the utilitarian assumption that people are 'disesmbodied entities, arranged and classified in categories and sub-categories of required qualifications' (pp. 275–276) and can be readily deployed in different ways. This fails to take account of the complexity of human beings, who are emotional as well as rational. Some change interventions, such as empowerment and involvement, can, from one perspective, be seen as emotion manipulation or control (Doorewaard and Benschop, 2002). These authors suggest that adopting a processual-relational perspective that is sensitive to emotional subroutines would involve designing change programmes that activated people's emotions, rather than sought to neutralize them, and would avoid conflict and dissent.

 Critical Reflection

In Chapter 4 we considered the role of the HR department in terms of the competing demands faced by HR professionals, and in Chapter 14 we considered HR's role in the context of corporate social responsibility. In the context of managing an organizational change programme, what do you think will be the key ethical, moral, and professional challenges for HR professionals and how would you go about addressing these?

In the next two sections, we focus on two areas that are particularly significant roles for HR professionals during change: managing personal transitions, and communication.

15.6 Managing personal transitions

One of the key aspects of managing change is leading and helping individuals through personal change. As By (2005) notes, the general view is that people in organizations need to be able to undergo constant change. The success of change programmes also rests on whether or not employees are able and willing to embrace change (Piderit, 2000), and helping people through change programmes often falls on HR's shoulders.

For many people going through a major organizational change, the experience can be quite traumatic and unsettling. Bamford and Daniel (2005: 391) write: 'many people come through the process of change feeling bruised, disenchanted and de-motivated'. Researchers

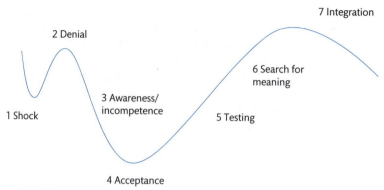

Figure 15.3   The change transition curve.

Source: based on Adams et al (1976) *Transition: Understanding and Managing Personal Change.* London: Martin Robertson & Co. Reproduced in Balogun and Hope-Hailey (2004: 142).

in the field of organizational change frequently use the **transition curve** or **coping cycle** model to understand how people respond at an emotional level to change (Fig. 15.3). This model was originally developed in the field of bereavement counselling to show how people respond to the trauma of losing a loved one. The fact that it has been so widely applied in organizational change management is indicative of the strength of feeling that can be experienced by individuals going through a major change at work.

 Key Concept

The **transition curve** or **coping cycle** is a model originally developed to explain the emotional process a person experiences after a bereavement. Research has shown that people experience similar emotions when confronted with change at work that affects them at a fundamental level.

There are seven stages in the curve, which measures the peaks and troughs in confidence and competence against time:

- Shock: the initial feeling of shock when confronted with the inevitability of change and the loss of self-confidence.
- Denial: when individuals have not really come to terms fully with what the changes will mean to them.
- Awareness/incompetence: starting to realize that change is inevitable and will affect them at a personal level.
- Acceptance: when individuals start to let go of the past.
- Testing: the identification of new behaviours and testing them out.
- Search for meaning: the assimilation and understanding of learning.
- Integration: the integration of new behaviours and ways of working into everyday life.
  (Adapted from Balogun and Hope-Hailey, 2004: 141–142)

The reality is that most people do not pass neatly and sequentially through the seven stages of the curve within a prescribed period of time. Many become 'stuck' at various stages or revert back to earlier stages before progressing. Factors such as personality, personal circumstances, and the extent to which organizational change affects the individual, and attitude towards the change, will all affect individual responses. When an organization is going through multiple and far-reaching changes, the likelihood of individuals failing to assimilate change effectively and raise their levels of confidence and competence is increased (Balogun and Hope-Hailey, 2004). However, it remains true that the way in which the change programme is managed will impact significantly on individual responses. HR functions can work in a variety of ways to help individuals cope with change. Strategies for helping people through the curve are shown in Table 15.1.

 Critical Reflection

Think back to the last time you experienced a major change in your life. Can you recognize the way in which you went through the transition curve?

Table 15.1   Strategies for helping people through the transition curve

Stage in the process	Strategies
Shock and denial	• Coaching/mentoring
	• Emotional support
	• Communication to enable mental preparation
	• Involvement and information sharing
	• Understanding the transition process
Awareness	• Factual information about the change
	• New goals/targets
	• Anticipating falling performance levels
	• Allowing expression
Acceptance/testing	• Focus on short-term goals
	• Rewarding new behaviours
	• Training/development
	• Enabling risk-taking
	• Leadership
Search for meaning/integration	• Rewarding success

Source: Balogun and Hope-Hailey (2004).

15.6.1 **Resistance to change**

Most commonly, the practitioner literature on change management tends to focus on how to overcome resistance to change. For instance, 91% of HR respondents in Crail's (2007) survey said that dealing with employee resistance to change was a significant problem for them. In this way, resistance is perceived in a negative light as employees not cooperating with managerial imperatives. However, Piderit (2000) notes that dismissing employees' objections to change is a manifestation of attribution error, whereby managers and employees blame each other for the failure of change, without taking account of their own role in the process. Individuals may resist change for a variety of reasons, most of which have little to do with resisting change for its own sake. For example, employees may resist change for ethical or communitarian reasons, or for genuine concerns for the organization that the change is not appropriate (Piderit, 2000; Balogun and Hope-Hailey, 2004). Equally, there may be a fear of the unknown, lack of perceived control, or fear of a perceived threat (Proctor and Doukakis, 2003; Holbeche, 2006). As Piderit (2000) argues, there are frequently negative consequences for individuals in the expression of negative attitudes, and so it is unlikely that people would resist change on wholly unreasonable grounds.

Many traditional frameworks for understanding the importance of change and processes for the effective management of change programmes tend to be based on rationalist views of human nature, and therefore emphasize the importance of rational arguments and the damping down of people's emotional responses. However, it can be useful to think of resistance as having three components, in a similar way to other attitudes:

- Behaviourally: resistance is manifest in terms of negative behaviours such as non-compliance, inaction, or defiance.
- Emotionally: resistance is seen as a set of emotions, including anxiety and frustration.
- Cognitively: resistance is regarded as a set of negative thoughts about change, such as 'unreadiness' to change or reluctance.

    (Piderit, 2000)

It is possible that individuals may experience different reactions or ambivalence on each of these dimensions; for instance, cognitively employees may not like the proposed change but not manifest this through their behaviour.

15.7 **Communication during change**

Communication has been found to have a significant impact on the success of organizational change initiatives (Kitchen and Daly, 2002; Balogun and Hope-Hailey, 2004). Proctor and Doukakis (2003) argue that poor communication can lead to the failure of change programmes, and so it is worrying that 90% of respondents to Crail's (2007) survey of HR managers cited communication breakdown as a problem they had experienced in managing change.

HR departments may be called upon to lead the development and implementation of a communication strategy in support of change initiatives. For example, Crail (2007) found that most HR departments were involved with communication. However, research by Harkness

(2000) discovered that employee satisfaction with communication peaked at 50% in 1987 and has since been on a downard trajectory, suggesting that there are some important gaps in internal communication capability.

At the organizational level, communication can influence:

- Employees' perceptions of the validity of the proposed change.
- The level of resistance to change.
- Employee morale and retention rates.
- The ability to challenge and question organizational norms and conventions.
- The overall success of the change programme.

At the individual level, communication can influence:

- Personal acceptance of the need for change.
- Understanding of how the change will impact on oneself.
- The speed and success with which individuals progress through the coping cycle.

  (Goodman and Truss, 2004)

However, communication is a complex issue. In particular, managers will need to consider the following interconnected factors:

- Purpose: the first thing to consider is what the aim of the communication is; for example, to raise awareness of the need for change, to disseminate factual information, to persuade people, to seek people's views, or to acknowledge people's contribution.
- Timing: the timing of communication before, during, and after a change programme can be crucial in determining its effectiveness. Also relevant here is the stage reached in the change programme.
- Target: who is expected to receive the communication? Is it aimed at everyone, or just certain groups of people?
- Sender: who will send the communication? For instance, the CEO, a senior line manager, individuals' direct line managers, or a dedicated change manager?
- Medium: how will people be reached, and what is the most appropriate means? Choices include verbally, for instance through presentations or videoclips, or in one-to-one meetings, in writing, for instance, via emails, letters, posters, or notices.
- Content: what information should be included? Klein (1996) divides content into what employees must know, should know, and could know.
- Context: what else is happening that might be relevant for the communication? For example, if employees are worried about losing their jobs or relocating, then these concerns need to be addressed. Equally, organizational history and norms in terms of patterns and style of communication may have influenced people's expectations

  (Kitchen and Daly, 2002; Balogun and Hope-Hailey, 2004; Goodman and Truss, 2004)

This would suggest that, for most large-scale change programmes, it is appropriate to have a communication strategy. However, as Klein (1996) argues, this strategy will usually need to be highly flexible to allow for change over time as events unfold through the stages of the change programme.

Communication theories also suggest that it is important to remember communication is a two-way process comprising not only the message, but also the sender and the receiver, as well as a feedback loop to check understanding (Klein, 1996; Johnson and Scholes, 2002). Equally, perceptual filters come into play, since both sender and receiver bring to bear their own subjective realities on the communication process.

In addition to the formal elements of communication, messages also contain an informal component, for instance, through the body language with which the message is delivered, the choice of language, and the environment within which the message is delivered (Kitchen and Daly, 2002).

Goodman and Truss (2004) suggest that communication during change programmes can be considered using their 'Change Wheel' model (Fig. 15.4).

The four central quadrants of the model identify the four overarching areas where decisions can be made about how to handle the communication: Message, Channel, Media, and Approach.

- Media: prior studies have shown that communication during change requires repetition through more than one medium to increase people's memory. Face-to-face communication has been found to be the most effective (Klein, 1996).

- Channel: messages delivered via line managers have been shown to have more impact, since they draw on the formal hierarchy, as well as informal leaders who are able to influence opinion (Klein, 1996).

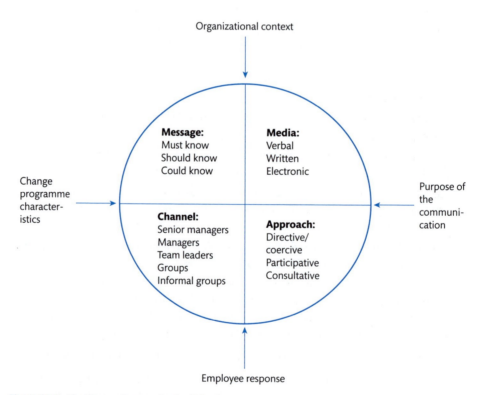

Figure 15.4   The Change Communication Wheel.

Source: Goodman and Truss (2004: 225).

- Message: Kitchen and Daly (2002) argue that there is information that people must know, which is important job-related information, should know, but is not essential, and could know, which is relatively unimportant. Part of the communication strategy involves working out what messages belong to these categories. Personally relevant information tends to be retained better by individuals (Klein, 1996).

- Approach: communication can be highly directive or even coercive, telling employees what they are expected to do, or more consultantive, inviting people to be involved and to comment (Goodman and Truss, 2004).

The optimal strategy is contingent upon the four contextual factors outside the circle: purpose of the communication, employee response, change programme characteristics, and organizational context. In this sense, the Change Communication Wheel is similar to the Change Kaleidoscope.

Communication is a two-way process, and so consideration needs to be given under each heading as to whether and how employees' views will be sought. Equally, although an organization may develop change communication strategies and activities, informal communication channels (including the 'grapevine') will inevitably spring up during periods of change.

Crail (2007) found that organizations used the following communication methods:

Cascade of information through line	
managers	85%
Departmental meetings	82%
Emails from top management	74%
Personal letters	70%
All-employee meetings	58%
Emails from HR	56%
Intranet postings	55%
Training sessions	46%
Noticeboards	44%
Video-conferencing	13%
Other	11%

 Case study 15.2 Communication during change at PubCo

PubCo is a small, public sector publishing organization. Successive periods of change have included the introduction of electronic production methods, changes to the senior management team, and relocation. These led to high levels of staff turnover. Recently, employees have been required to move to new working hours with a loss of overtime pay. In order to manage this change, senior managers sought to minimize impacts on productivity, efficiency, and staff morale but, at the same, time, ensure that staff moved willingly to the new contractual arrangement. Reflecting afterwards on the way the changes were communicated to staff, managers felt that communication could have been handled better. For instance, both staff and managers found out about the change at the same time and so managers were unable to prepare their staff. A third of staff would be financially affected and they were offered no compensation or transition arrangements, and so managers were not surprised by their negative reaction. The changes were announced in July, but staff meetings to ascertain people's views were not organized until October. There was no agreed communication strategy and so individual line managers developed their own approaches. Many of them felt not only ill-informed themselves about the changes, but also powerless to address issues of morale and retention amongst staff. No formal processes were put in place to reward or thank staff. It transpired that most staff actually found out about the proposed change from a public report, and the majority were not aware initially how the changes would impact on their pay. Few reported that they had been consulted or updated as the change progressed, although almost all wished they had been asked. Most said they wanted to find out about the change through face-to-face communication with their line manager. Very few said that senior managers had made their messages clear, and only one-quarter felt that managers were in touch with the concerns of employees.

Source

Goodman, J. and Truss, C. (2004) The medium and the message: communicating effectively during a major change initiative. *Journal of Change Management*, 4(3), pp. 217–228.

Activity

What could managers at PubCo have done differently to communicate the change more effectively? What impact would this have had on the way employees felt about the change, and about their managers?

15.8 Why does change often fail?

Given all the research that has taken place on the issue of change management, and all the expertise within management consultancy firms and individual organizations, why does the evidence continue to suggest that most change efforts fail to meet their objectives? By (2005: 370) suggests that change is frequently 'reactive, discontinuous, ad hoc and often triggered by a situation of organisational crisis', rather than managed and planned, and therefore more likely to fail.

Some of the specific reasons that have been identified are:

- Lack of strategic planning, including failure to look ahead and anticipate the impact of external changes on the organization.
- Failure to design and implement change quickly enough to keep up with competitors or with customer demands.
- Internal cultural weaknesses and, most importantly, adherence to familiar routines and ways of working that become increasingly irrelevant to the outside world. Such routines can be deeply embedded and hard to change.
- Failure to take account of employees' likely responses to change, at both an individual and a collective level.
- Past successes, which mean that organizations become blinkered and tend to keep trying to manage change in the same way.

- Poor communication during change programmes, particularly failure to identify a vision or a purpose for the change and communicate this effectively and failure to engage with employees.
- Allowing change programmes to lose impetus.
- Not building reinforcing mechanisms into the change programme so that the changes do not become embedded.
- Failure to devote sufficient resources in terms of time, money, and staff to managing and implementing change.
- Simply the fact that change is an inherently complex and ambiguous process.

  (Johnson and Scholes, 2002; Balogun and Hope-Hailey, 2004; Holbeche, 2006)

Crail's (2007) study of HR managers found that they felt the following factors acted as barriers to change:

Employee resistance	81%
Communication breakdown	90%
Lack of time to prepare	65%
Lack of time to implement	63%
Poor leadership from senior managers	60%
Lack of change management expertise	57%

 ## Conclusion

Change is inevitable in organizations, and it is very probable that all HR professionals will be called upon to help design, manage, and implement change programmes. However, managing change is complex and there is evidence that not only is there a lack of awareness in the practitioner community about theories and models of change, but also most efforts to manage change fail to meet their objectives. HR practitioners may therefore be called upon as subject experts within their organizations, and an understanding of the political and emotional dimensions of change is therefore important.

 ## Summary

- Most change programmes fail to meet their objectives.
- Change may be viewed as either planned or emergent. Planned approaches to change often fail to take account of the emotional and political aspects of change.
- It can also be seen as either transformational or incremental.
- Evidence suggests that most change programmes fail to meet their objectives.
- There is a clear role for HR professionals to play in helping organizations to manage change by being subject experts. HR may be called upon to be involved in either the process of managing change or the content of the change itself.
- Analytical models such as the Change Kaleidoscope can be used to help analyse the context within which change is taking place and to guide the choice of appropriate strategies.
- Individuals often go through the 'coping cycle' when faced with major organizational change, and an awareness of the phases of the coping cycle is important when designing change programmes.

- Communication plays a central role in the management of change programmes and organizations need to make decisions about how to communicate effectively with staff during a change, both to keep them informed and to hear their views.

 ## Review questions

1. What do you see as the most important roles that the HR department can play in managing change programmes and why?

2. How should HR professionals balance the needs of the organization against those of employees during change?

3. How would you go about analysing the context within which a change management programme will take place?

4. Why do people resist change and what can be done about it?

5. Why do you think that change programmes usually fail to meet their original expectations and what can be done to address this?

 ## End-of-chapter case study   Transforming the Learning and Skills Council (LSC)

In 2005, the LSC, the UK public body responsible for improving the quality and quantity of skills training for post-16-year-olds in the UK, took the decision to transform its way of operating, firstly to ensure greater efficiency and, secondly, to align itself more closely with the needs of industry and the colleges who delivered the training. The plan was to shift to a structure whereby the LSC's national office focused purely on strategic and national-level activities, whilst regional offices would take over locally based support functions and relationship building with regional partners, to ensure the local offices could collaborate closely with education providers.

This change programme involved a culture change, the upskilling of the workforce, the evaluation and grading of all jobs, and the requirement for all staff to reapply, alongside anticipated job losses of 1,300. The HR department was put in charge of the programme; a detailed project plan was created by a large, dedicated change team, including clear milestones and targets, with an end date of July 2006, and included a risk assessment exercise and an equality and diversity impact assessment, as well as a thorough communication strategy.

The communication strategy focused on ensuring that several channels of communication were used, including all-staff events, team briefings, an intranet site dedicated to providing information about the change, a helpline, training and development interventions, union and staff consultation, and regular briefings from the CEO, all overseen by the change communication team. Overall, the HR department expanded from 120 to 170 staff members during the change programme. However, due to the tight timeframe, not much time was allocated to 'unfreezing' the organization, letting go of old ways of working and moving on, and explaining the rationale for the change.

The most significant task was the re-evaluation and reassignment of almost all jobs within the LSC. This involved the development of role profiles, and the evaluation and categorization of jobs into bands. Roles were compared against the closest job description from the previous structure, and the result was that many jobs were upskilled to a higher band. Jobs were then categorized as: 'flow through', where changes were not substantial and employees could effectively be moved into their new jobs straight away; 'fewer', where role descriptions were similar to those in place previously but where there were fewer roles available, in which case employees were encouraged to express an interest in voluntary severance or apply for interview; or 'new', which were essentially newly created roles that people could apply for. For the latter two categories, formal applications were required and a selection process took place. Once these categorizations were announced, levels of staff insecurity rose. To allay staff fears, the LSC organized training sessions for staff on competency-based interviewing and gave information about how the selection process would work. A redeployment team helped staff find jobs elsewhere, and employees were given 2 days a week to job-hunt, as well as a £250 development and training grant.

Despite all the preparation, the union response was hostile; in particular it opposed the potential compulsory redundancies and questioned the business case for change. As the change progressed, a lack of understanding over the way the newly designed job roles would be structured and how people would work together began to emerge, which created uncertainty. In the end, following months of discussion and, finally, industrial action by the union, the LSC agreed to allow employees to reapply for more posts than originally intended. During the change, the HR helpline was inundated with calls and emails and could not respond within the planned 48-hour period. The HR team was under significant pressure, with many working 12-hour days over a long period of time. Finally, however, the change programme closed in November 2006, just 4 months after its planned completion, with no compulsory redundancies.

Source

Adapted from Alfes, K., Truss, C. and Gill, J. (2009) *Transforming the Learning and Skills Council. Case Studies A and B.* Cranfield: The European Case Clearing House.

Case study questions

1. What could the LSC have done differently to reduce levels of resistance amongst employees?

2. How effectively do you think the change was managed overall?

3. What do you see as the key challenges ahead for the LSC?

 ## Further reading

Balogun, J. and Hope-Hailey, V. (2004) *Exploring Strategic Change*, 2nd edn. London: Prentice Hall.
A thorough overview of change management from a practical perspective.

By, R.T. (2005) Organisational change management: a critical review. *Journal of Change Management*, 5(4), pp. 369–380.
A useful theoretical review of change management.

Crail, M. (2007) HR's role in managing organisational change. *IRS Employment Review*, 19 November.
Interesting data on HR's role in managing change programmes.

Holbeche, L. (2006) *Understanding Change. Theory, Implementation and Success.* Oxford: Butterworth-Heinemann.
Especially useful for understanding the human side of change.

 For additional material on the content of this chapter please visit the supporting Online Resource Centre www.oxfordtextbooks.co.uk/orc/truss.

Part 4

New forms of SHRM

16 | **New forms of SHRM**

 Learning Objectives

By the end of this chapter you should be able to:

- Discuss a number of possible scenarios for the future business world.
- Examine the implications for strategic approaches to HRM for the different possible scenarios.
- Discuss the kinds of competencies needed by HRM practitioners in these scenarios.
- Examine how specific future developments may influence approaches to SHRM.

 Key Concepts

Scenarios for the future
Competencies for HR professionals
Private equity

16.1 Introduction

Throughout the foregoing chapters in this book there have been several references made to wider developments and trends that are likely to affect the way in which business is done in the future and what these are likely to mean for the role of the HRM function and HRM strategies in organizations in the future. In this chapter we consider some of the scenarios that have been put forward about the future of business and examine what the implications of these would be for SHRM and for the role of the HR function. We also consider how these might influence the competencies required by those concerned with the HRM role and how these might change in the future. In addition we examine a number of more specific developments that may have consequences for strategic approaches to managing people in the future.

Conjecture is of course not an exact science. The future may be influenced by things we cannot anticipate or do not expect to be important from the standpoint we have at a particular point in time. As a result, we need to exercise some caution in relation to how we respond to different views of what the future will hold and what these will mean for managing people in organizations. However, we can be reasonably certain that in the foreseeable future organizations will continue to grapple with how best to manage their HR. Some commentators have suggested that people management issues will assume greater significance in organizations of the future, although there may be a need for a paradigm shift in the way the work of the HR function is conceptualized (The Work Foundation, 2009; CIPD, 2010f).

16.2 The future for SHRM

There is general agreement that HR strategies and the role of the HR function will in the future continue to be closely linked to what happens in business more generally. To this end a number of bodies (see, for example, CIPD, Microsoft, PwC, The Work Foundation) have attempted to envision the future business world and have developed a number of possible scenarios. Below we explore a number of these and examine what the different scenarios may mean for SHRM in the future.

 Key Concept

Scenarios for the future present an outline of a predicted set of developments and/or sequence of events. A number of different scenarios for the future may be examined in order to plan for and consider the consequences of different eventualities.

The professional services firm PwC has published a report entitled *Managing Tomorrow's People* and this starts by making a number of general observations about the future of business. First, it is proposed that the way in which businesses operate will continue to change in response to influences from developing information and communication technology, increasing globalization, and the effect of changing demographics on organizational structures and cultures. Second, it is suggested that in the future people management will present one of the greatest business challenges and that as a consequence the role of the HRM function will need to undergo fundamental change. Specifically, it proposes that the management of HR will become more important as:

- The boundaries between work and non-work life become less clear, as companies assume greater responsibility for the welfare of their employees.
- People performance metrics develop and become more sophisticated, and these will increasingly be used to monitor and control employee performance.
- Social capital and relationships play an important role in driving business success.

As such, it is argued that there will be three main developments in the HR function. Instead of being seen essentially as a passive, service-providing function it will:

- Become the heart of the organization, taking on a new remit which will incorporate and influence many other aspects of the business.
- Become centred around the corporate social responsibility agenda in the organization.
- Take on more of a transactor role where activity is outsourced.

The report sets out three possible scenarios for the future of business and in turn examines the implications of each scenario for HRM (PwC, 2007). Each of the scenarios proposed rests on a different set of assumptions. The first scenario is based on the idea that large corporations will become increasingly powerful, effectively turning into 'mini-states', and that they will take on a prominent and powerful role in societies. The second scenario is based on the proposition that businesses will place increasing emphasis on the importance of the environmental agenda and assumes that this will have a major impact on business strategies. The third scenario proposes that greater specialization of businesses will occur and that this will result in the increasing collaboration between organizations and the establishment of interorganizational networks. It is noteworthy that these are not necessarily seen as being mutually exclusive. We briefly examine each of the scenarios in turn. However, it is worth noting that the scenarios rely largely on a developed-world perspective and it may be that we see alternative developments in emerging economies in the future.

 Key Concept

Competencies for HR professionals refer to the skills and behaviours required in order to perform the professional work of HR effectively.

16.2.1 Scenario 1–corporate is king

In this scenario it is proposed that we will see growth in the size and power of major corporations. It is argued that in some cases the annual turnover of large corporations will equal or exceed the GDP of individual countries, especially those in the developing world. As a result these powerful organizations, looking to attract and retain high-calibre staff, will take on greater responsibility for looking after the welfare of employees, in some cases providing services traditionally provided by the state. This might include providing healthcare insurance or providing or assisting with the procurement of housing and education for employees' children. These types of policies will be designed to help 'lock' high-calibre employees into these organizations. Under these circumstances it is envisaged that a big divide will open between large and powerful organizations and those that are smaller and less powerful, in terms of their approach to managing people. Larger organizations will aim to look after and provide for their employees, whereas those working for smaller, less powerful organizations will need to access health, education, and housing for themselves and will be more vulnerable to shifts in the marketplace (e.g. the price of housing). This scenario is also based on certain assumptions about the nature of services that states will provide in the future. If national or regional governments seek to reduce the size and nature of state provision (Skelcher, 2007), or where that provision is perceived to be of inferior quality, there may be real opportunities for employers to attract and retain staff by providing alternative services for their employees. It is also anticipated that these organizations will take advantage of developments in technology, in order to refine and individualize their relationships with their employees. Technology will allow them to monitor employee performance more closely, which will be justified by the high costs of managing HR in this way.

Thus, in this scenario employers will become major providers of services for their employees. As such, the HR function will be concerned with broader aspects of employees' lives and with the provision of services to support them. Leadership teams will focus on the evolution of the organizational culture and hence will need to have rigorous assessment procedures to ensure recruits fit with the ideal, and existing staff will be subject to ongoing training and development to support the desired culture. These factors together mean that the HR costs will be high for organizations and as a result there will be a need for accurate metrics, to ensure that HR are performing, and to have an early warning if people are not performing or are displaying 'non-corporate' behaviour.

In this scenario the person responsible for people (e.g. Chief People Officer) will hold a powerful position, and sophisticated measures will allow him or her to demonstrate explicitly the contribution of people to organizational performance. The approach to managing people will be seen as crucial, since although people will be seen to have great significance to the business, they also carry a higher risk factor than other resources. In this scenario those who manage the people function will increasingly need financial and numeracy skills. They will also need to be good at marketing, and to attract quality HR they will need to be tuned into employee needs.

16.2.2 Scenario 2–the green world

In this scenario it is assumed that the actions of organizations will be driven by a powerful social conscience and sense of responsibility. Customers will expect organizations to act ethically and to have good environmental credentials. As a result, changing consumer values and attitudes will drive corporate behaviour. It is expected that as a consequence organizations will take greater control of their supply chain and that their values will be strongly infused into the way in which people are managed (for a discussion see Jabbour and Santos, 2008). Potential recruits will judge an employer on its social and environmental stance, and the retention of existing employees will be affected by how they behave in practice. Consequently, the HR function will need to play a key role in the development and promotion of the organization's CSR agenda and will need to take on responsibility for developing an employer brand consistent with this agenda.

Employees in turn will be expected to be committed to and uphold these values. For example, organizations may seek to reduce their carbon footprint by reducing the amount of travel for business. As such, employees, particularly in international organizations, may be expected to make greater use of information and communication technologies in order to reduce travel requirements. In response, the HR function may need to provide support, for example to assist employees who work in virtual teams. Additionally, employees may be encouraged to avoid unnecessary commuting travel and organizations may need to provide greater support to enable effective remote working, or alternatives such as corporate transportation to avoid individual car use. Under this scenario selection will be concerned with hiring not only high quality talent but also employees whose values are aligned with those of the organization. Retention of employees may not only be associated with traditional rewards, but may also include secondments to social projects, or the opportunity to take time out of work to volunteer for charitable causes. Employees will also expect their employers to behave responsibly towards them and this might, for example, involve the HR function in developing innovative solutions in times of business downturn in order to avoid redundancies.

In this scenario the head of HR (Head of People and Society) will be a senior member of the executive team and will drive the CSR programme. Since people in the organization and their behaviours will be seen to have a direct link to the success or failure of the organization, the CEO will also be closely involved in people strategy. Whilst evidence to date suggests that customers' expectations are changing and that they expect organizations with which they do business to uphold certain standards, the resilience of these views in a changing context (e.g. the global financial crisis) will influence whether this becomes a business imperative or an approach an organization may choose to take.

Pfeffer (2010) has picked up the sustainability and HR theme in a more specific sense. He notes that most attention in the sustainability debate has focused on the impact of organizations on the physical as opposed to the social environment. However, he argues that decisions made by organizations have implications for the health and wellbeing of their staff, since measures of population health are used as indicators of societal effectiveness and the level of development of a country. Thus, he argues that being a socially responsible organization should also mean that account is taken of the effects of management practices on the physical and psychological wellbeing of employees. Evidence shows that decisions taken by organizations about how to manage and reward their employees (working hours, job design, job security, pay and benefits, fairness) have significant effects on human health and mortality. As such, HR professionals concerned with human sustainability need to ensure that relevant data are collected and publicized on health outcomes.

16.2.3 Scenario 3—small is beautiful

This scenario is based on the assumption that big is bad for business, for people, and for the environment. As such, global businesses will fragment and localism will prevail. Small, low-impact, high-technology business will become the norm and the development of networks will be key in the form of loose clusters of organizations. These networks will be driven and sustained through the use of ICT, with tasks being transacted between organizations through an electronic exchange. There is evidence to show growth in networked organizations and other collaborative organizational forms (Gulati, 2007); however, this scenario relies on a continuance of this trend, which may have significant consequences for the ways in which organizations are managed.

These developments will be accompanied by individuals building portfolio careers, where they may only work with an organization on a short-term contractual basis. Specialism-based guilds, or similar bodies, are envisaged to help manage career opportunities and to provide training and development for individuals. They may also take on some of the roles traditionally undertaken by employers (e.g. sourcing talent, provision of healthcare insurance, pensions, training and development). Organizations will recognize that their employees and their relationships across networks will be crucial to their success. As such, they will seek to promote people networks. In addition to rewarding staff for specialist expertise, they will also reward collaborative behaviour and connectivity. In this context a people strategy is replaced by a sourcing strategy, since the people supply chain is crucial in this networked world. Individuals, not organizations, take responsibility for training and development, and loyalty is to the profession or network, rather than to a particular employing organization.

Discussions in practitioner forums about factors likely to influence the future of HRM lend support to networked and other collaborative organizational forms becoming increasingly important (see, for example, http://www.hr.toolbox.com). As such, relational competencies are deemed to be important for future HR professionals. In order to take advantage of these organizational forms, there is a need to develop greater collaboration, negotiation, conflict resolution, and knowledge management capabilities. HR professionals are seen to be responsible for leading the development of these core organizational competencies and to strengthen the alignment with actual business strategies. However, research has shown that where the HR function has taken on the role of internal consultant, this can be contested by other occupational groups also keen to take on this role (Wright, 2008). The need for HR to look beyond internal concerns is also emphasized in that it needs also to be concerned with how to select, engage, work with, and develop external partners to create value for the organization.

In a similar vein, but focusing more specifically on the management of people, Microsoft in a white paper entitled *The New World of Work* (2007) identified the main factors likely to influence the workforce in the future as increasing global integration, demographic change, and technological innovation occur. They argue that two major opportunities exist for businesses in the way in which they manage their people. First, there needs to be a focus on human capability. This means that businesses need to focus on the capabilities that amplify the skills and impact of people. For example, collaboration is cited as allowing individual expertise and experience to create increased value through networking, knowledge sharing, and the refinement of ideas. Second, there is a need to think strategically about the workforce, where people are seen as an asset rather than a cost, and that the benefits of diversity in the workforce need to be recognized and harnessed. Seeing the workforce in a more strategic and creative way will drive policies and practices to help retain key workers in an unpredictable labour market. In addition it is argued that organizations will need to take corporate responsibility into the heart of the organization in order to avoid tighter legal regulation. A more central role for corporate responsibility is also seen as an important tool in employee engagement.

 Critical Reflection

Based on your own knowledge of business, which of these scenarios do you think are likely? Are there other implications for the HR function and HR strategies that you can identify?

Faced with a number of possible future scenarios for the business world, it is important that HR professionals make plans to deal with the HR implications of the different scenarios, in both the long and the short term. It is also important to monitor the environment on an ongoing basis, in order to be able to adjust plans in line with actual developments. Boxall and Purcell (2003) argue that HR professionals should undertake scenario planning, where a number of future scenarios are developed taking the organization's context into account. Planning for each of these scenarios then creates a readiness to deal with a range of future circumstances. They propose a number of steps to achieve this:

- Step 1 involves identifying long-term business scenarios.
- Step 2 involves analysing the organization's readiness in HR terms for each scenario.
- Step 3 involves identifying key stakeholder trends relevant to the management of people.
- Step 4 involves developing HR strategies for the long-term business scenarios, taking stakeholder trends into account.

16.3 The professional association (CIPD) view

The CIPD report *Next Generation HR* (Sears, 2010) proposes that there will be a shift in the core purpose of the HR function over the next 5–10 years. It identifies three main challenges for HR in the future:

1. Future-proofing organizations.
2. Developing an insight-driven approach to HR.
3. Taking on the role of being partners *and* provocateurs.

16.3.1 Future-proofing organizations

In recent decades it has been acknowledged that the role of HR has shifted from a traditional personnel function supporting the employee's life cycle to a greater focus on people and performance, and as a result the development of a more strategic approach to HRM. However, it is argued that in moving forward HR needs to play a role in helping organizations prepare for ongoing sustainable success and that this will involve a move away from the 'one model fits all' orthodoxy (Sears, 2011). Following the global economic crisis, the CIPD reports evidence of senior business leaders (both within and outside the HR function) becoming more focused on sustainable business performance, which may challenge existing approaches to generating profit and business growth. They argue that in order to do this organizations need to build 'future-proof' cultures and develop 'future-fit' leaders and for the HR function to take on a role of organization guardians and commentators.

Future-proof cultures need to be productive and open, with high value being placed on the role of organizational development. This type of culture it is suggested needs to be based on the development of deep trust relations between employers and their employees. For many organizations, achieving a high level of emotional loyalty will mean going beyond current approaches to employee engagement. This type of relationship needs to be supported by a straight-talk, transparent, and dialogue-oriented culture. Employees need to trust what the organization stands for and this needs to be reinforced in their day-to-day experiences. This could prove to be a major challenge for organizations following the decline in trust observed in recent years, which it has been argued has been brought about by more general trends such as growing income inequality, globalization, and the economic downturn, resulting in redundancies and organizational restructuring (Uslaner, 2009).

The report also argues that in order to achieve brand alignment, organizations need to develop relationships with their staff which are based on the same principles as the relationships they aim to develop with their customers. This implies a role for the HR function in ensuring internal coherence and consistency, not just in policy but also supported through practice. Moving beyond healthy cultures, where employees at all levels feel supported and which makes it easier to do difficult work, there is a need for agile and adaptable cultures. The HR function as a result can play an important role in facilitating a more dynamic strategic planning process. The HR function can also help develop a more alert and enterprising approach to doing business—allowing for a living strategy that responds to trends and opportunities that arise.

Future-fit leaders will need to be developed by talent management strategies that go beyond just filling the organizational pipeline. There is a need to identify the abilities and mindsets that the leaders of tomorrow will require and how these may differ from what is needed in today's leaders. It is important that organizations do not spend their resources developing leaders able to run yesterday's or today's rather than tomorrow's business. The role for HR will then be in selecting and developing people for these roles.

Becoming organizational guardians and commentators would involve HR professionals using their knowledge and understanding of what really happens in the organization to provide a commentary on how decisions or behaviours may influence the long term for the organization. This might take the form of:

● Challenging actions that may have the potential to damage the internal and/or external brand of the organization.

● Designing HR policies that support progressive, sustainable ways of doing business, for example, managing performance, rewarding employees, and managing talent can be powerful mechanisms in organizations to reinforce existing or shape new behaviours.

● Challenging behaviour that does not correspond to what the organization stands for, even if it requires challenging senior business leaders. In this role HR becomes a guardian of what the organization stands for. Taking on the role of Chief Integrity Officer may be controversial and sometimes hard to do and therefore HR leaders will need courage and support from those at the top of the organization to do this. In addition the HR function will need a degree of independence and may need to be in dialogue with non-executive directors in order to do this.

16.3.2 An insight-driven approach to HR

The CIPD believes that HR functions in the future will be distinguished by the insight they bring to the organization that enables activities to be relevant, timely, and impactful. Organizational insight is described by the CIPD as a juxtaposition of an understanding of the key determinants of what makes the organization successful (taking account of the market, state of development, etc.), together with a deep understanding of what goes on in the organization and what makes things happen. These involve both an understanding of the key drivers of the business and organizational intelligence gathering in a variety of formal and informal ways. Insight of this nature is important for making good and sound decisions and for helping understanding of how changes may impact the organization more broadly. This insight may be both strategic and operational in nature. The CIPD argues that in order to develop this insight HR people need to be:

- Business savvy—this involves more than being financially literate, but having a broader understanding of how the business works.

- Context savvy—this requires understanding market trends and what affects the business, including more general economic and societal trends.

- Organization savvy—this is about understanding what contributes to the business success and failure (e.g. people, culture, leadership) and the ability to change. This needs to be understood in the context of the particular organization.

The CIPD proposes that being insight driven is the next stage of evolution of the HR function. In an update to the report, an example is cited of where economic growth in Asia has resulted in new approaches to HR developing, which are more enterprising and which go beyond traditional approaches to HR. An initiative carried out by a Hong Kong-based company expanding into mainland China is described, where HR, recognizing the importance of local knowledge and contacts in doing business in the mainland, recruited experienced, ex-senior management employees, who originally came from the parts of China where they wanted to do business, to act as navigators of these contexts (Sears, 2011).

16.3.3 Becoming partners and provocateurs

Finally, the CIPD argues that HR leaders in the future need to be seen by other business leaders as having a real share in the voice and influence in the organization. It is suggested that they need to act as provocateurs, in the sense that they encourage new ways of doing business and/or new areas of strategic focus and that they will need to do this in such a way that they are not seen as mavericks. Through providing insight, as discussed earlier, they will need to be able to offer different viewpoints, stimulate debate, and challenge existing world views. A number of characteristics are identified that these leaders will need to fulfil their roles. These include:

- Purpose, humility, and resolve, and in particular the ability to elevate the debate to look at what really matters. They need a strong sense of purpose connected to a fundamental goal or value which allows them to take the conversation beyond immediate objectives or targets. However, they also require a lightness of touch in the way they operate so that they explore and stimulate rather than challenge and 'browbeat'.

- A dynamic and holistic world view allied to real personal savvy. They will need to be able to see interconnections and to be 'joined-up' thinkers. This means they need to be attuned to their environment and may be more outward looking than other business leaders. Personal savvy is more than experience and requires the exercise of judgement about which issues to drive and where and how to build alliances.

- Personal presence involves the ability to engage in difficult conversations and challenge prevailing orthodoxies. They will need to be seen as people worth listening too, who can be trusted and who are not judgemental.

Becoming partners and provocateurs is a type of change that may be challenging to achieve and will have clear implications for the development and education of HR professionals. Whilst the technical foundations of the role are likely to remain important, the above suggests that there will be an increased need for HR professionals to develop a more holistic view of how organizations work, and a greater need for the development of personal skills in order to allow them to become real influencers. The above discussion would also suggest that if the nature of work is different, there may be a need for a different type of recruit to the profession. Likewise, a different role for the HR function may attract a different kind of person to work in the field.

16.4 Other influences

16.4.1 Regional and national policy

Taking a wider perspective, organizations operate in the context of national and regional government policy frameworks. As a consequence, these will have some degree of influence over an organization's approach to business and to managing its HR. Therefore when examining likely future developments it is useful to be aware of the strategies and plans that these bodies have in place. For example, countries within the European Union (EU) will be influenced by the EU's employment and social affairs policies. Recent EU policy has focused on economic growth and the creation of jobs in a sustainable manner. The approach has been to combine flexibility and mobility of labour, whilst at the same time maintaining a strong social security support network, an approach termed 'flexicurity'. In addition to the policy to support growth, the EU is active in promoting decent work, by ensuring that employees' rights are protected and that minimum standards are upheld across member countries. More recently, Europe 2020, the EU's growth strategy, aims to create more jobs throughout the EU and has set a target of having 75% of 20- to 64-year-olds in employment by the end of the decade. Member countries are obliged to develop national-level strategies to meet these targets. In addition there is ongoing dialogue about employment matters between the European Commission, national governments, trade unions, employers' bodies, and the other European institutions.

At national level a number of organizations will also seek to shape government policy and the way in which regional targets are attained. In the UK the employer's organization, the Confederation of British Industry (CBI), in a report entitled *Making Britain the Place to Work*, has argued that the UK needs to build on its competitive strategy on the dual platforms of skills and flexibility. It proposes that there need to be three strands to the government's employment strategy:

- Embracing flexibility in order to align the needs of individuals and the needs of businesses.
- Reshaping regulation in order to sustain and encourage employment, rather than undermining it.
- Adopting a fairer approach to workplace relations, reflecting mainstream employee views.

Embracing flexibility is seen as key to modern employment relationships and to competitive advantage. Employers are encouraged to recognize that flexibility needs to take account of the employees' needs as well as those of the organization. Training and technology are seen as key to helping organizations achieve greater flexibility. In order to have a wide pool of skills and experience, widespread participation in the labour market is advocated and the encouragement of government is seen as vital to increasing participation in those groups that are currently underrepresented.

The CBI argues that for sustainable jobs to be created there is a need for a regulatory and legislative framework which is supportive of employers, but which also safeguards basic standards for employees. As such they advocate that proposals for change should be subject to rigorous examination and evaluated in the light of what they are likely to mean for sustainable employment.

In the light of reduced levels of trade union membership amongst employees in the private sector, the CBI argues that the framework for employment relations needs to be widened in order to accommodate other patterns of employee–employer communication/voice. It is argued that whilst there should be encouragement to resolve disputes at workplace levels where at all possible, there is also a need to review the employment tribunal system.

As illustrated by the above, government policy may be subject to influences at different levels and from different sources, which may seek to shape policies in different ways. Employers are then faced with interpreting government policy in line with their own wider objectives and standpoints on the business world.

16.4.2 International strategies

As organizations are increasingly subject to greater global integration (as discussed in Chapter 1), a number of questions arise about strategic approaches to international HRM (IHRM). For example, there has been much debate about the extent to which global HR strategies are achievable and whether global pressures lead to convergence in the approaches to managing HR globally and across regions. Pinnington (2011) argues that there are three major challenges for IHRM. These are cross-cultural communication and diversity; global knowledge management; and local and global sustainability. Brewster and Mayrhofer (2011) suggest that one of the problems for IHRM is that much of our knowledge about HRM comes from the US and it is often assumed that this knowledge is more widely applicable. However, they argue that organizations that wish to manage HR effectively across different countries need to understand the different national cultures and institutional parameters they are dealing with. This would suggest that a 'best-fit' approach will vary according to national context. The challenge therefore that organizations face is to balance the desire to be coherent and consistent across their global operations, led by their overall HR strategy, with the need to be sensitive to differences in culture and national institutions which shape business activity. In more recent years there has been increasing empirical investigation into approaches to HRM employed in emerging economies; for example, in China (Zhu et al, 2007), India (Budhwar and Varma, 2010), and Russia (May et al, 1998). This growing body of evidence shows some variation in approaches to HRM in these different national contexts.

16.4.3 Outsourcing the HR function

Sako and Tierney (2007) examined the future of HR and argue that current developments may represent the most significant period of upheaval for the HR function since its establishment as an organizational function. The principal reason for this is the trend towards outsourcing of the HR function. Whilst cost savings may be the primary motivation on the part of employers for outsourcing HR, the move has also come to be seen as a way of transforming the HR function. Their research identified three principal ways of using outsourcing. First, employers may create a shared service centre and then outsource it. Second, processes may be outsourced, which a vendor then may improve. Third, organizations may take a 'big bang' approach of transforming and outsourcing all at once. Outsourcing and the transfer of staff to service providers will result in a smaller remaining HR function and changes to the roles of both those who remain and those who transfer to the service provider. Outsourcing has implications for the relationship between service providers and end users and as such this relationship is key to success. Sako and Tierney argue that there is a need to ensure alignment of interests and mutual understanding between parties if such deals are to be sustainable.

16.4.4 **Private equity finance**

In recent years we have seen growth in the private equity model of financing organizations. Private equity represents a rather different governance and accountability model from traditional approaches. When a company is subjected to a private equity buy-out, there may be significant implications for the employment contract of individuals who work for it and for the organization of work (Wood and Wright, 2010). Whilst the implications for private equity buy-outs for shareholders have been the subject of research attention, little attention has been paid to the implications for employees (Wood and Wright, 2010). Research in finance suggests that significant performance gains can be yielded for the companies that private equity funds invest in (Kaplan and Stromberg, 2009).

The term 'private equity' has been used in a broad sense. It might, for example, involve early investment in new endeavours, typically known as venture capital. It might also involve groups of investors buying out a mature organization, designed to change the governance and management style, in order to lead to greater returns (Wright et al, 2000) and may ultimately lead to the resale of the organization. These may take the form of buy-outs by outsiders, management buy-ins, and investor-led buy-outs. Private equity buy-outs have often been associated with restructuring and downsizing. Boselie and Koene (2010) suggest that private equity buy-outs may signal a major organizational transformation.

 Key Concept

Private equity companies invest in private companies and buy out public companies, resulting in the latter being delisted on a public exchange. The aim of buying out public companies is frequently to try to improve their financial performance in the short term and then sell the company on at a profit.

In general, mergers and takeovers are often associated with a reappraisal of the way in which people are managed (Conyon et al, 2001). Where the takeover is by outsiders, alterations to the contract of employment may also be facilitated. As Wood and Wright (2010) argue, there are many things that are implicit in the employment relationship, often originally designed to help attract and retain staff, but which may be subject to change following a takeover. They argue that private equity firms may have three reasons for wishing to do so. First, they may take advantage of the opportunity to make changes if the power in the employment relationship has shifted and employees are in a less strong position than they were when such arrangements were made. Second, demands from investors for returns may result in a reordering of priorities which necessitates changes to the relationship between the employer and the employee. Third, difficulties in valuing human capital in monetary terms (Harcourt and Wood, 2007) may result in reduced value being placed on the relationships with staff.

However, the business objectives of private equity firms may also differ from those normally assumed for organizations. If these businesses operate in such a way to increase the value of a business they have taken over in the short term, in order to sell on, concern with the long term is less likely to be a consideration. Employment issues tend to have a long-term payoff. For example, the development of and running out of a development programme may take some time to show a payoff. As a consequence, private equity companies are likely to be interested only in the types of activities that show short-term payoff. This may result in a reduction in staff numbers, through redundancy or natural wastage. In addition they may look for more efficient working practices in order to improve employee productivity. Practices that result in short-term improvements, via work intensification, however, may not be sustainable and may have negative longer-term consequences for employees and for the organization. Terms and conditions may also be reduced; in particular, benefits that incur long-term liability on the part of the organization may be terminated. Reward systems may also be linked more directly to some measure of performance.

 ## Critical Reflection

How useful are, and how might we evaluate, different scenarios of the future business world? How might professional development for HR professionals be designed to help prepare them for the future? To what extent can the HR function play a proactive role in developing its future? How might organizations respond to the influence of governments on their activity?

 ## Conclusion

This chapter has presented an overview of factors that may influence approaches to SHRM and the role of the HR function in the future. This has included examining a number of future scenarios for the business world and a discussion of what these would mean for SHRM. It has also examined the implications for the HR profession, based on research commissioned by the CIPD. In addition the chapter explored the possible influence of a number of other factors such as government policy, international strategies, outsourcing, and the structure of finance.

 ## Summary

- Developments in the business world will have implications for SHRM and for the role played by the HR function.

- Information and communication technologies, globalization, and changing demographics are commonly thought to be major influences on the future of the business world.
- Many commentators predict that managing people effectively will be an increasingly important activity for organizations.
- The growth of networks means that relational capabilities will assume greater significance.
- Insight-driven HR is proposed as the next stage in the evolution of the HR function, following from process and performance stages.
- Other factors may also be important in influencing the approaches adopted in the future, such as the context of government policy, pursuing international strategies, the outsourcing of the function, and the growth in private equity financing.

 ## Review questions

1. What are some of the main developments likely to influence the business world in the foreseeable future?
2. What are the potential roles for the HR function and strategic approaches to HR in the future?
3. Examine the competencies that are likely to be crucial to the success of HR in the future.
4. What additional factors may play an important role?
5. Explore the nature of their influence.

 ## Further reading

CIPD (2010) *Next Generation HR: Time for Change—Towards a Next Generation for HR.* London: CIPD.
This report provides some useful insight into the challenges that the HR profession is likely to encounter in the future and what kinds of competencies HR professionals will need to deal with these challenges.

PwC (2007) *Managing Tomorrow's People. The Future of Work to 2020.* London: PricewaterhouseCoopers LLP. http://www.pwc.com/gx/en/managing-tomorrows-people/future-of-work.
This report explores a number of possible scenarios for the world of business and discusses what the implications might be for the HRM function.

 For additional material on the content of this chapter please visit the supporting Online Resource Centre www.oxfordtextbooks.co.uk/orc/truss.

Glossary

Added value Added value is about identifying what really matters to key stakeholders and delivering the services and products that achieve this. In many respects it builds on the total quality management ethos of delivering products and services that create 'customer delight'.

Aesthetic labour Aesthetic labour refers to circumstances where physical appearance and 'embodied capacities and attributes' form the basis of employment. In other words, part of paid employment is concerned with how people look, sound, and present themselves.

AMO model The AMO model suggests that employees perform well when they have the necessary skills or ability to do so, the motivation to perform, and are given the opportunity to perform by their line managers. HR policies and practices can impact on AMO and thus give rise to higher levels of performance.

Balanced Scorecard The Balanced Scorecard was developed by Kaplan and Norton (1998) as a tool to help managers find holistic ways of measuring organizational performance.

Black box The 'black box' refers to the unknown processes that occur between HR interventions, on the one hand, and performance outcomes, on the other. One focus of research has been to find an appropriate theory to explain how this 'black box' works in order to better explain why and how HRM might impact on performance.

Blended learning Blended learning is where a range of learning methods, underpinned by a range of learning theories, are combined or blended together. This usually involves some form of e-learning as part of the combination.

Business ethics Business ethics 'is the study of business situations, activities, and decisions where issues of right and wrong are addressed' (Crane and Matten, 2007: 5).

Business strategy Business strategy sets out an organization's strategic scope or direction; essentially, the markets it wants to compete in (Grant, 2010). It is important to note that business strategy is often referred to as corporate strategy.

Capabilities Capabilities are 'the capacity of an organisation to use resources, get things done, and behave in ways that accomplish goals. They characterise how people think and behave in the context of the organisation. . . . Capabilities define what the organisation does well' (Ulrich and Brockbank, 2005b: 49). See also core competence.

Career development Career development is a planned and structured response to the career aspirations of key employees.

Change management Change management involves planned change and change agency. **Planned change** is an approach to managing change that assumes that change is an activity that can be managed and organized, and led by senior managers. **Change agency** is the practice of leading and managing change. A change agent is a person or group of people within an organization tasked with managing change.

Coaching Coaching is where a peer or manager works with an employee to motivate the employee, help him or her develop skills, and provide reinforcement and feedback (Noe, 2002: 452).

Code of conduct A code of conduct sets out the way in which employees or members of an occupational group are expected to behave when carrying out their work responsibilities. Also referred to as a code of ethics.

Codification Codification is based on the assumption that it is possible to encode knowledge as text, figures, or digital data. Many observers argue it is information rather than knowledge that is being encoded in this way. See also knowledge management.

Cognition Cognition involves the development of representations or mental models of the world around us within an individual's mind (Bowden and Marton, 2004). See also situated cognition.

Communities of practice 'Communities of practice are groups of people who share a concern, a set of problems, or a passion about a topic, and who deepen their knowledge and expertise in this area by interacting on an ongoing basis. . . . Over time, they develop a unique perspective on their topic as well as a body of common knowledge, practices and approaches. . . . They will tend to organise along friendship lines or within local geographical or organisational contexts rather than cover the whole organisation' (Wenger et al, 2002: 4–5, 13).

Competence Competence is the ability of an individual to do a particular job to a high standard.

Competencies Competencies are 'a broad grouping of knowledge, skills, and attitudes that enable a person to be successful at a number of similar tasks' (Blanchard and Thacker, 2004: 9).

Competitive strategy Competitive strategy is about *how* an organization will compete in those markets identified in the business strategy.

Contingency theories Contingency theories assume that approaches to SHRM will vary in different contexts.

Continuing professional development Continuing professional development (CPD) is an ongoing learning process that focuses on developing professional expertise and the ability to learn more effectively. Pivotal to CPD is the concept of reflective practice (i.e. the ability to reflect critically).

Core competence Core competence is the combination of an organization's technologies with the knowledge, skills, and abilities of its employees. It determines the viability and competitiveness of an organization. See also capabilities.

Corporate social responsibility (CSR) Corporate social responsibility 'encompasses the economic, legal, ethical, and philanthropic expectations placed on organisations by society at a given point in time' (Crane and Matten, 2007: 49).

Corporate university The corporate university is an extension of an old-style training school model found predominantly in the US. In many respects it is a branding exercise that copies the traditional university model and is designed to signal to stakeholders a strategic-level response to learning and development.

Development Development is much broader than training and usually has a longer-term focus. It is concerned with the enhancement of an individual's personal portfolio of knowledge, skills, and abilities (i.e. competencies). See also education.

Devolution Devolution refers to HR managers passing responsibility for HR tasks over to line managers. This can take various forms, varying from total devolution accompanied by the removal of the HR function entirely, to simply asking line managers to fill out relevant forms. It can apply across the full range of HR activity, or just certain areas, such as recruitment.

Education Education can range from courses in basic literacy and numeracy through to postgraduate qualifications such as an MBA. National HRD policies have a very strong focus on education.

E-learning E-learning is a learning and development delivery system that relies on technology and normally requires the learner to engage in self-directed study. It is not a learning theory.

Emotional intelligence Emotional intelligence is about dealing with emotions effectively and can be viewed as an ability or competency (McEnrue and Groves, 2006).

Emotional labour Emotional labour is where employees are expected to manage their emotions as part of their paid employment.

Employee engagement Employee engagement is a state experienced by individuals in relation to their work that involves investing intellectual energy into thinking about the task, physical energy and absorption in the task, and positive emotional energy and enthusiasm in relation to task fulfilment. It has also been variously proposed that engagement includes a social dimension and positive connections with others, or that it incorporates long working hours, but there is as yet no general agreement about these latter two.

Employee voice The term 'employee voice' refers to circumstances where employees are given the opportunity to have some input into organizational decision making.

Employer branding Employer branding is 'the practice of developing, differentiating and leveraging an organisation's brand message to its current and future workforce in a manner meaningful to them . . . [and] is aimed at motivating and securing employees' alignment with the vision and values of the company' (Price, 2004: 263).

Engagement strategies Engagement strategies are workplace approaches used by employers with the aim of raising levels of employee engagement.

Evaluation Evaluation is concerned with measuring the impact training or learning has had on individual performance in the workplace and the contribution this makes to overall organizational performance.

Explicit knowledge Explicit knowledge is formal, abstract, or theoretical knowledge which relies on an individual's conceptual skills and cognitive abilities.

External fit See vertical strategic alignment.

Facilitation Facilitation is about guiding and supporting a learner or group of learners with the minimum of input.

Free-market capitalism Free-market capitalism is characterized by the free markets, privatization, and deregulation. In theory free-market capitalism is characterized by self-correcting mechanisms that avoid any necessity for state intervention. These mechanisms are embedded in a globally integrated financial market which has been made possible through advances in technology.

Globalization Globalization is about the creation of a borderless global economy that allows unhindered movement of finance, products, services, information, and people.

High-performance work practices 'High-perform-ance work practices' refers to a bundle of HR practices that is expected to yield positive performance outcomes at the individual and organizational levels. However, there is little consensus as to the precise practices that should be in the bundle, and the evidence as to their impact is mixed.

Horizontal fit See horizontal strategic alignment.

Horizontal strategic alignment (also referred to as horizontal alignment and horizontal fit) Horizontal strategic alignment is the process by which HRD strategy, policies, plans, and practices are aligned with an organization's HRM strategy, policies, plans, and practices.

HR architecture HR architecture is where HR strategies are likely to be varied, with different approaches selected for different employee groups.

HR strategy HR strategy refers to the strategy that an organization adopts for managing its people. Some firms do not have an HR strategy, but all will be driven by employment law to have appropriate policies in place for managing people. Organizations may have one overarching HR strategy and/or different strategies for managing different groups of employees. HR strategies may be explicit and documented, or implicit.

Human capital Becker (1964, 1975) popularized Schultz's (1961) human capital theory that organizations derive economic value from employees' skills, competence, knowledge, and experience. Shultz (ibid) argued that human capital can be developed through education and training.

Human resource development (HRD) Human resource development encompasses a range of organizational practices that focus on learning: training, learning, and development; workplace learning; career development and lifelong learning; organization development; organizational knowledge and learning.

Informal learning Informal learning is essentially learning that is 'predominantly unstructured, experien-tial, and non-institutionalised', (Marsick and Volpe, 1999: 4), with the control of learning resting primarily in the hands of the learner (Marsick and Watkins, 1990).

Intellectual capital Intellectual capital comprises the intangible assets of an organization, including both human capital and social capital.

Internal fit See horizontal strategic alignment.

Knowledge Knowledge is a complex, multifaceted concept which lacks a universal definition. It is often discussed as comprising explicit and tacit dimensions. See also explicit knowledge and tacit knowledge.

Knowledge intensive firms Knowledge intensive firms (KIFs) are organizations that employ a significant number of employees who are engaged in knowledge work.

Knowledge management Knowledge management is a strategic approach to the control and/or nurturing of organizational knowledge.

Knowledge work Knowledge work involves being engaged in complex activities and tasks that are characterized by autonomy and judgement, such as that carried out by professionals, scientists, and consultants.

Knowledge workers Knowledge workers are employees who are engaged in knowledge work (i.e. those engaged in complex activities and tasks that are characterized by autonomy and judgement, such as that carried out by professionals, scientists, and consultants.

Learning There is no universal definition of learning. Learning at the individual level is about the acquisition of new knowledge and how this changes the individual in some way (e.g. in terms of how they think about something, or how they carry out a task, or how they behave). See also lifelong learning, social and situated learning, and reflective practice.

Lifelong learning Lifelong learning is the ongoing acquisition of knowledge and skills by study and experience throughout the duration of an individual's career.

Mentoring Mentoring involves a more experienced and usually more senior person helping a less experienced employee through discussion and guidance. It is a developmental relationship which is focused on supporting the employee's ability to achieve his/her career ambitions.

National human resource development (NHRD) National human resource development is intended to provide a coherent set of policies for the social and economic development of a country. It encompasses a wide range of concerns, including public health, environmental protection, diversity, education, and vocational training. The way in which NHRD is handled varies from country to country.

National vocational education and training (NVET) National vocational education and training is focused on developing a country's human capital and represents a strategic response to the long-term skills needs of its indigenous private, public, and non-profit sectors.

New institutionalism The new institutionalist framework is based on the idea that external pressures on organizations will exert a homogenizing effect, leading to similar solutions being adopted by firms in the same industry.

Organization development (OD) Organization development is a systematic and methodical approach to the management of change that is aimed at improving organizational performance and competitiveness.

Organizational change There are several types of organizational change, including the following. **Transformational change**: a wide-reaching and fundamental change of an organization's strategy, culture, and structure. **Incremental change**: a small-scale change affecting only part of what an organization does, such as introducing a new technology or restructuring a department. **Punctuated equilibrium**: periods of incremental change interspersed with transformational change.

Organizational culture Organizational culture is a pattern of shared basic assumptions that the group learned as it solved its problems of external adaptation and internal integration, which has worked well enough to be considered valid and, therefore, to be taught to new members as the correct way to perceive, think, and feel, in relation to those problems (Schein, 1992: 12).

Organizational structure Organizational structure is the way in which an organization is designed in order to support the competitive strategy.

Outsourcing Outsourcing involves contracting with external organizations or individuals who possess specialist expertise and can fulfil specific projects for an organization, instead of employing an in-house function or individual specialist.

Pluralistic ideology Conflict in the employment relationship is seen as inevitable, since both employers and employees are seen as seeking to maximize their own interests—employers might want higher productivity and reduced costs, whereas employees might want higher wages in return for their labour. In this perspective the approach for employers is to attempt to manage conflict, rather than to avoid or suppress it.

Psychological contract The psychological contract is the set of unwritten reciprocal expectations between an organization and an individual employee (Schein, 1992). It reflects the existence of an emotional as well as an economic attachment to the organization, which is highly subjective and subject to change (Boxall and Purcell, 2008).

Reflective practice Reflective practice involves thinking critically about specific incidents and examining what happened, how it happened, and why it happened. The outcome of this process is often some form of learning that involves an adjustment to how we think and act in the world.

Resource-based view (RBV) The resource-based view of the firm is based on the premise that firms can achieve sustained competitive advantage if they secure and effectively deploy resources that are not available to, or imitable by, their competitors.

Resource dependency Resource dependency theory argues that firms are dependent on others in their network for important resources, and that the nature of the dependency relationship will impact on the leeway available to the firm to choose its own solutions to managerial dilemmas.

Shared service centres Shared service centres can be established, often around a call centre or intranet that is accessible to everyone in the organization and that is set up to answer queries. Shared service centres benefit from economies of scale and accessibility; they can be in-house, part-outsourced, or fully outsourced.

Shareholder theory Shareholder theory gives priority to profit maximization based on a corporation's legal obligations to generate shareholder wealth (Key, 1999). This is consistent with an economic perspective on globalization.

Situated cognition Cognition is situated in the workplace and distributed across group members, and learning occurs as a result of social interaction between group members.

Social capital Social capital is 'the sum of actual and potential resources within, available through, and derived from the network of relationships possessed by an individual or social unit. Social capital thus comprises both the network and the assets that may be mobilised through that network' (Nahapiet and Ghoshal, 1998: 243). See also intellectual capital.

Social learning Social learning, or as it is often termed social cognitive theory, is where learning takes place as a result of engaging in social activities. This includes passive engagement, such as observation and listening, and active engagement, actually contributing to discussions.

Social networks Social networks are informal groups that emerge and evolve in the workplace but have weaker ties than communities of practice and tend to span organizational boundaries.

Stakeholder theory Stakeholder theory looks beyond profit maximization and focuses on social and environmental values, based on a corporation's moral obligations to all those who have a stake in the business (Freeman, 2011). This reflects a social perspective on globalization.

Strategic alignment See horizontal and vertical strategic alignment.

Strategic human resource development (SHRD) Strategic human resource development is when HRD strategy, policies, plans, and practices are vertically and horizontally aligned and learning is embedded in the organization's strategic processes.

Strategic management Strategic management is the process that enables organizations to turn strategic intent into action. It comprises four phases: analysis, selection, implementation, and review.

Strategic partner Strategic partner refers to the role adopted by the HR function whereby the focus is on HR activities in supporting the strategic direction of the organization.

Supply chain The supply chain is the network of organizations that are involved in the processes that create value for customers in the form of products and/or services.

Tacit knowledge Tacit knowledge is the practice or skills dimension of knowledge which accrues over time. It is often referred to as an individual's skills or expertise. Spender (1996) describes tacit knowledge as **automatic** knowledge in acknowledgement of Polanyi's assertion that 'we can know more than we can tell' (1967: 4). It is difficult to articulate tacit knowledge because it is so deeply embedded within an individual's experience, judgement, and intuition (Ahmed et al, 2002).

Talent development Talent development is the strategic allocation of HRD resources aimed at developing top talent in an organization.

Talent management Talent management focuses on 'key employees' or 'top talent'. Top talent can be defined as 'employees who routinely exceed expectations while

exhibiting the right behaviours and are agile in learning and approach. These are people who customers pay a premium to do business with and others strive to work with' (Morgan and Jardin, 2010: 24).

Training Training involves planned instruction in a particular skill or practice and is intended to result in changed behaviour in the workplace leading to improved performance.

Training method Training methods are the different ways in which specific elements within an intervention can be delivered to learners.

Unitary ideology The unitary ideology promotes a common purpose and shared values and ways of behaving. Teamwork and employee commitment are emphasized. Anyone who challenges this ideology is treated as dysfunctional and subjected to training or disciplinary action.

Universalist theories Universalist theories are predicated on the assumption that there is 'one best way' to manage people (e.g. best practice).

Vertical fit See vertical strategic alignment.

Vertical strategic alignment (also referred to as vertical alignment and vertical fit) Vertical strategic alignment is the process by which HRD strategy, policies, and plans are aligned with an organization's strategic goals and objectives.

References

Adler, P. (2003) Making the HR outsourcing decision. *Sloan Management Review*, Fall, pp. 53–60.

Ahmed, P.K., Kok, L.K. and Loh, A.Y.E. (2002) *Learning Through Knowledge Management*. Oxford: Butterworth-Heinemann.

Akerlof, G.A. and Shiller, R.J. (2009) *Animal Spirits: How Human Psychology Drives the Economy, and Why It Matters for Global Capitalism*. Oxford: Princeton University Press.

Aktharsha, U.S. and Anisa, H. (2011) Knowledge management system and learning organization: an empirical study in an engineering organization. *Journal of Knowledge Management*, IX(2), pp. 26–43.

Alfes, K., Truss, C., Soane, E., Rees, C. and Gatenby, M. (2010a) *Creating an Engaged Workforce*. Wimbledon: CIPD.

Alfes, K., Truss, C. and Gill, J. (2010b) The HR manager as change agent: evidence from the public sector. *Journal of Change Management*, 10(1), pp. 109–127.

Ali, Y., Lewis, N. and McAdams, K.C. (2010) Case study: building an internal coaching capacity—the American Cancer Society coach cadre model. *Industrial and Commercial Training*, 42(5), pp. 240–246.

Alis, D., Karsten, L. and Leopold, J. (2006) From gods to goddesses. *Time and Society*, 15, pp. 81–104.

Allen, W.C. (2006) Overview and evolution of the ADDIE training system. *Advances in Developing Human Resources*, 8(4), pp. 430–441.

Allen, N. and Meyer, J. (1990) Organisational socialisation tactics: a longitudinal analysis of links to newcomers' commitment and role orientation. *Academy of Management Journal*, 33(4), pp. 847–858.

Almeida, P., Phene, A. and Grant, R. (2005) Innovation and knowledge management: scanning, sourcing, and integration. In M. Easterby-Smith and M.J. Lyles (eds) *Handbook of Organisational Learning and Knowledge Management*. Oxford: Blackwell Publishing.

Alvesson, M. (2004) *Knowledge Work and Knowledge-Intensive Firms*. Oxford: Oxford University Press.

Alvesson, M. and Kärreman, D. (2001) Odd couple: making sense of the curious concept of knowledge management. *Journal of Management Studies*, 38(7), pp. 995–1018.

Amann, E. (2009) Technology, public policy, and the emergence of Brazilian multinationals. In L. Brainard and L. Martinez-Diaz (eds) *Brazil as an Economic Superpower? Understanding Brazil's Changing Role in the Global Economy*. Washington, DC: Brookings Institution Press.

Antila, E.M. (2006) The role of HR managers in international mergers and acquisitions: a multiple case study. *International Journal of Human Resource Management*, 17(6), pp. 999–1020.

Appelbaum, E., Bailey, T., Berg, P. and Kalleberg, A. (2000) *Manufacturing Advantage: Why High Performance Work Systems Pay Off*. Ithaca: ILR Press.

Aragón-Sánchez, A. and Sánchez-Marín, G. (2005) Strategic orientation, management characteristics, and performance: a study of Spanish SMEs. *Journal of Small Business Management*, 43(3), pp. 287–308.

Aras, G. and Crowther, D. (2010) *A Handbook of Corporate Governance and Social Responsibility (Corporate Social Responsibility)*. Farnham: Gower Publishing Limited.

Argyris, C. (1999) *On Organisational Learning*, 2nd edn. Oxford: Blackwell Business.

Arthur, J. (1994) Effects of human resource systems on manufacturing performance and turnover. *Academy of Management Journal*, 37(3), pp. 670–687.

Atkinson, C. and Hall, L. (2011) Flexible working and happiness in the NHS. *Employee Relations*, 33(2), pp. 88–105.

Atkinson, J. (1985) Flexibility: planning for an uncertain future. *Manpower Policy and Practice*. 1, pp. 26–29.

Authers, J. (2010) *The Fearful Rise of Markets*. Harlow: FT Prentice Hall.

Bahl, R. (2010) *Super Power? The Amazing Race Between China's Hare and India's Tortoise*. London: Portfolio/Penguin.

Baird, L. and Meshoulam, I. (1988) Managing two fits of strategic human resource management. *Academy of Management Review*, 13(1), pp. 116–128.

Bakan, J. (2004) *The Corporation: The Pathological Pursuit of Profit and Power*. London: Constable.

Bakker, A. and Xanthopoulou, D. (2008) The crossover of daily work engagement: test of an actor–partner interdependence model. *Journal of Applied Psychology*, 94(6), pp. 1562–1571.

Bakker, A.B. and Schaufeli, W.B. (2008). Positive organizational behavior: engaged employees in flourishing organizations. *Journal of Organizational Behavior*, 29(2), pp. 147–154.

Balogun, J. and Hope-Hailey, V. (2004) *Exploring Strategic Change*, 2nd edn. London: Prentice Hall.

Bamford, D. and Daniel, S. (2005) A case study of change management effectiveness within the NHS. *Journal of Change Management*, 5(4), pp. 391–406.

Barbera, R.J. (2009) *The Cost of Capitalism: Understanding Market Mayhem and Stabilizing Our Economic Future*. New York, NY: McGraw-Hill.

Barney, J. (1991) Firm resources and sustained competitive advantage. *Journal of Management*, 17(1), pp. 99–120.

Barney, J. (1995) Looking inside for competitive advantage. *Academy of Management Executive*, 9(4), pp. 49–61.

Barney, J. (2001) Is the resource-based view a useful perspective for strategic management research? Yes. *Academy of Management Review*, 26, pp. 41–56.

Barney, J.B. and Clark, D.N. (2007) *Resource-Based Theory: Creating and Sustaining Competitive Advantage*. Oxford: Oxford University Press.

Baron, J. and Kreps, D. (1999) Consistent human resource practices. *California Management Review*, 41(3), pp. 29–54.

Barr, D. (2004) *Getting it Together: Surviving Your Quarterlife Crisis*. London: Hodder and Stoughton.

Barros, G. (2009) Brazil: the challenges in becoming an agricultural superpower. In L. Brainard and L. Martinez-Diaz (eds) *Brazil as an Economic Superpower? Understanding Brazil's Changing Role in the Global Economy*. Washington, DC: Brookings Institution Press.

Bartholomew, D. (2008) *Building on Knowledge: Developing Expertise, Creativity and Intellectual Capital in the Construction Profession*. Chichester: Wiley-Blackwell.

Bateman, T. and Organ, D. (1983) Job satisfaction and the good soldier: the relationship between affect and organizational citizenship. *Academy of Management Journal*, 26(4), pp. 587–595.

Baumard, P. (1999) *Tacit Knowledge in Organisations*. London: Sage (translated by S. Wauchope).

Beardwell, J. (2007) Recruitment and selection. In J. Beardwell and T. Claydon (eds) *Human Resource Management: A Contemporary Approach*, 5th edn. Harlow: Pearson.

Beaumont, P.B. (1987) *The Decline of the Trade Union Organisation*. London: Croom Helm.

Beaumont, P.B. and Hunter, L.C. (2002) *Managing Knowledge Workers*. London: CIPD.

Becker, B. and Gerhart, B (1996) The impact of human resource management on organizational performance: progress and prospects. *Academy of Management Journal*, 39(4), pp. 779–801.

Becker, B. and Huselid, M. (1998) High performance work systems and firm performance: a synthesis of research and managerial applications. *Research in Personnel and Human Resources Management*, 16, pp. 53–101.

Becker, B., Huselid, M. and Ulrich, D. (2001) *The Balanced HR Scorecard: Linking People, Strategy and Performance*. Harvard: Harvard Business School Press.

Becker, G. (1964) *Human Capital: A Theoretical and Empirical Analysis with Special Reference to Education*. New York: Columbia University Press.

Becker, G. (1975) *Human Capital: A Theoretical and Empirical Analysis with Special Reference to Education*, 2nd edn. New York: Columbia University Press.

Beckett, H. (2005) Perfect partners. *People Management Supplement: The Guide to Recruitment Consultancies*, April, pp. 16–17, 19–20, 23.

Beckhard, R. (1969) *Organisation Development: Strategies and Models*. Reading, MA: Addison Wesley.

Beer, M. et al. (eds) (1984) *Managing Human Assets*. New York: Free Press.

Beer, M., Spector, B., Lawrence, P., Quinn Mills, D. and Walton, R. (1985) *Human Resource Management: A General Manager's Perspective*. Glencoe: Free Press.

Bélanger, P., Giles, A. and Murray, G. (2002) Workplace innovations and the role of institutions. In G. Murray, J. Bélanger, A. Giles and P. Lapointe (eds) *Work and Employment in the High Performance Workplace*. London: Continuum, pp. 150–180.

Berger, L.A. and Berger, D.R. (2011) *The Talent Management Handbook: Creating a Sustainable Competitive Advantage by Selecting, Developing and Promoting the Best People*. New York, NY: McGraw-Hill.

Billet, S. (2001) Learning through work: workplace affordances and individual engagement. *Journal of Workplace Learning*, 13(5), pp. 209–214.

Billet, S. (2004) Learning through work: workplace participatory practices. In H. Rainbird, A. Fuller and A. Munro (eds) *Workplace Learning in Context*. London: Routledge.

Birchall, D. (2006) Managing outsourcing. *HR Director*. 27, pp. 38–40.

Birkinshaw, J. (2010) *Reinventing Management: Smarter Choices for Getting Work Done*. San Francisco, CA: John Wiley and Sons.

Blanchard, P. N. and Thacker, J. W. (2004) *Effective Training Systems, Strategies, and Practices*. Upper Saddle River, NJ: Prentice Hall.

Blau, P.M. (1964) *Exchange and Power in Social Life*. New York: John Wiley.

Bloom, N. and Van Reenen, J. (2006) Management practices, work–life balance and productivity: a review of some recent evidence. *Oxford Review of Economic Policy*, 22, pp. 457–482.

Blowfield, M. and Murray, A. (2008) *Corporate Social Responsibility*. Oxford: Oxford University Press.

Bohdanowicz, P. and Zientara, P. (2008) Hotel companies' contribution to improving the quality of life of local communities and the well-being of their employees., *Tourism and Hospitality Research*, 9(2), pp. 147–158.

Bolton, S. and Boyd, C. (2003) Trolly dolly or skilled emotion manager? Moving on from Hochschilds Managed Heart. *Work Employment and Society*, 17(2), pp. 289–308.

Boselie, P. and Koene, B. (2010) Private equity and human resource management: barbarians at the gate! HR's wake-up call? *Human Relations*, 63(9), pp. 1297–1319.

Boselie, P., Paauwe, J. and Jansen, P. (2001) Human resource management and performance: lessons from the Netherlands. *International Journal of Human Resource Management*, 12(7), pp. 1107–1125.

Boselie, P., Paauwe, J. and Richardson, R. (2003) Human resource management, institutionalization and organizational performance: a comparison of hospitals, hotels and local government. *International Journal of Human Resource Management*, 14(8), pp. 1407–1429.

Boselie, P., Dietz, G. and Boon, C. (2005) Commonalities and contradictions in HRM and performance research. *Human Resource Management Journal*, 15(3), pp. 67–80.

Boudreau, J. and Ramstad, P. (2007) *Beyond HR: The New Science of Human Capital*. Boston, MA: Harvard Business School Press.

Bowden, J. and Marton, F. (2004) *The University of Learning: Beyond Quality and Competence*. London: Routledge-Falmer.

Bowen, D. and Ostroff, C. (2004) Understsanding HRM–firm performance linkages: the role of the 'strength' of the HRM system. *Academy of Management Review*, 29(2), pp. 203–221.

Bower, T. (2009) *The Squeeze: Oil Money and Greed in the 21st Century*. London: Harper Press.

Boxall, P. (1991) Strategic human resource management: beginnings of a new theoretical sophistication? *Human Resource Management Journal*, 2(3), pp. 60–79.

Boxall, P. (1996) The strategic HRM debate and the resource-based view of the firm. *Human Resource Management Journal*, 6(3), pp. 59–75.

Boxall, P. (1998) Achieving competitive advantage through human resource strategy: towards a theory of industry dynamics. *Human Resource Management Review*, 8(3), pp. 265–288.

Boxall, P. (2003) HR strategy and competitive advantage in the service sector. *Human Resource Management Journal*, 13(3), pp. 5–20.

Boxall, P. and Macky, K. (2009) Research theory on high-performance work systems: progressing the high-involvement stream. *Human Resource Management Journal*, 19(1), pp. 3–23.

Boxall, P. and Purcell, J. (2003). *Strategy and Human Resource Management*. Basingstoke: Palgrave Macmillan.

Boxall, P. and Purcell, J. (2008) *Strategy and Human Resource Management*, 2nd edn. Basingstoke: Palgrave Macmillan.

Boyd, R. (2011) *Fatal Risk: A Cautionary Tale of AIG's Corporate Suicide*. Hoboken, NJ: John Wiley and Sons.

Bracci, E. and Vagnoni, E. (2011) Understanding small family business succession in a knowledge management perspective. *IUP Journal of Knowledge Management*, 9(1), pp. 7–36.

Brainard, L. and Martinez-Diaz, L. (eds) (2009) *Brazil as an Economic Superpower? Understanding Brazil's Changing Role in the Global Economy*. Washington, DC: Brookings Institution Press.

Brandl, J., Madsen, M.T. and Madsen, H. (2009) The perceived importance of HR duties to Danish line managers. *Human Resource Management Journal*, 19(2), pp. 194–210.

Brassington, F. and Pettitt, S. (2003) *Principles of Marketing*. Harlow: Pearson Education Limited.

Brenner, R., Arrighi, G. and Harvey, D. (2010) Theorising the contemporary world. In R. Albritton, B. Jessop and R. Westra (eds) *Political Economy and Global Capitalism: The 21st Century, Present and Future*. London: Anthem Press.

Brewer, P.D. and Brewer, K.L. (2010) Knowledge management, human resource management, and higher education: a theoretical model. *Journal of Education for Business*, 85, pp. 330–335.

Brewster, C. (1999) Different paradigms in strategic human resource management: questions raised by comparative research. In P. Wright, L. Dyer, J. Boudreau and G. Milkovich (eds) *Research in Personnel and Human Resource Management: Strategic HRM In the 21st Century*. Supplement 4. Greenwich, CT: JAI Press.

Brewster, C. and Mayrhofer, W. (2011) Comparative human resource management. In A.-W. Harzing, and A.H. Pinnington (eds), *International Human Resource Management*. London: Sage, pp. 47–78.

Brooks, S.G. and Wohlforth, W.C. (2009) Reshaping the world order. *Foreign Affairs*, March/April, pp. 49–63.

Brown, D., Caldwell, R., White, K., Atkinson, H., Tansley, T., Goodge, P. and Emmott, M. (2004) *Business Partnering: A New Direction for HR*. London: CIPD.

Brown, J.S. and Duguid, P. (1998) Organising knowledge. *California Management Review*, 40(3), pp. 90–111.

Brown, P., Lauder, H. and Ashton, D. (2011) *The Global Auction: The Broken Promises of Education, Jobs and Income*. New York, NY: Oxford University Press.

Brown, S. and Leigh, T. (1996) A new look at psychological climate and its relationship to job involvement, effort and performance. *Journal of Applied Psychology*, 81, pp. 358–368.

Brown, W., Deakin, S., Hudson, M., Pratten, C. and Ryan, P. (1998) *The Individualisation of Employment Contracts in Britain*. Cambridge: Centre for Business Research, Department of Applied Economics, University of Cambridge.

Bryan, L.L. and Joyce, C.I. (2007) *Mobilising Minds: Creating Wealth from Talent in the 21st-Century Organisation*. New York, NY: McGraw-Hill.

Buchanan, D. and Huczynski, A. (2004) *Organizational Behaviour: An Introductory Text*, 5th edn. London: FT Prentice Hall.

Buckley, A. (2011) *Financial Crisis: Causes, Context and Consequences*. Harlow: FT Prentice Hall.

Budhwar, P. and Varma, A. (2010) Guest editors' introduction: Emerging patterns of HRM in the new Indian economic environment. *Human Resource Management*, 49(3), pp. 345–351.

Buller, P. (1988) Successful partnerships: HR and strategic planning at eight top firms. *Organizational Dynamics*, 17(2), pp. 27–53.

Bullock, R. and Batten, D. (1985) It's just a phase we're going through. *Group and Organisation Studies*, 10, pp. 383–412.

Burchell, J. and Cook, J. (2006) It's good to talk? Examining attitudes towards corporate social responsibility dialogue and engagement processes. *Business Ethics: A European Review*, 15(2), pp. 154–170.

Burgelman, R.A., Christensen, C.M. and Wheelwright, S.C. (2008) *Strategic Management of Technology and Innovation*. New York, NY: McGraw-Hill Irwin.

Burke, R.J. and Cooper, C.L. (eds) (2008) *The Long Work Hours Culture: Causes, Consequences and Choices*. London: Emerald Group.

Butler, P. and Glover, L. (2010) Employee participation and involvement. In J. Beardwell and T. Claydon (eds) *Human Resource Management: A Contemporary Approach*, 6th edn. Harlow: FT Prentice Hall, pp. 531–566.

Burnes, B. (2004) Kurt Lewin and the planned approach to change: a re-appraisal. *Journal of Management Studies*, 41(6), pp. 977–1002.

Buyens, D. and de Vos, A. (2001) Perceptions of the value of the HR function. *Human Resource Management Journal*, 11(3), pp. 70–89.

By, R.T. (2005) Organisational change management: a critical review. *Journal of Change Management*, 5(4), pp. 369–380.

Cable, V. (2009) *The Storm: The World Economic Crisis and What it Means*. London: Atlantic Books.

Cabrera, E. and Cabrera, A. (2005) Fostering knowledge sharing through people management practices. *International Journal of Human Resource Management* 16(5), pp. 720–735.

Caldwell, R. (2001) Champions, adapters, consultants and synergists: the new change agents in HRM. *Human Resource Management Journal*, 11(3), pp. 39–52.

Caldwell, R. (2003) The changing roles of personnel managers: old ambiguities, new uncertainties. *Journal of Management Studies*, 40(4), pp. 983–1004.

Caplan, J. (2011) *The Value of Talent: Promoting Talent Management Across the Organisation*. London: Kogan Page.

Cappelli, P. (2008) *Talent on Demand: Managing Talent in an Age of Uncertainty*. Boston, MA: Harvard Business School Press.

Cappelli, P., Singh, H., Singh, J. and Useem, M. (2010) *The India Way: How India's Top Business Leaders Are Revolutionizing Management*. Boston, MA: Harvard Business Press.

Carley, M., McKay, S. and Welz, C. (2009) *Industrial Relations Developments in Europe 2008*. Dublin: European Foundation for the Improvement of Living and Working Conditions.

Carmeli, A. and Weisberg, J. (2006) Exploring turnover intentions among three professional groups of employees. *Human Resource Development International*, 9(2), pp. 191–206.

Casey, B., Keep, E. and Mayhew, K. (1999) Flexibility, quality and competitiveness. *National Institute Economic Review*, 168, pp. 70–81.

Cates, K. and Rahimi, K. (2003) Algebra lessons for older workers. In J. Pickford (ed.) *Mastering People Management*. Harlow: FT Prentice Hall.

Chalmers Mill, W. (2010) Training to survive the workplace of today. *Industrial and Commercial Training*, 42(5), pp. 270–273.

Chalofsky, N. (1992) A unifying definition for the human resource development function. *Human Resource Development Quarterly*, 3(2), pp. 175–182.

Chandler, A.D. (1962) *Strategy and Structure: Chapter in the History of the Industrial Enterprise*. Cambridge, MA: MIT Press.

Chang, S.-J. (2008) *Sony vs Samsung: The Inside Story of the Electronics Giant's Battle for Global Supremacy*. Singapore: John Wiley and Sons (Asia).

Chang, W. and Huang, T. (2005) Relationship between strategic human resource management and firm performance: a contingency perspective. *International Journal of Manpower*, 26(5), pp. 434–474.

Chesbrough, H. (2011) *Open Services Innovation: Rethinking Your Business to Grow and Compete in a New Era*. San Francisco, CA: Jossey-Bass.

Cho, E. and McLean, G.N. (2004) What we discovered about NHRD and what it means for HRD. *Advances in Developing Human Resources*, 6(3), pp. 382–393.

Cho, Y. and McLean, G.N. (2009) Leading Asian countries' HRD practices in the IT industry: a comparative study of South Korea and India. *Human Resource Development International*, 12(3), pp. 313–331.

CIPD (2001) *Performance Through People: The New People Mangement*. London: CIPD.

CIPD (2003a) Press release: CIPD guide shows how HR policies give backbone to corporate social responsibility (6 August 2003). http://www.cipd.co.uk/pressoffice/_articles/06082003101501.htm?IsSrchRes=1 (accessed 25 August 2010).

CIPD (2003b) Press release: Corporate social responsibility is part of HR agenda argues CIPD (12 March 2003). http://www.cipd.co.uk/pressoffice/_articles/12032003111804.htm?IsSrchRes=1 (accessed 25 August 2010).

CIPD (2003c) Press release: Responsible business attracts the best people—and keeping them improves the bottom line (10 July 2003). http://www.cipd.co.uk/pressoffice/_articles/10072003123700.htm?IsSrchRes=1 (accessed 25 August 2010).

CIPD (2003d) *HR Survey: Where We Are, Where We're Heading*. London: CIPD.

CIPD (2006) *Reflections on Talent Management*. London: CIPD.

CIPD (2007) *The Changing HR Function*. London: CIPD.

CIPD (2008a) *HR Business Partnering*. October. London: CIPD.

CIPD (2008b) *HR Shared Service Centres*. February. London: CIPD.

CIPD (2008c) *Understanding and Attracting Strategic HR Talent: A Focus on the Business Partner Role*. London: CIPD.

CIPD (2009a) Factsheet: Corporate social responsibility (September). http://www.cipd.co.uk/subjects/corpstrtgy/corpsocres/csrfact.htm (accessed 25 August 2010).

CIPD (2009b) *Evaluating Human Capital*. London: CIPD.

CIPD (2009c) *Human Capital Factsheet*, http://www.cipd.co.uk/subjects/corpstrtgy/hmncapital (accessed 17 June 2009).

CIPD (2009d) Factsheet: Strategic human resource management (May).

CIPD (2010a) *Opening up Talent for Business Success: Integrating Talent Management and Diversity*. London: CIPD.

CIPD (2010b) *Talent Development in the BRIC Countries*. London: CIPD.

CIPD (2010c) *Fighting Back Through Talent Intervention: Talent Management Under Threat in Uncertain Times*. London: CIPD.

CIPD (2010d) *Learning and Talent Development*. London: CIPD.

CIPD (2010e) *Building Productive Sector Workplaces*. January. London: CIPD.

CIPD (2010f) *Next Generation HR: Time for Change— Towards a Next Generation for HR*. London: CIPD.

CIPD (2011) *The Economic Rights and Wrongs of Employment Regulation*. London: CIPD.

Clarke, C., Hope-Hailey, V. and Kelliher C. (2007) Being real or really being someone else? Change, managers and emotion work. *European Management Journal*, 25(2), pp. 92–103.

Clegg, H.A. (1979) *The Changing System of Industrial Relations in Great Britain*. Oxford: Blackwell.

Clegg, J. (2009) *China's Global Strategy: Towards a Multipolar World*. London: Pluto Press.

Cohan, W.D. (2009) *House of Cards: How Wall Street's Gamblers Broke Capitalism*. London: Allen Lane.

Colbert, B. (2004) The complex resource-based view: implications for theory and practice in strategic human resource management. *Academy of Management Review*, 29(3), pp. 341–358.

Collier, P. (2010) *Wars, Guns and Votes: Democracy in Dangerous Places*. London: The Bodley Head.

Collins, C. and Smith, K. (2006) Knowledge exchange and combination: the role of human resource practices in the performance of high-technology firms. *Academy of Management Journal*, 49(3), pp. 544–560.

Collinson, C. and Purcell, G. (2004) *Learning to Fly: Practical Knowledge Management from Leading and Learning Organisations*. Chichester: Capstone Publishing.

Comfort, P.J., Comfort, D., Hillier, D. and Eastwood, I. (2005) Corporate social responsibility: a case study of the UK's leading food retailers. *British Food Journal*, 107(6), pp. 423–435.

Conner, K. (1991) A historical comparison of resource-based theory and five schools of thought within industrial organization economics: do we have a new theory of the firm? *Journal of Management*, 17(1), pp. 121–154.

Conway, E. and Monks, K.(2009) Unravelling the complexities of high commitment: an employee-level analysis. *Human Resource Management Journal*, 19(2), pp. 140-158.

Conway, S. and Steward, F. (2009) *Managing and Shaping Innovation*. Oxford: Oxford University Press.

Conyon, M.J., Girman, S., Thompson, S. and Wright, P. (2001) Do hostile mergers destroy jobs? *Journal of Economic Behaviour and Organization*, 45(4), pp. 427-440.

Cooke, F.L. (2004a) Foreign firms in China: modelling HRM in a toy manufacturing corporation. *Human Resource Management Journal*, 14(3), pp. 31-52.

Cooke, F.L. (2004b) *Life is too short, so is the (employment) contract: the nature of work and implications for HRM in the voluntary sector*. Paper presented at the Work, Employment and Society Conference, Manchester.

Cooke, F.L. (2011) Talent management in China. In H. Scullion and D.G. Collings (eds) *Global Talent Management*. Abingdon: Routledge.

Cooke, F.L. and He, Q. (2010) Corporate social responsibility and HRM in China: a study of textile and apparel enterprises. *Asia Pacific Business Review*, 16(3), pp. 355-376.

Cooke, F.L., Shen, J. and McBride, A. (2005) Outsourcing HR as a competitive strategy? A literature review and an assessment of implications. *Human Resource Management*, 44(4), pp. 413-432.

Coombs, W.T. and Holladay, S.J. (2011) *Managing Corporate Social Responsibility: A Communication Approach*. Hoboken, NJ: Wiley-Blackwell.

Cooper, G. (2008) *The Origin of Financial Crises: Central Banks, Credit Bubbles and the Efficient Market Fallacy*. Petersfield: Harriman House Ltd.

Corporate Leadership Council (2004) *Driving Performance and Retention Through Employee Engagement: A Quantitative Analysis of Effective Engagement Strategies*. Arlington, VA: Corporate Leadership Council.

Craig, R.L. (1976) *Training and Development Handbook: A Guide to Human Resource Development*. New York, NY: McGraw-Hill.

Crail, M. (2007) HR's role in managing organisational change. *IRS Employment Review*, November 19, 2007.

Crane, A. and Matten, D. (2007) *Business Ethics*, 2nd edn. Oxford: Oxford University Press.

Cranfield School of Management (2008) *Flexible Working and Performance: Summary of Research*. London: Working Families.

Cropanzano, R. and Mitchell, M. (2005) Social exchange theory: an interdisciplinary review. *Journal of Management*, 31, pp. 874-900.

Cross, R., Borgatti, S.P. and Parker, A. (2002) An examination of work-environment support factors affecting transfer of supervisory skills training to the workplace. *Human Resource Development Quarterly*, 15(4), pp. 449-471.

Crouse, P., Doyle, W. and Young, J.D. (2011) Workplace learning strategies, barriers, facilitators and outcomes: a qualitative study among human resource management practitioners. *Human Resource Development International*, 14(1), pp. 39-55.

Crail, M. (2007) HR's role in managing organisational change. *IRS Employment Review*, November 19, 2007.

Csikszentmihalyi, M. (1990) *Beyond Boredom and Anxiety*. San Francisco: Jossey-Bass.

Cummins, T. and Huse, E. (1989) *Organisation Development and Change*. St Paul, MN: West.

Currie, G. and Procter, S. (2001) Exploring the relationship between HR and middle managers. *Human Resource Management Journal*, 11(3), pp. 53-69.

Dalkir, K. (2011) *Knowledge Management in Theory and Practice*. Cambridge, MA: Massachusetts Institute of Technology.

Das, G. (2006) The India Model. *Foreign Affairs*, 85(4), pp. 2-16.

Datta, D., Guthrie, J. and Wright, P. (2005) Human resource management and labor productivity: does industry matter? *Academy of Management Journal*, 48(1), pp. 135-145.

Daud, S., Fadzilah, W. and Yusoff, W. (2010) Knowledge management and firm performance in SMEs: the role of social capital as a mediating variable. *Asian Academy of Management Journal*, 15(2), pp. 135-155.

Davenport, T.H. and Prusak, L. (2000) *Working Knowledge: How Organisations Manage What They Know*. Boston, MA: Harvard Business School Press.

Davies, I.A. and Crane, A. (2010) Corporate social responsibility in small- and medium-size enterprises: investigating employee engagement in fair trade companies. *Business Ethics: A European Review*, 19(2), pp. 126-139.

Davies, J. and Kourdi, J. (2010) *The Truth About Talent*. Chichester: John Wiley and Sons Ltd.

De Man, A.-P., Berends, H., Lammers, I., van Raaij, E. and van Weele, A. (2008) Knowledge and innovation in networks: a conceptual framework. In A.-P. de Man (ed.) *Knowledge Management and Innovation in Networks*. Cheltenham: Edward Elgar Publishing.

De Vries, P. and Lukosch, H. (2009) Supporting informal learning at the workplace. *International Journal of Advanced Corporate Learning*, 2(3), pp. 39 -44.

Deephouse, D. (1999) To be different, or to be the same? It's a question (and theory) of strategic balance. *Strategic Management Journal*, 20, pp. 147–166.

Delbridge, R. and Keenoy, T. (2011) Beyond managerialism? *International Journal of Human Resource Management*, 21(6), pp. 799–817.

Delery, J. and Doty, D. (1996) Modes of theorising in strategic human resource management: tests of universalistic, contingency and configurational performance predictions. *Academy of Management Journal*, 39(4), pp. 289–309, 802–835.

Delery, J. and Shaw, J (2001) The strategic management of people in work organizations: review, synthesis and extension. *Research in Personnel and Human Resources Management*, 20, pp. 165–197.

Demuijnck, G. (2009) Non-discrimination in human resources management as a moral obligation. *Journal of Business Ethics*, 88, pp. 83–101.

Deng, Y. (2008) *China's Struggle for Status: The Realignment of International Relations*. Cambridge: Cambridge University Press.

Devanna, M., Fombrun, C. and Tichy, N. (1984) A framework for strategic human resource mangement. In C. Fombrun, N. Tichy and M. Devanna (eds) *Strategic Human Resource Management*. New York: Wiley.

Dewey, J. (1916) *Democracy and Education*. London: Macmillan.

Diamond, J. (2005) *Collapse: How Societies Choose to Fail or Survive*. London: Penguin Books.

Dietz, G., Gillespie, N. and Chao, G. (2010) Unravelling the complexities of trust across cultures. In M. Saunders (ed.) *Organizational Trust: A Cultural Perspective*. Cambridge: Cambridge University Press, pp. 3–41.

DiMaggio, P. and Powell, W. (1983) The iron cage revisited: institutional isomorphism and collective rationality in organizational fields. *American Sociological Review*, 48, pp. 147–160.

Dirks, K. and Ferrin, D. (2001) The role of trust in organizational setting. *Organization Science*, 12, pp. 450–467.

Dixon, N. (1992) Organisational learning: a review of the literature with implications for HRD professionals. *Human Resource Development Quarterly*, 3, pp. 29–49.

Dobers, P. (2009) Corporate social responsibility: management and methods. *Corporate Social Responsibility and Environmental Management*, 16, pp. 185–191.

Donate, M.J. and Guadamillas, F. (2010) The effect of organizational culture on knowledge management practices and innovation. *Knowledge and Process Management*, 17(2), pp. 82–94.

Doorewaard, H. and Benschop, Y. (2002) HRM and organizational change: an emotional endeavour. *Journal of Organisational Change Management*, 16(3), pp. 272–286.

Doornbos, A.J., Bolhus, S. and Simons, P.R.-J. (2004) Modeling work-related learning on the basis of intentionality and developmental relatedness: a noneducational perspective. *Human Resource Development Review*, 3(3), pp. 250–274.

Dowling, P.J. and Welch, D.E. (2004) *International Human Resource Management: Managing People in a Multinational Context*, 4th edn. London: Thomson.

Doz, Y., Santos, J. and Williamson, P. (2001) *From Global to Metanational: How Companies Win in the Knowledge Economy*. Boston, MA: Harvard Business School Press.

Drucker, P. (1961) *The Practice of Management*. London: Mercury Books.

Dyer, L. (1985) Strategic human resources management and planning. *Research in Personnel and Human Resources Management*, 3, Washington: BNA.

Edwards, P. (2003) The employment relationship and the field of industrial relations. In P. Edwards (ed.) *Industrial Relations Theory and Practice*. Oxford: Blackwell Publishing, pp. 1–37.

Edwards, P. (2008) The employment relationship in strategic human resource management. In J. Storey, P. Wright and D. Ulrich (eds) *Routledge Companion to Strategic Human Resource Management*. Abingdon: Routledge, pp. 40–51.

Edwards, P. (2010) The employment perspective in strategic HRM. In J. Storey, P.M. Wright and D. Ulrich (eds) *The Routledge Companion to Strategic Human Resource Management*. Abingdon: Routledge.

Eichengreen, B. (2011) *Exorbitant Privilege: The Rise and Fall of the Dollar*. New York, NY: Oxford University Press.

Ellinger, A.D. (2005) Contextual factors influencing informal learning in a workplace setting: the case of "reinventing itself company". *Human Resource Development Quarterly*, 16(3), pp. 389–415.

Elliott, L. and Atkinson, D. (2009) *The Gods That Failed: How the Financial Elite Have Gambled Away Our Futures*. London: Vintage Books.

Emelo, R. (2010) Increasing productivity with social learning. *Industrial and Commercial Training*, 42(4), pp. 203–210.

Emerson, R.M. (1976) Social exchange theory. *Annual Review of Sociology*, 2, pp. 335–362.

Engardio, P. (2007) *Chindia: How China and India Are Revolutionizing Global Business*. New York, NY: McGraw-Hill.

Epple, D., Argote, L. and Murphy, K. (1996) An empirical investigation of the micro structure of knowledge acquisition and transfer through learning by doing. *Operations Research*, 44, pp. 77–86.

Eraut, M. (2004) Transfer of knowledge between education and workplace settings. In H. Rainbird, A. Fuller and A. Munro (eds) *Workplace Learning in Context*. London: Routledge.

Ericksen, J. and Dyer, L. (2005) Toward a strategic human resource management of high reliability organisational performance. *International Journal of Human Resource Management*, 16(6), pp. 907–928.

Esty, D.C. and Winston, A.S. (2006) *Green to Gold: How Smart Companies Use Environmental Strategy to Innovate, Create Value, and Build Competitive Advantage*. London: Yale University Press.

European Commission (2008) *Industrial Relations in Europe 2008*. Luxembourg: Publications Office of the European Communities.

European Commission (2011) *Industrial Relations in Europe 2010*. Luxembourg: Publications Office of the European Union.

European Foundation for the Improvement of Living and Working Conditions (2007) *ERM Report 2007: Restructuring and Employment in the EU: The Impact of Globalisation*. Luxembourg: Office for Official Publications of the European Communities.

European Foundation for the Improvement of Living and Working Conditions (2008). *Annual Review of Working Conditions in the EU 2007–2008*. Luxembourg: Office for Official Publications of the European Communities.

Eurostat (2010) *Europe in Figures, Eurostat Year Book 2010*. Luxembourg: Publications Office of the European Union.

Farndale, E., Kelliher, C. and Hope-Hailey, V. (2011) The influence of perceived employee voice on organisational commitment: an exchange perspective. *Human Resource Management*, 50(1), pp. 113–129.

Ferguson, N. (2004) *Empire: How Britain Made the Modern World*. London: Penguin.

Fernandez, S. and Rainey, H.G. (2006) Managing successful organizational change in the public sector. *Public Administration Review*, 66(2), pp. 168–176.

Fitz-enz, J. (2009) *The ROI of Human Capital: Measuring the Economic Value of Employee Performance*. New York, NY: AMACOM.

Fleming, J., Coffman, C. and Harter, J. (2005) *Manage Your Human Sigma*. Boston, MA: Harvard Business Press.

Flood, P., Gannon, M. and Paauwe, J. (1995) *Managing Without Traditional Methods*. Wokingham: Addison-Wesley.

Folger, R. (1977) Distributive and procedural justice: combined impact of "voice" and improvement on experienced inequity. *Journal of Personality and Social Psychology*, 35, pp. 108–119.

Folger, R. and Konovsky, M.A. (1989) Effects of procedural and distributive justice on reactions to pay raise decisions. *Academy of Management Journal*, 32, pp. 115–130.

Fombrun, C., Tichy, N. and Davanna, M. (eds) (1984) *Strategic Human Resource Management*. New York: Wiley.

Forth, J., Bewley, H. and Bryson, A. (2006) *Small and Medium Sized Enterprises: Findings from the 2004 Workplace Employment Relations Survey*. London: Department of Trade and Industry.

Foss, N. (1996) Research in strategy, economics and Michael Porter. *Journal of Management Studies*, 33(1), pp. 1–24.

Fox, A. (1966) *Industrial Sociology and Industrial Relations*. London: HMSO.

Fox, A. (1974) *Beyond Contract*. London: Faber.

Fox, J. (2010) *The Myth of the Rational Market: A History of Risk, Reward and Delusion on Wall Street*. Petersfield: Harriman House Publishing.

Francis, H. (2003) HRM and the beginning of organizational change. *Journal of Organizational Change Management*, 16(3), pp. 309–327.

Francis, H. and Keegan, A. (2006) The changing face of HRM: in search of balance. *Human Resource Management Journal*, 16(3), pp. 231–249.

Freedman, M. (2003) *The Art and Discipline of Strategic Leadership*. New York, NY: McGraw-Hill.

Freeman, R.B. and Medoff, J.L. (1984) *What Do Unions Do?* New York: Basic Books.

Freeman, R.E. (2011) *Strategic Management: A Stakeholder Approach*. Cambridge: Cambridge University Press.

Freeman, R.E., Wicks, A.C. and Parmar, B. (2004) Stakeholder theory and 'the corporate objective revisited'. *Organization Science*, 15(3), pp. 364–369.

French, W. (1969) Organization development, objectives, assumptions and strategies. *California Management Review*, 69(12), pp. 23–34.

Frenkel, S.J. (2000) Introduction: service work and its implications for HRM. *International Journal of Human Resource Management*, 11(3), pp. 469–476.

Friedman, T.L. (2006) *The World Is Flat: The Globalised World in the Twenty-First Century*. London: Penguin.

Friedman, T.L. (2008) *Hot, Flat and Crowded: Why the World Needs a Green Revolution—and How We Can Renew our Global Future*. London: Allen Lane.

Fung, V.K., Fung, W.K. and Wind, Y. (2008) *Competing in a Flat World: Building Enterprises for a Borderless World*. Upper Saddle River, NJ: Wharton School Publishing.

Gainey, T. and Klaas, B. (2002) Outsourcing the training function: results from the field. *Human Resource Planning*, 25(1), pp. 16–22.

Galanou, E. and Priporas, C.-V. (2009) A model for evaluating the effectiveness of middle managers' training courses: evidence from a major banking organization in Greece. *International Journal of Training and Development*, 13(4), pp. 221–246.

Gallup (2006) *Engagement Predicts Earnings per Share*.

Garrow, V. and Hirsh, W. (2008) Talent management: issues of focus and fit. *Public Personnel Management*, 37(4), pp. 389–402.

Gatenby, M., Alfes, K., Rees, C., Soane, E. and Truss, C. (2009a) *Employee Engagement in Context*. Wimbledon: CIPD.

Gatenby, M., Alfes, K., Rees, C., Soane, E. and Truss, C. (2009b) *Harnessing employee engagement in the UK public services*. Paper to the 10th Public Management Research Association Conference, Ohio, October.

Gates, S. (2004) *Measuring More than Efficiency*. Research Report R-1356-04-RR. New York: Conference Board.

Gerdes, L. (2009) Bad economy hasn't changed Gen Y's desire for work–life balance. Bloomberg Business Week, http://www.businessweek.com.

Gerhart, B. (2005) Human resources and business performance: findings, unanswered questions and an alternative approach. *Management Revue*, 16(2), pp. 174–185.

Gerhart, B., Wright, P. and McMahan, G. (2000) Measurement error in research on the human resource and firm performance relationship: further evidence and analysis. *Personnel Psychology*, 53, pp. 855–872.

Ghoshal, S. and Moran, P. (2005) Towards a good theory of management. In J. Birkinshaw and G. Piramal (eds) *Sumantra Ghoshal on Management: A Force for Good*. Harlow: Prentice Hall.

Golden, K. and Ramanujam, V. (1985) Between a dream and a nightmare: on the integration of the human resource management and strategic business planning process. *Human Resource Management*, 24(4), pp. 429–452.

Goldman, M. (2008) *Oilopoly: Putin, Power and the Rise of the New Russia*. London: One World.

Gooderham, P., Nordhaug, O. and Ringdal, K. (1999) Institutional and rational determinants of organisational practices: HRM in European firms. *Administrative Science Quarterly*, 44(3), pp. 507–531.

Gooderham, P., Parry, E. and Ringdal, K. (2008) The impact of bundles of strategic human resource management practices on the performance of European firms. *International Journal of Human Resource Management*, 19(11), pp. 2041–2056.

Goodman, J. and Truss, C. (2004) The medium and the message: communicating effectively during a major change initiative. *Journal of Change Management*, 4(3), pp. 217–228.

Gould-Williams, J. (2007) HR practices, organizational climate and employee outcomes: evaluating social exchange relationships in local government. *International Journal of Human Resource Management*, 18(9), pp. 1627–1647.

Graham, H.T. and Bennett, R. (1992) *Human Resource Management*, 7th edn. M&E Handbook Series. London: Pitman.

Granovetter, M. (1995) *Getting a Job: A Study of Contracts and Careers*, 2nd edn. Chicago: University of Chicago Press.

Grant, R.M. (1991) The resource-based theory of competitive advantage: implications for strategy formulation. *California Management Review*, 33(3), pp. 114–135.

Grant, R.M. (2010) *Contemporary Strategy Analysis*, 7th edn. Chichester: John Wiley and Sons.

Gratton, L. and Truss, C. (2003) The three-dimensional people strategy: putting human resources policies into action. *Academy of Management Executive*, 17(3), pp. 74–86.

Gratton, L., Hope-Hailey, V., Stiles, P. and Truss, C. (1999). *Strategic Human Resource Management: Corporate Rhetoric and Human Reality*. Oxford: Oxford University Press.

Gray, J. (2000) *False Dawn: The Delusions of Global Capitalism*. London: Granta Books.

Gray, J. (2009) *Gray's Anatomy: John Gray's Selected Writings*. London: Allen Lane.

Green, F. (2004) Why has work effort become more intense? *Industrial Relations*, 43(4), pp. 709–741.

Griffin, R.P. (2010) Means and ends: effective training evaluation. *Industrial and Commercial Training*, 42(4), pp. 220–225.

Grundy, A. (1998) How are corporate strategy and HR strategy linked? *Journal of General Management*, 23(3), pp. 49–72.

Guerra, F. and Chung, J. (2009) Fear of falling. *Financial Times*, 6 January, p. 11 (Analysis).

Guerrero, S. and Barraud-Didier, V. (2004) High-involvement practices and the performance of French firms. *International Journal of Human Resource Management*, 15(8), pp. 1408–1423.

Guerrier, Y. and Adib, A. (2003) Work at leisure and leisure at work: a study of the emotional labour of tour reps. *Human Relations*, 56(11), pp. 1399–1417.

Guest, D. (1987) Human resource management and industrial relations. *Journal of Management Studies*, 24(5), pp. 503–521.

Guest, D. (1989) Human resource management: its implications for industrial relations and trade unions. In J. Storey (ed.) *New Perspectives on Human Resource Management*. London: Routledge.

Guest, D. (1997) Human resource management and performance: a review and research agenda. *International Journal of Human Resource Management*, 8(3), pp. 263–276.

Guest, D. (2001) Human resource management: when research confronts theory. *International Journal of Human Resource Management*, 12(7), pp. 1092–1106.

Guest, D. (2011) Human resource management and performance: still searching for some answers. *Human Resource Management Journal*, 21(1), pp. 3–13.

Guest, D. and King, Z. (2004) Power, innovation and problem-solving: the personnel manager's three steps to heaven?' *Journal of Management Studies*, 41(3), pp. 401–423.

Guest, D., Michie, J., Conway, N. and Sheehan, M. (2003) Human resource management and performance. *British Journal of Industrial Relations*, 41(2), pp. 291–314.

Guest, D., Conway, N. and Dewe, P. (2004) Using sequential tree analysis to search for 'bundles' of HR practices. *Human Resource Management Journal*, 14(1), pp. 79–96.

Gulati, R. (2007) *Network resources: alliances, affiliations and other relational assets*. Oxford: Oxford University Press.

Gupta, V. (2010) A culturally sensitive approach to sustainable business in emerging markets: how to manage the challenges and opportunities in view of the global economic crisis?, *Global Management Journal*, 2(1), pp. 17–30.

Guthrie, J., Flood, P., Liu, W. and MacCurtain, S. (2009) High performance work systems in Ireland: human resource and organizational outcomes. *International Journal of Human Resource Management*, 20(1), pp. 112–125.

Haberberg, A. and Rieple, A. (2008) *Strategic Management: Theory and Application*. Oxford: Oxford University Press.

Haier (2011a) http://www.haier.com/abouthaier/corporateprofile/ (accessed 20 January 2011).

Haier (2011b) http://www.haier.com/AboutHaier/HaierWorldwide/management.asp (accessed 20 January 2011).

Halbesleben, J.R.B., Harvey, J. and Bolino, M.C. (2009) Too engaged? A conservation of resources view of the relationship between work engagement and work interference with family. *Journal of Applied Psychology*, 94(6), pp. 1452–1465.

Haldar, U.K. (2009) *Human Resource Development*. New Delhi: Oxford University Press.

Hall, B.W. (2008) *The New Human Capital Strategy*. New York, NY: American Management Association.

Hall, E. (1976) *Beyond Culture*. Garden City, NY: Doubleday.

Hall, K. (2005) Global division. *People Management*, 24 March, pp. 44–45.

Hallin, A. and Gustavsson, T.K. (2009) Managing death—corporate social responsibility and tragedy. *Corporate Social Responsibility and Environmental Management*, 16, pp. 206–216.

Hamel, G. (2007) *The Future of Management*. Boston, MA: Harvard Business School Press.

Hamel, G. and Prahalad, C. (1993) Strategy as stretch and leverage. *Harvard Business Review*, 71(2), pp. 75–84.

Hamel, G. and Prahalad, C.K. (1996) *Competing for the Future*. Boston, MA: Harvard Business School Press.

Hamm, S. (2007) *Bangalore Tiger: How Indian Tech Upstart Wipro Is Rewriting the Rules of Global Competition*. New York, NY: McGraw-Hill.

Harcourt, M. and Wood, G. (2007) The importance of employment protection for skill development in coordinated market economies. *European Journal of Industrial Relations*, 13(2), pp. 141–159.

Harford, T. (2007) *The Undercover Economist*. London: Abacus.

Harkness, J. (2000) Measuring the effectiveness of change—the role of internal communication in change management. *Journal of Change Management*, 1(1), pp. 66–73.

Harley, B. and Hardy, C. (2004) Firing blanks? An analysis of discursive struggle in HRM. *Journal of Management Studies*, 41(3), pp. 377–400.

Harney, A. (2008) *China Price: The True Cost of Chinese Competitive Advantage*. New York, NY: Penguin Press.

Harris, C., Cortvriend, P. and Hyde, P. (2007) Human resource management and performance in healthcare organisations. *Journal of Health Organization and Management*, 21(5), pp. 448–459.

Harris, L.C. (2002) The emotional labour of barristers: an exploration of emotional labour by status profession-als. *Journal of Management Studies*, 39(4), pp. 553–584.

Harter, J.K., Schmidt, F.L. and Hayes, T.L. (2002) Business-unit-level relationship between employee satisfaction, employee engagement, and business outcomes: a meta-analysis. *Journal of Applied Psychology*, 87(2), pp. 268–279.

Harvey, D. (2010) *The Enigma of Capital: And the Crises of Capitalism*. London: Profile Books Ltd.

Harvey, M., Fisher, R., McPhail, R. and Moeller, M. (2009) Globalisation and its impact on global managers' decision processes. *Human Resource Development International*, 12(4), pp. 353–370.

Hatcher, T. (2006) An editor's challenge to human resource development. *Human Resource Development Quarterly*, 17(1), pp. 1–4.

Hayes, J. (2006) *The Theory and Practice of Change Management*, 2nd edn. Basingstoke: Palgrave Macmillan.

Hayton, B. (2010) *Vietnam: Rising Dragon*. London: Yale University Press.

Heracleous, L., Wirtz, J. and Pangarkar, N. (2006) *Flying High in a Competitive Industry: Cost-Effective Service Excellence at Singapore Airlines*. Singapore: McGraw-Hill.

Herling, R.W. (2001) Operational definitions of expertise and competence. In R.A. Swanson and E.F. Holton (eds) *Foundations of Human Resource Development*. San Francisco: Berrett-Kochler.

Hesketh, A. and Fleetwood, A. (2006) Beyond measuring the human resources management–organizational performance link: applying critical realist meta-theory. *Organization*, 13(5), pp. 677–699.

Hinton, M. (2006a) Introduction: managing the information management function. in M. Hinton (ed.) *Introducing Information Management: The Business Approach*. Oxford: Elsevier Butterworth-Heinemann.

Hinton, M. (2006b) Managing information in modern organisations. In M. Hinton (ed.) *Introducing Information Management: The Business Approach*. Oxford: Elsevier Butterworth-Heinemann.

Hirshman, A.O. (1970) *Exit, Voice and Loyalty: Responses to Decline on Firms, Organizations and States*. Cambridge, MA: Harvard University Press.

Hislop, D. (2005) *Knowledge Management in Organizations*. Oxford: Oxford University Press.

Hislop, D. (2009) *Knowledge Management in Organizations*, 2nd edn. Oxford: Oxford University Press.

Ho, J.S.-Y., Downe, A.G. and Loke, S.-P. (2010) Employee attrition in the Malaysian service industry: push and pull factors. *Journal of Organisational Behaviour*, IX(1 and 2), pp. 16–31.

Hochschild, A.R. (1983) *The Managed Heart: Commercialization of Human Feeling*. Berkeley: University of California Press.

Hofmeister, J. (2010) *Why We Hate the Oil Companies*. New York, NY: Palgrave Macmillan.

Holbeche, L. (2001) *Aligning Human Resources and Business Strategy*. Oxford: Elsevier Butterworth-Heinemann.

Holbeche, L. (2005) *Understanding Change. Theory, Implementation and Success*. Oxford: Butterworth-Heinemann.

Holbeche, L. (2009) *Aligning Human Resources and Business Strategy*, 2nd edn. Oxford: Butterworth-Heinemann.

Holbeche, L. (2010) *HR Leadership*. Oxford: Butterworth-Heinemann.

Honey, P. and Mumford, A. (1992) *The Manual of Learning Styles*. Maidenhead: Peter Honey.

Hood, C. (2005) Public management: the word, the movement, the science. In E. Ferlie, L. Lynn and C. Pollitt (eds) *The Oxford Handbook of Public Management*. Oxford: Oxford University Press.

Hope-Hailey, V., Gratton, L., McGovern, P., Stiles, P. and Truss, C. (1997) A chameleon function? HRM in the 90s. *Human Resource Management Journal*, 7(3), pp. 5–18.

Hope-Hailey, V., Farndale, E. and Truss, C. (2005) The HR department's role in organisational performance. *Human Resource Management Journal*, 15(3), pp. 49–66.

Huang, Y. (2008) *Capitalism with Chinese Characteristics: Entrepreneurship and the State*. Cambridge: Cambridge University Press.

Humphrey, R.H., Pollack, J.M. and Hawver, T.H. (2008) Leading with emotional labor. *Journal of Managerial Psychology*, 23(2), pp. 151–168.

Huselid, M. (1995) The impact of human resource management practices on turnover, productivity and corporate financial performance. *Academy of Management Journal*, 38(3), pp. 635–672.

Hutton, T. (2003) *The World We're In*. London: Abacus.

Hutton, W. (2007) *The Writing on the Wall: China and the West in the 21st Century*. London: Little, Brown.

Hutton, W. (2010) *Them and Us: Changing Britain—Why We Need a Fair Society*. London: Little, Brown.

Hyman, J. and Mason, B. (1995) *Managing Employee Involvement and Participation*. London: Sage Publications.

Idowu, S.O. and Papasolomou, I. (2007) Are the corporate social responsibility matters based on good intentions or false pretences? An empirical study of the motivations behind the issuing of CSR reports by UK companies. *Corporate Governance*, 7(2), pp. 136–147.

Jabbour, C.J.C. and Santos, F.C.A. (2008) The central role of human resource management in the search for sustainable organizations. *International Journal of Human Resource Management*, 19(12), pp. 2133–2154.

Jacques, M. (2009) *When China Rules the World: The Rise of the Middle Kingdom and the End of the Western World*. London: Allen Lane.

Jamrog, J. and Overholt, M. (2004) Building a strategic HR function: continuing the evolution. *Human Resource Planning*, 27(1), pp. 51–63.

Jarvis, P. (2006) *Towards a Comprehensive Theory of Human Learning*. Abingdon: Routledge.

Jashapara, A. (2010) *Knowledge Management: An Integrated Approach*. Harlow: Pearson Education.

Jelavic, M. (2010) Knowledge management views in Eastern and Western cultures: an integrative analysis. *Journal of Knowledge Globalization*, 3(2), pp. 51–69.

Johnson, G. and Scholes, J. (2002) *Exploring Corporate Strategy*. London: FT Prentice Hall.

Johnson, M. (2004) Otherwise engaged. *Training*, 41(10), p. 4.

Kahn, W. (1990) Psychological conditions of personal engagement and disengagement at work. *Academy of Management Journal*, 33, pp. 692–724.

Kaletsky, A. (2010) *Capitalism 4.0: The Birth of a New Economy*. London: Bloomsbury.

Kalling, T. and Styhre, A. (2003) *Knowledge Sharing in Organisations*. Copenhagen: Copenhagen Business School Press.

Kamoche, K. (1996) Strategic human resource management within a resource-capability view of the firm. *Journal of Management Studies*, 33(2), pp. 213–233.

Kang, S. and Snell, S. (2009) Intellectual capital architectures and ambidextrous learning: a framework for human resource management. *Journal of Management Studies*, 46(1), pp. 65–92.

Kang, S., Morris, S. and Snell, S. (2007) Relational archetypes, organizational learning and value creation: extending the human resource architecture. *Academy of Management Review*, 32(1), pp. 236–256.

Kanti Srikantaiah, T. (2010) *Convergence of Project Management and Knowledge Management*. Lanham, MD: Scarecrow Press.

Kaplan, R. and Norton, D. (1998) Using the Balanced Scorecard as a strategic management system. *Harvard Business Review*, Jan-Feb.

Kaplan, R.D. (2009) Centre stage for the twenty-first century. *Foreign Affairs*, March/April, pp. 16–32.

Kaplan, R.D. (2010) *Monsoon: The Indian Ocean and the Future of American Power*. New York, NY: Random House.

Kaplan, R.S. and Norton, D.P. (1996) *Translating Strategy into Action—The Balanced Scorecard*. Boston, MA: Harvard Business School Press.

Kaplan, R.S. and Norton, D.P. (2004) *Strategy Maps: Converting Intangible Assets into Tangible Outcomes*. Boston, MA: Harvard Business School Press.

Kaplan, S.N. and Stromberg, P. (2009) Leveraged buyouts and private equity. *Journal of Economic Perspectives*, 23(1), pp. 121–146.

Käser, P.A.W. and Miles, R.E. (2001) Knowledge activists: the cultivation of motivation and trust properties of knowledge sharing relationships. *Academy of Management Proceedings*, ODC: D1–D6.

Katou, A. and Budhwar, P. (2006) Human resource management systems and organizational performance: a test of a mediating model in the Greek manufacturing context. *International Journal of Human Resource Management* , 17(7), pp. 1223–1253.

Kaufman, B. (2007) The development of HRM in historical and international perspective. In P. Boxall, J. Purcell and P. Wright (eds) *The Oxford Handbook of Human Resource Management*. Oxford: Oxford University Press.

Kelliher, C. and Gore, J. (2006) Functional flexibility and the intensification of work: transformation within service industries. In P. Askenazy, D. Cartron, F. de Connick, et al (eds) *Organisation et Intensité du Travail*. Toulouse: Octares, pp. 93–102.

Kelliher, C., Truss, C., and Hope-Hailey, V. (2004) Disappearing between the cracks: HRM in permeable organisations. *Management Revue*, 15(3), pp. 305–323.

Kelly, K. (2008) *CEO: The Low-Down on the Top Job*. Harlow: Prentice Hall.

Kersley, B.A.C., Forth, J., Bryson, A., Bewley, H., Dix, G. and Oxenbridge, S. (2006) *Inside the Workplace: Findings from the 2004 Workplace Employment Relations Survey*. London: Routledge.

Key, S. (1999) Toward a new theory of the firm: a critique of stakeholder 'theory'. *Management Decision*, 37(4), pp. 317–328.

Khilji, S. and Wang, X. (2006) 'Intended' and 'implemented' HRM: the missing linchpin in strategic human resource management research. *International Journal of Human Resource Management*, 17(7), pp. 1171–1189.

Kim, J.-K. (2011) Effects of corporate social responsibility on B to B relational performance, *International Journal of Business and Management*, 6(2), pp. 24–34.

Kim, M.O. and Jaffe, S. (2010) *The New Korea: An Inside Look at South Korea's Economic Rise*. New York, NY: AMACOM.

Kingsnorth, P. (2008) *Real England: The Battle Against the Bland*. London: Portobello Books.

Kinnie, N., Hutchinson, S., Purcell, J. and Swart, J. (2005a) Satisfaction with HR practices and commitment to the organisation: why one size does not fit all. *Human Resource Management Journal*, 15, pp. 9–29.

Kinnie, N., Swart, J. and Purcell, J. (2005b) Influences on the choice of HR system: the network organization perspective. *International Journal of Human Resource Management*, 16(6), pp. 1004–1028.

Kitay, J. and Marchington, M. (1996) A review and critique of workplace industrial relations typologies. *Human Relations*, 49(10), pp. 1263–1290.

Kitchen, P. and Daly, F. (2002) Internal communication during change management. *Corporate Communications*, 7(1), pp. 46–53.

Klaas, B., Gainey, T., McClendon, J. and Hyeukseung, Y. (2002) Professional employer organisations and their impact on HR outcomes: a field study of HR outsourcing in small and medium enterprises. *Academy of Management Proceedings*, pp. 1–7.

Klein, N. (2008) *The Shock Doctrine: The Rise of Disaster Capitalism*. London: Penguin.

Klein, S. (1996) A management communication strategy for change. *Journal of Organizational Change Management*, 9(2), pp. 32–42.

Koch, R. (2011) *FT Guide to Strategy: How to Create, Pursue and Deliver a Winning Strategy*. Harlow: Pearson Education.

Kochan, T. (2007) Social legitimacy of the human resource management profession: a US perspective. In P. Boxall, J. Purcell and P. Wright (eds) *The Oxford Handbook of Human Resource Management*. Oxford: Oxford University Press.

Kochan, T. and Barocci, T. (1985) *Human Resource Management and Industrial Relations*. Boston: Little Brown.

Kochan, T.A. (2000) On the paradigm guiding industrial relations theory and research: comment on John Goddard and John T. Delaney. Reflections on the 'high performance' paradigm's implications for industrial relations as a field. *Industrial and Labor Relations*, 53(4), pp. 704–711.

Kolb, D.A. (1984) *Experiential Learning: Experience as the Source of Learning and Development*. Englewood Cliffs, NJ: Prentice-Hall.

Konrad, A. (2006) Engaging employees through high-involvement work practices. *Ivey Business Journal*, March/April, pp. 1–6.

Kor, Y. and Mahoney, T. (2004) Edith Penrose's (1959) contributions to the resource-based view of strategic management. *Journal of Management Studies*, 41(1), pp. 183–191.

Korczynski, M. (2003) Communities of coping: collective emotional labour in service work. *Organization*, 1(1), pp. 55–79.

Korczynski, M. (2002) *Human Resource Management in Service Work*. Basingstoke: Palgrave Macmillan.

Korsgaard, M.A., Schweiger, D.M. and Sapienza, H.J. (1995) Building commitment, attachment, and trust in strategic decision-making teams—the role of procedural justice. *Academy of Management Journal*, 38, pp. 60–84.

Koulopoulos, T.M. and Roloff, T. (2006) *Smartsourcing: Driving Innovation and Growth Through Outsourcing*. Avon, MA: Adams Media.

Kular, S., Gatenby, M., Rees, C., Soane, E. and Truss, C. (2008) *Employee Engagement: A Literature Review*. Kingston Business School Working Paper Series No. 19.

Kumar, N., Mohapatra, P.K. and Chandrasekhar, S. (2009) *India's Global Powerhouses: How They Are Taking on the World*. Boston, MA: Harvard Business Press, p. 56.

Kynge, J. (2006) *China Shakes the World: The Rise of a Hungry Nation*. London: Weidenfeld and Nicolson.

Lado, A. and Wilson, M. (1994) Human resource systems and sustained competitive advantage: a competency-based perspective. *Academy of Management Review*, 19(4), pp. 699–727.

Lam, A. (2000) Tacit knowledge, organizational learning and societal institutions: an integrated framework. *Organization Studies*, 21(3), pp. 487–513.

Lansbury, R.D., Kwon, S.-H. and Suh, C.-S. (2006) Globalisation and employment relations in the Korean auto industry: the case of the Hyundai Motor Company in Korea, Canada and India. *Asia Pacific Business Review*, 12(2), pp. 131–147.

Lantos, G.P. (2001) The boundaries of strategic corporate social responsibility. *Journal of Consumer Marketing*, 18(7), pp. 595–630.

Lantos, G.P. (2002) The ethicality of altruistic corporate social responsibility. *Journal of Consumer Marketing*, 19(3), pp. 205–230.

Larsen, H.H. and Mayrhofer, W. (eds) (2006) *Managing Human Resources in Europe*. Abingdon: Routledge.

Larsson, R., Brousseau, K.R., Driver, M.J. and Sweet, P.L. (2004) The secrets of mergers and acquisition success: a co-competence and motivational approach to synergy realisation. In A.L. Pablo and M. Javidon (eds) *Mergers and Acquisitions: Creating Integrative Knowledge*. Oxford: Blackwell Publishing.

Lasserre, P. (2007) *Global Strategic Management*, 2nd edn. Basingstoke: Palgrave Macmillan.

Lave, J. and Wenger, E. (1991) *Situated Learning: Legitimate Peripheral Participation*. Cambridge: Cambridge University Press.

Lawler, E. and Mohrman, S. (2003) HR as a strategic partner: what does it take to make it happen? *Human Resource Planning*, 26(3), pp. 15–30.

Le Deist, F.D. and Winterton, J. (2005) What is competence? *Human Resource Development International*, 8(1), pp. 27–46.

Legge, K. (1978) *Power, Innovation and Problem-Solving in Personnel Management*. London: McGraw-Hill.

Legge, K. (1989) Human resource management: a critical analysis. In J. Storey (ed.) *New Perspectives on Human Resource Management*. London: Routledge.

Legge, K. (1995) *Human Resource Management: Rhetorics and Realities*. Basingstoke: Macmillan.

Legge, K. (2005) *Human Resource Management: Rhetorics and Realities*, 2nd edn. Basingstoke: Palgrave Macmillan.

Lehmann, S. (2009) Motivating talents in Thai and Malaysian service firms. *Human Resource Development International*, 12(2), pp. 155–170.

Leimbach, M. (2010) Learning transfer model: a research-driven approach to enhancing learning effectiveness. *Industrial and Commercial Training*, 42(2), pp. 81–86.

Leiter, M.P. and Maslach, C. (2005) A mediation model of job burnout. In A.S.G. Antoniou and C.L. Cooper (eds) *Research Companion to Organizational Health Psychology*. Cheltenham: Edward Elgar, pp. 544–564.

Lengnick-Hall, C. and Lengnick-Hall, M. (1990) *Interactive Human Resource Management and Strategic Planning*. Westport, CT: Quorum Books.

Leonard, D. (1998) *Wellsprings of Knowledge: Building and Sustaining the Sources of Innovation*. Boston: Harvard Business School Press.

Leopold, J., Harris, L. and Watson, T. (2005) *The Strategic Managing of Human Resources*. London: Pearson.

Lepak, D. and Snell, S. (1998) Virtual HR: strategic human resource management in the 21st century. *Human Resource Management Review*, 8(3), pp. 215–235.

Lepak, D. and Snell, S. (1999a) The human resource architecture: toward a theory of human capital allocation and development. *Academy of Management Review*, 24, pp. 31–48.

Lepak, D. and Snell, S. (1999b) The strategic management of human capital: determinants and implications of different relationships. *Academy of Management Review*, 24(1), pp. 1–18.

Lepak, D. and Snell, S. (2002) Examining the human resource architecture: the relationships among human capital, employment and human resource configurations. *Journal of Management*, 28(4), pp. 517–543.

Lepak, D., Liao, H., Chung, Y. and Harden, E. (2006) A conceptual review of human resource management systems in strategic human resource management

research. *Research in Personnel and Human Resource Management*, 25, pp. 217–271.

Leppitt, N. (2006a) Challenging the code of change: Part 1. Praxis does not make perfect. *Journal of Change Management*, 6(2), pp. 121–142.

Leppitt, N. (2006b) Challenging the code of change: Part 2. Crossing the Rubicon: extending the integration of change. *Journal of Change Management*, 6(3), pp. 235–256.

Lesser, E. and Cohen, D. (2004) How to invest in social capital. In E. Lesser and L. Prusak (eds) *Creating Value with Knowledge: Insights from the IBM Institute for Business Value*. New York, NY: Oxford University Press.

Lesser, E. and Prusak, L. (eds) (2004) *Creating Value with Knowledge: Insights from the IBM Institute for Business Value*. New York, NY: Oxford University Press.

Levin, D.Z., Cross, R., Abrams, L.C. and Lesser, E.L. (2004) Trust and knowledge sharing: a critical combination. In E. Lesser and L. Prusak (eds) *Creating Value with Knowledge: Insights from the IBM Institute for Business Value*. New York, NY: Oxford University Press.

Levis, K. (2009) *Winners & Losers: Creator and Casualties of the Age of the Internet*. London: Atlantic Books.

Lewin, K. (1951) *Field Theory in Social Science*. New York: Harper & Row.

Lewis, J. (2002) Did HR fuel the demise of Enron? *Personnel Today*, 19 March.

Lewis, P. (2005) Suppression or expression: an exploration of emotion management in a special care baby unit. *Work, Employment and Society*, 19(3), pp. 565–581.

Liker, J.K. and Hoseus, M. (2008) *Toyota Culture: The Heart and Soul of the Toyota Way*. New York, NY: McGraw-Hill (written in collaboration with the Center for Quality People and Organizations).

Lincoln, Y.S. and Lynham, S.A. (2011) Criteria for assessing theory in human resource development from an interpretive perspective. *Human Resource Development International*, 14(1), pp. 3–22.

Lindgren, A, and Sederblad, P. (2003) Team work and emotional labour in call centres. In C. Garstan and K. Jacobsson (eds) *Learning to Be Employable—New Agendas on Work, Responsibility and Learning in a Globalising World*. Basingstoke: Palgrave Macmillan, pp. 172–188.

Lippman, S. and Rumelt, R. (1982) Uncertain imitability: an analysis of inter-firm differences in efficiency under competition. *Bell Journal of Economics*, 13, pp. 418–438.

Little, B. and Little, P. (2006) Employee engagement. conceptual issues. *Journal of Organizational Culture, Communication and Conflict*, 10(1), p. 111.

Liu, G., Liston-Heyes, C. and Ko, W.-W. (2006) Employee participation in cause-related marketing strategies: a study of management perceptions from British consumer service industries. *Journal of Business Ethics*, 92, pp. 195–210.

Lohman, M.C. (2009) A survey of factors influencing the engagement of information technology professionals in informal learning activities. *Information Technology, Learning, and Performance Journal*, 25(1), pp. 43–53.

Long, B. (2007) Strategic human resource management and the workers' experience. *Journal of Individual Employment Rights*, 12(3), pp. 265–282.

Loretto, W., White, P. and Vickerstaff, S. (2005) *Older Workers and Options for Flexible Work*. Working Paper No. 31. Manchester: Equal Opportunities Commission.

Lybeck, J.L. (2011) *A Global History of the Financial Crash: 2007-10*. Cambridge: Cambridge University Press.

Lynn, M. (2011) *Bust: Greece, the Euro, and the Sovereign Debt Crisis*. Hoboken, NJ: John Wiley and Sons.

Maas, P. (2009) *Crude World: The Violent Twilight of Oil*. London; Allen Lane.

MacDuffie, J. (1995) Human resource bundles and manufacturing performance: organizational logic and flexible production systems in the world auto industry. *Industrial and Labor Relations Review*, 48, pp. 197–221.

Macey, W. and Schneider, B. (2008) The meaning of employee engagement. *Industrial and Organizational Psychology*, 1, pp. 3–30.

MacLeod, D. and Clarke, N. (2009) *Engaging for Success: Enhancing Performance Through Employee Engagement*. Norwich: Office of Public Sector Information.

Magnus, G. (2011) *Uprising: Will Emerging Markets Shape or Shake the World Economy?* Chichester: John Wiley and Sons.

Mankin, D.P. (2007) *The implications of knowledge sharing in academic communities for academic development*. Proceedings 8th Conference on HRD Research and Practice Across Europe, Oxford, June.

Mankin, D.P. (2009) *Human Resource Development*. Oxford: Oxford University Press.

Mankin, D. and Cohen, S.G. (2004) *Business Without Boundaries: An Action Framework For Collaborating Across Time, Distance, Organisation, and Culture*. San Francisco: Jossey-Bass.

Marchand, D. (1998) Competing with intellectual capital. In G. von Krogh, G. Roos and D. Kleine (eds) *Knowing in Firms*. London: Sage.

Marchington, M. and Grugulis, I. (2000) 'Best practice' human resource management: perfect opportunity or dangerous illusion? *International Journal of Human Resource Management*, 11, pp. 1104–1124.

Marchington, M. and Wilkinson, A. (2008) *Human Resource Management at Work*, 4th edn. London: CIPD.

Marin, G.S. (2008) The influence of institutional and cultural factors on compensation practice around the world. In L.R. Gomez-Mejia and S. Werner (eds) *Global Compensation: Foundations and Perspectives*. Abingdon: Routledge.

Marquardt, M.J. (2005) Globalisation: the pathway to prosperity, freedom and peace. *Human Resource Development International*, 8(1), pp. 127–129.

Marquardt, M.J. and Engel, D.W. (1993) *Global Human Resource Development*. Englewood Cliffs, NJ: Prentice Hall.

Marsick, V. (2006) Informal strategic learning in the workplace. In J.N. Streumer (ed.) *Work-Related Learning*. New York, NY: Springer.

Marsick, V. and Volpe, F.M. (1999) Informal learning on the job. *Advances in Developing Human Resources*, 1, pp. 5–8.

Marsick, V.J. (2003) Invited reaction: informal learning and the transfer of learning: how managers develop proficiency. *Human Resource Development Quarterly*, 14(4), pp. 389–395.

Marsick, V.J. and Watkins, K.F. (1994) The learning organisation: an integrative vision for HRD. *Human Resource Development Quarterly*, 5(4), pp. 353–360.

Martenson, C. (2011) *The Crash Course: The Unsustainable Nature of Our Economy, Energy and Environment*. Hoboken, NJ: John Wiley and Sons.

Martin, G. and Groen-In't-Woud, S. (2011) Employer branding and corporate reputation in global companies: a signalling model and case illustration. In H. Scullion and D.G. Collings (eds) *Global Talent Management*. Abingdon: Routledge.

Martin-Alcazar, F., Romero-Fernandez, P. and Sanchez-Gardey, G. (2005) Strategic human resource management: integrating the universalistic, contingent and configurational perspectives. *International Journal of Human Resource Management*, 16(5), pp. 633–659.

Maslach, C. and Leiter, M.P. (2008) Early predictors of job burnout and engagement. *Journal of Applied Psychology*, 93(3), pp. 498–512.

Masters, M.F. Gibney, R., Shevchuk, I. and Zagenczyk, T. (2008) The state as employer. In P. Blyton, E. Heery, N. Bacon and J. Fiorito (eds) *The Sage Handbook of Industrial Relations*. London: Sage Publications, pp. 305–324.

Matthewman, J. (2011) *The Rise of the Global Nomad*. London: Kogan Page.

May, D.R., Gilson, R.L. and Harter, L.M. (2004) The psychological conditions of meaningfulness, safety and availability and the engagement of the human spirit at work. *Journal of Occupational and Organizational Psychology*, 77(1), pp. 11–37.

May, R., Borman Young, C. and Ledgerwood, D. (1998) Lessons from Russian human resource management experience. *European Management Journal*, 16(4), pp. 447–459.

Maycunich Gilley, A., Callahan, J.L. and Bierema, L.L. (2003) *Critical Issues in HRD: A New Agenda for the Twenty-First Century*. Cambridge, MA: Perseus Publishing.

McCabe, D. and Lewin, D. (1992) Employee voice: a human resource management perspective. *California Management Review*, 34, pp. 112–123.

McCarthy, A.M. and Garavan, T.N. (1999) Developing self-awareness in the managerial career development process: the value of 360-degree feedback and the MBTI. *Journal of European Industrial Training*, 23(9), pp. 437–445.

McDonnell, A. and Collings, D.G. (2011) The identification and evaluation of talent in MNEs. In H. Scullion and D.G. Collings (eds) *Global Talent Management*. Abingdon: Routledge.

McGovern, P., Gratton, L., Stiles, P., Hope-Hailey, V. and Truss, C. (1997) Human resource management on the line? *Human Resource Management Journal*, 7(4), pp. 12–29.

McGregor, R. (2010) *The Party: The Secret World of China's Communist Rulers*. London: Allen Lane.

McLagan, P. (1989) *Models of HRD Practice*. Alexandria, VA: ASTD Press.

McLoughlin, I. and Gourlay, S. (1992) Enterprise without unions: the management of employee relations in non-union firms. *Journal of Management Studies*, 29(5), pp. 669–691.

McLuhan, R. (2008) Shared services: a problem shared. *Personnel Today*, 8 December.

Merrifield, R., Calhoun, J. and Stevens, D. (2008) The next revolution in productivity. *Harvard Business Review*, June, pp. 72–80.

Mertens, K, Heisig, B. and Vorbeck, J. (2011) Introduction. In K. Mertens, B. Heisig and J. Vorbeck (eds) *Knowledge Management: Concepts and Best Practices*. London: Springer.

Meyer, T.A. (2010) *Innovate! How Great Companies Get Started in Terrible Times*. Hoboken, NJ: John Wiley and Sons.

Microsoft (2007) *The New World of Work: Evolution of the UK Workforce*. www.microsoft.com/uk/peopleready.

Midler, P. (2009) *Poorly Made in China: An Insider's Account of the Tactics Behind China's Production Game*. Hoboken, NJ: John Wiley and Sons.

Miles, R. and Snow, C. (1984) Designing strategic human resources systems. *Organizational Dynamics*, Summer, pp. 36–52.

Millmore, M., Lewis, P., Saunders, M., Thornhill, A. and Morrow, T. (2007) *Strategic Human Resource Management: Contemporary Issues*. Harlow: Pearson.

Minsky, H.P. (2008 [1986]) *Stabilising an Unstable Economy*. New York, NY: McGraw-Hill.

Mintzberg, H. (1978) Patterns in strategy formation. *Management Science*, 24(9), pp. 934–948.

Mintzberg, H. (1994) *The Rise and Fall of Strategic Planning*. New York, NY: The Free Press.

Mintzberg, H. (1996) Five Ps for Strategy. In H. Mintzberg and J.B. Quinn (eds) *The Strategy Process*. London: Prentice Hall.

Mintzberg, H. and Lampel, J. (1999) Reflecting on the strategy process. *Sloan Management Review*, Spring.

Mirvis, P. (1997) Human resource management: leaders, laggards and followers. *Academy of Management Executive*, 11(2), pp. 43–56.

Molm, L.D., Peterson, G. and Takahashi, N. (1999) Power in negotiated and reciprocal exchange. *American Sociological Review*, 64, pp. 876–890.

Monks, K. (1993) Models of personnel management: a means to understanding the diversity of personnel practices? *Human Resource Management Journal*, 3(2), pp. 29–41.

Monks, K. and McMackin, J. (2001) Designing and aligning an HR system. *Human Resource Management Journal*, 11(2), pp. 57–72.

Mooney, P. (2001) *Turbo-Charging the HR Function*. London: CIPD.

Moore, G., Slack, R. and Gibbon, J. (2009) Criteria for responsible business practice in SMEs: an exploratory case of U.K. Fair Trade Organisation. *Journal of Business Ethics*, 89, pp. 173–188.

Moran, J. and Brightman, B. (2001) Leading organizational change. *Career Development International*, 6(2), pp. 111–118.

Morgan, H. and Jardin, D. (2010) HR + OD = integrated talent management. *OD Practitioner*, 42(4), pp. 23–29.

Morgan, M., Levitt, R.E. and Malek, W. (2007) *Executing Your Strategy: How to Break it Down and Get it Done*. Boston, MA: Harvard Business School Press.

Morris, C.R. (2008) *The Two Trillion Dollar Meltdown: Easy Money, High Rollers, and the Great Credit Crunch.* New York: Public Affairs.

Moyo, D. (2011) *How the West Was Lost: Fifty Years of Economic Folly and the Stark Choices Ahead.* London: Allen Lane.

Mueller, F. (1996) Human resources as strategic assets: an evolutionary resource-based theory. *Journal of Management Studies*, 33(6), pp. 757–785.

Mundra, N., Gulati, K. and Vashisth, R. (2011) Achieving competitive advantage through knowledge management and innovation: empirical evidences from the Indian IT sector. *IUP Journal of Knowledge Management*, 9(2), pp. 7–25.

Nadeem, S. and Metcalf, H. (2007) *Work–Life Policies in Great Britain: What Works, Where and How?* London: Department for Business, Enterprise and Regulatory Reform.

Nadler, L. and Nadler, Z. (1989) *Developing Human Resources.* Austin: Learning Concepts.

Nahapiet, J. and Ghoshal, S. (1998) Social capital, intellectual capital, and the organisational advantage. *Academy of Management Review*, 23(2), pp. 242–266.

Nair, C. (2011) *Consumptionomics.* Oxford: Infinite Ideas Ltd.

Naisbitt, J. and Naisbitt, D. (2010) *China's Megatrends: The 8 Pillars of a New Society*, New York, NY: Harper Collins.

New York Times (2009a) http://www.nytimes.com/2009/06/29/business/global/29oil.html?ref=business (accessed 27 June 2009).

New York Times (2009b) http://www.nytimes.com/2009/06/29/technology/companies/29google.html?_r=1&ref=technology (accessed 29 June 2009).

New York Times (2010) http://www.nytimes.com/2009/06/29/business/global/29oil.html?ref=business (accessed 26 June 2010).

Nie, W. and Xin, K. (2009) *Made in China: Secrets of China's Dynamic Entrepreneurs.* Hoboken, NJ: John Wiley and Sons.

Nie, W., Xin, K. and Zhang, L. (2009) *Made in China: Secrets of China's Dynamic Entrepreneurs.* Singapore: John Wiley and Sons (Asia).

Nilekani, N. (2008) *Imagining India: Ideas for the New Century.* London: Allen Lane.

Nishii, L., Lepak, D. and Schneider, B. (2008) Employee attributions of the 'why' of HR practices: their effects on employee attitudes and behaviors, and customer satisfaction. *Personnel Psychology*, 61, pp. 503–545.

Nolan, J., Wichert, I. and Birchell, B. (2000) Job insecurity, psychological well-being and family life. In E. Heery and J. Salmon (eds) *The Insecure Workforce.* London: Routledge, pp. 181–209.

O'Dell, C. and Hubert, C. (2011) *The New Edge in Knowledge.* Hoboken, NJ: John Wiley and Sons.

Ogilvie, J. and Stork, D. (2003) Starting the HR and change conversation with history. *Journal of Organizational Change Management*, 16(3), pp. 254–271.

Ohmae, K. (2005) *The Next Global Stage: Challenges and Opportunities in Our Borderless World.* Upper Saddle River, NJ: Wharton School Publishing.

Oliver, C. (1997) Sustainable competitive advantage: combining institutional and resource-based views. *Strategic Management Journal*, 18(9), pp. 697–713.

Orlitzky, M. and Frenkel, S. (2005) Alternative pathways to high-performance workplaces. *International Journal of Human Resource Management*, 16(8), pp. 1325–1348.

Orr, J.E. (1990) Sharing knowledge, celebrating identity: community memory in a service culture. In D. Middleton and D. Edwards (eds) *Collective Remembering.* London: Sage.

Osman-Gani, A.M. and Chan, T.H. (2009) Trends and challenges of developing human capital in Singapore: an analysis of current practices and future potentials. *Human Resource Development International*, 12(1), pp. 47–68.

Osono, E., Shimizu, N. and Takeuchi, H. (2008) *Extreme Toyota: Radical Contradictions That Drive Success at the World's Best Manufacturer.* Hoboken, NJ: John Wiley and Sons.

Paauwe, J. (2004) *HRM and Performance: Achieving Long-Term Viability.* Oxford: Oxford University Press.

Paauwe, J. and Boselie, P. (2003) Challenging 'strategic HRM' and the relevance of the institutional setting. *Human Resource Management Journal*, 13(3), pp. 56–70.

Paauwe, J. and Boselie, P. (2005) Best practices . . . in spite of performance: just a matter of imitation? *International Journal of Human Resource Management*, 16(6), pp. 987–1003.

Paetzold, K. (2010) *Corporate Social Responsibility: An International Marketing Approach.* Hamburg: Diplomica Verlag GmBH (in English).

Palade, A. (2010) Significant aspects regarding career management. Means for a better career planning and development. *Bulletin: Economic Sciences Series*, LXII(2), pp. 124–134. Petroleum-Gas University of Ploiesti.

Pasher, E. and Ronen, T. (2011) *The Complete Guide to Knowledge Management: A Strategic Plan to Leverage Your Organisation's Intellectual Capital.* Hoboken, NJ: John Wiley and Sons.

Pass, S. (2006) *The HR Function: Today's Challenges, Tomorrow's Direction.* London: CIPD.

Patriotta, G. (2003) *Organizational Knowledge in the Making: How Firms Create, Use and Institutionalize Knowledge*. Oxford: Oxford University Press.

Patterson, M., West, M., Lawthom, R. and Nickell, S. (1997) *The Impact of People Management Practices on Business Performance*. London: CIPD.

Patterson, M., Rick, J., Wood, S., Carroll, C., Balain, S. and Booth, A. (2007) *Review of the Validity and Reliability of Measures of Human Resource Management*. Report for the National Co-ordinating Centre for Research Methodology and the National Co-ordinating Centre for NHS Service Delivery and Organisation R and D (NCCSDO). Report No. RM03/JH10/MP. Sheffield: Institute of Work Psychology, Sheffield University, August.

Peacock, L. (2008) Fast pace of change means opportunity knocks for HR. *Personnel Today*, 3 June, p.1.

Pedersen, E.R. (2006) Making corporate social responsibility (CSR) operable: how companies translate stakeholder dialogue into practice. *Business and Society Review*, 111(2), pp. 137–163.

Penrose, E. (1959) *The Theory of the Growth of the Firm*. New York: Wiley.

Perkowski, J. (2008) *Managing the Dragon: Building a Billion-Dollar Business in China*. London: Bantam Press.

Personnel Today (2007) Change management is role for human resources professionals, 5 November.

Peston, R. (2008) *Who Runs Britain? . . . And Who's to Blame for the Economic Mess We're in*. London: Hodder.

Pettigrew, A and Whipp, R (1993) *Managing Change for Corporate Success*. London: Blackwell.

Pettigrew, A.M., Woodman, R.W. and Cameron, K.S. (2001) Studying organizational change and development: challenges for future research. *Academy of Management Journal*, 44(4), pp. 697–713.

Pfeffer, J. (1994) *Competitive Advantage Through People*. Boston: Harvard Business School Press.

Pfeffer, J. (1998) *The Human Equation: Building Profits by Putting People First*. Boston: Harvard Business School Press.

Pfeffer, J. (2005) Producing sustainable competitive advantage through the effective management of people. *Academy of Management Executive*, 19(4), pp. 95–106.

Pfeffer, J. (2010). Building sustainable organizations: the human factor. *Academy of Management Perspectives*, February.

Pfeffer, J. and Sutton, R. (1999) *The Knowing–Doing Gap: How Smart Companies Turn Knowledge into Action*. Boston, MA: Harvard Business School Press.

Piderit, S. (2000) Rethinking resistance and recognizing ambivalence: a multidimensional view of attitudes towards an organizational change. *Academy of Management Review*, 25(4), pp. 783–794.

Pinnington, A.H. (2011) Strategic management in IHRM. In A.-W. Harzing, and A.H. Pinnington (eds) *International Human Resource Management*. London: Sage, pp. 13–46.

Polanyi, M. (1962) *Personal Knowledge: Towards a Post-Critical Philosophy*. London: Routledge.

Polanyi, M. (1967) *The Tacit Dimension*. London: Routledge.

Pollert, A. (2005) The unorganised worker: the decline in collectivism and new hurdles to individual employment rights. *Industrial Law Journal*, 34(3), pp. 217–238.

Porter, M. (1980) *Why are firms successful?* Paper presented to the Fundamental Issues in Strategy Conference, Napa, CA.

Porter, M.E. (1985) *Competitive Advantage: Creating and Sustaining Superior Performance*. New York: Free Press.

Porter, M.E. (1990) *The Competitive Advantage of Nations*. London: Macmillan.

Porter, M.E. (2008) The five competitive forces that shape strategy. *Harvard Business Review*, January, pp. 78–93.

Porter, M.E. and Kramer, M.R. (2006) Strategy and society: the link between competitive advantage and corporate social responsibility. *Harvard Business Review*, December.

Porter, M.E. and Nohria, N. (2010) What is leadership? The CEO's role in large, complex organizations. Boston, MA: Harvard Business Press.

Prahalad, C.K. (2009) *The Fortune at the Bottom of the Pyramid: Eradicating Poverty Through Profits*. Upper Saddle River, NJ: Wharton School Publishing.

Prahalad, C.K. and Hamel, G. (1990) The core competence of the corporation. *Harvard Business Review*, May-June, pp. 79–91.

Preuss, L., Haunschild, A. and Matten, D. (2009) The rise of CSR: implications for HRM and employee representation. *International Journal of Human Resource Management*, 20(4), pp. 953–973.

Price, A. (2004) *Human Resource Management in a Business Context*. London: Thomson.

Priem, R. and Butler, J (2001) Is the resource-based 'view' a useful perspective for strategic management research? *Academy of Management Review*, 26(1), pp. 22–40.

Proctor, T. and Doukakis, I. (2003) Change management: the role of internal communication and employee development. *Corporate Communications*, 8(4), pp. 268–277.

Purcell, J. (1981) *Good Industrial Relations.* London: Macmillan.

Purcell, J. (1987) Mapping management styles in employee relations. *Journal of Management Studies,* 24(5), pp. 533–548.

Purcell, J. (1989) The impact of corporate strategy on human resource management. In J. Storey (ed.) *New Perspectives on Human Resource Management.* London: Routledge.

Purcell, J. (1999) Best practice and best fit: chimera or cul-de-sac? *Human Resource Management Journal,* 9(3), pp. 26–41.

Purcell, J. and Hutchinson, S. (2007) Front-line managers as agents in the HRM–performance chain. *Human Resource Management Journal,* 17(1), pp. 3–17.

Purcell, J. and Kinnie, N. (2007) HRM and business performance. In P. Boxall, J. Purcell and P. Wright (eds) *The Oxford Handbook of Human Resource Management.* Oxford: Oxford University Press.

Purcell, K., Hogarth, T. and Simms, C. (1999) *Whose Flexibility? The Cost and Benefits of Non-Standard Working Arrangements and Contractual Arrangements.* York: Joseph Rowntree Foundation.

Purcell, J., Kinnie, N., Hutchinson, S., Rayton, B. and Swart, J. (2003) *Understanding the People and Performance Link: Unlocking the Black Box.* Wimbledon: CIPD.

PwC (2007) *Managing Tomorrow's People. The Future of Work to 2020.* London: PricewaterhouseCoopers LLP. http://www.pwc.com/gx/en/managing-tomorrows-people/future-of-work.

Rachman, G. (2010) *Zero-Sum World: Power and Politics after the Crash.* London: Atlantic Books.

Ramamurti, R. (2009) Why study emerging-market multinationals? In R. Ramamurti and J.V. Singh (eds) *Emerging Multinationals in Emerging Markets.* Cambridge: Cambridge University Press.

Rao, T.V. and Varghese, S. (2009) Trends and challenges of developing human capital in India. *Human Resource Development International,* 12(1), pp. 15–34.

Rau, B. L. and Hyland, M.A. (2002) Role conflict and flexible work arrangements: the effects of applicant attraction. *Personnel Psychology,* 55(1), pp. 111–136.

Reed, R. and DeFillippi, R. (1990) Causal ambiguity, barriers to imitation and sustainable competitive advantage. *Academy of Management Review,* 15, pp. 88–102.

Rees, C., Alfes, K., Gatenby, M., Soane, E. and Truss, K. (2009) Work organisation, employee voice and engagement: exploring the connections. *British Universities Industrial Relations Association (BUIRA) Annual Conference—Capitalism in Crisis: The Changing Context of IR and the World of Work,* Cardiff University, 2–4 July.

Reich, R. (2009) *Supercapitalism: The Battle for Democracy in an Age of Big Business.* London: Icon Books.

Rettab, B., Brik, A.B. and Mellahi, K. (2009) A study of management perceptions of the impact of corporate social responsibility on organisational performance in emerging economies: the case of Dubai. *Journal of Business Ethics,* 89, pp. 371–390.

Reynolds, J., Caley, L. and Mason, R. (2002) *How Do People Learn?* London: CIPD.

Rich, B., Lepine, J. and Crawford, E. (2010) Job engagement: antecedents and effects on job performance. *Academy of Management Journal,* 53(3), pp. 617–635.

Rigg, C. (2007) Corporate technocrats or world stewards: what's the point of management development? In R. Hill and J. Stewart (eds) *Management Development: Perspectives from Research and Practice.* Abingdon: Routledge.

Riley, M.W. and Riley J. (1994) Age integration and the lives of older people. *The Gerontologist,* 34, pp. 110–115.

Rivlin, G. (2010) *Broke, USA.* New York, NY: HarperCollins.

Robinson, I. (2006) *Human Resource Management in Organisations.* London: CIPD.

Rodgers, F.S. and Rodgers, C. (1989) Business and the facts of family life. *Harvard Business Review,* 67, pp. 121–129.

Rodwell, J. and Teo, S. (2004) Strategic HRM in for-profit organizations in a knowledge-intensive industry. *Public Management Review,* 6(3), pp. 311–331.

Rose, E. (2008) *Employment Relations.* London: Pearson Education.

Rothbard, N. (2001) Enriching or depleting? The dynamics of engagement in work and family roles. *Administrative Science Quarterly,* 46, pp. 655–730.

Rother, M. (2009) *Toyota Kata: Managing People, for Improvement, Adaptiveness, and Superior Results.* New York, NY: McGraw-Hill.

Royle, T. (1998) Avoidance strategies and the German system of co-determination. *International Journal of Human Resource Management,* 9(6), pp. 1026–1047.

Royle, T. (2005) The union recognition dispute at McDonald's Moscow food-processing factory. *Industrial Relations Journal,* 36(4), pp. 318–332.

Royle, T. (2006) The dominance effect? Multinational corporations in the Italian quick food service sector. *British Journal of Industrial Relations,* 44(4), pp. 757–780.

Rusaw, A. (2007) Changing public organizations: four approaches. *International Journal of Public Administration,* 30, pp. 347–361.

Russell, J. and Barrett, L. (1999) Core affect, prototypical emotional episodes, and other things called emotion: dissecting the elephant. *Journal of Personality and Social Psychology*, 76, pp. 805–819.

Sachs, J.D. (2008) *Common Wealth: Economics for a Crowded Planet*. London: Allen Lane.

Sako, M. and Tierney, A. (2007) *The Future of HR: How Human Resource Outsourcing Is Transforming the HR Function*. London: Advanced Institute of Management Research.

Saks, A.M. (2006) Antecedents and consequences of employee engagement. *Journal of Managerial Psychology*, 21(7), pp. 600–619.

Salamon, M. (2000) *Industrial Relations: Theory and Practice*. London: FT Prentice Hall.

Sallis, E. and Jones, G. (2002) *Knowledge Management in Education: Enhancing Learning and Education*. London: Kogan Page.

Sanchez R (1995) Strategic flexibility in product competition. *Strategic Management Journal*, 16, pp. 135–159.

Santos-Rodrigues, H., Dorrego, P.F. and Jardon, C.F. (2010) The influence of human capital on the innovativeness of firms. *International Business and Economics Research Journal*, 9(9), pp. 53–63.

Saul, J.R. (2005) *The Collapse of Globalism*. London: Atlantic Books.

Schaper, M. (2010) *Making Ecopreneurs*, Corporate Social Responsibility Series. Farnham: Gower Publishing.

Schaufeli, W.B. and Bakker, A.B. (2004) Job demands, job resources, and their relationship with burnout and engagement: a multi-sample study. *Journal of Organizational Behavior*, 25(3), pp. 293–315.

Schaufeli, W.B., Martínez, I., Marqués-Pinto, A., Salanova, M. and Bakker, A.B. (2002) Burnout and engagement in university students: a cross-national study. *Journal of Cross-Cultural Psychology*, 33, pp. 464–481.

Schein, E.H. (1992) *Organizational Culture and Leadership*, 2nd edn. San Francisco, CA: Jossey-Bass.

Scholtens, B. (2009) Corporate social responsibility in the international banking industry. *Journal of Business Ethics*, 86, pp. 159–175.

Schön, D.A. (1983) *The Reflective Practitioner: How Professionals Think in Action*. Aldershot: Ashgate.

Schramm, J. (2004). Perception on ethics. *HR Magazine*, 49, p. 176.

Schuler, R. and Jackson, S. (1987) Linking competitive strategies with human resource management practices. *Academy of Management Executive*, 1(3), pp. 207–219.

Schuler, R. and Walker, J. (1990) Human resource strategy: focusing on issues and actions. *Organizational Dynamics*, Summer, pp. 5–19.

Schuler, R.S., Briscoe, D.R. and Claus, L. (2008) *International Human Resource Management*. London: Routledge.

Schuler, R.S., Jackson, S.E. and Tarique, I.R. (2011) Framework for global talent management: HR actions for dealing with global talent challenges. In H. Scullion and D.G. Collings (eds) *Global Talent Management*. Abingdon: Routledge.

Scullion, H. and Collings, D.G. (2011) Global talent management: introduction. In H. Scullion and D.G. Collings (eds) *Global Talent Management*. Abingdon: Routledge.

Sears, L. (2011) A new way of seeing: insight-led HR. *People Management*, April.

Segerlund, L. (2010) *Making Corporate Social Responsibility a Global Concern*, Non-State Actors in International Law, Politics and Governance Series. Farnham: Ashgate Publishing.

Seijts, G. and Crim, D. (2006) What engages employees the most, or the 10 C's of employee engagement. *Ivey Business Journal*, March/April, pp. 1–5.

Seiler, T.B. (2004) The human foundation of knowledge management. In H. Tsoukas and N. Mylonopoulos (eds) *Organisations as Knowledge Systems*. Basingstoke: Palgrave Macmillan.

Seshadri, D.V.R. and Tripathy, A. (2006) Reinventing a giant corporation: the case of Tata Steel. *Vikalpa*, 31(3), pp. 131–134.

Shantz. A., Wright, K., Alfes, K., Soane, E. and Truss, C. (2010) *Too much or too little? Gender differences in employee engagement*. Gender, Work and Organisation Conference, Keele, June.

Shih, H., Chiang, Y. and Hsu, C. (2006) Can high performance work systems really lead to better performance? *International Journal of Manpower*, 27(8), pp. 741–763.

Shiller, R. (2009) A failure to control the animal spirits. *Financial Times*, 9 March, p. 15.

Shimazu, A., Schaufeli, W., Kosugi, S., Suzuki, A., Nashiwa, H., Kato, A., Sakamoto, M., Irimajiri, H., Hirohata, K., Goto, R. and Kitaoka-Higashiguchi, K. (2008) Work engagement in Japan: validation of the Japanese version of the Utrecht work engagement scale. *Applied Psychology*, 57(3), pp. 510–523.

Simon, H.A. (1985) Human nature in politics: the dialogue of psychology with political science. *American Political Science Review*, 79(2), pp. 293–304.

Singh, A. and Soltani, E. (2010) Knowledge management practices in Indian information technology companies. *Total Quality Management*, 21(2), pp. 145–157.

Sirmon, D., Hitt, M. and Ireland, R. (2007) Managing firm resources in dynamic environments to create value: looking inside the black box. *Academy of Management Review*, 32(1), pp. 273–292.

Sisson, K. (2001) Human resource management and the personnel function—a case of partial impact? In J. Storey (ed.) *Human Resource Management: A Critical Text*, 2nd edn. Mitcham: Thomson Learning.

Sisson, K. and Marginson, P. (2003) Management: systems, structures and strategy. In P. Edwards (ed.) *Industrial Relations: Theory and Practice*, 2nd edn. London: Blackwell Publishing, pp. 157–188.

Skelcher, C. (2007) Public–private partnerships and hybridity. In E. Ferlie, L.E. Lynn Jr and C. Pollitt (eds) *The Oxford Handbook of Public Management*. Oxford: Oxford University Press, pp. 347–370.

Slotte, V., Tynjälä, P. and Hytönen, T. (2004) How do HRD practitioners describe learning at work? *Human Resource Development International*, 7(4), pp. 481–499.

Smith, D. (2008) *The Dragon and the Elephant: China, India and the New World Order*. London: Profile Books.

Smith, P.J. and Sadler-Smith, E. (2006) *Learning in Organisations: Complexities and Diversities*. London: Routledge.

Snell, S., Youndt, M. and Wright, P. (1996) Establishing a framework for research in strategic human resource management: merging resource theory and organizational learning. *Research in Personnel and Human Resources Management*, 14, pp. 61–90.

So, S.J. and Westland, J.C. (2010) *Red Wired: China's Internet Revolution*. London: Marshall Cavendish Business.

Soane, E., Alfes, K., Gatenby, M., Rees, C. and Truss, C. (2009) The direct and indirect influences of leadership and management on employee engagement. *Capitalizing on Diversity in HRM Research. Proceedings 6th International Conference of the Dutch HRM Network*, Amsterdam, November.

Soane, E., Alfes, K., Truss, C., Rees, C. and Gatenby, M. (2010) Managing a positive environment: engagement, wellbeing, performance and the role of meaningful-ness. *Academy of Management Conference*, Chicago, September.

Som, A. (2008) Innovative human resource management and corporate performance in the context of economic liberalization in India. *International Journal of Human Resource Management*, 19(7), pp. 1278–1297.

Soros, G. (2008) *The New Paradigm for Financial Markets: The Credit Crisis for Financial Markets*. New York: Public Affairs.

Sostrin, J. (2009) A conceptual framework of barriers to workplace learning and performance. *OD Practitioner*, 41(3), pp. 42–49.

Sparrow, P., Brewster, C. and Harris, H. (2004) *Globalising Human Resource Management*. London: Routledge.

Sparrow, P., Hird, M., Hesketh, A. and Cooper, C. (2010) Introduction: Performance-led HR. In P. Sparrow, M. Hird, A. Hesketh and C. Cooper (eds) *Leading HR*. Basingstoke: Palgrave Macmillan.

Sparrow, P., Scullion, H. and Farndale, E. (2011) Global talent management: new roles for the corporate HR function? In H. Scullion and D.G. Collings (eds) *Global Talent Management*. Abingdon: Routledge.

Sparrow, S. (2006) We don't need HR. *Personnel Today*, 14 March.

Spear, S.J. (2010) *The High-Velocity Edge: How Market Leaders Leverage Operational Excellence to Beat the Competition*. New York, NY: McGraw-Hill.

Spender, J.C. (1996) Organisational knowledge, learning and memory: three concepts in search of a theory. *Journal of Organisational Change*, 9(1), pp. 63–78.

Spulber, D.F. (2007) *Global Competitive Strategy*. Cambridge: Cambridge University Press.

Starbuck, W.H. and Hedberg, B. (2001) How organiza-tions learn from success and failure. In M. Dierkes, A.B. Antal, J. Child and I. Nonaka (eds) *Handbook of Organizational Learning and Knowledge*. Oxford: Oxford University Press.

Steinberg, G. (2008) *The War for Wealth: The True Story of Globalization, or Why the Flat World Is Broken*. New York, NY: McGraw-Hill.

Steinbock, D. (2010) *Winning Across Global Markets: How Nokia Creates Strategic Advantage in a Fast-Changing World*. San Francisco, CA: Jossey-Bass.

Stewart, J. and Kringas, P. (2003) Change management: strategy and values in six agencies from the Australian Public Service. *Public Administration Review*, 63(6), pp. 675–688.

Stewart, J. and Tansley, C. (2002) *Training in the Knowledge Economy*. London: CIPD.

Stewart, T.A. (2002) *The Wealth of Knowledge: Intellectual Capital and the Twenty-First Century Organisation*. London: Nicholas Brealey.

Stiglitz, J. (2007) *Making Globalisation Work*. London: Penguin Books.

Storey, J. (1989) Introduction: from personnel management to human resource management. In J. Storey (ed.) *New Perspectives on Human Resource Management*. London: Routledge.

Storey, J. (1992) *Developments in the Management of Human Resources*. Oxford: Blackwell.

Storey, J. (2005) *Adding Value Through Information and Consultation*. Basingstoke: Palgrave Macmillan.

Storey, J. (ed.) (2001) *Human Resource Management: A Critical Text*. London: Thomson Learning.

Story, J. (2010) *China Uncovered: What You Need to Know to Do Business in China*. Harlow: Pearson Education.

Sukserm, T. and Takahashi, Y. (2010) A prospective process for implementing human resource development (HRD) for corporate social responsibility (CSR). *Interdisciplinary Journal of Contemporary Research in Business*, 2(1), pp. 10–32.

Sullivan, D. and Marvel, M. (2011) How entrepreneurs' knowledge and network ties relate to the number of employees in new SMEs. *Journal of Small Business Management*, 49(2), pp. 185–206.

Sumardi, W.A. and Othman, R. (2010) The three facets of talent management in Malaysia. *International Journal of Business Research*, 10(1), pp. 181–185.

Swanson, R.A. (2001) Human resource development and its underlying theory. *Human Resource Development International*, 4, pp. 299–312.

Swanson, R.A. and Holton, F.E. (2001) *Foundations of Human Resource Development*. San Francisco: Berrett-Kochler.

Swart, J. and Kinnie, N. (2003) Sharing knowledge in knowledge-intensive firms. *Human Resource Management Journal*, 13(2), pp. 60–75.

Swart, J., Kinnie, N. and Purcell, J. (2003) *People Performance in Knowledge-Intensive Firms*. London: CIPD.

Tamkin, P., Reilly, P. and Strebler, M. (2006) *The Changing HR Function: The Key Questions*. London: CIPD.

Tappin, S. and Cave, A. (2008) *The Secrets of CEOs: 150 Global Chief Executives Lift the Lid on Business, Life and Leadership*. London: Nicholas Brealey Publishing.

Tappin, S. and Cave, A. (2010) *The New Secrets of CEOs: 200 Global Chief Executives on Leading*. London: Nicholas Brealey Publishing.

Tapscott, D. and Williams, A.D. (2008) *Wikinomics: How Mass Collaboration Changes Everything*. London: Atlantic Books.

Teece, D., Pisano, G. and Shuen, A. (2007) Dynamic capabilities and strategic management. *Strategic Management Journal*, 28(13), pp. 509–533.

Tett, G. (2009) Lost through destructive creation. *Financial Times*, 10 March, p. 11.

The Work Foundation (2009) *Quality People Management for Quality Outcomes*. London: The Work Foundation.

Thornhill, A., Lewis, P., Saunders, M. and Millmore, M. (2000) *Managing Change: A Human Resource Strategy Approach*. Harlow: FT Prentice Hall.

Tomer, J. (1987) *Organizational Capital: The Path to Higher Productivity and Well-being*. New York: Praeger.

Torrens, C. (2010) *Doing Business in China*. London: Profile Books.

Torrington, D., Hall, L. and Taylor, S. (2005) *Human Resource Management*, 2nd edn. London: Prentice Hall.

Towers, B. (1997) *The Representation Gap: Change and Reform in the British and American Workplace*. Oxford: Oxford University Press.

Towers Perrin (2005) *HR Outsourcing: New Realities, New Expectations*. Stamford, CT: Towers Perrin.

Towers Perrin (2007) *Executive Briefing: Engagement in the Public Sector*. London: Towers Perrin.

Towers Perrin–ISR (2006) *The ISR Employee Engagement Report*. London: Towers Perrin.

Trompenaars, F. and Hampden-Turner, C. (1997) *Riding the Waves of Culture: Understanding Cultural Diversity in Business*. London: Nicholas Brealey.

Truss, C. (2001) Complexities and controversies in linking human resource management and organisational outcomes. *Journal of Management Studies*, 38(8), pp. 1121–1150.

Truss, C. (2004) Who's in the driving seat? Managing human resources in a franchise firm. *Human Resource Management Journal*, 14(4), pp. 57–75.

Truss, C. (2009) Changing HR functional forms in the UK public sector. *International Journal of Human Resource Management*, 20(4), pp. 717–737.

Truss, C. and Gill, J. (2005) *Dynamic HR processes: a complexity-capability perspective*. Paper to the BAM Conference, Oxford, September.

Truss, C. and Gratton, L. (1994) Strategic human resource management: a conceptual approach. *International Journal of Human Resource Management*, 5(3), pp. 663–686.

Truss, C. and Katz, S. (2003) *The Challenge of Devolution: Human Resource Management at Inchcape UK*. Cranfield: European Case Clearing House.

Truss, C., Gratton, L., Hope-Hailey, V. and Stiles, P. (1997) Soft and hard models of human resource management: a reappraisal. *Journal of Management Studies*, 34(1), pp. 53–73.

Truss, C., Soane, E., Edwards, C., Wisdom, K., Croll, A. and Burnett, J. (2006) *Working Life: Employee Attitudes and Engagement 2006*. Wimbledon: CIPD.

Truss, C., Soane, E., Alfes, K., Gatenby, M. and Rees, C. (2010) How to engage the 'pole vaulters' on your staff. *Harvard Business Review*, March, p. 24.

Tsoukas, H. and Vladimirou, E. (2005) What is organizational knowledge? In H. Tsoukas (ed.) *Complex Knowledge: Studies in Organizational Epistemology*. Oxford: Oxford University Press.

Turner, A. (2001) *Just Capital: The Liberal Economy*. London: Macmillan.

Tyson, S. (1995) *Human Resource Strategy*. London: Pitman.

Tyson, S. and Fell, A. (1986) *Evaluating the Personnel Function*. London: Hutchinson.

Tyson, S. and Witcher, M. (1994) Human resource strategy: emerging from the recession. *Personnel Management*, August.

Ubias, U. and Alas, R. (2010) The innovation climate—predictor for corporate social responsibility (CSR). *EBS Review*, 27, pp. 70–86.

Ulrich, D. (1997a) A new mandate for human resources. *Harvard Business Review*, Jan–Feb, pp. 124–134.

Ulrich, D. (1997b) Measuring human resources: an overview of practice and a prescription for results. *Human Resource Management*, 36, pp. 303–320.

Ulrich, D. (1997c) *Human Resource Champions: The Next Agenda for Adding Value and Delivering Results*. Boston: Harvard Business School Press.

Ulrich, D. and Beatty, D. (2001) From partners to players: extending the HR playing field. *Human Resource Management*, 40(4), pp. 293–307.

Ulrich, D. and Brockbank, W. (2005a) Role call. *People Management*, 16 June, pp. 23–28.

Ulrich, D. and Brockbank, W. (2005b) *The HR Value Proposition*. Boston, MA: Harvard Business School Press.

Ulrich, D. and Ulrich, W. (2010) *The Why of Work: How Great Leaders Build Abundant Organizations that Work*. New York, NY: McGraw-Hill.

Ulrich, D., Allen, J., Brockbank, W., Younger, J. and Nyman, M. (2009) *HR Transformation: Building Human Resources from the Outside In*. New York, NY: McGraw-Hill.

United Nations Department of Economics and Social Affairs/Population Division (2009) *World Population Ageing*. Working paper. New York: United Nations.

Urip, V. (2010) *CSR Strategies: Corporate Social Responsibility for a Competitive Edge in Emerging Markets*. Hoboken, NJ: John Wiley and Sons.

US Bureau of Labor Statistics (2010) *International Comparison of Annual Labor Force Statistics*. http://www.bls.gov/ilc/flscomparelf.htm.

Uslaner, E. (2009) *Trust and the economic crisis of 2008*. Prepared for the Ruffin Summit on Public Trust in Business, Darden School of Business, University of Virginia, 18–20 September.

Vaiman, V. (2010) Managing talent of non-traditional knowledge workers: opportunities, challenges, and trends. In V. Vaiman (ed.) *Talent Management of Knowledge Workers: Embracing the Non-Traditional Workforce*. Basingstoke: Palgrave Macmillan.

Valentine, S. and Godkin, L. (2009) Ethics, social responsibility, and ethical reasoning in an education-based health science center: when doing good results in good employees. *Journal of Leadership, Accountability and Ethics*, 7(3), pp. 61–77.

Van Agtmael, A. (2008) *The Emerging Markets Century: How a New Breed of World-Class Companies Is Overtaking the World*. London: Simon and Schuster.

Van de Ven, F. (2007) Fulfilling the promise of career development: getting to the 'heart' of the matter. *Organization Development Journal*, 25(3), pp. 45–50.

Van de Heijden, B., Boon, J., van der Klink, M. and Meijs, E. (2009) Employability enhancement through formal and informal learning: an empirical study among Dutch non-academic university staff members. *International Journal of Training and Development*, 13(1), pp. 19–37.

Varese, F. (2011) *Mafias on the Move: How Organised Crime Conquers New Territories*. Princeton, NJ: Princeton University Press.

Varma, A., Budhwar, P.S. and DeNisi, A. (2008) Performance management around the globe: introduction and agenda. In A. Varma, P.S. Budhwar and A. DeNisi (eds) *Performance Management Systems: A Global Perspective*. Abingdon: Routledge.

Vashisth, R., Kumar, R. and Chandra, A. (2010) Barriers and facilitators to knowledge management: evidence from selected Indian universities. *Journal of Knowledge Management*, VIII(4), pp. 7–24.

Vettori, S. (2010) Introduction. In S. Vettori (ed.) *Ageing Populations and Changing Labour Markets (Corporate Social Responsibility)*. Farnham: Gower Publishing.

Victor, D.G. (2011) *Global Warming Gridlock: Creating More Effective Strategies for Protecting the Environment*. Cambridge: Cambridge University Press.

Von Krogh, G. (1998) Care in knowledge creation. *California Management Review*, 40(3), pp. 133–153.

Von Krogh, G., Ichijo, K. and Nonaka, I. (2000) *Enabling Knowledge Creation: How to Unlock the Mystery of Tacit Knowledge and Release the Power of Innovation*. Oxford: Oxford University Press.

Wagner, J. (2010) Personalise your career development plan. *Strategic Finance*, March, pp.17–18.

Wagner, J.A. (1994) Participation's effects on performance and satisfaction: a reconsideration of research evidence. *Academy of Management Review*, 19, pp. 312–330.

Wall Street Journal (2010) http://online.wsj.com/article/SB100014240527487041980045753103916 69390852.html?KEYWORDS=nokia (accessed 19 June 2010).

Wall, T. and Wood, S. (2005) The romance of human resource management and business performance, and the case for big science. *Human Relations*, 58(4), pp. 429–462.

Wang, G.G., Rothwell, W.J. and Sun, J.Y. (2009) Management development in China: a policy analysis. *International Journal of Training and Development*, 13(4), pp. 205–220.

Warhurst, C., Nickson, D., Witz, A. and Cullen, A.M. (2000) Aesthetic labour in interactive service work: some case study evidence from the 'new' Glasgow. *Service Industries Journal*, 20(3), pp. 1–18.

Warner, M. and Rowley, C. (2010) Chinese management at the crossroads: setting the scene. *Asia Pacific Business Review*, 16(3), pp. 273–284.

Watkins, K.E. and Cervero, R.M. (2000) Organisations as contexts for learning: a case study in certified public accountancy. *Journal of Workplace Learning*, 12(3), pp. 187–194.

Watkins K.E. and Marsick V.J. (1992) Towards a theory of informal and incidental learning in organisations. *International Journal of Lifelong Education*, 11(4), pp. 287–300.

Watson, T. (2004) HRM and critical social science analysis. *Journal of Management Studies*, 41(3), pp. 447–467.

Weiss, H.M. and Cropanzano, R. (1996). Affective events theory: a theoretical discussion of the structure, causes and consequences of affective experiences at work. *Research in Organizational Behavior*, 19, pp. 1–74.

Welch, J. (2005) *Winning*. London: HarperCollins.

Wellins, R., Bernthal, P. and Phelps, M. (2005) *Employee Engagement: The Key to Realising Competitive Advantage*. Development Dimensions International (DDI), http://www.ddiworld.com.

Wenger, E. (1998) *Communities of Practice: Learning, Meaning, and Identity*. Cambridge: Cambridge University Press.

Wenger, E., McDermott, R. and Snyder, W. M. (2002) *Cultivating Communities of Practice*. Boston, MA: Harvard Business School Press.

Wernerfelt, B. (1984) A resource-based view of the firm. *Strategic Management Journal*, 5(2), pp. 171–180.

Werther, W.B. and Chandler, D.B. (2011) *Strategic Corporate Social Responsibility: Stakeholders in a Global Environment*. London: Sage Publications.

West, M., Borrill, C., Dawson, J., Scully, J., Carter, M., Anelay, S., Patterson, M. and Waring, J. (2002) The link between the management of employees and patient mortality in acute hospitals. *International Journal of Human Resource Management*, 13(8), pp. 1299–1310.

Whitener, E. (2001) Do high commitment human resource practices affect employee commitment? A cross-level analysis using hierarchical linear modelling. *Journal of Management*, 27, pp. 515–535.

Whittington, R. (2001) *What Is Strategy—And Does it Matter?* London: Thomson Learning.

Wildavsky, B. (2010) *The Great Brain Race: How Global Universities Are Shaping the World*. Princeton, NJ: Princeton University Press.

Wilkinson, A., Dundon, T., Marchington, M. and Ackers, P. (2004) Changing patterns of employee voice: case studies from the UK and Republic of Ireland. *Journal of Industrial Relations*, 46, pp. 298–322.

Williamson, O. (1975) *Markets and Hierarchies*. New York: Free Press.

Wolf, M. (2005) *Why Globalization Works*. New Haven: Yale Nota Bene/Yale University Press.

Wolf, M. (2009) Seeds of its own destruction. *Financial Times*, 9 March, p. 13.

Wong, J. (2010) *Chinese Whispers: A Journey into Betrayal*. London: Atlantic Books.

Wood, G. and Wright, M. (2010) Private equity and human resource management: an emerging agenda. *Human Relations*, 63(9), pp. 1279–1296.

Wood, S. (2003) Organisational performance and manufacturing practices. In D. Holman, T. Wall, C. Clegg, P. Sparrow and A. Howard (eds) *The New Workplace: A Guide to the Human Impact of Modern Working Practices*. London: Wiley.

Wood, S. and de Menezes, L. (1998) High commitment management in the UK: evidence from the Workplace Industrial Relations Survey and Employers' Manpower and Skills Practices Survey. *Human Relations*, 51(4), pp. 485–515.

Worrall, L. and Cooper, C. (2007) *The Quality of Working Life: Managers' Health, Motivation and Productivity*. London: Chartered Management Institute.

Wright, C. (2008) Reinventing human resource management: business partners, internal consultants and the limits to professionalization. *Human Relations*, 61(8), pp. 1063–1086.

Wright, M., Hoskisson, R. and Busenitz, L. (2000) Entrepreneurial growth through privatization: the upside of management buyouts. *Academy of Management Review*, 25(3), pp. 591–601.

Wright, P. and Boswell, W. (2002) Desegregating HRM: a review and synthesis of micro and macro human resource management research. *Journal of Management*, 28(3), pp. 247–276.

Wright, P. and McMahan, G. (1992) Theoretical perspectives for strategic human resource management. *Journal of Management*, 18(2), pp. 295–320.

Wright, P. and Snell, S. (1998) Toward a unifying framework for exploring fit and flexibility in strategic human resource management. *Academy of Management Review*, 23(4), pp. 756–772.

Wright, P. and Snell, S. (2005) Partner or guardian? HR's challenge in balancing value and values. *Human Resource Management*, 44(2), pp. 177–182.

Wright, P., McMahan, G. and McWilliams, A. (1994) Human resources and sustained competitive advantage: a resource-based perspective. *International Journal of Human Resource Management*, 5(2), pp. 301–326.

Wright, P., Dunford, B. and Snell, S. (2001) Human resources and the resource based view of the firm. *Journal of Management*, 27, pp. 701–721.

Wright, P., Gardner, T. and Moynihan, L. (2003) The impact of HR practices on the performance of business units. *Human Resource Management Journal*, 13(3), pp. 21–36.

Wright, P., Scott, S., Peder, H. and Jacobsen, H. (2004) Current approaches to HR strategies: inside-out versus outside-in. *Human Resource Planning*, 27(4), pp. 35–47.

Wright, P., Gardner, T., Moynihan, L. and Allen, M. (2005) The relationship between HR practices and firm performance: examining causal order. *Personnel Psychology*, 58(2), pp. 409–446.

Yang, B. and Wang, X. (2009) Successes and challenges of developing human capital in the People's Republic of China. *Human Resource Development International*, 12(1), pp. 3–14.

Yorks, L. (2005) *Strategic Human Resource Development*. Mason, OH: Thomson South-Western.

Youndt, M. and Snell, S. (2004) Human resource configurations, intellectual capital, and organizational performance. *Journal of Managerial Issues*, 16(3), pp. 337–360.

Zaugg , R. and Thom, N. (2003) Excellence through implicit competencies: human resource management–organisational development–knowledge creation. *Journal of Change Management*, 3(3), pp. 199–211.

Zerk, J.A. (2011) *Multinationals and Corporate Social Responsibility: Limitations and Opportunities in International Law*. Cambridge: Cambridge University Press.

Zhu, Y., Warner, M. and Rowley, C. (2007) Human resource management with 'Asian' characteristics: a hybrid people-management system in East Asia. *International Journal of Human Resource Management*, 18(5), pp. 745–768.

Zink, K.J. (2005) Stakeholder orientation and corporate social responsibility as a precondition for sustainability. *Total Quality Management*, 16(8/9), pp. 1041–1052.

Index

Important Notice to All Customers

Bellwether Books has made every effort to inspect each book prior to shipment to ensure there are no markings and/or inscriptions of an offensive nature in the book you have purchased. However, the majorities of our titles are publisher returns, and while appearing in 'like new' condition, they may have some markings that we did not catch.

If you do find offensive markings in this book, please return the book and upon receipt back to us, we will ship another copy, if available, to you at no additional charge, or credit your account back the full amount (purchase price plus shipping & handling) should this copy be unavailable.

Thanks for purchasing from Bellwether Books, and we hope you enjoy your book!

For any questions or concerns, kindly email us at info@bellwetherbookstore.com